Reconquest and Crusade
in Medieval Spain

THE MIDDLE AGES SERIES

Ruth Mazo Karras, Series Editor
Edward Peters, Founding Editor

A complete list of books in the series
is available from the publisher.

Reconquest and Crusade in Medieval Spain

Joseph F. O'Callaghan

PENN

University of Pennsylvania Press
Philadelphia

Production of this volume was assisted by a grant from the Program for Cultural Cooperation between Spain's Ministry of Education, Culture, and Sports and United States Universities

First paperback edition 2004

10 9 8 7 6 5 4 3 2

Published by
University of Pennsylvania Press
Philadelphia, Pennsylvania 19104-4011

Library of Congress Cataloging-in-Publication Data

O'Callaghan, Joseph F.
    Reconquest and crusade in medieval Spain / Joseph F. O'Callaghan.
        p. cm. — (The Middle Ages series)
    Includes bibliographical references and index.
    ISBN 0-8122-3696-3 (cloth : alk. paper) —ISBN 0-8122-1889-2 (pbk. : alk. paper)
    1. Spain—History—711–1516. 2. Spain—History, Military. 3. Migration, Internal—Spain—History. 4. Land settlement—Spain—History. 5. Crusade bulls. I. Title. II. Series.

DP99 .O33 2002
946'.02—dc21   2002028952

For Anne
Her children rise up and call her blessed . . .
Give her the fruit of her hands,
and let her work praise her in the gates
—Proverbs 31: 28, 31

Contents

List of Illustrations   ix

Preface   xi

Genealogical Tables   xv

1   Reconquest, Holy War, and Crusade   1

2   From Barbastro to Almería, 1063–1157   23

3   From Almería to Las Navas de Tolosa, 1157–1212   50

4   From Las Navas de Tolosa to Córdoba, 1212–1236   78

5   From Córdoba to Seville, 1236–1248   99

6   Warfare in the Crusading Era   124

7   Financing Reconquest and Crusade   152

8   The Liturgy of Reconquest and Crusade   177

9   Epilogue   209

Abbreviations   217

Notes   221

Bibliography   277

Index   309

Illustrations

Illustrations

1. Calatrava la Vieja   53
2. Pendón of Las Navas de Tolosa   73
3. Alfonso Téllez and Military Orders besiege a castle   86
4. Entrance to Real Alcázar of Seville   115
5. Count García of Castile fights al-Manṣūr   131
6. King of Granada attempts to capture Chincoya Castle   136–37
7. Christian Knights defeat the Marīnids   145
8. Pendón of Baeza   192

Maps

1. Muslim Spain, 711–1031   2
2. Spain at the death of Fernando I   28
3. Spain at the death of Alfonso VIII   77
4. Spain at the death of Fernando III   121

Preface

The epic battle between Islam and Christianity for dominance in the Mediterranean, extending over many centuries, occupies a principal place in the history of medieval Europe. Historians of the Middle Ages, however, have tended to take a narrow view of that conflict by focusing primarily on the crusades directed to the Holy Land in the twelfth and thirteenth centuries. This book attempts to redress the balance in part by emphasizing that the clash of arms between Christians and Muslims in the Iberian peninsula from the early eighth century onward, commonly labeled the reconquest, was transformed into a crusade by the papacy during the twelfth and thirteenth centuries. Successive popes accorded to Christian warriors willing to participate in the peninsular wars against Islam the same crusading benefits offered to those going to the Holy Land. Thus if one wishes to study the history of the crusades one has to take a broader view of the entire Mediterranean to include medieval Spain.

The beginnings of crusading historiography help to explain the limited vision of the crusades that prevailed until recent years. Because generations of French nobles and kings participated in expeditions to liberate Jerusalem, crusading was seen as an integral part of French national history. English and American medievalists, concentrating their attention initially on France and England, were inevitably drawn to the crusades to the Holy Land, but either ignored or mentioned only cursorily the war against Islam in Spain. Spanish historians were themselves responsible for this neglect in that, while they wrote much about the reconquest, they gave scant heed to the fact that the popes were granting remission of sins, the hallmark of crusading bulls, to those exposing their lives in combat against Islam. José Goñi Gaztambide's history of the bull of crusade in Spain, published in 1958, changed the focus entirely through his detailed study of papal documents according crusading indulgences and other privileges to those engaged in the reconquest.

My interest in this project was first awakened when I reviewed Goñi Gaztambide's book. In 1987, while directing a National Endowment for the Humanities Summer Institute on Medieval Spain: Land of Three Religions, I explored the topic further. I am indebted to the participants in the Institute, my good friends Manuel González Jiménez, Angus MacKay, Teofilo Ruiz, and Robert I. Burns, whose perspective on medieval Spain is always helpful. Father Burns also provided me with transcripts of several papal bulls. My students Theresa Earenfight, Donald Kagay, Nina Melechen, James Todesca, and Theresa Vann have always been a source of inspiration for me. Paul Chevedden has also been most helpful.

In writing this book I have attempted to utilize all the sources known to me, although, in comparison to other European countries, the number of Christian and Muslim chronicles is limited. The principal Latin narrative source for the twelfth century is the *Chronicle of Alfonso the Emperor*, a contemporary account of the reign of Alfonso VII of León-Castile by an anonymous cleric. For the thirteenth century there are three major narratives for the history of Castile and León, namely, *The Latin Chronicle of the Kings of Castile*, probably written by the royal chancellor, Bishop Juan of Osma (d. 1246); the *History of the Affairs of Spain* by Rodrigo Jiménez de Rada, archbishop of Toledo (d. 1247); and the uncritical *Chronicle of the World* by Lucas, bishop of Túy (d. 1249). All three works, concluding with the fall of Córdoba in 1236, were written by contemporaries who participated in many of the events they described and who were favorable to the monarchy. For the subsequent years to the fall of Seville in 1248 the vernacular *History of Spain* undertaken at the direction of Alfonso X provides a detailed narrative.

For the Crown of Aragón the chief narrative sources are the *Deeds of the Counts of Barcelona*, written by the monks of Ripoll between 1162 and 1276 in its first redaction, and the *Chronicle of San Juan de la Peña*, composed at the direction of Pedro IV (1336–87). A unique thirteenth-century source is the *Chronicle of Jaime I* of Aragón, written in Catalan; though some scholars have questioned its authorship, there is general agreement that it was written or dictated by the king himself and thus reflects his point of view. The Catalan *Chronicle* of Bernat Desclot dating from the later thirteenth century is generally exact in its relation of earlier events.

Annals from all the Christian kingdoms provide specific dates for many events mentioned in the chronicles.

Official documentation for the Christian kingdoms is ample, especially from the second half of the twelfth century. Besides numerous papal bulls conceding crusading privileges, hundreds of charters of the kings of Castile, León, Portugal, and Aragón are extant. These documents are particularly helpful because they often were dated during sieges, recorded the capture of castles or towns, or rewarded those assisting in the conquest.

Muslim chronicles include the memoir of ʿAbd Allāh, the last Zīrid king of Granada (1073–90), written in exile in Morocco. Ibn Ṣāḥib al-Salā, secretary to the Almohad caliph, wrote an official account of conquests in Spain between 1159 and 1184. In the early thirteenth century al-Marrākushī, while residing in Baghdad, wrote a history of the Almohads, drawing upon his memory of his years in Spain. Al-Ḥimyarī's description in alphabetical order of the cities and towns of Islamic Spain frequently includes pertinent historical data. The late thirteenth- or early fourteenth-century account of the Almoravids and the Almohads by the Moroccan historian Ibn ʿAbī Zarʿ tends at times to hyperbole and is not always trustworthy. Especially valuable is the history of Ibn ʿIdhārī, completed in 1306. Drawing on earlier accounts, he provides an abundance of detail and seems quite judicious in his assessment of events. Dating from the late fourteenth century is the work of the great philosopher of history, Ibn Khaldūn (d. 1406), whose history of the Berbers includes many references to the peninsula. Finally, one should mention al-Maqqarī (d. 1631) whose historical compendium includes many extracts from earlier writers.

There is a scarcity of documentary material for Islamic Spain, though at times documents were included in Muslim chronicles. Moreover, Lévi-Provençal has published some documents relative to the Almohad empire.

Literary sources such as the *Poem of the Cid* and the *Poem of Fernán González*, both written in the thirteenth century, mirror the attitudes and customs of that epoch. Several troubadours enjoying the patronage of peninsular rulers also commented on specific crusades. The legal codes compiled by Alfonso X reflect military and naval customs developed by the middle of the thirteenth century and his *Cantigas de Santa Maria* provides anecdotal and illustrative material. Citations of all these sources and others will be found in the endnotes and the bibliography.

With respect to language I have tried to be consistent in using Castilian, Portuguese, or Catalan forms when speaking of people and places in those kingdoms. For Arabic transliteration I have generally followed the guidelines of the *International Journal of Middle East Studies*.

I also wish to thank the rector of La Iglesia colegiata de San Isidoro of León for permission to reproduce a photograph of the *pendón de Baeza*, and the Patrimonio Nacional de España for permission to include a photograph of the *pendón de las Nava de Tolosa*, as well as illustrations from the Escorial manuscript of the *Cantigas de Santa Maria*. The Biblioteca Nazionale of Florence also kindly gave permission to use illustrations from the Banco Rari manuscript of the *Cantigas*.

Although the events described in this book occurred eight or nine hundred years ago, the tragedy of 11 September 2001 forcibly reminded the world that the rhetoric of crusade, holy war, and *jihād*, with all the intensity of feeling that those words conjure, is a powerful weapon and is still with us.

**The Kings of León, Castile, and Portugal
in the Eleventh, Twelfth, and Thirteenth Centuries**

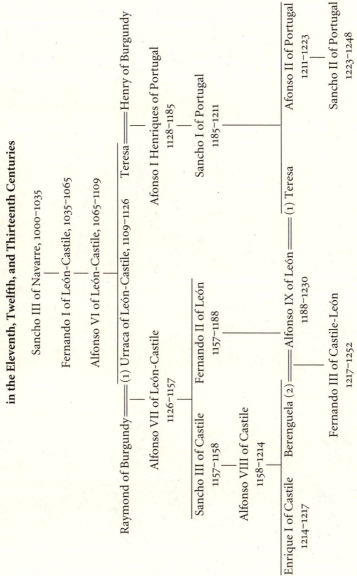

Sancho III of Navarre, 1000–1035

Fernando I of León-Castile, 1035–1065

Alfonso VI of León-Castile, 1065–1109

Raymond of Burgundy ══ (1) Urraca of León-Castile, 1109–1126   Teresa ══ Henry of Burgundy

Alfonso VII of León-Castile
1126–1157

Afonso I Henriques of Portugal
1128–1185

Fernando II of León
1157–1188

Sancho I of Portugal
1185–1211

Sancho III of Castile
1157–1158

Alfonso VIII of Castile
1158–1214

Alfonso IX of León ══ (1) Teresa
1188–1230

Afonso II of Portugal
1211–1223

Sancho II of Portugal
1223–1248

Enrique I of Castile
1214–1217

Berenguela (2)

Fernando III of Castile-León
1217–1252

The Kings of Aragón and Navarre and the Counts of Barcelona

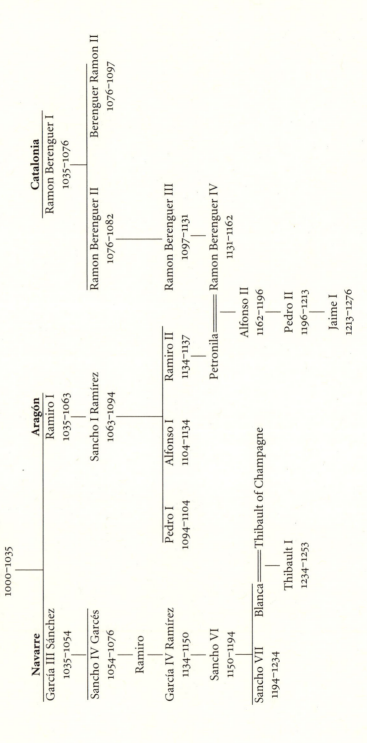

Sancho III of Navarre
1000–1035

Navarre

García III Sánchez
1035–1054

Sancho IV Garcés
1054–1076

Ramiro

García IV Ramírez
1134–1150

Sancho VI
1150–1194

Sancho VII
1194–1234

Blanca ═══ Thibault of Champagne

Thibault I
1234–1253

Aragón

Ramiro I
1035–1063

Sancho I Ramírez
1063–1094

Pedro I
1094–1104

Alfonso I
1104–1134

Ramiro II
1134–1137

Petronila ═══ Ramon Berenguer IV
1131–1162

Alfonso II
1162–1196

Pedro II
1196–1213

Jaime I
1213–1276

Catalonia

Ramon Berenguer I
1035–1076

Ramon Berenguer II
1076–1082

Berenguer Ramon II
1076–1097

Ramon Berenguer III
1097–1131

The Almoravid Rulers

Yūsuf ibn Tāshufīn
1061–1106

ʿAlī ibn Yūsuf
1106–1143

Tāshufīn ibn ʿAlī
1143–1145

Ibrāhīm ibn Tāshufīn
1145

Isḥaq ibn ʿAlī
1145–1147

The Almohad Caliphs

1. ʿAbd al-Muʾmin
1129–1163

2. Abū Yaʿqūb Yūsuf I
1163–1184

3. Abū Yūsuf Yaʿqūb al-Manṣūr
1184–1199

4. Abū ʿAbd Allāh Muḥammad al-Nāṣir
1199–1214

5. Abū Yaʿqūb Yūsuf II al-Mustanṣir
1214–1224

6. Abū Muḥammad ʿAbd al-Wāḥid I al-Makhlūʿ
1224

7. Abū Muḥammad ʿAbd Allāh al-ʿĀdil
1224–1227

8. Abū Zakariyāʾ Yaḥyā al-Muʿtaṣim
1227–1229

Abū Ibrāhīm Isḥaq al-Ṭāhir

9. Abū-l-ʿUlā Idrīs al-Maʾmūn
1232

11. Abū-l-Hasan ʿAlī al-Saʿīd al -Muʿtadid
1242–1248

12. Abū Hafs ʿUmar al-Murtaḍā
1248–1266

Chapter 1
Reconquest, Holy War, and Crusade

When the crusaders assaulted and captured Jerusalem in July 1099 the struggle between Christians and Muslims in Spain had been in progress for nearly four hundred years. From 711, when a mixed force of Arabs and Moroccan Berbers crossed the Strait of Gibraltar and overthrew the Visigothic kingdom, until the collapse of the Umayyad Caliphate of Córdoba in 1031, Muslim supremacy in Spain was unquestioned. As the seat of Islamic power was Córdoba, an eccentric location in the southern part of the peninsula, the Muslims did not permanently occupy large stretches of mountainous zones in the north. That made it possible for small groups of Christians to form the tiny, independent states of Asturias, León, Castile, Navarre, Aragón, and Catalonia. Clinging to the Cantabrian and Pyrenees mountains, this congeries of Christian enclaves, variously ruled by kings or counts, was kept on the defensive for nearly three hundred years, as Muslim armies marched northward every summer to ravage their lands but never to conquer them. In those early centuries a no-man's land stretching along the Duero River from the Atlantic to the borders of Aragón separated Christian and Muslim territory, but it was many years before the Christians dared to venture southward to occupy that zone (see Map 1). As the Christian population increased a gradual movement toward the Duero occurred and the process of settling that frontier zone commenced. In the northeast, however, Muslim rule reached as far north as the foothills of the Pyrenees until the late eleventh century.[1]

After the occupation of the Duero valley, the Christians took advantage of the breakup of the Caliphate to move into the Tagus valley, capturing Toledo in 1085. The invasions of the Almoravids (*al-murābiṭūn*) from Morocco soon afterward and of the Almohads (*al-muwaḥḥidūn*) in the middle of the twelfth century put the Christians on the defensive again, however, and temporarily checked their advance. Early in the thirteenth century victory over the Moroccans enabled the Christians to press forward to the Guadiana River and to capture the principal towns of the Guadalquivir valley. By

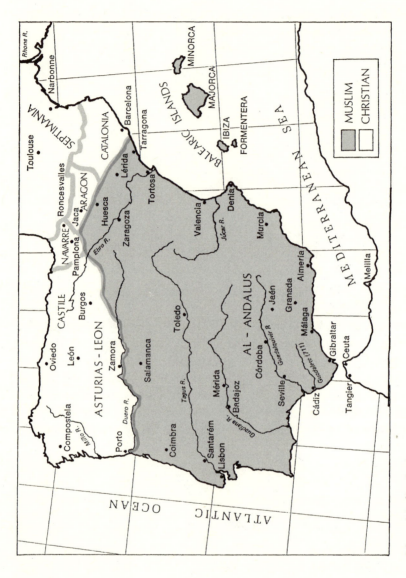

Map 1. Muslim Spain, 711–1031.

mid-century all of Islamic Spain was in Christian hands except the tiny kingdom of Granada, and that was reduced to tributary status to Castile-León. Occupying the central meseta, the largest segment of the peninsula, the kingdom of Castile-León maintained a contiguous frontier with the Muslims until Ferdinand and Isabella conquered Granada in 1492. Meanwhile, the kingdoms of Portugal on the west and Aragón-Catalonia on the east had expanded as fully as possible by the middle of the thirteenth century, and their boundaries would remain fixed thereafter save for some minor adjustments. Thus in the closing centuries of the Middle Ages the conquest of Islamic lands remained the primary responsibility of the kings of Castile-León.[2]

The Reconquest: Evolution of an Idea

The preceding historical sketch summarizes a long period in the history of medieval Spain that Spanish historians have called the *Reconquista*. The reconquest has been depicted as a war to eject the Muslims, who were regarded as intruders wrongfully occupying territory that by right belonged to the Christians. Thus religious hostility was thought to provide the primary motivation for the struggle. In time, the kings of Asturias-León-Castile, as the self-proclaimed heirs of the Visigoths, came to believe that it was their responsibility to recover all the land that had once belonged to the Visigothic kingdom. Some historians assumed that that ideal of reconquest persisted without significant change throughout the Middle Ages until the final conquest of Granada and the inevitable union of Castile and Aragón under Ferdinand and Isabella.[3]

Nevertheless, in the last thirty years or so historians have challenged these assumptions, asking whether it is even appropriate to speak of reconquest. Did the reconquest really happen or was it merely a myth? If it is legitimate to speak of reconquest, then what exactly is meant by that term? Doubts about the validity of this idea are reflected, for example, in Jocelyn Hillgarth's consistent placement of the word "Reconquest" in quotation marks.[4] However that may be, Derek Lomax pointed out that the reconquest was not an artificial construct created by modern historians to render the history of medieval Spain intelligible, but rather "an ideal invented by Spanish Christians soon after 711" and developed in the ninth-century kingdom of Asturias. Echoing Lomax's language, Peter Linehan remarked that "the myth of the Reconquest of Spain was invented" in the "880s or thereabouts."[5] Like all ideas, however, the reconquest was not a static concept brought to perfection in the ninth century, but rather one that evolved and was shaped by the influences of successive generations. In order to assess these views it is best first to trace the origins of the idea of the reconquest in the historiography of the early Middle Ages.

The Loss of Spain and the Recovery of Spain

The idea of the reconquest first found expression in the ninth-century chronicles written in the tiny northern kingdom of Asturias, the so-called *Prophetic Chronicle*, the *Chronicle of Albelda*, and the *Chronicle of Alfonso III*, which proposed to continue the *History of the Gothic Kings* of Isidore of Seville (d. 636).[6] These texts, written in Latin no doubt by churchmen, have generally been associated with the royal court and probably reflect the views of the monarch and the ecclesiastical and secular elite. What ordinary people thought is unknown, but the chroniclers developed an ideology of reconquest that informed medieval Spanish historiography thereafter. The *Chronicle of Alfonso III* also served as the basis for subsequent continuations in the eleventh and twelfth centuries by Sampiro, bishop of Astorga (d. 1041), Bishop Pelayo of Oviedo (d. 1129), and the anonymous author of the *Chronicle of Silos*.[7]

The history of the idea of the reconquest may be said to begin with the collapse of the Visigothic *Monarchia Hispaniae* of which Isidore of Seville spoke. From their seat at Toledo, the Visigoths were believed to have extended their rule over the whole of Spain, including Mauritania in North Africa, in other words over the whole Roman diocese of Spain.[8] Given the interest of medieval and early modern Spaniards in the possibility of conquering Morocco, it is well to remember that they knew that Mauritania or Tingitana was anciently one of the six provinces of the diocese of Spain.[9] In the early fourteenth century Alfonso XI of Castile (1312–50), repeating the language of the canonist Álvaro Pelayo, laid claim to the Canary Islands because, as part of Africa, the Islands were said to have once been subject to Gothic dominion. In the fifteenth century Alfonso de Cartagena made much the same argument.[10] The concept of a unified and indivisible kingdom embracing the entire Iberian peninsula, though it hardly corresponded to reality, was one of the most significant elements in the Visigothic legacy. That idea was reflected in the thirteenth-century account of Infante Sancho's protest against the plans of his father, Fernando I (1035–65), king of León-Castile, to partition his dominions among his sons: "In ancient times the

Goths agreed among themselves that the empire of Spain should never be divided but that all of it should always be under one lord."[11]

The Muslim rout of King Rodrigo (710–711), the "last of the Goths," at the Guadalete river, on 19 July 711, brought the Visigothic kingdom crashing to the ground and changed the course of Spanish history in a radical way. The contemporary Christian *Chronicle of 754*, written in Islamic Spain, deplored the reign of King Rodrigo, "who lost both his kingdom and the fatherland through wicked rivalries." Decrying the disaster that befell the Visigoths, the chronicler lamented that "human nature cannot ever tell all the ruin of Spain and its many and great evils."[12] The *Prophetic Chronicle* declared that "through fear and iron all the pride of the Gothic people perished . . . and as a consequence of sin Spain was ruined." In varying degrees the ninth-century Asturian chroniclers mourned the loss or extermination of the Gothic kingdom, the ruin of Spain, and the destruction of the fatherland. Similar language appears in the chronicles of later centuries.[13]

By contrast with the catastrophic loss of Spain, the chroniclers tell us that through Divine Providence liberty was restored to the Christian people and the Asturian kingdom was brought into being. This reportedly occurred when the majority of the Goths of royal blood came to Asturias and elected as king Pelayo (719–737), son of Duke Fáfila, also of the royal line. Pelayo, formerly a *spatarius* or military officer in the Visigothic court, supposedly was King Rodrigo's grandnephew. When faced with an overwhelming Muslim force demanding that he surrender, Pelayo, in the chronicler's words, responded:

I will not associate with the Arabs in friendship nor will I submit to their authority . . . for we confide in the mercy of the Lord that from this little hill that you see the salvation of Spain (*salus Spanie*) and of the army of the Gothic people will be restored. . . . Hence we spurn this multitude of pagans and do not fear [them].

The ensuing battle of Covadonga, fought probably on 28 May 722, was a great victory for Pelayo, for "thus liberty was restored to the Christian people . . . and by Divine Providence the kingdom of Asturias was brought forth."[14] Among the Asturians the battle of Covadonga became the symbol of Christian resistance to Islam and a source of inspiration to those who, in words attributed to Pelayo, would achieve the *salus Spanie*, the salvation of Spain.

The inevitability and the inexorability of the struggle that Pelayo commenced was stressed by the *Chronicle of Albelda*, which declared that "the

Christians are waging war with them [the Muslims] by day and by night and contend with them daily until divine predestination commands that they be driven cruelly thence. Amen!" Recording the prophecy that the Muslims would conquer Spain, the *Prophetic Chronicle* expressed the hope that "Divine Clemency may expel the aforesaid [the Muslims] from our provinces beyond the sea and grant possession of their kingdom to the faithful of Christ in perpetuity. Amen.!"[15]

Identifying the Goths with Gog and the Arabs with Ishmael, the author of the *Prophetic Chronicle* offered this reflection on the words of the Prophet Ezekiel (Ezek. 38–39) addressed to Ishmael: "Because you abandoned the Lord, I will also abandon you and deliver you into the hand of Gog . . . and he will do to you as you did to him for one hundred and seventy times [years]." Although the Goths were punished for their crimes by the Muslim invasion, the chronicler proclaimed that "Christ is our hope that upon the completion in the near future of one hundred and seventy years from their entrance into Spain the enemy will be annihilated and the peace of Christ will be restored to the holy church." Calculating that those one hundred and seventy years would be reached in 884, the author predicted that "in the very near future our glorious prince, lord Alfonso, will reign in all of Spain."[16] Aware of Alfonso III's (866–910) recent successes against the Muslims, as well as internal disorders afflicting Islamic Spain, the chronicler was confident that the days of Muslim domination were numbered. This anticipation of the imminent destruction of Islam proved illusory, but the hope persisted for centuries.

The notion of continuity existing between the new kingdom of Asturias and the old Visigothic kingdom, whether actual or imagined, had a major influence on subsequent development of the idea of reconquest. The ninth-century chroniclers were at pains to establish the connection between the old and new monarchies, identifying the people of Asturias with the Goths, and linking the Asturian kings to the Visigothic royal family. Indeed, the chroniclers consciously conceived of themselves as continuing Isidore's *Gothic History*. According to the *Chronicle of Albelda*, Alfonso II (791–842) "established in Oviedo both in the church and in the palace everything and the entire order of the Goths as it had been in Toledo."[17] Exactly what that meant is not entirely certain, but the purpose of the statement was to affirm the link between Asturias and the Visigothic kingdom, however tenuous that might be.

The Gothic connection thus established was repeated again and again in subsequent centuries, though without any further attempt at proof. For example, the twelfth-century author of the *Chronicle of Silos* described Alfonso VI, king of León-Castile (1065–1109) as "born of illustrious Gothic lineage." Two centuries later, Álvaro Pelayo recalled that Alfonso XI was descended from the Goths. When Enrique of Trastámara claimed the throne in opposition to his half-brother Pedro the Cruel (1350–69), he declared that "the Goths from whom we are descended" chose as king "the one whom they believed could best govern them."[18] Fifteenth-century expressions of this sort were commonplace, and even Ferdinand and Isabella were reminded of their Gothic ancestry. By asserting, though not demonstrating, the bond between the medieval kings and their supposed Visigothic forebears, the chroniclers also underscored the close link between the Visigothic monarchy and its purported successor in Asturias-León-Castile. In doing so they justified the right of the medieval kings, as heirs of the Visigoths and of all their power and authority, to reconquer Visigothic territory and restore the Visigothic monarchy.[19]

The emergence of the kingdoms of Portugal and Aragón-Catalonia in the twelfth century, and to a lesser extent, of Navarre, necessitated some readjustment in Castilian thinking as it became apparent that the eastern and western monarchies would also have their share of the old Visigothic realm. In expectation of the inevitability of conquest, the kings of Castile, León, and Aragón optimistically made several treaties that will be discussed in later chapters, partitioning Islamic Spain. Even more optimistically the kings of Castile and Aragón concluded a treaty in 1291 providing for the partition of North Africa, allotting to Castile Morocco—ancient Mauritania—over which the Visigoths reportedly had once held sway, and to Aragón Algeria and Tunis.[20]

Reconquest and Holy War

The Christian struggle against Islamic Spain can be described as a war of both territorial aggrandizement and of religious confrontation. In speaking of the warlike activities of the Asturian kings the chroniclers tell us that the king "extended the kingdom" or "expanded the land of the Christians with the help of God." The greatest encomium that could be bestowed on the monarch was that he had increased the extent of his dominions. The thirteenth-century *Latin Chronicle*, for example, emphasized that Fernando I "liberated Coimbra from the hands of the Moors." Later in the century, Fray Juan Gil de Zamora remarked that Alfonso III had "liberated from Arab dominion" Gallia Gothica (southeastern France and Catalonia), Vasconia (the Basque provinces), and Navarre. Then, after repeatedly noting that "Spain was re-covered" (*recuperata fuit Hispania*) or "liberated" (*liberata fuit*) by this king or that, he summed up the process by commenting that "Spain was recov-ered by many noble kings." [21]

Among them was Fernando III (1217–52), who, as he lay on his death-bed, admonished his son, the future Alfonso X (1252–84), as follows:

My Lord, I leave you the whole realm from the sea hither that the Moors won from Rodrigo, king of Spain. All of it is in your dominion, part of it conquered, the other part tributary. If you know how to preserve in this state what I leave you, you will be as good a king as I; and if you win more for yourself, you will be better than I; but if you diminish it, you will not be as good as I.[22]

In effect, after recalling the reconquest of lands lost by Rodrigo, the last Visigothic king, Fernando III urged his son to continue a policy of territorial aggrandizement and expansion.

While the king might hope to increase the size of his kingdom, the sol-diers who did his bidding often were motivated, as we shall see, by the desire to enrich themselves and to raise their social standing by the acquisition of booty. Beyond that, they looked for pasturage for their flocks, and over the centuries extended the sheepwalks or *cañadas* from the northern stretches of Castile into Andalucía (Ar. al-Andalus). They were also anxious to secure land for cultivation, to acquire the wealth of Islamic Spain, and ultimately to control markets and means of production. In order to accomplish all that they had first to dominate a given territory and to hold it by the establish-ment of fortified settlements or by taking possession of old Roman towns then in Muslim hands.

The ideas of territorial aggrandizement and religious expansion were coupled in the late eleventh century, just before the First Crusade, when San-cho I Ramírez, king of Aragón and Navarre (1063–94), expressed his aspira-tions in this way:

Let it be known to all the faithful that for the amplification of the Church of Christ, formerly driven from the Hispanic regions, I, Sancho . . . took care to settle inhabi-tants in that place [Montemayor] . . . for the recovery and extension of the Church of Christ, for the destruction of the pagans, the enemies of Christ, and the building up and benefit of the Christians, so that the kingdom, invaded and captured by the Ish-maelites, might be liberated to the honor and service of Christ; and that once all the people of that unbelieving rite were expelled and the filthiness of their wicked error was eliminated therefrom, the venerable Church of Jesus Christ our Lord may be fos-tered there forever.[23]

In other words, the liberation of the kingdom, following the destruction and expulsion of the Muslims and the extirpation of their rite, would result in the recovery, growth and fostering of the Christian religion.

Damian Smith suggested that the reforming popes of the late eleventh and twelfth centuries influenced the idea of reconquest by their use of such words as *recuperare, restituere, liberare, reparare, reddere, reuocare, restaurare,* and *perdere.* Urban II, for example, referred to the liberation of the church of Toledo and commended the efforts of the count of Barcelona to restore the church of Tarragona. Noting the restoration of the metropolitan see of Toledo, Paschal II remarked that the church there "was ripped from the yoke of the Moors and the Moabites." Such language, although referring primarily to the restoration or liberation of churches, likely reinforced the idea of territorial liberation or reconquest.[24]

Muslim authors were aware of the Christian ambition to dispossess them. 'Abd Allāh, king of Granada (1073–90), commented in his memoirs that "the Christians' thirst for al-Andalus became quite evident."[25] The early fourteenth-century Moroccan chronicler, Ibn 'Idhārī, whose work reliably reflects traditions handed on by his sources, reported that Fernando I made the following reply to a deputation from Islamic Toledo seeking his help against their fellow Muslims of Zaragoza:

We seek only our own lands which you conquered from us in times past at the beginning of your history. Now you have dwelled in them for the time allotted to you and we have become victorious over you as a result of your own wickedness. So go to your own side of the Strait [of Gibraltar] and leave our lands to us, for no good will come to you from dwelling here with us after today. For we shall not hold back from you until God decides between us.[26]

Thus the Christians made plain their belief that the Muslims had no right to the lands they held and would eventually be driven out.

Territorial conquest undoubtedly prompted many military actions along the frontier and may have been uppermost in the minds of many warriors over the centuries. Religious considerations, however, also fueled the struggle against Islam. Menéndez Pidal remarked that "the war of reconquest always had a religious character" and Sánchez Albornoz emphasized that the struggle with the Muslims "was not only a war of reconquest, but also of religion, and it was maintained, not only by the desire to recover territory, but also by hatred between creeds."[27]

Such a war may be described as a holy war, though to do so is surely a travesty. War, which of its very nature entails the destruction of life, the infliction of extreme harm on human beings, and the ruination of crops, homes, churches, temples, and other structures, is not holy or sacred. The type of war of which we are speaking was not holy but rather religious. A religious war was a conflict between two societies, in each of which the spiritual and the temporal, the sacred and the secular, were wholly integrated. In such a society religion and religious values were paramount, touching upon and regulating every aspect of individual and community life. Full participation in the community was dependent upon one's adhering to the community's religion.[28]

By proclaiming oneself a Christian, a Muslim, or a Jew, one espoused not only specific religious doctrines such as the Christian dogma of the Trinity, or the absolute monotheism of the Muslims or the Jews, but one also accepted an entire system of cultural values affecting one's daily life, habits, traditions, laws, and even language. Thus Christian and Muslim societies were mutually exclusive, by reason not only of social and legal differences, but above all because of religion which suffused every facet of life. Daily interaction between Christians and Muslims did contribute to a degree of acculturation, especially in matters of language and social usage, but there was no real possibility of the full integration of Christians into Muslim society or Muslims into Christian society. In each instance Christians or Muslims could only be protected minorities with limited political and legal rights.

The purpose of war against Islam was not to convert the Muslims. Aside from the challenge to Islamic rule by the ninth-century martyrs of Córdoba, and some Mozarabic apologetic treatises of the eleventh and twelfth centuries,[29] Hispanic Christians were remarkably passive in confronting Muslim theology. Those who did make an attempt to preach the Gospel among the Muslims tended to come from beyond the peninsula. One of the first recorded efforts of this sort was undertaken around 1074 by a Cluniac monk, Anastasius, who offered to prove the certitude of the Christian faith by undergoing an ordeal by fire; but when the Muslims proved obdurate, he "shook the dust from his feet" and returned home.[30] Less than a century later, Peter the Venerable, abbot of Cluny, visited Spain and obtained a translation of the Qur'ān (done by the Englishman Robert of Ketton) so he could refute Islamic doctrine, but he did not initiate any serious effort at conversion. Although Mark, a canon of Toledo, also translated the Qur'ān early in the thirteenth century, that apparently did not prompt any missionary campaign.[31] From time to time individual Muslims converted, but the popes and northern Europeans expressed greater interest than peninsular Christians in persuading the Muslims to adopt the Christian faith.

In time the Muslims came to be regarded as invaders wrongfully occupying territory that by right belonged to the Christians, and whose entire way of life was foreign to that of the Christians. Thus the aim of the conflict was to drive the Muslims from the peninsula. Sampiro of Astorga put that succinctly when he remarked that Fernando I appeared on the scene "to expel the barbarians." The difficulty, if not the impossibility, of reconciling or assimilating different religious and cultural points of view was at the root of the conflict between the Christians and Muslims. Both sides came to understand that it would end only when the Christians completed the subjugation of the Muslims or ousted them from the peninsula. Though the discord was obviously based on religious antagonism, the term holy war or *guerra santa* appeared for the first time that I am aware of in fifteenth-century peninsular sources.[32]

Some scholars have argued that a holy or religious war was totally contrary to Christian belief. Jaime Oliver Asín, for example, stated emphatically that "neither here [Spain] nor in any Christian country could there be born by itself alone a kind of war whose spirit was essentially anti-Christian: the propagation of religious faith by the violence of arms." This statement misunderstands the nature of the war in Spain as well as the crusades to the Holy Land. Neither the reconquest nor the crusades were intended to convert anyone by force, but rather to evict them from territory claimed by the Christians or at least to subject them to Christian rule. Américo Castro, following Oliver Asín, argued that because warfare is inconsistent with the tenets of Christianity the source of the holy war must be sought in the teachings of Muḥammad. Castro concluded that "the holy war against the Muslims in Spain and Palestine, leaving aside the difference in its aims and consequences, was inspired by the *jihād* or Muslim holy war." He also believed that the idea that those who fell in war against the "infidels" were martyrs to the faith was borrowed from Islam and was "simply a reflection of Islamic ideas and emotions."[33]

The Islamic concept of *jihād* (a word etymologically signifying any effort aimed at a specific objective) was a precept established in the Qur'ān. A religious duty incumbent upon all male members of the community, its aim was the subjugation of all people to the rule of Islam. This was an obligation that would continue until the rule of Islam had been extended throughout the entire world. Given the universal and unified nature of the Islamic community in theory, there could be no holy war against other adherents of the faith. Warfare against non-Muslims might be interrupted by truces (though these ought to be limited to a ten-year period), but there could never be permanent peace with them until they had finally submitted to Islam. Service in the holy war, according to Muḥammad, was the most meritorious of all works, bringing spiritual benefit to the participants. In several places in the Qurʾān God promised the reward of heavenly bliss to those dying in the holy war, who were accounted as martyrs (*shuhadāʾ*) to the faith.[34]

It was understood that all peoples should be invited to embrace Islam, and only after they had refused to do so would the holy war be declared against them. In practice, pagan peoples were forced to accept Islam, but Christians and Jews, as "Peoples of the Book" (*ahl al-kitāb*), peoples who had received a revelation from the one true God, contained in their respective scriptural texts, were allowed to worship freely, provided that they submitted to Muslim rule, and paid both the poll tax (*jizya*) and the land tax (*kharāj*). The opportunity to participate in the holy war in Spain and to obtain religious merit and even entrance into paradise drew many volunteers to the peninsula. Al-Andalus, according to al-Ḥimyarī, was "a territory where one fights for the faith and a permanent place of the *ribāṭ*." Following an ascetic regimen, volunteers (*al-murābiṭūn*) were stationed in frontier garrisons (*ribāṭ*) in defense of Islam.[35]

The argument that the Christians had to borrow from Islam in this respect because of Christianity's repugnance to the use of force needs to be subjected to close scrutiny. Given the obvious similarities between Christian and Muslim concepts of holy war, one could argue that the idea ultimately derives from the Hebrew Scriptures, a common source for both Christian and Muslim teaching. Even though the Fifth Commandment, "Thou shalt not kill," explicitly and without qualification prohibited killing, God directed Joshua, Judah Maccabee, and other Jewish leaders to take up arms and gave them victory over their enemies. Victory was attributable to God's care for his people, and defeat was construed as a sign of his wrath, a punishment for sins. When the continuator of Lucas of Túy, described Fernando III as a new Joshua, he was doubtless aware of God's promise to Joshua: "Your domain is to be all the land of the Hittites." With that promise in mind Joshua instructed his officers: "Prepare your provisions, for three days from now you shall cross the Jordan here, to march in and take possession of the land which the Lord, your God, is giving you" (Josh. 1: 4, 10). After noting that Joshua "had conquered the kings who occupied the promised land," the continuator went on to say that, like Joshua, Fernando III, had conquered the Muslim kings and "established the people of León and Castile, who are the sons of Israel, in the land of the Moors."[36]

Christians clearly were aware of the use of violence at God's command in the Hebrew Scriptures, but they also knew that the fundamental message of the Gospel is peace. Jesus seemed to condemn all warlike activity when he declared that "all that take the sword shall perish by the sword" (Matt. 26: 52). Early Christian writers condemned the use of force to spread the Gospel and questioned or even denied the moral right of a Christian to follow a military career. Nevertheless, there is no explicit condemnation of war or of the military profession in the New Testament. Christians were expected to avoid the shedding of blood under any circumstances and especially in defense of religion. Once the empire became Christian after the conversion of Constantine, these attitudes began to change as more and more Christians held civil or military positions, where they exercised the authority to condemn guilty persons to death or to order men to kill in battle. In effect Christians accepted the authority of the state and its coercive power.[37]

In these circumstances, St. Augustine of Hippo (d. 430), basing himself on Roman legal concepts, developed the western theological tradition concerning the legitimacy of warfare. He held that warfare is licit when undertaken for just cause under the direction of a duly constituted authority. The purpose of warfare was to establish peace and order. To achieve that end the state, like the individual, had an inherent, natural right of self-defense, against both internal and external enemies. Offensive war to punish those who inflicted harm without cause or to recover property seized wrongfully might also be undertaken. Thus, warfare, though abhorrent, was necessary at times. On the other hand, Augustine condemned the waging of war "through mere lust of dominion to crush and subdue people who do you no harm." He asked: "What else is this to be called than great robbery?"[38]

A just war was not identical with a religious war, but that transformation was not long in coming. The establishment of Christianity as the state religion of the Roman Empire eventually meant that sacred and secular interests were united in war which was thought of as being carried out in God's name. In the Carolingian age the church was identified with the community that was often described simply as the *populus christianus*. The concept of the Christian people transcended ethnic, racial, or linguistic barriers. As members of the church, of the one Body of Christ, all Christians had responsibility for one another. The defense of Christian values was tantamount to the defense of society itself. Eventually Christians acknowledged that the use of force to achieve that purpose was justifiable.[39]

Reflecting on papal attitudes toward Islam, John Gilchrist argued that from the eighth century onward the popes justified hostilities against the Muslims threatening southern Italy and the Mediterranean world by referring to the wars waged at God's command in Sacred Scripture. Scant mention of Augustine's theory of the just war appeared in papal and canonistic texts of the central Middle Ages. In general until the eleventh century Christians taught that warfare was sinful and inappropriate behavior for a follower of Christ. H. E. J. Cowdrey argued that Gregory VII played a decisive role in transforming Christian attitudes toward the use of force, "so that from being inherently sinful, it was, or at least might be, meritorious to engage in it, and so to promote 'right order' in human society by force of arms." Gregory VII and the other reform popes of the late eleventh century and beyond justified their wars by branding their enemies as Anti-Christ and sanctioning the shedding of blood to maintain the rights of Christ and his Church. In that sense warfare was made holy or sacred.[40]

One can fairly say that both Christian and Islamic societies, founded upon the unity of the sacred and the secular, drew upon the Hebrew Scriptures and their own respective traditions to arrive at a similar acceptance of warfare. One should also emphasize that the participation of Spanish Christians in the struggle against Islam was not based on any evangelical precept; nor was it their aim to convert the Muslims or to subjugate them to their rule, but rather to dispossess them entirely. Nevertheless, once the Christians in the thirteenth century began to occupy extensive Muslim lands, they found there an overwhelming Muslim presence which they could not easily get rid of. Thus, they treated subject Muslims, known as Mudejars, as a protected minority, whose status was similar to that of Christians living in Muslim lands.[41]

The *Populus Christianus* Against the "Pagans"

The gulf separating Christians and Muslims in Spain is reflected in the language they used to refer to one another. Language mirrored their respective attitudes and often made plain their bitter animosity toward those whom they perceived as enemies.[42] We may begin our inquiry by considering the names by which they identified one another.

Muslim authors referred to Christians in several ways. *Rūm*, meaning the Romans, was essentially an ethnic or political term without any pejorative connotations. In the eastern Mediterranean it referred to the Byzantines, but it was also extended to the entire Christian population. The words *al-Ishban* (from *Hispani* or Spaniards), or *al-Franj*, the Franks or Catalans, both ethnic references, were also used. From time to time, reference was made to Christians or Nazarenes (*naṣrānī*), a description of their religious affiliation and their devotion to Jesus of Nazareth, but without implying any negative judgment. Terms such as boor (*ʿilj*) and foreigner or barbarian (*ʿajamī*), of course, suggested people of inferior social status. Very commonly used were the words infidel (*kāfir*), polytheist (*mushrik*), or idolater (*ʿabid al-aṣnām*), all of which reflected the Muslim opinion (expressed in the Qurʾān) that the Christians, by holding to the dogma of the Trinity, actually believed in three Gods rather than the one true God. On this account, one chronicler could say that "the land of the Christians is a land of idolatry (*arḍ al-shirk*)." Muslim authors also often described Christians as enemies of God (*ʿadūw Allāh*), and Christian rulers as tyrants (*ṭāghiya*). The mention of a ruler's name was followed frequently by an imprecation: "May Allāh curse him!" "May Allāh damn him!" Despite these negative remarks Muslim authors, realizing that a triumph over a worthy adversary enhanced the quality of victory, at times exhibited a grudging respect for the abilities of Christian warriors.[43]

The earliest Christian sources written immediately after the Muslim invasion are surprisingly silent concerning the nature of the religion professed by their conquerors. However, as the Muslim presence grew stronger and appeared more threatening, especially from the ninth century onward, Christian authors began to speak more often and more negatively about their adversaries, employing a variety of words, some of biblical derivation, some ethnic, and some condemnatory. *Saraceni*, *Agareni*, and *Ismaelitae*, all derived from the Book of Genesis (Gen. 16–17, 21, 25), appear primarily in the early Latin sources. As Sarah, the wife of the patriarch Abraham, failed to conceive, he turned to Sarah's Egyptian slave girl, Hagar, who bore him a son Ishmael. The *Prophetic Chronicle* explained these terms to ninth-century readers: "The perverse Saracens think that they descend from Sarah; more truly the Agarenes are from Hagar, and the Ishmaelites from Ishmael." Noting that "Abraham sired Ishmael from Hagar," the chronicler then gave a genealogy from Ishmael to Muḥammad "who is thought by his followers to be a prophet." A pejorative note was injected when Christians stressed that the Muslims were descended from the slave girl Hagar, rather than from Abraham's legitimate wife Sarah.[44]

Also of biblical origin, but quite anachronistic, were the words Chaldeans, used in the Hebrew Bible with reference to Babylon, and Moabites, a people settled east of the Dead Sea; the word Moabites was used most often to refer to the Almoravids, a Muslim sect who invaded Spain in the late eleventh century. The ethnic origin of one of the principal elements in the Muslim community was stressed when the sources mentioned the Arabs, though they were a distinct minority. When Christian authors referred to the Muslims as "pagans" they were in effect condemning them in much the same way as the ancient Romans who were charged as idolators because they did not believe in the Christian God.[45]

Muslims were also commonly described as "infidels," a term that literally designated men without faith, here meaning that they did not share the Christian faith. By calling them barbarians, Christian authors emphasized that the Muslims did not belong to the Christian community, but there was also an implication that they were less civilized than the Christians. The description of the Muslims as enemies of the cross of Christ (*inimici crucis Christi*), which became more common during the era of the crusades, emphasized the religious nature of the opposition to them.[46]

Finally, we have the word *mauri*. The earliest citation of *mauri* that I have encountered is in the *Chronicle of 754*, but it does not appear in the Christian chronicles of Asturias-León until Bishop Sampiro used it in the eleventh century. *Mauri* referred to natives of Mauritania, the old Roman province in North Africa, and eventually appeared in the vernacular as *moros*, whence our Moors. *Mauri* or *moros*, an ethnic description not implying any condemnation, eventually supplanted nearly all of the other biblical and ethnic terms in common usage.[47]

Although Muslims referred to Jesus respectfully, believing him to be one of the prophets, they pointed out the error of the Christians who declared him to be God. Eighth-century Christian chroniclers had little to say about Islam or Muḥammad, though the *Byzantine-Arabic Chronicle of 741* recorded that the Muslims "worshipped him with great honor and reverence and affirmed in all their sacraments and scriptures that he was an apostle of God and a prophet." By contrast, ninth-century Mozarabic writers, such as Eulogius (d. 859) and Alvarus (d. 861) of Córdoba, felt no compunction in denouncing Muḥammad as a perfidious and false prophet, and his religion as a false or damnable sect.[48] The *Chronicle of Albelda*, for example, described him as the "wicked Muḥammad." After remarking that he "was thought to be a prophet by his followers," the *Prophetic Chronicle* included a life of Muḥammad, the pseudo-prophet, the heresiarch, who was buried in hell.[49] Archbishop Rodrigo incorporated a life of Muḥammad into his *History of the Arabs* and also reported that the prophet was buried in hell.[50] The twelfth-century *Chronicle of Nájera* spoke of the "superstitious Muḥam-madan sect" and the thirteenth-century *Poem of Fernán González* con-demned Muḥammad as "the man of wicked belief." Comparing the Muslim leader al-Manṣūr, known to the Christians as Almanzor, and the count of Castile Fernán González respectively to Goliath and King David, the poet put these words in the mouth of the defeated Muslim: "Ay, Muḥammad, in an evil hour I trusted in you . . . all your power isn't worth three fruit trees." The *Libro de Alexandre* of the same century called the Muslims a "renegade peo-ple who pray to Muḥammad, a proven traitor," and the *Chronicle of 1344* re-ferred to Muḥammad's "wicked sect" and "wicked law." Reminding Alfonso XI that his ancestors, the Gothic kings, were "the shield and protection of the faith of Christ," a contemporary poet urged him "to honor the holy law [of Christ] by destroying the wicked law [of Muḥammad]." A century later, Fray Martín de Córdoba, spoke of the "dirty flies of Muḥammad."[51] These exam-ples could be multiplied.

Muslim rulers were also mentioned with contempt. The *Chronicle of Si-los*, recording the death of al-Manṣūr, the Muslim leader who ravaged the Christian states in the late tenth century, remarked that "he was seized by the devil who had possessed him in life and he was buried in hell." The thirteenth-century poet Gonzalo de Berceo described the caliph as "lord of the pagans, the mortal enemy of all the Christians."[52] On the other hand, the *History of Rodrigo*, after recording the victories over the Muslims of Rodrigo Díaz de Vivar, known as the Cid, uttered no word of condemnation and used no pe-jorative adjective to describe them.

Finally, one ought to observe that when Christian chroniclers speak of warfare against the Muslims, they generally speak of Christian armies and Christian soldiers, rather than Castilians, Leonese, Portuguese, Navarrese, Aragonese, or Catalans. In doing so they were highlighting the religious dif-ferences between the combatants.

Reconquest and Crusade

Now we may return to the question: is it appropriate to speak of reconquest, and if so what was it? Did the reconquest really happen? One may suppose that initial resistance to Islam in the northernmost sectors was prompted by a desire to protect one's own and did not have any ideological coloration. Al-though Abilio Barbero and Marcelo Vigil argued that northern moun-taineers opposing Muslim rule had previously been equally hostile to Roman and Visigothic attempts to subdue them, Bonnaz, Montenegro, and others have emphasized the continuing Gothic presence in Asturias.[53] Whether or not Pelayo and his followers thought of themselves as engaged in the reconquest of the lost Visigothic kingdom is unknown, but in time an ideological framework for Christian opposition to Islam developed. The historiography of the late ninth century supposed a direct link between the Visigothic realm destroyed by Muslim invaders in 711 and the kingdom of Asturias-León-Castile. By implication the neo-Gothic peoples of the north, after resisting Muslim expansion, were merely reconquering land once belonging to their ancestors. Emphasizing that Divine Providence was on their side, the Christians concluded that the Muslims would inevitably be driven from Spain.

Richard Fletcher, however, declared unacceptable Menéndez Pidal's suggestion that the ideal of reconquest set forth by the ninth-century chroniclers "remained the dominant concern of Spanish rulers, especially those of the succcessor-states in the Asturian kingdom in León and Castile, until the process was complete."[54] Indeed for most of the ninth, tenth, and eleventh centuries the Christians were at the mercy of the Muslims and could only make weak and ineffectual efforts to oppose their intrusions. The chroniclers of the tenth and eleventh centuries scarcely touched on the theme of reconquest, inasmuch as the Christians had all they could do to survive the overwhelming power of the Caliphate. To speak of the expulsion of the Muslims and the recovery of Spain in such circumstances one would have had to have had great faith in God's promises.

In the twelfth century, however, given changing political conditions, the possibility of reconquest became very real and from that point on reconquest ideology fills the pages of the Christian chronicles. According to Julian Bishko "the last years of the eleventh century witnessed a profound transformation in the nature, tempo, and course of the Spanish and Portuguese reconquest." In much the same way, Roger Collins commented that "the eleventh century and the early twelfth marked a period of profound change in the peninsula, in which the ideology of the *Reconquista* was first born." While an idea such as reconquest may not be tangible, it was nevertheless real in that it influenced the actions of Spanish kings and princes from the late eleventh century onward. Spain may not have been reconquered by the descendants of the Visigoths, but it certainly was reconquered by the Christians, who again and again expressed their belief that the recovery of Spain from Muslim hands was their ultimate objective. As Lomax remarked: "The Reconquest really did happen, in the sense already defined, and the Christians involved really did believe that they were recovering Spain for Christian political predominance."[55]

Too often the reconquest has been presented in a monolithic, institutionalized way, without nuance or variation. On the contrary, it was a process unfolding in the context of the changing political, religious, social, and economic circumstances of each epoch. It was characterized by a slow and intermittent advance from one river frontier to another and was accompanied by the colonization or repopulation of occupied territory. Thus Angus MacKay, following Sánchez Albornoz, emphasized that most historians "would agree . . . that the related concepts of the frontier and the reconquest provide the key to Spanish historical development."[56]

The reconquest has also been described as a crusade, although in a strict canonical sense crusades did not appear in Western Europe until the end of the eleventh century. Prior to that time northern Europeans had paid scant heed to peninsular events, but thereafter northern influences, including crusading ideology, permeated Spain in every way. In time the notion of crusading fueled traditionalist and nationalist fervor as generations of Spaniards were taught that for seven hundred years their ancestors almost singlehandedly had waged a crusade to hold back the Muslim hordes threatening to engulf Christian Europe. During the Spanish Civil War the effort of General Franco's forces to bring down the Republic and destroy the republican opposition was described by propagandists as "our crusade" (*nuestra cruzada*), a term that suggested a religious struggle against the forces of godless communism.[57] The twentieth-century crusade was an appeal to the medieval tradition of a crusade to drive the "infidels" from the peninsula.

Nevertheless, the study of crusading influences on the idea of the reconquest did not receive significant scholarly attention until more than forty years ago when José Goñi Gaztambide wrote his monumental study of the papal bull of crusade in Spain. A crusade, in his view, was "an indulgenced holy war" (*una guerra santa indulgenciada*), a war sanctioned by ecclesiastical authority (popes, councils, or bishops) who granted remission of sins to those taking part in it. Since then Spanish historians, perhaps assuming that everything had been said about the subject, have paid only minimal attention to it.[58] Emphasizing the crusading nature of the thirteenth-century wars against the Muslims Robert I. Burns, however, commented that he had "relentlessly used the phrase 'Crusader Valencia' " in the titles of his books and articles.[59]

Students of the crusades usually tended to concentrate on the struggle

to liberate the Holy Land in the twelfth and thirteenth centuries and to ig-
nore or even to deny that crusades also were undertaken in the Iberian
peninsula. Some, however, have spoken of the war against Spanish Islam
prior to the twelfth century as a pre-crusade and the wars of the twelfth and
thirteenth centuries as crusades. Paul Rousset summed up the arguments in
favor of the crusading character of those wars: they had papal encouragement, an international character because of French participation, and they
were part of a general Christian offensive against Islam. On the contrary, he
argued, the wars of the reconquest lacked the distinctive crusading indulgence, the wearing of the cross, and the intention of delivering the Holy
Land. In much the same vein Hans Eberhard Mayer argued that the wars in
Spain were holy wars, but not crusades. However, they "became a substitute
for a crusade. French knights, chary of the difficult journey to Jerusalem,
could instead fight Islam in Spain. The popes promoted this, recognizing it
as the equivalent of a crusade."[60]

The collaborative *A History of the Crusades* published under the general
editorship of Kenneth Setton tried to broaden that outlook by taking into account crusades against the Muslims in Spain, the pagan Slavs of Eastern Europe, the Albigensian heretics, and political opponents of the papacy. Julian
Bishko's lengthy chapter on the Spanish Reconquest was a notable contribution to that series.[61] In spite of such major works as Steven Runciman's *A
History of the Crusades*, crusading historians did not fully appreciate the nu-
ances of canon law relating to the crusaders until the publication of James
Brundage's studies.[62] In recent years English scholars have sparked a renewal
of interest in the crusades and have incorporated the wars of the reconquest
into the general theme of crusading history. Jonathan Riley-Smith, for example, defined the crusade as "an expedition authorized by the pope, the leading participants in which took vows and consequently enjoyed the privileges
of protection at home and the Indulgence, which, when the campaign was
not destined for the East, was expressly equated with that granted to crusaders to the Holy Land." Quite recently, however, Christopher Tyerman has
raised many questions, pointing to the ambiguity surrounding the notion of
the crusade, especially in the twelfth century, and emphasizing the lack of a
coherent crusading organization and structure.[63]

The same may be said of the idea of the reconquest, which did not have
an institutional or structural foundation; nor can one say that everyone involved in it was motivated in precisely the same way. The reconquest can best
be understood as an ongoing process, which, though often interrupted by
truces, remained the ultimate goal toward which Christian rulers directed

their efforts over several centuries. Claiming descent from the Visigoths, they argued that they had a right, indeed an obligation, to recover the lands of the Visigothic kingdom; once Christian, those lands were now believed to be held unjustly by the Muslims. Thus the struggle for territory was placed in a religious context and the reconquest became a religious war between Christians and Muslims.

The central theme of this book is the evolution of the reconquest from the late eleventh century until the middle of the thirteenth, with particular attention to the influence of crusading ideology on peninsular warfare. While the "traditionalists" among crusading historians limited the crusade to expeditions directed to Jerusalem, the "pluralists" (to use Tyerman's characterization) emphasized the multiplicity and diversity of crusades proclaimed by the popes. My position obviously is with the "pluralists," as I do not believe that the term crusade can only be applied to expeditions to the east. From the beginning the popes acknowledged that the war against Islam in Spain was as worthy of spiritual and material support as the effort to recover the Holy Land. In many instances the popes stated explicitly that Hispanic crusaders would gain the same spiritual benefits as those going to Jerusalem.

Unlike the reconquest, the crusade in Spain can be viewed as an event, a specific campaign, resulting from a proclamation by the pope, a council, a papal legate, or a bishop who granted remission of sins to those who would take up arms against the Muslims. Whereas kings often made donations of property for "the remission of my sins," waging war against the Muslims as a way of atoning for sin was a new development principally of the late eleventh and twelfth centuries. The proclamation of a crusade presupposed that the benefits offered would be preached to the faithful so that they could be recruited. Preachers presumably expected some declaration of intent on the part of the listener. Only in that way and by confessing his sins and receiving absolution could he obtain remission of sins. Thus the Hispanic crusader, like his eastern counterpart, probably took a vow to participate in the planned expedition and placed a cross on his garments as a sign of his intention. From time to time kings, nobles, and others took the crusader's vow and set out to meet the enemy, fortified by the knowledge that their sins would be forgiven and that if they were killed in battle they would be rewarded with eternal life in heaven. Christian rulers recognized the recruiting value that a promise of remission of sins entailed and were quite prepared to take advantage of the spiritual and material benefits accruing from the crusade. Thus the canonical apparatus relating to crusading was adapted to the peninsular war against Islam. While the reconquest was a constant aim of the

Christian kings, not every campaign of the reconquest was a crusade, but just as one might refer to Reconquest Spain, I believe it is entirely appropriate to speak of Crusading Spain. Papal crusading bulls are strewn across the pages of Spanish history and crusading ideas and wars had a profound impact on peninsular life.

In addition to following these developments due attention will also be directed to the business of the organization and financing of armies as well as the rituals associated with military campaigns. As one might expect the process provoked tensions between popes who thought to use the crusade in defense of Christendom and kings who often were motivated not by the crusading ideal or even by the tradition of reconquest, but rather by mutual rivalry and jealousy.

The focus of this study is medieval Spain, the Hispania of the Romans, the term employed by popes and others to describe the entire Iberian peninsula. Consideration of the reconquest and crusade in all the Hispanic kingdoms, namely Aragón, Catalonia, Navarre, Castile, León, and Portugal, ought to advance our understanding of the war between Christianity and Islam as a general European phenomenon. How the idea of the reconquest was modified and transformed by the concept of the crusade is the subject of the pages that follow.

Chapter 2
From Barbastro to Almería, 1063–1157

From the middle of the eleventh century to the middle of the twelfth the Christian reconquest made important advances at the same time that crusading ideas were introduced into the peninsula. Following the disintegration of the Umayyad Caliphate of Córdoba early in the eleventh century a significant alteration of the political situation occurred with the emergence of a series of statelets known as *taifas*: Badajoz in the west; Seville, Granada, and Málaga in the south; Toledo in the center; Valencia and Denia on the east coast; the Balearic Islands; and in the northeast, Zaragoza, and Lleida (Lérida). None of them was strong enough to reunite Islamic Spain and their quarrels made them an easy prey to the Christians of the north who manipulated them to their own profit.[1]

The Christian states of León, Castile, Navarre, Aragón, and Catalonia, however, were as much rivals of one another as of the kings of the *taifas*. Rather than present a united front in opposition to Islam, Christian rulers vied with one another in imposing tribute on the *taifas* and later contended over rights of conquest. Just as the Muslim kings concluded that it was prudent to become vassals of their Christian neighbors, paying tribute and joining in attacks on their fellow Muslims, so too, when it suited their purpose, Christian princes did not hesitate to make alliances with Muslims. From time to time, individual knights, including the Cid, often hailed as the great hero of the Christian reconquest, entered the service of Muslim rulers and fought against their fellow Christians.[2]

The strongest of the Christian monarchs, Fernando I, king of León and Castile (1035–65), and his contemporary, Count Ramon Berenguer I of Barcelona (1035–76), demanded tribute from the *taifas*, the former from Zaragoza, Toledo, and Badajoz, and the latter from Zaragoza and Lleida. Meantime Fernando I's conquest of Coimbra (1064) and other towns gave him control of northern Portugal.[3] After his death his sons quarreled, but one of them, Alfonso VI (1065–1109), emerged as master of his father's entire inheritance. Until this time the reconquest was mainly a war for the recovery of territory believed to be held unjustly by the Muslims. The twelfth-century *Chronicle of Silos* made the point that Fernando I "expelled the madness of the Moors from Portugal," and that his son Alfonso VI labored "in expanding the kingdom of the Spaniards" and "in taking provinces back from their sacrilegious hands and converting them [the provinces] to the faith of Christ."[4] Insofar as the reconquest pitted Christians against Muslims, it was at this time a religious war, not a crusade.

The transformation of the reconquest into a crusade came about as a consequence of the opening of the peninsula to French and papal influences in the second half of the eleventh century. The principal vehicles of this process were the pilgrimage to Santiago de Compostela; the introduction of Cluniac monasticism; and marriages between the Christian rulers of the Pyrenean states of Navarre, Aragón, and Barcelona with their neighbors in southern France, and between the royal house of León-Castile and the French ducal house of Burgundy. Thus the sense of isolation in which Hispanic Christians had lived was relieved, and as the century wore on, many French knights who had familial and feudal ties south of the Pyrenees discovered an outlet for their aggression in the war against the peninsular Muslims. The influx of Frenchmen into Spain coincided with the beginning of the crusades to liberate the Holy Land.[5]

Barbastro: A Crusade Before the Crusades

Papal interest in the war against the Spanish Muslims first became manifest when Alexander II (1062–73) and Gregory VII (1073–85) encouraged French knights to carry out expeditions into Spain. The former, probably in 1063, addressed a bull to the *Clero Vulturnensi* (the clergy of Voltorno, perhaps Castel Voltorno in Campania in southern Italy) instructing "those knights destined to set out for Spain" to confess their sins and to receive an appropriate penance. He declared: "We, by the authority of the Holy Apostles Peter and Paul, relieve them of penance and grant them remission of sins." Although some questioned the authenticity of the bull, Goñi Gaztambide argued that it was genuine and that there was no serious reason for rejecting it.[6]

Pope Alexander offered two things to knights planning an expedition into Spain: relief from penance and remission of sins. With respect to the first, it was clear that once the knight confessed his sins and received absolution, his involvement in the expedition would satisfy any necessary penance. The pope and those who heard him likely understood remission as the blotting out of all the knight's sins up to that time. In the past one might atone for sin by entering a monastery or going on pilgrimage, but from this time on remission might be gained by taking up arms against the enemies of Christian society. In that respect, Cowdrey emphasized that a revolution in Christian thinking about the liceity of warfare was effected. Although the pope's bull did not use the word indulgence, Goñi Gaztambide asserted that Alexander II "granted a plenary indulgence . . . an indulgence in the strict sense." Brundage affirmed that this was "the earliest known papal grant of anything approaching an indulgence proper. . . . In this letter the pope for the first time claimed to relieve the participants in a military expedition of the penance which they had merited for their sins." Nevertheless, Brundage concluded that this commutation of penance was not technically an indulgence remitting the temporal punishment due to sin. Indeed that modern doctrine of the indulgence had yet to be elaborated. The term indulgence as used in subsequent papal crusading bulls was rather ambiguous, but probably meant that the sins of the one who confessed, received absolution, and did penance by taking part in the struggle against Islam would be remitted; his soul having been washed clean of sin, the crusader who fell in battle would gain immediate entrance into heaven.[7]

The pope did not explicitly refer to a military expedition, but it is apparent that that is what he had in mind. The suggestion that the knights were intent on pilgrimage to Santiago, rather than war against the Muslims, is not likely. In a letter addressed to the bishops of Spain and the province of Narbonne, he declared that he was pleased to hear

that you protect the Jews who live among you, so that they may not be killed by those who are setting out for Spain against the Saracens . . . for the situation of the Jews is greatly different from that of the Saracens. One may justly fight against those [the Saracens] who persecute Christians and drive them from their towns and their own homes.

In those few words Alexander II provided a general justification for warfare against the Muslims, a point he reiterated in a letter to Bishop Guifré of Narbonne.[8]

In Goñi Gaztambide's view, Alexander II "transformed the Spanish holy war into a true crusade." While historians may demur, one must acknowledge that Alexander II not only lent papal encouragement to the war against the Muslims in Spain, but also recognized for the first time that the sins of those taking part in it would be remitted and the penance imposed by a confessor would be satisfied by their participation. There seems no significant difference, therefore, between his concession to "the knights destined to set out for Spain" and later bulls of crusade to the Holy Land. In Menéndez Pidal's memorable phrase, the pope launched "a crusade before the crusades."[9]

Although the pope may not have taken the initiative in organizing an expedition into Spain, he obviously was aware of it and may have been responding to an appeal for assistance. His letters were not written in a vacuum and should be put in the context of peninsular developments. In April 1063, for example, he expressed satisfaction at the liberation of the Catalan town of Ager "from the power of the pagans."[10] During the Council of Jaca also in 1063, presided by the southern French archbishop of Auch, Ramiro I of Aragón (1035–63), who aspired to collect tribute from the neighboring Muslims, may have decided to seek both French and papal help for an offensive against them. His death at the hands of a joint Muslim-Castilian force in May removed him from the scene, but his son Sancho I Ramírez (1064–94) inherited his ambitions. Count Ramon Berenguer I, perhaps in preparation for an offensive, promulgated the Peace and Truce of God in a Curia at Barcelona in May 1064. In a Curia held at León in December 1063, Fernando I probably planned the siege of Coimbra, which surrendered after six months on 9 July 1064.[11] Alexander II may have known of these plans and may have attempted to coordinate them.

In the summer of 1064 troops from Burgundy, Normandy, and Aquitaine, with Normans from Italy, and other Italians, Catalans, and Aragonese set out against the Muslims.[12] Their leaders included Robert Crispin of Normandy, William VIII, duke of Aquitaine, and Count Ermengol III of Urgell, who, six years before, had agreed to share the tribute of the *taifas* with the count of Barcelona. Ibn Ḥayyān's mention of "the commander of the cavalry of Rome" (*qā'id khayl rūmah* or *rūmiyah*), prompted speculation concerning the commander's identity and the possibility that Alexander II entrusted him with the banner of St. Peter. Although that cannot be proved, it seems likely that Ibn Ḥayyān understood that the Christians were acting with papal approbation. Paul Chevedden's identification of Robert Crispin as "the commander of the cavalry of Rome" has merit.[13]

At the beginning of August 1064, after a siege of forty days, the Christians captured Barbastro, about sixty miles northeast of Zaragoza. The defenders were assured that they could depart in safety, but the Christians massacred them, raped their women, and enslaved their children. Giving themselves up to the luxuries of Muslim life, their pleasure was cut short when al-Muqtadir, king of Zaragoza (c. 1049–c. 1083), recovered Barbastro, around the end of

April 1065. Ibn Ḥayyān remarked that "the city was purified from the filth of idolatry, and cleansed from the stains of infidelity and polytheism." Not until 1100 would Barbastro fall to the Christians again. Despite this loss, the expedition made manifest that French knights could reap substantial spiritual and material rewards by taking part in the wars in Spain. The northerners also displayed a fanaticism toward the Muslims that differed from the comparative tolerance of peninsular Christians who, over centuries, had learned to accommodate the Islamic presence. The same phenomenon later became apparent during the oriental crusades[14] (see Map 2).

Gregory VII and the Spanish Reconquest

Henceforth the papacy maintained a continuing interest in and assumed an increased responsibility for the struggle against Islam in Spain. Encouraged by the initial conquest of Barbastro, Sancho I Ramírez, in the hope of enlisting support for further military action, became a papal vassal in 1068 and married the sister of Count Ebles de Roucy; with papal approval, the latter agreed to undertake an expedition into Spain.[15]

The proposed expedition was part of the unfinished agenda that Alexander II left to his successor, Gregory VII. Following his election, he reminded his legates in southern France to lend every encouragement to Ebles de Roucy, who had concluded a pact with the papacy concerning the *terra Hispanie*. Suitable persons chosen by the legates would determine whether the rights of St. Peter were being safeguarded in accordance with that agreement. As other princes were also planning to go to Spain, the pope required that they too be made aware of papal rights and enter an equitable pact "on behalf of St. Peter." On the same day, he wrote to "all the princes wishing to go to Spain":

We believe that it is not unknown to you that the kingdom of Spain belonged from ancient times to St. Peter in full sovereignty (*proprii iuris*) and though occupied for a long time by the pagans, it belongs even now—since the law of justice has not been set aside—to no mortal, but solely to the Apostolic See.

That being so, he was prepared to dispose of Spanish lands to any Frenchman who conquered them. He announced that Count Ebles intended to "enter that land and to rip it from the hands of the pagans for the honor of St. Peter" and "obtained this concession from the Apostolic See: that he

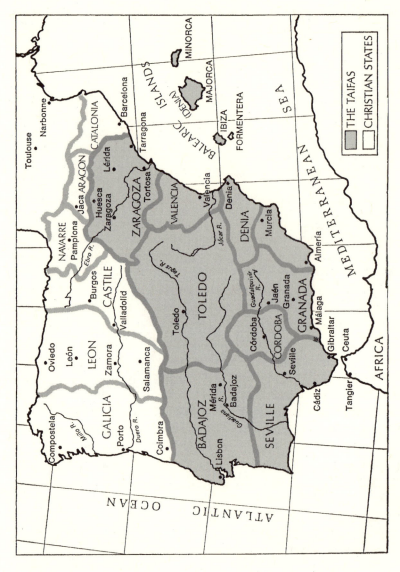

Map 2. Spain at the death of Fernando I, 1065.

should hold on behalf of St. Peter under the conditions of the pact made between us that region from which he is able, on his own or with the help of others, to expel the pagans." In effect, whatever land the count conquered would be held in vassalage from the papacy. Encouraging the princes to join the count, Gregory VII admonished them, if they intended to act independently, to do nothing to injure the rights of St. Peter in Spain, "as do the ones ignorant of God who now occupy it." Unless the princes entered an equitable pact to maintain those rights, the pope prohibited them from entering the country.[16] Although he made no offer of remission of sins, that may have been included in the agreement between Count Ebles and Alexander II. One may reasonably suppose that the count expected the same spiritual benefit as the expeditionaries to Barbastro, but Gregory VII's overriding concern was to guarantee respect for papal rights in Spain.

There is scant evidence of the outcome of this affair, save that Suger, abbot of St. Denis, reported that Ebles de Roucy led a great army such as kings command into Spain. Nevertheless, as none of the peninsular sources mention the expedition, it seems not to have achieved any important success. Describing the expedition to Barbastro and that of Count Ebles as crusades, José María Lacarra remarked: "It is interesting to note that the small kingdom of Aragón succeeded in attracting the interest of the papacy in order to serve as a scenario for the first crusades known to Christendom. The fame of the great crusades to the Holy Land in European historiography has eclipsed the memory of this peninsular precedent."[17]

A few years later, Gregory VII, likely basing himself on the false Donation of Constantine, claimed that "the kingdom of Spain was given by ancient constitutions to Blessed Peter and to the Holy Roman Church in right and ownership." While he congratulated the Christian rulers for having reconquered the land, he exhorted them to render the *servitium*—apparently a monetary tribute—once paid to St. Peter which had been abandoned because of the Saracen invasion. Even though the Muslims had occupied the peninsula for centuries, he firmly believed that papal rights were still valid. His apparent intention to treat reconquered land as fiefs held of the papacy clashed with the peninsular idea of reconquest. Alfonso VI, by declaring himself "emperor of all Spain" or "emperor established over all the nations of Spain," asserted his hegemony over the entire peninsula and implicitly rejected Gregory VII's pretensions.[18]

At this time the reconquest assumed a different character as the Christian rulers intensified their pressure on the *taifas*. When Alfonso VI sent

Count Sisnando to collect tribute, 'Abd Allāh, king of Granada, recorded the count's explicit expression of Christian intentions:

Al-Andalus originally belonged to the Christians. Then they were defeated by the Arabs. . . . Now that they are strong and capable, the Christians desire to recover what they have lost by force. This can only be achieved by weakness and encroachment. In the long run, when it has neither men nor money, we'll be able to recover it without any difficulty.[19]

After wasting away the enemy by levying tribute, Alfonso VI initiated a new aggressive policy when he captured Toledo on 6 May 1085.[20] At the installation of Bernard de Sauvetot as archbishop in the following year, the king described his motivation:

The city, by the hidden judgment of God, for three hundred and seventy-six years had been held by the Moors who commonly blasphemed the name of Christ. . . . In the place where our holy fathers adored the God of faith, the name of the cursed Muḥammad was invoked. . . . I took up arms against the barbarous peoples. . . . I directed my army against this city . . . thinking that it would be pleasing in the sight of the Lord, if I, Alfonso, the emperor, under the leadership of Christ, were able to restore to the devotees of his faith, the city which wicked people under the evil guidance of their leader Muḥammad had taken from the Christians.

The theme of restoration was reiterated by Pope Urban II (1088–99) who commented that "through the efforts of the most glorious King Alfonso and the labor of the Christian people, after the Saracens were expelled, the city of Toledo was restored to the law of the Christians."[21]

The rulers of the *taifas*, recognizing that all would eventually be swallowed up by Alfonso VI, summoned to their aid the Almoravids (the "Moabites" of the Christian chroniclers) who had recently subjugated Morocco. The invaders promptly routed Alfonso VI at Zallāqa (Sagrajas) a few miles northeast of Badajoz on 23 October 1086. Responding to his appeal, a French army, including Eudes, duke of Burgundy and Count Raymond of Toulouse, crossed the Pyrenees but, after unsuccessfully attacking Tudela on the Ebro River, they returned home. In the next several years the Almoravids overwhelmed the *taifas* and incorporated them into their empire. As a consequence of Almoravid expansion, the Christians were kept on the defensive for the next fifty years.[22]

The last of the *taifas* still independent of the Almoravids were Zaragoza and Valencia. For some years the Castilian exile, Rodrigo Díaz de Vivar, the

Cid, protected Zaragoza from domination by Aragón or Barcelona. He also extended his protection to al-Qādir, the former king of Toledo now ruling in Valencia, but after his assassination the Cid seized the city in 1094, and not long after defeated the Almoravids at Cuart de Poblet. Only after his death in 1099 and the abandonment of Valencia by the Christians in 1102 were the Almoravids able to take possession. For the time being only Zaragoza escaped their grasp.[23]

Nevertheless, King Pedro I (1094–1104) of Aragón made the conquest of Zaragoza his principal objective. As a first step toward that goal, he continued his father's siege of Huesca, a town giving access to the Ebro River valley and ultimately to Zaragoza about fifty miles to the south. After he defeated al-Mustaʿīn, the king of Zaragoza, at Alcoraz in 1096, the defenders abandoned Huesca, thus allowing the Aragonese to take possession. Four years later Pedro I captured Barbastro, thereby removing two obstacles to his advance on Zaragoza. Inspired by the proclamation of the First Crusade, he soon appeared before Zaragoza at the head of a crusading army.[24]

Urban II and the Restoration of the See of Tarragona

The second invasion of Spain by the Almoravids in 1089 brought home to Urban II, as Guibert de Nogent noted, the threat not only to Christian Spain but also to southern France. In order to counteract Islam the pope encouraged Archbishop Bernard of Toledo to restore the other metropolitan sees still under Muslim rule (namely, Tarragona, Braga, Mérida, and Seville) and to bring about the conversion of the "infidels." The latter admonition— almost an afterthought—is the first indication of papal interest in a mission to Spanish Islam.[25]

In practical terms the restoration of the archbishopric of Tarragona in the northeast, though deserted, seemed most feasible.[26] With that intention, Urban II in 1089 exhorted the Catalan bishops and nobles, in remission of their sins, to rebuild Tarragona:

We encourage those who will set out for Jerusalem or other places in a spirit of penitence or devotion to expend all the labor of that journey on the restoration of the church of Tarragona, so that that city . . . may be celebrated as a barrier and a bulwark against the Saracens for the Christian people, to whom, out of the mercy of God, we offer that indulgence which they would gain if they had fulfilled the journey [to Jerusalem].[27]

In effect, the pope offered to those helping to restore the archbishopric the same indulgence and remission of sins that they would gain if they went on pilgrimage to Jerusalem or elsewhere. Encouraged by his words, Count Berenguer Ramon II of Barcelona pledged to restore Tarragona and "delivered the city and all the land of his power to Blessed Peter and his vicars," promising to pay an annual tribute. In gratitude for this generosity, Urban II in 1091 appointed Bishop Berenguer of Vic as metropolitan of Tarragona, and pleaded with Count Ermengol of Urgell to undertake the recovery of Tarragona: "You should not hesitate to offer an acceptable sacrifice to the almighty Lord and to receive the indulgence of your sins." Whatever aid the count could give to Bishop Berenguer would be taken as "penance and absolution of sins."[28]

By providing military support for those settling in Tarragona the Catalan counts would merit remission of sins, absolution, and indulgence, the same spiritual benefits later offered for the oriental crusade. In spite of the pope's pleas, however, the restoration of Tarragona would not soon be accomplished. Archbishop Berenguer, as McCrank pointed out, "seems to have experimented with an organization closely resembling a military confraternity for the recovery of Tarragona." He encouraged a band of knights, living a communal life in several frontier fortresses, to restore Tarragona "for the redemption of all their sins."[29] All efforts at repopulation, however, were unavailing.

Pope Urban's letters reveal that he was fully cognizant of the efforts of Christian Spain to conquer lands held by the Muslims. Indeed, he seems to have had a broad view of the relationship between the Islamic world and Christendom. If he could offer remission of sins and indulgence to the Catalans striving to repopulate and defend Tarragona, he could extend the same benefit some years later to those going on crusade to the Holy Land. Just ten years after the fall of Toledo and four to six years after urging the restoration of Tarragona, he launched the First Crusade at the Council of Clermont in 1095. The same remission of sins offered by Alexander II in 1063 and Urban II in 1089–91 was now offered to those who would deliver the holy places from the "infidels." In seeking the genesis of the First Crusade one must look to these Spanish antecedents.[30]

Spanish Crusaders to the Holy Land

The pope's appeal evoked an enthusiastic response in Spain, but he soon had to direct Spanish Christians to their own struggle against Islam. For example, he urged Counts Bernat of Besalú, Guislabert of Rousillon, and Guillem of Cerdanya:

for the remission of sins to strive for the restoration of the city and church of Tarragona. . . . If, therefore, the warriors of other provinces unanimously propose to aid the churches in Asia and to liberate their brothers from the tyranny of the Saracens, so also should you, with one heart, strive . . . to help the neighboring churches suffering from the incursions of the Saracens. If anyone should die for God and for the love of his brethren in that expedition, he should not doubt that by the mercy of our most clement God he will truly receive indulgence of his sins and participation in life eternal. If anyone of you, therefore, plans to go to Asia, let him try to fulfill the desire of his devotion here. For there is no virtue in delivering Christians from Saracens there while exposing Christians here to the tyranny and oppression of the Saracens.[31]

The pope stated quite bluntly that it made no sense to journey to the east to liberate the Christian people from the Muslim yoke while ignoring those closer to home. Anyone who took up arms against the Muslims in Spain was assured of gaining indulgence, remission of sins, and life eternal, just the same as the oriental crusaders.

The pull toward the Holy Land was strong especially after the fall of Jerusalem in 1099, an event reported in the peninsular annals. The thirteenth-century author Archbishop Rodrigo noted that Urban II "was the first to establish that those going to the aid of the Holy Land should be signed on the right shoulder with the sign of the cross."[32]

Among those responding to the papal summons to the crusade was Pedro I of Aragón, who had renewed his father's tie of vassalage to the papacy, pledging an annual tribute.[33] In 1100 he "accepted the cross to go to the region of Jerusalem" but, perhaps at the urging of Pope Paschal II (1099–1118)—as Cardinal Rainier, a former legate in Spain—he opted instead to engage the Muslims at home. As a *crucifer* or cross-bearer he appeared before Zaragoza in February 1101 "with the banner of Christ," the first reference to the cross as the emblem of the crusade. As a base of attack on Zaragoza he also began construction of a castle called *Juslibol* (*Deus le veult*—"God wills it") just opposite the city.[34] Although he did not achieve the conquest of Zaragoza Pedro I, who had obviously heard of the message of Clermont, ought to be considered one of the first crusaders in Spain.

Meantime pilgrims and crusaders from Portugal, León, Castile, Aragón, Navarre, and Catalonia made the journey to the east. Among those participating in the First Crusade were Count Guillem Ramon of Cerdanya (whose son Guillem Jordà did so in 1102); Count Fernando Díaz of Asturias, and Pedro Gutiérrez. Count Rodrigo González de Lara, after quarreling with Alfonso VI, went to the Holy Land and eventually entered the Order of the Temple. Count Berenguer Ramon II of Barcelona, accused of murdering his brother, was forced to go into exile to the east in 1097.[35]

When Archbishop Bernard of Toledo, a former Cluniac monk, "signed with the sign of the cross," appeared in Rome in May 1099 on his way to the Holy Land, Urban II, who had a clearer vision of the nature of the struggle against Islam, absolved him of his vow and sent him home. The archbishop's action was an example of northern European incomprehension of the Spanish situation. Another Frenchman, Count Henry of Burgundy, the husband of Alfonso VI's daughter Teresa, reportedly journeyed to the Holy Land about 1103. Maurice Bourdin, the French archbishop of Braga, did so between 1104 and 1108.[36]

As the kingdom of León-Castile was hard pressed by the Almoravids after 1086 there is little reason to think that Alfonso VI ever contemplated participating in the oriental crusade. On the contrary, he appealed to the pope to restrain his people from exposing the kingdom to Muslim attacks by making the journey to Jerusalem. In 1101 Paschal II forbade the people of Spain to abandon their own land "which the ferocity of the Moabites [the Almoravids] so frequently assails." At the same time he offered remission of sins to those who would fight the Muslims in King Alfonso's realm. In effect, he was proposing an alternate crusade in Spain.[37]

In the following spring the pope expressed his concern that the people of León-Castile failed to obey his command:

We wrote to you previously that you should not abandon your country because of the expedition to Jerusalem. . . . For we are not a little fearful of the tyranny [of the Muslims] in the western regions if you depart. . . . We command you to stay in your country; fight with all your strength against the Moabites and the Moors. There with God's help, you will do your penances. There you will receive the remission and the grace of the Holy Apostles Peter and Paul and of their Apostolic Church.

Paschal II ordered all the pilgrims to return home, including the bearers of this letter, but no one was to blame them for not having completed their pilgrimage to Jerusalem. Although this letter of 25 March has usually been dated in 1101, it may have been prompted by the Almoravid defeat of Infante Sancho, the heir to the Leonese-Castilian throne, at Uclés in 1108. The pope's assurance that those fighting the Muslims in Spain would gain remission of sins emphasized that he considered that war a crusade in precisely the same way as the expeditions to the Holy Land.[38]

Both Urban II and Paschal II understood much better than many would-be Spanish crusaders to the Holy Land the importance of the struggle against Islam in Spain. By conceding to those who fought the Spanish Muslims the same remission of sins granted to the oriental crusaders, they evinced a global outlook not necessarily shared by the Christian rulers in Spain or in any other European country. There is no record that Alfonso VI ever took the crusader's vow but he and his people certainly understood that they would benefit from the remission of sins offered by Paschal II. Similarly several French knights who had been to the Orient, for example, Gaston IV of Béarn, Rotrou of Perche, William VI of Montpellier, and Alphonse Jourdain, count of Toulouse, realizing that they could obtain the same remission of sins in Spain, eventually took part in the Spanish wars. Their presence helped to diffuse knowledge of the Holy Land and of crusading, especially in Catalonia and Aragón. Therefore, it is not incorrect to describe as crusades the wars against the Muslims in Spain in the years immediately following the First Crusade.[39]

The Crusade to the Balearic Islands

While crusading ideas penetrated Spain across the Pyrenees, the Atlantic and the Mediterranean also put Spain in contact with the crusading world. In 1108, for example, King Sigurd of Norway, with sixty ships, embarked on a crusade to the Holy Land. After plundering Galicia, he sailed along the coast of Portugal, defeating a Muslim fleet and massacring the Muslims of Sintra who refused to accept Christianity. Unable to take Lisbon, he sacked Alcácer do Sal before passing through the Strait of Gibraltar; after dispersing another Muslim fleet, he raided Formentera, Ibiza, and Menorca, and then continued on to the east in 1109.[40] This assault foreshadowed the crusade soon to be launched against the Balearic Islands.

Meanwhile, Pisa and Genoa had been actively attacking Muslim positions in the western Mediterranean. They collaborated with Alfonso VI in an unsuccessful attack on Valencia in 1092, and then joined Sancho I Ramírez in besieging Tortosa, again without success. In 1113 in response to Pisa's request, Paschal II (whose bull is no longer extant) presented a cross to Archbishop Pietro of Pisa and Roman standards to the military leaders, while also offering a crusade indulgence to everyone who participated in an expedition to deliver Christian captives held in the Balearic Islands. Cardinal Boso was named as legate.[41]

Sailing from Pisa on 6 August 1113, the fleet wintered in Catalonia. Count Ramon Berenguer III (1097–1131), hoping perhaps that they might eventually collaborate in the conquest of the Catalan coastal towns, agreed to be their standard-bearer whenever they came to Spain "against the Saracens." At Girona on 7 September he "received on his shoulder the sign of the most holy cross" from Archbishop Pietro. Other participants included William VI, lord of Montpellier (who been on crusade to the Holy Land); Aimery, viscount of Narbonne; contingents from Nîmes, Arles, and Béziers; Bishop Ramon Guillem of Barcelona and other bishops; and people from Catalan maritime communities. The crusading fleet, numbering about eighty Pisan ships, forty-seven French, and probably forty or fifty from Catalonia, reached the Balearic Islands in June 1114. After occupying Ibiza, the crusaders overran Mallorca and besieged the chief town, Palma, taking it by assault on 3 April 1115.[42]

The success of this venture led Ramon Berenguer III to make agreements with Genoa and Pisa for an assault on Tortosa, the chief port at the mouth of the Ebro River. Paschal II, whom he asked to concede a crusading indulgence, congratulated him for his victory in Mallorca and for intending "to oppose the Moors and Moabites [Almoravids] in Spain and to besiege their fortress of Tortosa." The bull of crusade no longer exists, but the pope appointed Cardinal Boso as his legate with the task of preaching the crusade. In preparation, the count levied tribute on the Muslim kings of Valencia, Tortosa, and Lleida, but the projected crusade seems not to have taken place.[43]

The conquest of Mallorca was ephemeral, as the Almoravids seized the islands within a year and another century would pass before a new crusade was launched against them. Meantime, at an unspecified date, the consuls of Pisa, recalling their friendship and alliance with Ramon Berenguer III and their joint conquest of Mallorca, emphasized that, even though the Muslims held Mallorca, the island still remained under Pisan and Catalan protection.[44] The crusade to the Balearic Islands taught the Catalans the value of Pisan or Genoese naval support in future twelfth-century efforts.

The Crusade Against Zaragoza

Soon afterward, Alfonso I of Aragón-Navarre (1104–34), known as the Battler, a king inspired perhaps more than any of his peninsular contemporaries by the crusading ideal, appealed for French assistance in capturing Zaragoza, the last independent *taifa*, which had fallen to the Almoravids in 1110.[45] His representative, Bishop Esteban of Huesca, probably attended the Council of Toulouse in 1118 which "confirmed the way of Spain"—language that can be understood to mean that the French bishops proclaimed a crusade for Spain. Several French nobles, namely, Gaston IV of Béarn (who had been to the Holy Land), his brother, Centulle of Bigorre, and Bernard Ató of Carcassonne responded to the king's plea, as did Diego López de Haro, lord of Vizcaya, and Count Ramon of Pallars. The siege of Zaragoza commenced on 22 May 1118.[46]

Later in the year Bishop-elect Pedro of Zaragoza was sent to Pope Gelasius II (1118–19), then journeying through southern France. In response, the pope declared that "If anyone of you receives penance for his sins and is killed in this expedition, we, by the merits of the saints and the prayers of the whole Catholic Church absolve you from your sins." Moreover, he offered "remission and indulgence of their sins" to those laboring in the "service of the Lord," and contributing to the repair of the church of Zaragoza. Although he assured those who were killed in the siege of remission of sins, it seems reasonable to suppose that anyone taking part would also enjoy that benefit. It is likely that the Council of Toulouse had previously given that assurance. Goñi Gaztambide pointed out that the concession of remission of sins not only to the warriors but also to those contributing to the construction of the church and the maintenance of its clergy was an entirely new element in the bull of crusade. Bishop Pedro exhorted the faithful if they could not come to Zaragoza at least to make a donation for the church and the clergy. On the authority of the pope and of all the bishops of Spain, the papal legate, Archbishop Bernard of Toledo, offered remission of sins to everyone who did so.[47]

Alfonso I's defeat of an Almoravid army attempting to relieve the city on 6 December compelled the defenders to surrender on 18 December. Muslims wishing to depart were allowed to do so, but those opting to remain would retain their possessions provided that they paid an annual tribute. Early in the new year the king extended certain customs and privileges to those choosing to settle there. In the next two years he seized Tudela, Tarazona, Borja, Calatayud, and Daroca, thereby pushing his frontier well south of the Ebro River. When the Almoravids attempted to recover their losses, he triumphed over them at Cutanda, near Daroca, on 18 June 1120. Five years later he made a triumphal march into al-Andalus, bypassing Valencia, Denia, Játiva, and Murcia, and moving on toward Granada. Marching westward he inflicted a severe defeat on the Muslims at Lucena on 10 March 1126 and then set out on the homeward journey, accompanied by several thousand Mozarabic Christians who were later settled in the Ebro valley.[48]

Crusades East and West

Alfonso I's conquest of Zaragoza likely encouraged Pope Calixtus II (1119–24) to attempt to broaden the Christian offensive in Spain, where as, Cardinal Guy of Burgundy, he had served as legate. By proposing an assault against Islam in both east and west he made explicit the policy of Urban II and Paschal II who endeavored to dissuade Spanish Christians from going to the Holy Land and to direct their energy to the peninsular war against Islam, where they could also obtain remission of sins.

The First Lateran Council of 1123, convened by Calixtus II, decreed that those who "had placed the cross on their clothing and made a vow" to go to the Holy Land *or* to Spain but had not done so, should do so by Easter next (canon 13). Thus the Council acknowledged that one could gain the crusading privilege both in the east and in the west. The Council also stipulated that incendiaries might atone for their crimes by participating "in the service of God either in Jerusalem *or* in Spain." Later, in the Council of Clermont in 1130, Pope Innocent II (1130–43) obliged incendiaries to render one year's military service either in Jerusalem *or* in Spain. The Catalan assembly of Barcelona in 1131 ordered the observance of this canon, which was subsequently repeated by other councils.[49]

Echoing the Lateran Council, Calixtus II, probably contemplating a Catalan crusade paralleling Alfonso I's Aragonese crusade, in 1123 offered "to all those who fight persistently in this expedition [in Spain] the same remission of sins that we gave to the defenders of the eastern church." If, however, those "who placed the sign of the cross on their garments for this reason" did not fulfill their vow within a year they would be excommunicated. Unable to visit the army "as we would wish," he appointed Archbishop Oleguer of Tarragona as his legate.[50] The pope's expectation that the participants in the expedition would take a vow and wear a cross as an outward manifestation of their intention suggests that this custom was known in Spain and probably had been followed by Alfonso I.

As bishop of Barcelona and archbishop of the still-not-populated see of Tarragona, Oleguer preached at the Council. A disastrous defeat in which many Christians perished at Corbins near Lleida in 1124 may have been the consequence of his preaching. Undeterred, in order to encourage settlement of Tarragona, in 1129 he gave the city in fief to the Norman knight Robert Burdet. Moreover, he also appears to have established a confraternity for the redemption of captives. French and Catalan prelates, gathered in the Council of Narbonne in 1129 to consider how "they might succor Christendom which had suffered so much oppression and death from the Saracens," agreed to form a broader confraternity whose members would each contribute at least twelve *denarii* every year for the restoration of Tarragona. There is no further evidence of the confraternity's activities. After Oleguer's death in 1137 Pope Lucius II (1144–45) exhorted the Catalan bishops to restore Tarragona and to aid "in the defense of Christendom."[51] Nevertheless, restoration was protracted and only in 1146 did the archbishop take up residence there.

Calixtus II's proclamation of a crusade also reached the ears of Archbishop Diego Gelmírez of Santiago de Compostela who, in the Council held there in 1125, tried to widen its scope:

Just as the soldiers of Christ . . . opened the road to Jerusalem, so let us become soldiers of Christ and . . . let us open . . . a road toward the same Holy Sepulchre by way of Spain which is shorter and much less difficult. Thus, let anyone who wishes to take part in this expedition [*militia*] examine his sins . . . hasten to make a true confession and sincere penance, and then, taking up arms, let him not delay in going to the camp of Christ in the service of God and for the remission of their sins.[52]

Archbishop Diego proposed a grand scheme, whereby "soldiers of Christ," earning remission of sins, would open the road to the Holy Sepulchre by way of Spain. The idea of proceeding through Spain to Africa and thence to the Holy Land was put forward in the fourteenth century in several treatises on the recovery of the Holy Land. Nevertheless, the death of Queen Urraca (1109–26), whose turbulent reign had precluded any significant action by León-Castile against the Muslims, distracted the archbishop from his projected crusade.[53]

The *Militia Christi* of Belchite and Monreal and the Will of Alfonso I

Meantime, Alfonso I's concern for the security of his new conquests led him to institute in 1122 a military organization comparable to the Order of the Temple, recently founded for the protection of pilgrims going to Jerusalem. Members of the *militia Christi* established at Belchite, about twenty-two miles southeast of Zaragoza, were offered a variety of spiritual benefits. A brother who confessed and dedicated his life to the defense of the Christian people would be absolved of all his sins as though he were making a monastic profession. Anyone serving at Belchite for a year would obtain the remission of sins gained by those going to Jerusalem. Lesser spiritual benefits were given to those serving for a month or contributing financially. Elena Lourie argued that Belchite reflected the Muslim *ribāṭ* in that individual members of the confraternity served for limited times, but I believe that that was true only of associates; members rather were committed to a lifetime of service. Alfonso VII's confirmation of the *militia* indicates that it was still in existence in 1136.[54]

Around 1124 Alfonso I founded a similar *militia Christi* with the extraordinary goal of overcoming all the Muslims beyond the sea and opening a route to Jerusalem. The castle of Monreal, about sixty miles south of Zaragoza, whose name was reminiscent of a crusader fortress in Palestine, was the seat of this new *militia*. The king exempted the members from every service and from the royal fifth of booty, just like the Templars. In likely imitation of these efforts, in 1138 Bishop Guifré of Barbastro and Roda, joined by several other bishops organized a confraternity for the resettlement and defense of Barbastro and offered absolution and remission of sins to all those who aided the work.[55] None of these confraternities seems to have flourished and all soon disappeared from view, but the need for a permanent military force to defend Christian Spain was becoming more apparent.

Alfonso I, meanwhile, resumed his efforts to capture all the fortresses along the Ebro River. With a relic of the true cross carried before him, he seized Mequinenza, about sixty miles southeast of Zaragoza, in 1133. However, he was defeated at Fraga, about fifteen miles north of Mequinenza, on 19 July 1134; falling ill, he died on 7 September. Ordericus Vitalis's description of the king and his warriors as "crusaders of Christ" (*Christi crucesignatos*) suggests that they dedicated themselves to the war against Islam in the knowledge that they would earn remission of sins and that they wore the sign of the cross on their clothing as evidence of their intention.[56] From the beginning of the siege of Zaragoza until his death Alfonso I likely considered himself a crusader meriting the indulgence offered by Gelasius II.

Perhaps because he failed to create a *militia* for the defense of his realm, the king, a crusader to the last, bequeathed his kingdoms to the Military Orders of the Hospital and the Temple and to the canons of the Holy Sepulchre in Jerusalem.[57] Nevertheless, the Aragonese and Navarrese refused to be bound by his wishes and elected their respective monarchs, Ramiro II (1134–37) and García Ramírez (1134–50). Refusing to recognize either one, Pope Innocent II demanded fulfillment of the will. Eventually Ramiro II's son-in-law, Count Ramon Berenguer IV of Barcelona and Prince of Aragón, made a settlement with the Hospital and the Holy Sepulchre, whereby they ceded their rights in Aragón to him. Then in 1143, expressing his concern "for the defense of the western church in the Spains" and the expulsion of the Muslims, and in memory of his father, Ramon Berenguer III, who had become a member of the Order of the Temple, he ceded several castles to the Templars, thereby settling their claims.[58] Thus even though the will was not implemented, both the Temple and the Hospital acquired property in the peninsula and influenced the establishment of indigenous Military Orders.

The Second Crusade and the Fall of Lisbon

In the third decade of the twelfth century a significant political restructuring took place and for a brief time tipped the balance of power in favor of the Christians. Revolts among Spanish Muslims and a grave challenge in Morocco by the Almohads, a new Muslim sect, brought the Almoravid empire to the verge of collapse.[59] The Portuguese *Chronicle* welcomed this internecine conflict as a sign that God, who had visited His wrath on the Christians because of their sins by allowing the Muslims to ravage their lands, was now pleased to bring about the dissolution of Islamic power. The emergence of new *taifas* again enabled the Christians to make territorial gains at Muslim expense.[60]

In 1135 Alfonso VII of León-Castile (1126–57), whose vassals included García IV of Navarre, Ramon Berenguer IV of Barcelona, William, lord of Montpellier, and Count Alphonse Jourdain of Toulouse, declared himself emperor of Spain, thereby asserting his supremacy over the entire peninsula.[61] Despite that act of bravado, new challenges to his ascendancy arose simultaneously. Ramon Berenguer IV, by his marriage in 1137 to Petronila, the daughter of Ramiro II, linked Catalonia and Aragón in what proved to be an indissoluble union. Farther west, Portugal, originally part of the kingdom of León, developed as an autonomous entity under Alfonso VI's daughter Teresa and her husband Count Henry of Burgundy. Their son Afonso I Henriques (1128–85), following his victory over the Muslims at Ourique (whose exact location is debated) in 1139, began to call himself king of Portugal.[62] As protection against the overwhelming power of León-Castile, he promised to pay four ounces of gold annually to the papacy as a sign of vassalage. Although Pope Lucius II commended his intention to "oppose the pagans," he acknowledged him only as duke of Portugal.[63]

Indeed, the three principal Christian rulers, Alfonso VII, Afonso I, and Ramon Berenguer IV, each of whom had relations among the crusading families of France, were intent on "opposing the pagans" and took advantage of Pope Eugenius III's (1145–53) proclamation of the Second Crusade to extend their respective realms. Archbishop Raimundo of Toledo, who was in Rome when the pope issued the crusading bull *Quantum predecessores* in December 1145, likely informed him of Alfonso VII's triumphs over the Muslims, to which the pope alluded in another bull two years later.[64] In 1146 all three men were actively planning military operations against the Muslims of Lisbon, Almería, and Tortosa.

About six years previously, Afonso I had an initial opportunity to collaborate with a northern fleet of about seventy ships, "full of armed men vowed to go to Jerusalem." Elated by news of their arrival at Porto at the mouth of the Douro (Duero), he made an agreement with them to besiege Lisbon. Though blockaded by land and by sea, the city could not be taken, and the northerners continued on their way. From the later account of the conquest of Lisbon in 1147 we know that tension developed between him and the northerners. Two of the crusading leaders, William Viel and his brother Ralph, who had participated in the earlier siege, distrusted Afonso I and accused him of failing to fulfill the terms of their agreement.[65]

After the crusaders departed Afonso I subjected the petty Muslim lords of Lisbon and Santarém to tribute and then seized Santarém, about forty-six miles to the north of the city, on 15 March 1147. The arrival of another northern crusading fleet a few months later prompted him to besiege Lisbon again.[66]

The fleet's coming was once considered a matter of chance, but Livermore and Phillips argued that Afonso I, the son of a crusader, learning of plans for the Second Crusade, sent his brother Pedro to discuss with St. Bernard of Clairvaux, the principal crusade preacher, the possibility of assistance to Portugal. In an undated letter (perhaps issued in July 1146), Bernard responded positively and forwarded to the king "documents which set forth the liberality of the Holy See." That was probably an allusion to papal bulls granting crusading indulgences. Phillips contended that in Bernard's preaching tour of the Low Countries he brought the Portuguese proposals to the attention of potential participants in the Second Crusade. Thus, when the fleet, bearing crusaders from Cologne, Flanders, Frisia, and Normandy, set out on 27 April, Phillips concluded that they had already agreed to collaborate with Afonso I, who was expecting their arrival. The early departure date indicates that a stop in Portugal was planned; otherwise the fleet would have arrived in the Holy Land well before the main crusading armies.[67]

The continental crusaders, joined by Englishmen and Scotsmen, sailed from Dartmouth on 19 May 1147. Count Arnold of Aerschot led the Rhinelanders; Christian of Gistel (whom Bernard met during his preaching tour of the Low Countries) commanded the Flemings, while the Anglo-Normans were headed by Hervey de Glanvill, Simon of Dover, Andrew of London, and Saher of Archelle.[68] Reaching the coast of Galicia, they made a pilgrimage to Santiago de Compostela on 7–8 June; setting out again on 15 June, they arrived at Porto at the mouth of the Douro on the next day, Monday.

There Bishop Pedro Pitões informed them that the king, who "had known in advance" of their coming, had already set out ten days previously for Lisbon. The bishop, on the king's command, urged them to take part in a just war, acting "like good soldiers, for the sin is not in fighting war, but in fighting for the sake of booty." Without reaching a decision, they sailed to Lisbon, arriving on 28 June. Although Afonso I appealed to them directly, they were of mixed minds, for as noted above, some did not trust him. Others pointed out that there was plunder aplenty to be had by preying on shipping along the coasts of Africa and Spain. Still others believed that they should continue to the Holy Land. After Hervey de Glanvill appealed to their sense of honor and spoke in favor of collaborating with the king, they concluded an alliance with him and were guaranteed their right to all the plunder of Lisbon and the ransom of captives. Once they had sacked it thoroughly, they would surrender it to him; those who wished to settle there would be given lands to hold "according to the most honorable customs and liberties of the Franks," and they and their descendants would be exempted from tolls throughout his kingdom. His promise to continue the siege unless forced to desist by mortal illness or by an attack from another quarter probably reflects their distrust.[69]

Archbishop João of Braga, sent to invite the Muslims to surrender, contended that they had "unjustly held our cities and lands already for 358 years," and exhorted them "to return to the homeland of the Moors whence you came, leaving to us what is ours." Rather than press that demand, however, he concluded by asking only that the citadel be surrendered while the Muslims remained in the city, enjoying their traditional customs. The Muslim spokesman, complaining of Christian greed, rejected this plea and declared his intention to hold out until God should determine otherwise.[70]

The siege began in earnest on 1 July. Blockading the city by land and sea, the crusaders constructed siege machines and movable towers while attempting to undermine the walls. Although the defenders successfully thwarted these efforts and destroyed the crusaders' machines, as the siege progressed and hunger set in, some inhabitants fled. Some accepted baptism, while others were beheaded; the hands of still others were cut off and they were sent back to the city where their fellow citizens hurled stones at them. Any hope the defenders had of receiving aid from their fellow Muslims was soon shattered and the crusaders were able to gain entrance by breaking through the wall. After a siege of five months the Muslims offered to capitulate, but discord between the king and the crusaders threatened to disrupt the process. At last, an agreement was reached allowing the Muslims to depart freely. When the crusaders entered the city on 24 October 1147, they ransacked it and killed many, including the Mozarabic bishop whose name is not recorded. The nearby fortress of Sintra (about fifteen miles to the west) as well as Almada south of the Tagus, directly opposite Lisbon, and Palmela, about fifteen miles to the south, were also captured. Gilbert of Hastings, an Englishman, was installed as bishop. Although some crusaders opted to settle there, most resumed their journey to Jerusalem on 1 February 1148.[71] The capture of Lisbon was one of the enduring consequences of the Second Crusade, indeed, one of its few successes.

Alfonso VII and the Crusade of Almería

While Afonso I was engaged in the siege of Lisbon, Alfonso VII was besieging the Mediterranean port of Almería. The Genoese, viewing Almería as a nest of pirates, attacked the town in 1146, but allowed themselves to be bought off. They then proposed a joint assault to Alfonso VII, who was besieging Córdoba.[72] The royal chronicle stated that he agreed to pay 30,000 *maravedís* in return for ships, arms, and supplies to be ready by 1 August (probably in 1147). He also invited his vassals, Ramon Berenguer IV and William of Montpellier, to participate "for the redemption of their souls." The treaty concluded in September 1146, however, required the king to pay 10,000 gold dinars within a month and another 10,000 at Easter in return for a Genoese fleet, troops, and siege machinery to be ready in the following May. Besides a third of all conquests and the right to establish factories and markets, the Genoese were exempted from tolls in his dominions. Ramon Berenguer IV subscribed to a similar pact and also obtained a promise of Genoese assistance in taking Tortosa after the conquest of Almería.[73]

About the same time that he seized Calatrava, about sixty miles south of Toledo, in January 1147, the king probably asked Eugenius III to grant crusading privileges. In *Divina dispensatione*, a new version of the crusading bull issued in April, the pope not only encouraged a crusade against the pagan Wends, but also acknowledged that "the king of the Spains [Alfonso VII] is strongly arming against the Saracens." In effect, the pope affirmed that the wars against the Muslims in Spain and the Wends were equivalent to the crusade to the Holy Land. In the minds of contemporaries a three-pronged offensive was being undertaken against the "infidels" in the Orient, in Spain, and in Eastern Europe. A year later the pope commented that he had willingly granted the royal petition concerning "an expedition against the tyranny of the infidels." That implies that Alfonso VII had asked that remission of sins be offered to participants in the assault on Almería. The contemporary *Poem of Almería* also declared that "pardon of sins was granted" and that the archbishop of Toledo and the bishop of León, while reminding crusaders of the likely temporal rewards of gold and silver, extended pardon of sins to them.[74]

A Genoese fleet of sixty-three galleys and 163 other ships arrived before Almería probably in July 1147. The count of Barcelona appeared with one ship and fifty-three knights, while Alfonso VII had 400 knights and 1,000 footsoldiers.[75] Bishop Arnaldo of Astorga exhorted the troops saying: "Now it is necessary that each one confess himself well and fully and know that the gates of paradise are open." In effect he suggested that those who fell in battle would gain entrance into heaven as martyrs to the faith. The Genoese Caffaro tells us that the Muslims offered 100,000 *maravedís* if Alfonso VII would withdraw, but the Genoese refused and determined to attack by themselves. Almería fell on 17 October 1147, a week before the fall of Lisbon. Although Caffaro described the assault as solely the work of the Genoese, it is certain that without the Spanish Christians the city would not have been taken.[76]

In February of the new year at Palencia the king probably discussed a continued offensive with his bishops (whom the pope had summoned to the Council of Rheims), and with Ramon Berenguer IV at Almazán on 5 April. A week after Easter, on 27 April, Eugenius III, recalling that he had granted the king's petition concerning an expedition against the "infidels," and was ready to do so in the future, now rejoiced "for the victory given to you by the Lord God of Hosts against the enemies of the name of Christ." He encouraged him to "strive to subjugate the barbarous nations," and as a sign of his good will sent him a golden rose, customarily carried by the pontiff on Laetare Sunday, the fourth Sunday of Lent. Then at some time during the summer of

1148 Alfonso VII laid siege to Jaén, but was compelled to withdraw after some of his commanders were captured. Simon Barton described this as a forgotten crusade.[77]

Ramon Berenguer IV's Crusade of Tortosa

Meantime, the Genoese, in return for a third of the city and exemption from tolls, pledged to collaborate with Ramon Berenguer IV in attacking Tortosa at the mouth of the Ebro River. Eugenius III, on 22 June 1148, promised the faithful who joined the assault against "the infidels and enemies of the cross of Christ . . . that remission of sins which . . . Pope Urban established for all those going abroad for the liberation of the oriental church." Those who completed "such a holy journey" or died there, if they confessed their sins, were assured of absolution and an eternal reward. Goñi Gaztambide pointed out that this was the first time that papal protection of crusaders' wives and children was cited in a bull of crusade directed to Spain.[78]

The Catalans and the Genoese, joined by William of Montpellier and crusaders from France, and others who had recently taken part in the capture of Lisbon, initiated the siege on 1 July. After five months the defenders asked for forty days in which to seek help, but when that was not forthcoming they surrendered on 31 December 1148. In the following year Ramon Berenguer IV captured Fraga, Mequinenza, and Lleida all on 24 October, thus completing the conquest of Catalonia and gaining control of the Ebro as far as Tortosa.[79] A bishopric was restored there and the Genoese were rewarded for their services.[80] The conquest of Tortosa, like the capture of Lisbon and Almería, was facilitated by the disintegration of the Almoravid empire, but also by collaboration between peninsular and extrapeninsular Christians, all inspired by the papal concession of the crusading indulgence.

The Peninsular Aftermath of the Second Crusade

Aware of French frustration over the failure of the Second Crusade and the possibility of still another expedition to rescue the Holy Land, the peninsular rulers likely hoped that they could again expect help from crusading fleets. Two poems by the troubadour Marcabrú may relate to these efforts to induce French participation in a crusade. Declaring that God summoned Alfonso VII "to take vengeance on the lineage of Pharaoh," he lamented that the French had abandoned "the enterprise of Spain and of the Sepulchre." It was left to Alfonso VII, with divine assistance, to repulse the Muslims, who took comfort in knowing that the northerners were mired in jealousy. Assured by preachers that they would gain "honor, wealth, and merit," the Spanish Christians, with their combined strength and shouting *"reial,"* would "defeat the pagan nation." In another poem he charged the French with degeneracy if they refused to take up "the affair of God."[81]

Representatives of Afonso I and Alfonso VII, meeting at Toledo in May 1150, agreed to seek northern assistance. Afonso I, who was contemplating an attack on Seville, dispatched Bishop Gilbert of Lisbon to his native England to seek recruits. Aided by northern ships the king twice unsuccessfully besieged Alcácer do Sal, about forty miles southeast of Lisbon, in the 1150s.[82] In the summer of 1150 Alfonso VII besieged Córdoba and in the following summer Jaén, but in each case without success. While at Jaén, he waited in vain for French ships coming to blockade Seville. Despite those setbacks he remained optimistic and concluded a treaty with Ramon Berenguer IV at Tudellén on 27 January 1151 delimiting future zones of conquest. The east coast, including Valencia, Denia, and Murcia, was allotted to the count to hold as a vassal of Alfonso VII, who reserved the remaining Muslim lands to himself.[83]

With his eye on those coastal towns, Ramon Berenguer IV in 1149 compelled Ibn Mardanīsh, the Muslim ruler of Valencia, to pay an annual tribute of 100,000 gold *dinars*. In 1152, Eugenius III, in response to the count's plea, extended to all the faithful who joined him in a crusade the indulgence given for the Holy Land. In the following year Anastasius IV (1153–54) reissued the crusading bull, but the campaign was limited largely to consolidating the count's control of the Ebro valley.[84]

Nevertheless, the need for a concerted Christian effort to halt Almohad expansion was becoming more evident. From their initial landing in Spain in 1146 the Almohads had begun to devour the petty Muslim kingdoms. Surely with the pope's approval, his legate, Cardinal Hyacinth (the future Pope Celestine III), attempted to organize a crusade at the Council of Valladolid in January–February 1155; Alfonso VII attended. Besides promulgating the Peace and Truce of God, the Council assured the defenders of Christendom of the same remission of sins obtained by making the journey to Jerusalem, and placed their persons and property under papal protection (canons 1, 18, 32).[85] Cardinal Hyacinth declared further that he had placed the sign of the cross on his own breast and proposed to lead an army against the "enemies of the cross of Christ." Alfonso VII's capture of Andújar and some other towns in the summer of 1155 was likely the immediate outcome of this crusade. In the following year, however, the Almohads undid his work.[86]

As they swept eastward, the king hastened to relieve Almería, but arrived too late and the town was lost. Returning home, he died on 21 August 1157. Lamenting his death, the troubadour, Peire d'Alvernha, cried out: "O King, by Christ, do not abandon us, because the Almohads are superior to us."[87]

In the ninety years or so from the siege of Barbastro to the death of Alfonso VII soldiers taking up arms against the Muslims in Spain were frequently promised remission of sins in return for their labors. Indeed, concession of that benefit by Alexander II in 1063 and by Urban II in 1089–91 antedated the First Crusade by some years and must be taken into account when discussing the origin of the crusading movement. Whether the military actions in Spain following the issuance of these papal bulls constituted a crusade, a pre-crusade, or an anticipation of the crusade will likely be disputed for many years. Nevertheless, there seems to be no significant difference in the benefits offered by both popes and by the early twelfth-century bulls of crusade. After the proclamation of the First Crusade, Urban II, Paschal II, Gelasius II, Calixtus II, Eugenius III, and Anastasius IV all emphasized that anyone engaged in the struggle against Islam in Spain merited the remission of sins given for the oriental crusade. Indeed, Spaniards were so stirred by the appeal to deliver Jerusalem that the popes had to offer that benefit to persuade them to combat the Muslims at home. In 1125 Archbishop Diego Gelmírez linked the western and eastern crusades when he proposed opening the way to Jerusalem via Spain.

Spanish crusaders were often aided by others coming from abroad. Thus the Pisans joined the Catalans in the Mallorcan Crusade and French knights collaborated with Alfonso I in the Crusade of Zaragoza and thereafter. In some respects the king of Aragón was a quintessential crusader devoted to the destruction of Islam until his dying day. His experiments with the *militia Christi* of Belchite and Monreal anticipated the later development of the indigenous Military Orders so typical of the crusading era. By bequeathing his realms to the Templars and Hospitallers and the canons of the Holy Sepulchre he not only testified to his crusading ideal but furthered the expansion of those Orders in Spain. Papal legates were named for only two crusades, Archbishops Pietro of Pisa in 1114 and Oleguer of Tarragona in 1123, but Cardinal Hyacinth placed himself at the head of a crusading army in 1155.

Seeking to benefit from the Second Crusade Spanish rulers welcomed crusaders from abroad. A fleet of northerners on their way to the Holy Land enabled Afonso I to conquer Lisbon at the same time that a Genoese fleet aided Alfonso VII in capturing Almería; later in the year Ramon Berenguer IV, again with Genoese assistance, seized Tortosa. The capture of these three cities was among the few successes achieved by the Second Crusade.

The custom of taking the crusading vow and wearing the cross was known in Spain at least from the time of the First Crusade. Intending to go to Jerusalem, Pedro I took the cross but then directed his energy against the Muslims in Spain. Ramon Berenguer III received the crusader's cross from the archbishop of Pisa and Ordericus Vitalis described Alfonso I and his warriors as *crucesignati*. Both the First Lateran Council in 1122 and Calixtus II in 1123 acknowledged that one might take the vow either for the oriental or the Spanish crusade. Explicit evidence that Alfonso VII, Afonso I, Ramon Berenguer IV, and their nobles took the vow or wore the cross is lacking, but, considering the circumstances, it would be foolish to let the argument from silence prevail. Surely these men thought of themselves as crusaders and expected to gain remission of sins. At the close of this period Cardinal Hyacinth gave an example to all when he announced that he had placed the sign of the cross on his breast as an outward sign of his crusading vow. That as well as the participation in the Spanish wars of both Spanish and French knights who had been to the Holy Land helped to disseminate the idea of the crusade and plant it firmly in Hispanic soil.

Chapter 3

From Almería to Las Navas de Tolosa,
1157–1212

In spite of the successes achieved in Spain during the Second Crusade, the disaster in the Holy Land dampened enthusiasm for crusading throughout Europe. Contributing to that was the rivalry and even outright hostility that developed following Alfonso VII's division of his dominions between his sons, Sancho III of Castile (1157–58) and Fernando II of León (1157–88). The resources that either monarch could employ against the Almohads were necessarily diminished, and whatever claims to hegemony they may have had were seriously challenged by both Portugal and the kingdom of Aragón, now united with the county of Barcelona.[1] Meanwhile, the Almohads subjugated Muslim Spain and gravely threatened all of Christian Spain. At the beginning of the new century the Christians finally put aside their quarrels and engaged the Almohads in a decisive battle that spelled the eventual ruin of Islamic Spain.

Given the recent failure in the Holy Land Pope Adrian IV (1154–59) was reluctant to launch an international crusade in Spain, even though he had the opportunity. In 1154, when Louis VII of France came on pilgrimage to Santiago de Compostela, Alfonso VII vainly attempted to enlist him in a Spanish crusade. After concluding a truce with Henry II of England, Louis may have suggested a joint expedition into Spain. The pope, however, counseled him not to enter an alien land unless he was first invited by the princes and people, and reminded him that his crusade, undertaken "without consulting the people" of Jerusalem, had worked to the detriment of Christendom. These words likely cut to the quick and prompted Louis VII to abandon all thoughts of a Spanish crusade. Adrian IV, unlike his predecessors Alexander II and Gregory VII, realized the folly of promoting foreign expeditions into Spain without taking into account the wishes of the faithful there. A few years later, in 1163, when Bishop Gilbert of Lisbon attended the Council of Tours, he may have solicited Louis VII's assistance for a Portuguese crusade; if so, nothing came of it.[2]

However that may be, the new kings of Castile and León, at Sahagún in

1158, delimited future zones of reconquest in Islamic Spain and agreed to partition Portugal. Fernando II would have the right to all Muslim territory from Lisbon southward in the Alentejo through Évora and Mértola on the Guadiana as far as Niebla, and westward along the coast to Silves; in addition he would have Mérida and Badajoz on the upper reaches of the Guadiana. All the rest was reserved for Sancho III, except that Seville and its revenues and all the castles from Seville westward to Niebla would be divided between the two kings. The remainder of the Guadalquivir valley and the land southward to Granada fell to Castile.[3]

The treaty of Sahagún reflected a sense of optimism about the future that would not be borne out by the course of events in the next half century. The death of Sancho III and the minority of his son, Alfonso VIII (1158–1214), threw Castile into disorder, prompting the Council of Segovia in 1166 to condemn anyone disturbing the peace or entering the service of the Muslims (canons 11, 17). Moreover, penance enjoined on anyone responding to the royal summons to defend the realm against invasion would be remitted, as if the individual had gone to Jerusalem (canon 2). Once again the war against Spanish Islam was equated with the oriental crusade.[4] In the western lands south of the Tagus River and in the valley of the Guadiana flowing westward and then turning in a southerly direction after passing Badajoz, Afonso I and Fernando II vied for position but their advances were undone by the Almohads. In the east Pope Adrian IV lauded Ramon Berenguer IV's intention "to dominate the barbarous peoples and wild nations, that is, the madness of the Saracens who are a most destructive pestilence," but he apparently did not issue a crusading bull.[5]

The principal obstacle to Almohad expansion in Murcia and Valencia was Ibn Mardanīsh, who turned for protection to Alfonso II (1162–96), the new king of Aragón and count of Barcelona. Although Ibn Mardanīsh pledged a tribute of 25,000 *maravedís* in 1168, a month later Alfonso II and Sancho VI of Navarre (1150–94) agreed to share equally in the conquest of Ibn Mardanīsh's dominions. In the next year Alfonso II seized Teruel, about ninety miles directly south of Zaragoza, which provided him with a base for incursions into the kingdom of Valencia. Two years later he concluded a friendship pact with Alfonso VIII, who guaranteed that Ibn Mardanīsh, who had failed to pay the promised tribute, would be compelled to pay 40,000 gold *maravedís* for five years. Payment of tribute ceased, however, after Ibn Mardanīsh's death in 1172. Seizing his lands, the Almohads now had effective control of Islamic Spain.[6]

The Military Orders

As an immediate defense against the Almohads several Military Religious Orders were established in Spain in imitation of the Orders of the Temple and the Hospital of St. John of Jerusalem. Founded in the Holy Land, those Orders benefited from Alfonso I's will. Renouncing claims to his dominions in 1143, the Templars agreed, in terms expressive of the ideal of reconquest, that a militia, on the model of the Order established in Jerusalem, should be constituted

for the defense of the western Church which is in the Spains, for the suppression, conquest, and expulsion of the nation of the Moors and the exaltation of the faith and religion of holy Christendom of the militia of the Temple of Solomon in Jerusalem which defends the oriental church, in subjection and obedience according to the rule and institutes of blessed obedience.[7]

While the Templars had their principal base at Monzón, about thirty miles northwest of Lleida, the seat of Hospitallers was at Amposta about eight miles south of Tortosa. Ramon Berenguer IV expected that the Hospitallers would strive "for the exaltation of the church of Christ, the propagation of the faith . . . and the defeat and confounding of the Moorish race."[8] Although both Orders acquired property in all the Christian kingdoms, their principal holdings were in Aragón and Catalonia..[9] As they tended to use their revenues to support their brethren in the Holy Land, Afonso I insisted that the Templars employ their Portuguese income in Portugal "while the war between the Saracens and Christians lasts."[10]

Sensing that they could not rely fully on the oriental Orders, the Christian rulers welcomed the newly established Military Orders of Calatrava, Alcántara, and Santiago, whose foundation helped to disseminate the crusading spirit. The argument that these Orders merely imitated the *ribāṭ*, a fortress in which Muslim volunteers dedicated themselves for limited periods to war against the Christians, ignores the Christian tradition of warfare in defense of the faith and the influence of the Templars and Hospitallers.[11]

In 1147 Alfonso VII had given Calatrava, a fortress in the Guadiana valley guarding the approaches to Toledo (see Figure 1), to the Templars, but their inability or unwillingness to defend it created a crisis. In 1158 Sancho III granted Calatrava to Abbot Ramón of the Cistercian monastery of Fitero, who had responded to his plea for help, "to defend it against the pagans, the enemies of the cross of Christ . . . so that the Christian religion may be propa-

Figure 1. Calatrava la Vieja, original seat of the Order of Calatrava. Photograph by J. F. O'Callaghan.

gated and the kingdom may be protected." Archbishop Juan of Toledo "on hearing this holy intention, gave thanks to God and immediately provided help from his goods and caused it to be preached publicly that all those who went to the aid of Calatrava would merit remission of all their sins." This would appear to be the second time that a Spanish bishop (the first was Diego Gelmírez) offered a crusading privilege. In effect, the first of the indigenous Hispanic Orders had been brought into being. The friars received a *vivendi forma* or way of life from the Cistercian General Chapter and papal approval in 1164, and were affiliated to the Order of Cîteaux in 1187.[12]

Calatrava soon set down roots in the neighboring kingdoms. Alfonso II entrusted the Order with the fortress of Alcañiz, about sixty miles southeast of Zaragoza.[13] In the kingdom of León the Order of San Julián del Pereiro, first documented in 1176, appears to have been a branch of Calatrava at least by 1187. Lucius III in 1183 expressed the hope that the friars would labor "in the defense of Christianity" especially because San Julián was set in "the jaws of the Saracens." Once its headquarters was transferred to Alcántara on the Tagus river in 1218, the Order assumed that new name.[14] The first notice of the Order of Évora in Portugal is also dated 1176, ten years after Afonso I conquered the town. Évora also seems to have been affiliated to the Order of Calatrava by 1187. After transferring their headquarters to Avis, about seventy miles east of Lisbon, around 1223–24, the friars were known as the Order of Avis.[15]

The most powerful and most widely diffused of the Spanish Military Orders was Santiago, whose foundations were laid at Cáceres in the kingdom of León in 1170.[16] In the following year the friars concluded a friendship pact with Archbishop Pedro of Compostela, who placed them under the protection of the Apostle St. James. Although the Almohads soon recovered Cáceres, the knights were richly endowed elsewhere in the kingdom of León. The Order was further augmented in 1172 by the incorporation of the friars of Ávila. The agreement stipulated that once the Muslims were driven from Spain, the friars of both Santiago and Ávila would cross into Morocco and advance on Jerusalem. The recurrence of the idea that once Spanish Islam was eradicated, Morocco could be conquered and Christian forces could march across North Africa to Jerusalem, is especially noteworthy. In 1175 Santiago received papal approval. The friars quickly expanded into the neighboring kingdoms of Portugal, where they received the castles of Monsanto and Abrantes, and Castile where their principal seat was at Uclés, about sixty miles east of Toledo.[17] Before the decade was over Santiago held property in France, England, and as far away as Carinthia.

There were also several ephemeral Orders such as Trujillo, a Castilian branch of the Order of San Julián. First noted in 1188, the Order disappeared after the loss of Trujillo, situated about twenty-five miles east of Cáceres, in 1195. The Order of Mountjoy (Monte Gaudio) in Aragón was absorbed by the Templars in 1196; the Castilian friars attempted to maintain an independent existence at Monfrag (Monfragüe) but they were united with Calatrava in 1221. The Order of San Jorge de Alfama was also established on the Catalan frontier, but little is known of its activities [18]

By entrusting important castles to the Military Orders, the Christian rulers attempted to establish a defensive perimeter stretching from southern Aragón along the Tagus River valley to Lisbon. In Portugal the Order of Avis was dominant, though Santiago was close behind; defense of the Leonese frontier was shared principally by Santiago and Alcántara. The Order of Calatrava controlled the direct route northward from Córdoba to Toledo, while Santiago (and to some extent the Hospital) defended the eastern approaches. In Aragón and Catalonia the Temple and the Hospital were paramount, but south of the Ebro Calatrava, through its commandery at Alcañiz, had the chief role until the end of the twelfth century. By maintaining permanent garrisons along the frontier, the Military Orders were the first to respond to the call to war.

Cardinal Hyacinth, Alexander III, Clement III, and the Crusade

About the very time that the peninsular Orders came into existence, the Almohad Caliph Abū Yaʿqūb Yūsuf I (1163–84) made a major effort to push back the Christians. When he besieged Huete, about thirty miles west of Cuenca, in July 1172, Alfonso VIII prepared to relieve the town and the papal legate Cardinal Hyacinth, who had previously visited Spain in 1155, offered pardon of sins (*grandes solturas*) to the defenders; in other words he granted the remission of sins habitually given to those participating in a crusade. It is likely that in extending the crusading indulgence he acted with papal authorization. The resistance of Huete, aided by heavy rains, and the imminent arrival of Alfonso VIII, compelled the Almohads to abandon the siege within two weeks. Despite that setback, in ensuing years the Almohads forced the Leonese frontier back to the Tagus.[19]

Perhaps in hope of uniting the peninsular rulers against the Muslims, Cardinal Hyacinth, on returning to Rome after two years in Spain, persuaded Pope Alexander III (1159–81) on 23 March 1175 to summon the Christian people of Spain to a crusade. Remission of sins was tendered to anyone fighting to expel the Almohads; anyone dying in the struggle was assured of pardon of all his sins, and anyone enlisted for a year at his own expenses, after confessing his sins, would gain the indulgence given crusaders to the Holy Land. Kings entering alliances with the Muslims injurious to the very faith that they ought to defend would be subject to excommunication and interdict. This bull established the parameters for later papal intervention in Spain.[20]

It is reasonable to believe that Alexander III's bull encouraged the Christian rulers, now that the caliph had returned to Morocco, to take the offensive, knowing that they could gain the spiritual benefits of a crusade. In June 1177 Fernando II, Alfonso VIII, and Alfonso II met at Tarazona, about forty miles northwest of Zaragoza, probably to coordinate a unified campaign. While the king of León led an expedition as far south as Arcos and Jerez, the kings of Castile and Aragón initiated the siege of Cuenca, and concluded a treaty agreeing to act jointly against both Christians and Muslims, except Fernando II.[21] The defenders of Cuenca, after a siege of nine months, realizing that relief would not be forthcoming, surrendered in September.[22] The capture of Cuenca, about 110 miles east of Toledo, was a key to further Castilian and Aragonese expansion southeastward into the kingdoms of Valencia and Murcia.

Acknowledging that Cuenca was "liberated from the dominion of the pagans and brought to the cult of Christianity," Lucius III on 1 June 1182 approved the foundation of the see of Cuenca:

just as the bounds of Christendom were expanded by your [Alfonso VIII] triumphal and magnificent actions, so it behooves us to be solicitous in every way so that the cultivation of the faith and religion may prosper in those places from which, by your warlike efforts, you have expelled the enemies of the cross of Christ and where, through you, Christian dominion is initiated and the church of Christ is beginning to be placed on a stable foundation.[23]

Given their success Alfonso II and Alfonso VIII decided to partition the *terra hispanie* in a treaty signed at Cazola in the province of Jaén on 20 March 1179. Valencia, Biar, Játiva, Denia, and Calpe were reserved for Aragonese conquest; but this treaty differed from that of Tudellén in 1151 in that Murcia, originally included in the Aragonese zone, was now assigned to Castile. Moreover, whatever lands Aragón might conquer in the future would not be under any feudal subordination to Castile. The two kings also proposed to partition the kingdom of Navarre.[24]

During the next six years conflict between the Christians and the Almohads occurred all along the frontier. In the west Afonso I, opting not to break his truce with the Almohads, did not immediately take advantage of Alexander III's crusading bull, but in 1178 he raided Andalucía. The Almohads retaliated in force over the next three years. Both Alfonso VIII and Fernando II also had truces with the Almohads but in 1183 they agreed that, after Christmas, they would resume warfare against them. In view of this aggression, Caliph Abū Yaʿqūb Yūsuf I invaded Spain and laid siege to Santarém in 1184, but had to withdraw five days later, when Fernando II came to Afonso I's aid. Wounded in the engagement, the caliph retreated to Seville, where he died.[25]

Afonso I soon followed him to the grave, dying in 1185. Hailing him as "an intrepid extirpator of the enemies of the Christian name and a diligent defender of the Christian faith," in 1179 Alexander III recognized Afonso I as king of Portugal and placed his kingdom under papal protection, including lands taken from the Muslims in which no other Christian prince had a claim. His kingdom now passed to his son, Sancho I (1185–1211). On the death of Fernando II of León, his son, Alfonso IX (1188–1230), then about seventeen years of age, acknowledged Castilian overlordship in order to avert Alfonso VIII's attempt to dispossess him. Regarding that as a great humiliation, he adopted a hostile attitude toward the king of Castile during times of grave crisis.[26]

Meanwhile, the fall of Jerusalem in 1187 prompted Pope Gregory VIII, who reigned for only a few months, to summon the Third Crusade. His successor Clement III (1187–91) in 1188 guaranteed that Spanish Christians who took up arms against the Muslims would gain the same remission of sins offered to crusaders going to Jerusalem. Lamenting the continued discord among the Spanish kings, which made his sorrow over the disaster in the Holy Land all the greater, he demanded that they settle their differences and agree to a perpetual peace or at least a truce for ten years and join in opposing the Muslims. He also exhorted the Spanish prelates to assist crusaders both in person and economically, and to urge those who could not take part to offer financial aid. The bishops could determine in accordance with the amount of the contribution and the quality of the person the degree of remission to be granted to those providing financial aid or sending substitutes. A crusader who had sworn to pay interest on a loan would be dispensed from his oath and the repayment of the principal would be postponed until his return or until his death was certified. Crusaders and their families would remain under papal protection for the duration of the crusade. The pope concluded by noting that while he had appealed to the people of Europe to rescue the Holy Land, he expected the people of Spain to arm themselves against the Muslims in their own land.[27]

Clement III's letter is significant because it fully extended the terms of Gregory VIII's bull of crusade to Spain. Not only were Spanish crusaders promised remission of sins and the temporal privileges accorded to crusaders going to the Holy Land, but for the first time the pope authorized the collection of ecclesiastical revenues to support the Spanish crusade. Rivera Recio commented that this letter is of "colossal importance" because it linked for the first time the ideas of reconquest and crusade. He also argued that Clement III (whose bull was hitherto unknown), rather than Celestine III, should be credited with the first papal encouragement of the Spanish crusade. The antecedent discussion of papal efforts to encourage crusading in Spain, however, suggests that Clement III was following in the footsteps of his predecessors.

In a second letter the pope commanded the bishops to prepare a report concerning disputes among the Christian monarchs, so that a settlement could be arranged. Meantime the kings were required to terminate their quarrels and take up arms against the Muslims. Although Archbishop Gonzalo of Toledo proposed a meeting for this purpose, Archbishop Pedro of Compostela demurred, suggesting a more convenient time, but there is no evidence that the meeting took place.[28]

The Crusade of Silves, 1189

Whether the papal plan for the taxation of the clergy to support the crusade was executed is unknown; surely the clergy would have opposed it, but just as surely the Christian rulers would have welcomed the opportunity to obtain funds in this way. Inspired probably to act on the pope's offer of the crusading indulgence, Alfonso VIII seized several towns south of the Guadiana River, and then turned southeastward toward the Mediterranean in the summer of 1189.[29]

The most important response to the papal appeal for a crusade came, however, from northern Europeans who collaborated with Sancho I of Portugal before continuing their journey to the Holy Land. In the spring of 1189, a fleet of crusaders from Denmark and Frisia stopped at Lisbon, where they were joined by many Portuguese. Cruising around Cape São Vicente, they attacked the fortress of Alvor, about four miles equidistant from Lagos and Portimão in the Algarve, the southernmost sector of Portugal. After massacring about 6,000 inhabitants (a Muslim historian expressed the hope that "God would reward them for their martrydom on the day of resurrection"), they next set their sights on the city of Silves, about seven miles northeast of Portimão.[30]

A second fleet of thirty-seven large ships bearing crusaders from England, France and Germany (including Louis, landgrave of Thuringia, Count Henry of Bar, Count Airald of Braine, and Saindo of Sandwich) reached Lisbon in July and accepted Sancho I's proposal for a joint attack on Silves. Not only did he provide an additional thirty-seven ships, but he also promised the northerners all the gold and silver they could take from the city. While he marched southward the fleet made its way to Silves where the crusaders, including Templars, Hospitallers, and knights of Santiago, Calatrava and Évora, seized the suburbs and established a siege. Silves was gradually starved into submission and surrendered on 1 September. Although Sancho I agreed to allow the Muslims to depart taking their movable goods, the crusaders objected and refused his offer of 10,000 *maravedís* if they would desist from sacking the city; in the end they had their way, and after pillaging the city on 3 September, they resumed their pilgrimage three days later. One of them, Nicholas, a Fleming, was consecrated as bishop.[31]

This Christian triumph was shortlived, however, as Caliph Abū Yūsuf Ya'qūb, known as al-Manṣūr, the Victorious (1184–99), made his first expedition into Spain in April 1190. The Christians of Silves successfully resisted the assault of one army, while he attacked Torres Novas and Tomar about sixteen miles north of Santarém; he besieged Santarém but Sancho I and a band of English crusaders led by Robert de Sabloil and Richard of Camwill were able to hold the city. In the following year the caliph seized Alcácer do Sal and compelled the surrender of Silves on 20 July. Recent Portuguese gains in the Alentejo and in the Algarve, except for Évora, were thus erased.[32]

Pope Celestine III's Promotion of the Crusade

Thereafter the Almohads concluded a series of truces with the Christian monarchs, who resumed their quarrels. Alfonso VIII, according to Muslim sources, even offered to pay tribute and to wage war against his coreligionists. Perceiving him as domineering, the kings of León, Navarre, Aragón, and Portugal formed alliances to counterbalance Castilian power.[33] Soon after his election, Pope Celestine III (1191–98), the former Cardinal Hyacinth, who knew the peninsular situation quite well, deplored the fact that while all of

Christendom was struggling against the Muslims in the Holy Land "only the Spaniards" were allied with them; he demanded that the Christian kings make peace for ten years and take up arms against the Muslims. As a further inducement he later authorized the absolution of those who injured the clergy, "so long as they make satisfaction for the injury done and do not hesitate to provide appropriate support from their goods for those going to Jerusalem or to Spain to fight against the Saracens."[34]

In 1192 in order to establish peace, the pope dispatched his nephew Cardinal Gregory of Sant'Angelo to Spain, instructing him to urge the Christian kings "to expel them [the Muslims] and drive them far from the lands which the Christian people had cultivated for a long time before." Here Celestine III expressed the idea of Christian reconquest in much the same way as peninsular writers. Lest anyone have any scruples about undertaking such a war, he cited the Book of Maccabees to justify his argument that the Christians were not claiming the lands of others but merely trying to recover what had once belonged to their fathers, which "the enemies of the cross of Christ" had unjustly occupied. He also cited the law of nations as justification for expelling enemies from lands that they occupied to the injury of Divine Majesty.[35]

Expressing his dismay that the Christian rulers of Spain were at peace with the Muslims and at war with one another at a time when the Holy Land was under "pagan" dominion, he commanded the Spanish prelates in 1193 to compel their kings to make peace and to terminate all truces with the Muslims. Whatever the kings might do, he ordered the friars of the Hospital, the Temple, Calatrava, and Santiago, as well as the laity, not to hesitate to wage war against the Muslims because of a truce. They could earn remission of sins and, like crusaders going to the Holy Land, would enjoy the same protection of their persons and goods. Anyone falling in battle would receive not only pardon of sins but also an eternal reward.[36] The suggestion that the Military Orders and the laity ought to attack the Muslims, whether the kings did so or not, would seem to run directly counter to royal intentions and confer on the papacy a superior right to determine the direction of the reconquest in Spain. We have no evidence of the reaction of the kings or the Military Orders to that idea.

Celestine III also directly exhorted Alfonso II (and probably the other kings), like "a true knight of Jesus Christ," to take up arms against the Muslims and to settle his quarrels in order to share in this "privilege of liberty and remission." Sancho I was preparing for a crusade, as the pope indicated when he commended the bishops of Lisbon and Évora who wished to accompany their king "against the enemies of the faith."[37] In 1194 in expectation that the truce with the Almohads would soon expire the kings of Castile, León, and Aragón finally made peace.[38]

The Crusade of Alarcos

Upon the expiration of the truce with the Almohads in 1194, Archbishop Martín of Toledo and the knights of Calatrava ravaged the Guadalquivir area. On hearing this, the caliph, al-Manṣūr, who had been ill and concerned about internal conflicts in Morocco, informed Alfonso VIII's ambassador that "my response to your lord, the traitor, will arrive soon."[39] Both sides now prepared for an offensive in the summer of 1195. One may reasonably suppose that Alfonso VIII understood that the pope's concession of crusading indulgences two years before would apply to himself and his army, and so one may describe the ensuing campaign as a crusade. Addressing the other Christian rulers, Celestine III lauded Alfonso VIII's intention, prompted by the legate Cardinal Gregory, to invade the lands of the Muslims, and he threatened with excommunication and interdict anyone who dared to take hostile action against Castile.[40]

That, unfortunately, could not save the king from a disastrous defeat at Alarcos. In order to provide an additional barrier against attacks on Toledo, Alfonso VIII had begun to construct a fortress at Alarcos on the left bank of the Guadiana River about eight miles west of modern Ciudad Real. Al-Manṣūr, convinced of the need to curb Castilian incursions into Andalucía, invaded in the spring of 1195. As he moved northward, Alfonso VIII requested aid from the kings of León and Navarre, but rather than wait for support, he determined to resist the enemy at Alarcos.

After passing through the Puerto del Muradal (Despeñaperros) at the beginning of July, the Almohads encamped in the plain of Salvatierra, annihilating a detachment of knights of Calatrava issuing from that castle. Moving on to Alarcos, the caliph engaged Alfonso VIII in one of the great battles of the reconquest on 19 July 1195. Overwhelmed by superior numbers, the king fled to Toledo while the remnants of his army scattered over the countryside. Those taking refuge in the castle of Alarcos soon negotiated its surrender. In the next few days the victors occupied numerous castles belonging to the Order of Calatrava, all within easy striking distance from Alarcos. Despite that success, al-Manṣūr opted to terminate the campaign and returned triumphantly to Seville about three weeks later.[41] The battle of Alarcos was the worst defeat suffered by any Christian king since Alfonso VI's rout at Zallāqa a century before. Nevertheless, the territorial losses to the kingdom of Castile were limited to the campo de Calatrava, and for the time being Toledo was still secure.[42]

The Papal Crusade Against Alfonso IX

Returning to Toledo, Alfonso VIII met his Leonese cousin Alfonso IX, who had arrived too late to participate in the battle. They quarreled bitterly, and soon Alfonso IX and Sancho VII of Navarre (1194–1234) entered an alliance with the Almohads against Castile. The protagonist of an earlier anti-Castilian coalition, Alfonso II of Aragón, however, tried to restore harmony and "to establish an alliance of love to wage war against the Agarenes," but he died early in 1196.[43] Once again Celestine III lamented that God, "in punishment for our sins, allowed the violence of the pagans to occupy both the eastern and western frontiers of the Christians;" he urged everyone to "drop everything for Him and take up the sign of the cross in imitation of Him." For the moment, however, his words fell on deaf ears.[44]

The Almohads invaded Castile again in the spring of 1196, ravaging the Tagus valley west of Toledo, while Alfonso IX, with the help of Almohad money and troops, plundered western Castile and Sancho VII pillaged near Logroño.[45] As the king of León seemed to be the principal obstacle to peace, Celestine III on 31 October 1196 accused him of allying himself with the Muslims, an alien people who were attacking Spain. The pope commanded the archbishops of Toledo and Compostela to publish the sentence of excommunication and to rouse the people to take up arms against their king, knowing that they could gain that remission of sins already conceded to those fighting against the Muslims. If the king persisted and dared to introduce Muslim troops into his kingdom, the pope ordered that "the men of his realm shall be absolved from their fidelity and his dominion by authority of the apostolic see." As directed, Cardinal Gregory, again dispatched to Spain, excommunicated the king and several bishops, and placed the kingdom of León under interdict.[46]

Prodded by the legate, Sancho VII made peace by the end of 1196 and Celestine III exhorted him to attack the Muslims in remission of his sins, "with the certain hope of obtaining the worthy prize of victory." Sancho I of Portugal appealed to the pope for crusading indulgences, not against the Almohads but against Alfonso IX, his former son-in-law. In response, Celestine III on 10 April 1197 conceded to those who attacked the king of León the remission of sins given to oriental crusaders. A month later, the pope informed the archbishops of Bordeaux and Auch and the people of southern France that they might fulfill the crusading vow by going to Spain rather than to the Holy Land.[47] Although it has been suggested that this was in reaction to the disaster of Alarcos, I suspect that the pope's real intention was to increase pressure on Alfonso IX. Celestine III's concession of the crusading indulgence to those waging war against a Christian prince was apparently not the first time that that was done, but it provided a more immediate precedent for later papal crusades against political opponents.

In the spring of 1197 al-Manṣūr undertook his third and final campaign against Castile. Once again his forces devastated the Tagus valley, moving eastward toward Cuenca, but he then agreed to a truce for ten years. Free of any concern from the Almohad quarter, Alfonso VIII and Pedro II, the new king of Aragón (1196–1213), invaded León while Sancho I penetrated Galicia. In desperate need of the caliph's assistance, Alfonso IX journeyed to Seville in August or September, but his plea was unavailing. Peninsular narratives say nothing of a crusade against him, nor of his excommunication, nor of the release of his subjects from their oath of allegiance, but the threat of all those disasters surely prompted him to come to terms with Alfonso VIII. As a guarantee of future peace and friendship he married Alfonso VIII's daughter Berenguela in October 1197.[48]

The contentious behavior of the Christian rulers was a scandal that drew a sharp condemnation from the troubadour Peire Vidal, who remarked:

> I am irked by the kings of Spain
> because they so prefer to fight among themselves,
> that they give warhorses and bays
> in tribute to the Moors,
>
> whose pride is doubled thereby;
> so they [the Christians] are defeated and conquered.
> It would be better, if it pleased them
> to maintain peace, loyalty, and faith among themselves.

In another poem he declared:

> It is very wrong that the four kings of Spain
> do not wish to keep the peace among themselves. . . .
> They ought to make their war
> against the people who do not believe in our law,
> until Spain is all of one faith.

Another troubadour, Raimbaut de Vaqueiras, expressed his hope that just as the Fourth Crusade would undo the Turks, so also "the valiant kings of Spain will gather a great host to conquer the Moors."[49] That became a major objective of the new pope, Innocent III (1198–1216).

The ten-year truce with the Almohads enabled the Christian kings to continue their quarrels despite papal appeals. The kings of Castile and Aragón, intending to partition Navarre, invaded in 1198, compelling Sancho VII to seek financial aid from the Almohads in Morocco. Relations between Castile and León deteriorated when Alfonso IX and Berenguela, who were first cousins once removed, bowed to papal demands and separated in 1204.[50] Active intevention by the pope and his legates eventually resulted in the restoration of harmonious relationships among all the Christian realms.[51] Inasmuch as the truce with the Almohads was about to expire the restoration of peace among the Christian rulers by the end of 1209 was indeed a happy circumstance.

The Projected Crusade of Pedro II of Aragón

In the midst of this wrangling, Pedro II, probably late in 1203, informed Innocent III of his desire to make war against the Muslims, but emphasized that he alone did not have sufficient strength to "rip from the hands [of the Muslims] the land that the most Christian kings and Catholic princes had formerly purchased by shedding their own blood." Thus he asked that a legate be sent to induce his colleagues to join him. Although he did not mention it, he likely envisioned the concession of the crusading indulgence. Early in 1204 Innocent III counseled him "not to lead an army against the Saracens at this time" because of continuing dissension among the Christian rulers and the recent conquest of Mallorca by the Almohads. The king was probably contemplating an assault on Mallorca, which the pope now thought unwise, given the changed political circumstances.[52]

Despite those cautionary words, the king set out for Rome, visiting Genoa and Pisa in the hope of enlisting their support in an offensive against Mallorca; he also asked the pope to send a legate to establish peace between those cities and to persuade them to collaborate with him. Anxious, no doubt, to discuss the king's plans with him in person, Innocent III asked him to proceed directly to Rome, assuring him that on his return a legate would accompany him. There, Pedro II, on 10 November 1204, surrendered his kingdom to the papacy, agreeing to hold it henceforth in vassalage and to pay an annual tribute. After being anointed by the cardinal bishop of Porto and crowned by the pope, who girded him with his sword, the king sailed for home, evidently unaccompanied by a legate.[53] Nevertheless, he had demonstrated his firm loyalty to the Catholic faith, and; as a papal vassal, he could now call upon his overlord for protection against all enemies.

Whether Pedro II stopped at Pisa or Genoa is uncertain, but he seems to have come away from Rome with two very different objectives in mind, one reflecting his own preference, the other that of the pope. While he seemed resolved to attack Mallorca or the Muslims in Spain, the pope apparently hoped to direct his efforts against the Albigensian heretics of southern France. Several papal letters written in 1205 bear dramatic witness to the tension between these two aims. Commending the king because "you manfully gird yourself to gain the island of Mallorca," the pope promised to establish a bishopric there, if it were conquered. In a second letter, he again commended the king because "you manfully gird yourself to expel the heretical depravity from the bounds of your realm." In a third letter the pope urged the Aragonese prelates to support the royal offensive against the heretics. Finally, the pope agreed that the knights of Calatrava and Santiago, idled by the Castilian truce with the Almohads, could, if they deemed it expedient, join Pedro II against the Muslims. Presumably the knights would not be permitted to violate the Castilian truce, but they could cross the border into the zone reserved for Aragonese reconquest.[54]

These are mixed messages. The king contemplated an assault on Mallorca or against the peninsular Muslims, while also promising to attack the heretics. The papal counsel of a year before against an offensive against the Muslims had obviously been forgotten and now the pope seemed to acquiesce in whatever military action the king might take. However, the other Christian rulers ignored his plan of campaign, and the lack of support from Pisa and Genoa compelled him to abandon any idea of an attack on Mallorca. Nor did the Military Orders respond to his plea to join him on the frontier. Because of the truce with the Almohads, it was proposed that the knights of Calatrava offer their services to the Latin Kingdom of Jerusalem; but as they lacked the necessary funds, Innocent III encouraged the Spanish monarchs and the faithful, in remission of their sins, to provide them with financial aid. Whether they were able to establish themselves in the Holy Land at this time is unknown.[55]

King Pedro's infeudation of his realm to the pope greatly annoyed his barons, who were even more provoked when, in November 1205 at Huesca, in preparation for his projected campaign—whatever direction it might

take—he imposed an extraordinary property tax, the *montaticum.* The organized hostility of the baronage must surely have forced him to postpone any
serious military operations, whether against Muslims or heretics.[56]

Several years elapsed before he was able to mount an offensive against
the Almohads. Reports that he was preparing to do so reached the ears of Innocent III, who endeavored to persuade Alfonso VIII to imitate his royal col-
league's example. If not, he was forbidden to prevent his subjects from aiding
the king of Aragón, and thus gaining remission of their sins. Whether they
did so in any numbers is unknown. In the summer of 1210, after so many
years of preparation, Pedro II's crusade got underway as he moved southward from Teruel, seizing Ademuz, Castielfabib, and Sertella, the first important Aragonese conquests in the old Muslim kingdom of Valencia.[57]

Preparations for the Crusade of Las Navas de Tolosa

The king of Aragón's success undoubtedly inspired Alfonso VIII's oldest son
and heir, Infante Fernando, "to dedicate the first fruits of his knighthood to
Almighty God by driving the enemies of the Christian name from the
bounds of his inheritance which they impiously occupied." Lauding the
prince's intention, Innocent III announced that kings not bound by truces
with the enemy would also be promised remission of sins, as would pilgrims
helping to carry on the work. Although the pope did not say so, his words
seem to imply that Infante Fernando, and perhaps also his father, had taken
the crusader's vow. Early in the next year Alfonso VIII, now actively preparing to resume hostilities, appealed to the pope to appoint a legate for Spain,
probably to arouse support for the campaign. Although he threatened to excommunicate any king who violated the peace while Alfonso VIII and his
son were attacking the Muslims, the pope, citing the disturbed condition of
the times, denied that request, but hinted that he might name a legate later.[58]

On the expiration of the truce with the Almohads the Christians resumed provocative incursions into Muslim territory. Accepting their challenge, Caliph Abū ʿAbd Allāh al-Nāṣir (1199–1213), whom the Christians
consistently dubbed Miramamolín, that is, *amīr al-muʾminīn* or commander
of the faithful, crossed the Strait of Gibraltar in May 1211, intent on making
war against the king of Castile, whom he described as the nearest and strongest of the Christian princes. While at Seville he received an embassy from
King John of England, who seemingly believed that an alliance with the Almohads might offset the threat of a French invasion of his realm. The En-

glish chronicler Matthew Paris, who despised John, asserted that he over-heard a royal ambassador relate that, in return for the Moroccan alliance John supposedly offered to pay an annual tribute as a sign of his dependence on the caliph, and even agreed to convert to Islam. Concluding that John was a fool, the caliph broke off negotiations. Nevertheless, according to Matthew, the caliph "not without, as it is said, the consent of King John, powerfully prepared to occupy the land of Spain." As Alfonso VIII was married to John's sister Leonor, the accuracy of these remarks must be doubted.[59]

Marching through the Puerto del Muradal in July, the caliph besieged the castle of Salvatierra, about eighteen miles south of modern Ciudad Real protecting the road to Toledo. Salvatierra had served as the headquarters of the Order of Calatrava since the loss of Calatrava itself in 1195. As Alfonso VIII was not prepared to engage the Almohads at this time, he authorized the hard-pressed knights to surrender in September, after a gallant defense of about fifty-one days. Proclaiming that he had cut off "the right hand of the king of Castile," and that the king's failure to respond was "the clearest proof of his weakness," al-Nāṣir, despite that triumph, terminated the campaign. In Christian eyes Salvatierra was a "fortress of salvation" whose resistance de-layed the Almohads until the usual season for campaigning was over.[60]

Well aware that al-Nāṣir intended to invade Castile in the following spring, Alfonso VIII required his vassals to be ready for war at Toledo on Trinity Sunday next. Despite his sorrow over the death on 14 October of his son and heir Infante Fernando, the king was not deterred from his prepara-tions. Appealing to King Philip Augustus of France, he expressed his confi-dence that, although few in numbers, his forces would gain strength from heaven. If perchance he were killed in the coming battle, he believed that he would "truly be counted among the martyrs." In anticipation of the later campaign he seized several castles in the western reaches of the kingdom of Valencia.[61]

Noting that the king chose "to die rather than witness the ruin of the Christian people," Innocent III commanded the bishops of France and Provence to offer remission of sins to everyone who participated in the cru-sade or provided financial support. According to the *Anales Toledanos I*, the pope granted "such liberty throughout the whole world that all should be absolved from their sins, and this pardon was [granted] because the king of Morocco said that he would fight against those who adored the cross throughout the world." Bishop Juan of Osma, the probable author of the *Latin Chronicle*, also reported that the king of Morocco proclaimed his inten-tion to make "war against all who adored the sign of the cross." Archbishop

Arnald Amaury of Narbonne said much the same: "As we have heard from
many people, Miramamolín declared war on all those who adore the cross"
but "he was defeated in a pitched battle by the same ones who venerate the
cross and fled."[62]

The sources cited no doubt had seen or heard of a forged Latin letter of
the caliph dated 8 October 1211 and addressed "to all the kings and princes
of the Christians and especially the king of Aragón and count of Barcelona."
The caliph supposedly pointed out that the Muslims had "cleansed Jerusalem
of the filthiness of the Christians" and that he had now taken Salvatierra, a
source of great pride. Inasmuch as "the law of the Saracens is better than
yours," he urged the Christians to "submit to our empire and convert to our
law." If they refused, he demanded that "all those who adore the sign of the
cross . . . hasten to battle with us where you will feel our swords." Complaining that the king of Aragón, at the pope's suggestion, had caused great harm
to the Muslims, he pledged to carry the war to Rome itself and to subject the
"lord of Rome" to contumely and misery. The letter's language is quite unlike
that of authentic Almohad letters, though, if asked, al-Nāṣir would likely
have subscribed to the sentiments expressed. Nevertheless, one can safely
conclude that it is a piece of propaganda concocted by the Christians and
that preachers quoted the caliph's purported comments in order to stir the
faithful to war.[63]

Troubadours such as Gavaudan and Folquet de Marselha also endeavored to rouse the French. In language reminiscent of the caliphal letter,
Gavaudan, for example, lamented:

> Lord, on account of our sins
> the strength of the Saracens increases.
> Saladin took Jerusalem
> and it has not yet been recovered.
> Now the king of Morocco announces
> that he will fight against
> all the kings of the Christians
> with his treacherous Andalusians and Arabs,
> armed against the faith of Christ.

The caliph, he continued, has assembled all his "captains, Mazmutz [Al-
mohads], Moors, Goths, and Berbers," who in their pride think that the
world belongs to them. "They bluster: 'Frenchmen, make room for us! Provence and the Toulousain and everything as far as Puy belongs to us!' "
Gavaudan then appealed to the emperor, the kings of France and England,

and the count of Poitou to serve God by aiding the king of Spain: "With Him you will conquer all the dogs and renegade turncoats that Muḥammad has bamboozled." Through penance the sin of Adam would be forgiven, and those believing in Christ, their guide against "those vile, false felons," would be exalted. Gavaudan exhorted his hearers: "Firm in the faith, let us not abandon our heritage to the black dogs from oversea." When crusaders from France, Cambrai, England, Brittany, Anjou, Béarn, Gascony, and Provence joined the Spaniards, they would annihilate the enemy and share the gold. In a final peroration Gavaudan, proclaiming himself a prophet, shouted: "Let the dogs die and God will be honored and served where Muḥammad was praised!"[64]

Another troubadour, Guilhem Ademar, affirmed that if King Alfonso and the best count in Christendom—perhaps the count of Toulouse—summoned their host in the name of God they would do great good against "the pagan Saracen traitors." The Cistercian monk, Caesarius of Heisterbach, offered an improbable rationale for the Almohad invasion when he reported that the Albigensians, before Innocent III launched a crusade against them, appealed to al-Nāṣir for help. Hoping to subjugate all of Europe, he gathered a great army and notified "Pope Innocent that he intended to lodge his horses in the portico of St. Peter's Church and to fix his standard on top of it."[65]

Meanwhile, Archbishop Rodrigo of Toledo was sent to France to beg for military assistance. Offering "remission of sins," he urged defenders of the faith to "fortify themselves with the sign of the cross" but his hearers unfortunately turned a deaf ear to his preaching. For his part, Philip Augustus was preoccupied with his own struggle with King John. On the other hand, Master Arnaldo, Alfonso VIII's physician, gathered numerous recruits in Poitou and Gascony.[66]

As Trinity Sunday approached, Innocent III in April 1212 admonished the Spanish kings to keep the peace and truce and urged them to aid one another "against the enemies of the cross of the Lord who not only aspire to the destruction of the Spains, but also threaten to vent their rage on Christ's faithful in other lands and, if they can, which God forbid, oppress the Christian name." Should anyone—and here he specifically mentioned Alfonso IX—join forces with the Muslims or give them aid and counsel, he would be subject to excommunication and interdict. All pending disputes would be resolved at a later date before the papal court. Informed of this directive, Alfonso IX insisted, as a condition for participating in the crusade, that Alfonso VIII surrender certain disputed castles. As the latter was not prepared to do so, Alfonso IX remained at home.[67]

In Rome, meantime, men, women, and clergy, observing the fast, went in procession on Wednesday 16 May to the Lateran basilica, where they prayed "that God might be propitious to those engaged in battle" with the Muslims in Spain. Alberic of Trois Fontaines also reported that "litanies and prayers were offered in France for the Christians who were about to fight in Spain."[68]

The Crusade of Las Navas de Tolosa

The first crusade of which we have direct contemporary information about its proclamation, organization, and execution took place in the summer of 1212.[69] During the octave of Pentecost (13–20 May) "the faithful of Christ gathered at Toledo from all parts of the world because of the remission granted by the Lord Pope, the vicar of the Lord Jesus Christ, to those going off to give battle in support of Christendom in Spain." The "army of the Lord" included Alfonso VIII, Pedro II, Archbishops Arnald Amaury of Narbonne and Guillaume of Bordeaux, the bishop of Nantes, several counts and viscounts from southern France, the knights of the Military Orders of Calatrava, Santiago, the Temple, and the Hospital, as well as Castilian nobles and urban militias. On his way to Toledo, Archbishop Arnald Amaury visited Sancho VII of Navarre, then hostile to Castile, and persuaded him to collaborate. The kings of León and Portugal did not participate in the crusade, but many of their subjects did. The *Anales Toledanos I* related that some northern crusaders who had arrived by Quinquagesima Sunday (5 February) killed many Jews in Toledo, and did a great deal of damage there. None of the sources mentions the taking of a vow, though many crusaders probably did so in Toledo prior to setting out. Both Archbishop Rodrigo and Archbishop Arnald remarked that the warriors bore the sign of the cross on their garments. Infanta Berenguela described the northern soldiers as *peregrini*, a word typically used to refer to crusaders, and not in this instance pilgrims enroute to Compostela.[70]

Alfonso VIII promised to pay the expenses of the 2,000 knights with their squires, 10,000 sergeants on horseback and up to 50,000 sergeants on foot who came to Toledo. Whether those figures are exact or not, his resources were severely strained, but he was able to take care of everyone. Pedro II was so poor and burdened with debt that Alfonso VIII had to pay the stipends for his troops even before they left Aragón and had to give him a daily stipend during the campaign. As the French lacked suitable horses and pack animals, the king had to supply them, dispensing "gold as though it were water." In order to meet these expenses he demanded that the clergy surrender half their annual revenues; they surely were not pleased but had little recourse except to consent. Thus, a substantial part of the money needed to finance the crusade came from ecclesiastical sources, and the king might indeed say that "God ministered abundantly to us."[71]

The Christians set out from Toledo on 20 June on the "way of the Lord" while al-Nāṣir marched out of Seville two days later. On St. John's Day, the French crusaders in the vanguard, "wishing to die for the name of Christ" captured Malagón, about forty-five miles south of Toledo, and slaughtered the defenders. Calatrava capitulated on 1 July after a siege of four days and was restored to the knights of Calatrava. Two days later most of the French crusaders, complaining of the excessive heat and the fact that they had not encountered al-Nāṣir as the preachers had assured them, and certainly protesting Alfonso VIII's refusal to allow them to plunder Calatrava, withdrew, despite all efforts to dissuade them. Only a few, including the archbishop of Narbonne and about 130 knights, remained. Archbishop Rodrigo commented that thereafter "only Spaniards and a few northerners" participated in the crusade. Juan of Osma, the likely author of the *Latin Chronicle*, thanked God who assured that the glory of victory in battle would be attributed "to the famous Spaniards and not to the northerners." The Toledan annalist reported that the French attempted to take Toledo, but the towns-people, reviling them as disloyal traitors, closed the gates against them. Meantime, on 5–6 July the crusading army took several other strongholds in the campo de Calatrava. At this point Sancho VII of Navarre joined the host. After bypassing Salvatierra, the crusaders, guided by a mysterious shepherd, crossed the Puerto del Muradal (Despeñaperros, about 110 miles south of Toledo) and advanced to Las Navas de Tolosa, about twenty-two miles north of Baeza and Úbeda.[72]

There they came face to face with the caliph's army on 13 July. In preparation for the "the battle of the Lord" Archbishop Rodrigo and other prelates exhorted the crusaders who confessed their sins and received absolution. On the day of battle they again confessed, participated in the celebration of mass and received the eucharist; that done, they took up arms and called on divine assistance. While Pedro II commanded the left wing and Sancho VII the right, the Castilians, including the Military Orders, occupied the center, with Alfonso VIII in the rear. Troops from Morocco and al-Andalus formed the bulk of the caliph's army, with light companies of Arab and Berber cavalry on the first line. Al-Nāṣir held the rear, surrounded by his bodyguard of blacks.[73]

When the battle was joined on Monday, 16 July, the Christians broke the enemy lines and achieved an extraordinary triumph. The caliph fled, leaving behind an immense treasure and many dead warriors. Declaring that Divine Providence had granted the victory, Archbishop Rodrigo led the victors in singing *Te Deum laudamus*. Among the many trophies of war, the tapestry covering the entrance to the caliph's tent was sent to the monastery of Las Huelgas near Burgos, where it still hangs in testimony of the victory (see Figure 2). The caliph's lance and his standard worked in gold, as well as his tent, all of silk, were sent to Rome, where the standard was hung in St. Peter's basilica. An exultant Alfonso VIII sent a detailed account of the crusade to Innocent III:

On their side 100,000 armed men or more fell in the battle, according to the estimate of the Saracens whom we captured. But of the army of the Lord . . . incredible though it may be, unless it be a miracle, hardly twenty-five or thirty Christians of our whole army fell. O what happiness! O what thanksgiving! though one might lament that so few martyrs from such a great army went to Christ in martyrdom.[74]

Elated, Innocent III summoned the clergy and people of Rome to give thanks to God and ordered the royal letter to be read publicly. He declared that it was "the sword of God not of man . . . that struck down the enemies of the cross of the Lord." The king's daughter Berenguela communicated news of the victory to her sister, Blanca, better known as Blanche of Castile, the wife of the future Louis VIII of France: "Our father, the king and lord, conquered Miramamolín in a pitched battle; we believe this to be a signal honor, because until now it was unheard of that the king of Morocco should be overcome on the battlefield." Archbishop Arnald Amaury praised Jesus who "gave victory to Catholic Christians under the happy apostolate of the Lord Pope Innocent over three kinds of wanton men and enemies of his holy church, namely, the eastern schismatics, the western heretics, and the southern Saracens." In this way the archbishop linked the Fourth Crusade which assaulted Constantinople and nearly destroyed the Byzantine Empire; the Albigensian Crusade against the heretics in southern France; and the Crusade of Las Navas de Tolosa. Diego García, the royal chancellor, drew a parallel between Rodrigo, the last king of the Visigoths, whose defeat in 711 resulted in the destruction of his kingdom, and Archbishop Rodrigo. As a result of the

Figure 2. The pendón of Las Navas de Tolosa. Las Huelgas de Burgos.

battle of the Guadalete "miserable Spain was almost entirely devastated," but because of Las Navas "victorious Spain not only won out against the Ishmaelites, but also vigorously beat them down."[75]

After gathering immense booty, the crusaders moved southward on 18 July; occupying several nearby castles, and continuing on to Baeza, whose Muslim population had fled. After a siege of three days they took Úbeda by assault. The shortage of supplies and the outbreak of pestilence, however, compelled the king to end the campaign. Although he abandoned Baeza and Úbeda, he had advanced the frontier well south of the Guadiana River and the Castilians were now poised to enter Andalucía. On the return march he greeted Duke Leopold VI of Austria, who had come too late to participate in the crusade. Entering Toledo, Alfonso VIII proceeded to the cathedral where he was received by the people praising God "because He had restored to them their king safe and unharmed and crowned with the crown of victory."[76]

By this time al-Nāṣir had regained the safety of Seville, where, on 31 July, he reassured his people that the disaster was not as great as it seemed. After recounting how Alfonso VIII had appealed for help to his coreligionists from Portugal to Constantinople, and complaining that the king of Navarre, threatened by the pope, violated his alliance with the Almohads, the caliph briefly described the ensuing clash of arms. "God," he said, "wished to purify the believers and to be done with the infidels." He argued that the consequences for the Christians were bad, while the Muslims remained under divine protection, hardly suffering any harm; nor were their numbers diminished. After admonishing his hearers not to be sad because he was not, he assured them that God would not abandon them and would not open a path for the "infidels." In essence the caliph tried to pretend that a great disaster had not occurred.[77]

The Aftermath of the Crusade of Las Navas de Tolosa

Aware that he had dealt a severe blow to Almohad power, Alfonso VIII resumed his campaign early in the new year, seizing several castles, including Dueñas adjacent to Salvatierra, which he gave to the knights of Calatrava; naming it Calatrava la nueva, they made it their new headquarters. At the same time he recognized the necessity of resolving outstanding differences with Alfonso IX, who had attacked the Castilian frontier during the crusade. After reaching a settlement, Alfonso IX decided to collaborate in a continuing assault on Islamic Spain and captured Alcántara, on the Tagus River about fifty miles west of Cáceres. He entrusted its defense to the knights of Calatrava, who gave it over to the knights of San Julián, who were known thereafter as the Order of Alcántara. His attempt to take Cáceres and Mérida was unsuccessful, as was Alfonso VIII's siege of Baeza.[78]

Pedro II, who had distinguished himself at Las Navas, intended to return to the wars against the Muslims, but had to defend his interests in Languedoc, where Innocent III in 1209 had launched a crusade against the Albigensians. Simon de Montfort, the leader of the crusade, was busy carving out a new principality for himself, thereby putting in jeopardy the rights of the king's brother-in-law, Count Raymond VI of Toulouse, and several of his vassals. Meantime, the pope, convinced that a new crusade to liberate the Holy Land was necessary, and believing that "the king of the Saracens"— probably al-Nāṣir—was preparing to go on the offensive, determined to wrap up the Albigensian affair. Thus he instructed his legate, Archbishop Arnald Amaury of Narbonne, another veteran of Las Navas, to dissuade the faithful from seeking the indulgence granted for the Albigensian crusade.[79]

At a Council held at Lavaur Pedro II proposed that the count of Toulouse and others be permitted to atone for whatever excesses they had committed "either by going on the Saracen frontier to aid the Christians . . . or in the regions overseas." In other words they could expiate their faults and their suspected leanings toward heresy by participating in the war against Islam in Spain, for which the king seemed to be planning, or by going to the Holy Land. The assembled prelates, however, objected.[80] By then the king realized that he had no recourse but to aid Raymond VI and to destroy Simon de Montfort, who engaged them in the battle of Muret, just south of Toulouse, on 12 September 1213. Although the king and his allies enjoyed a numerical advantage, they were utterly defeated and he was killed. As a consequence long-standing Catalan hopes of domination north of the Pyrenees were destroyed once and for all.[81]

Although Pedro II had intimated to the pope that the "king of the Saracens" was readying himself for war, the fact is that the al-Nāṣir, on returning to his capital at Marrakech after his humiliation at Las Navas, made no further effort to challenge the Christians, and departed this life on 25 December 1213. His great adversary, Alfonso VIII, succumbed on 5 October 1214 (see Map 3).[82]

As we have seen, the popes, in the third quarter of the twelfth century, smarting from the failure of the Second Crusade in the east, were disinclined to initiate crusades. Despite that, the development of the Military Orders founded in imitation of the Temple and the Hospital helped to keep alive the crusading ideal in Spain. Papal policy changed in the last quarter of the century as the Almohad menace loomed and the reconquest again benefited from the concession of crusading indulgences. Offering remission of sins, Cardinal Hyacinth placed himself at the head of a crusade in 1172 and three years later induced Alexander III to offer Spanish crusaders the same spiritual benefits as were given for the Holy Land. In 1188 Clement III reiterated the importance of the Spanish crusade as well as that of the orient and introduced a new element by proposing that the clergy be taxed in support of the crusade. These documents did not exist in a vacuum. Given the family and ecclesiastical ties between Spain and France, we can be certain that Afonso I, Fernando II, Alfonso II, and Alfonso VIII were fully prepared to take advantage of this spiritual largesse.

In a campaign reminiscent of the Second Crusade, northerners participating in the Third Crusade aided Sancho I in taking Silves in 1189, though the conquest was not permanent. Alfonso VIII, probably encouraged by Celestine III's concession of the indulgence in 1193, took up the struggle at Alarcos two years later, only to suffer a disastrous defeat. In the aftermath, the pope, frustrated by his inability to bring about peace among the contentious Christians, launched a crusade against Alfonso IX, thereby opening the way to the use of the crusade against non-Muslims. As the Christians gradually resolved their disputes, Pedro II contemplated a crusade perhaps against Mallorca, and Alfonso VIII prepared for Las Navas de Tolosa, the culmination of this crusading period. The Christian victory at Las Navas marked the end of Muslim ascendancy in Spain and helped to undermine the Almohad empire, which now entered a period of rapid decline. The balance of power was now tipped decisively in favor of the Christians, thus making possible the subjugation of the greater part of al-Andalus in the next forty years.

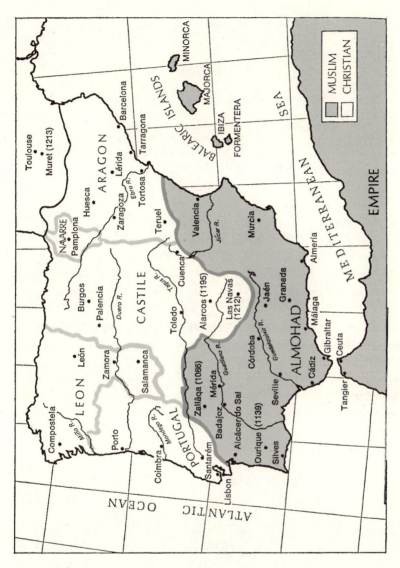

Map 3. Spain at the death of Alfonso VIII, 1214.

Chapter 4

From Las Navas de Tolosa to Córdoba, 1212–1236

An extraordinary transformation of the political landscape occurred in the nearly forty years following the Crusade of Las Navas de Tolosa. As the Almohads struggled to survive in Morocco, Spanish Muslims asserted their independence, but the Christians, taking advantage of Muslim disunity, demanded tribute, set rival Muslim leaders against one another, and eventually conquered Muslim cities and towns. Once again northern crusaders collaborated with the Portuguese in taking Alcácer do Sal, while the Catalans conquered Mallorca, the Leonese captured Mérida and Badajoz, and the Castilians seized Córdoba, once the seat of the Caliphate.

Innocent III, convinced that the danger posed by the Almohads to Spain and to Christendom had been repulsed and that the Albigensian heresy had been contained, determined to direct western energy to the recovery of the Holy Land. When he convoked the Fourth Lateran Council in 1213, he "revoked the remissions and indulgences granted by us to those going to Spain against the Muslims or against the heretics in Provence," because of the success achieved in both regions. The Council, in 1215, launched the Fifth Crusade and also imposed a tax of one-twentieth on ecclesiastical income for three years to support the enterprise. When the Spanish bishops attending the Council asked the pope to extend the crusading indulgence to those fighting the Muslims in Spain, he replied that if a war against the Muslims were undertaken there he would gladly do so.[1] In making that response he was no doubt well aware that a decade might pass before any of the Christian kings (except Alfonso IX of León) would be in condition to undertake a crusade against Spanish Islam. The minorities of Enrique I of Castile (1214–17), Jaime I of Aragón (1213–76), and the Almohad Caliph Abū Yaʿqūb Yūsuf II al-Mustanṣir (1213–24) precluded any significant military action and dictated the necessity of seeking a truce and prolonging it until more favorable circumstances.[2]

Pope Innocent's death in 1216 left this issue as well as the prosecution of the Fifth Crusade to his successor, Honorius III (1216–27), who exhorted everyone who had taken the cross to fulfill their crusading vows. The details of his efforts to collect the twentieth and not to divert it to the peninsular wars will be discussed more fully in a later chapter.[3]

The Crusade of Alcácer do Sal

The Fifth Crusade, in which the Spanish Cardinal Pelagius served as papal legate, had a direct impact in Spain when a fleet of about 300 ships carrying crusaders from Frisia and the Rhineland reached Galicia in June 1217.[4] After making a pilgrimage to Santiago de Compostela they sailed to Lisbon, arriving on 10 July. Afonso II of Portugal (1211–23) apparently made no effort to use their services, lest he be seen as violating the truce with the Almohads. Nevertheless, Bishops Sueiro of Lisbon and Sueiro of Évora, joined by the Cistercian abbot of Alcobaça, the commander of Palmela, the Templars, Hospitallers, and magnates tried to persuade the crusaders to collaborate in an attack on Alcácer do Sal on the river Sado about forty miles south of Lisbon. Alcácer had changed hands more than once and had been lost again in 1191. Besides offering to provide food and expenses, the Portuguese attempted to rouse the crusaders by announcing that the Almohads demanded an annual tribute of 100 Christians. Citing Innocent III's revocation of crusading indulgences in Spain, however, the Frisians departed for the Holy Land with about eighty ships on 26 July. After plundering Santa María de Faro and Rota on the southern coast, they stopped at Cádiz, whose terrified people fled; passing through the Strait of Gibraltar, they sailed up to Tortosa and Barcelona and thence to the orient. Despite that defection, Count William of Holland and Count George of Wied concluded that their presence in the Holy Land would be of limited use, because the Holy Roman Emperor Frederick II and many German princes had not yet set out; thus they opted to remain with 180 ships.[5]

The fleet reached Alcácer do Sal on 30 July and the arrival of the Portuguese three days later completed the siege. The bishops preached and imposed the sign of the cross "on almost everyone in our dioceses and indeed in all the dioceses of the realm." The crusaders attempted to mine the walls but the Muslims impeded them; however, one tower collapsed in part around 24 August. The Muslim governors of Seville, Córdoba, Jaén, and Badajoz attempted to relieve the beleaguered fortress but were thoroughly defeated on 11 September. The crusaders attributed their victory to three miracles: first, the day before the battle, "at evening the triumphant sign of the holy cross appeared in the sky as a sign of victory;" secondly, after midnight, Pedro Alvítiz, the master of the Temple in Spain, arrived with reinforcements; thirdly, a heavenly host of knights all clad in white appeared in the battle, blinding the Muslims in a shower of arrows. The defenders of Alcácer attempted to hold on, but as no further succor appeared, they had to surrender on 18 October 1217.[6]

The Portuguese then appealed to the pope to permit the northerners to remain for a year "for the liberation of Spain" and "the extirpation of the perfidious cult of the pagans." In addition they asked that Portuguese crusaders and those who might assume the cross be granted the indulgence merited by persons going to the Holy Land and that the twentieth should be used for their war, as Innocent III had stipulated. Furthermore, crusaders who had been away for too long, or whose infirmity or poverty made it impossible for them to continue to the Holy Land, should be allowed to return home with full remission of sins. Torn between his pledge to go to the Holy Land and the prospect of more victories in Spain, Count William of Holland informed the pope that Alfonso IX of León, Sancho VII of Navarre, and many Spanish prelates and nobles had taken the cross and broken their truces with the Muslims in the hope that the northerners would continue the crusade in the following summer. Though he congratulated them on their victory, Honorius III commanded the northerners to continue to the Holy Land, leaving Alcácer do Sal to the Portuguese; those lacking the means to do so could be absolved of their crusade vow. Thus at the end of March the northern crusaders set sail from Lisbon, arriving at Acre in late April and May 1218.[7]

Alcácer do Sal, whose conquest was the only positive outcome of the Fifth Crusade, was turned over to the knights of Santiago, who made it their headquarters and began the advance further into the Alentejo and the Algarve.

The Crusades of Archbishop Rodrigo of Toledo and Alfonso IX

About the same time as the fall of Alcácer do Sal, Rodrigo Jiménez de Rada, archbishop of Toledo, hoping perhaps to lay hands on the twentieth intended for the Fifth Crusade, resolved to organize his own crusade, in spite of the truce with the Almohads. Appointing the archbishop as his legate, Honorius III on 30 January 1218 authorized him to lead a crusade: "When kings with one accord set out to war against" the Muslims, Rodrigo "like another Joshua will lead you to wrest from their hands the land which they have occupied and where they have profaned the sanctuaries of God."[8] The legate's first task, however, was to bring about peace between Castile and León.

After the sudden death of Enrique I of Castile, his older sister Berenguela was acclaimed as queen, but she ceded her rights to her son, Fernando III (1217–52). His father, Alfonso IX of León, from whom she had been divorced because of consanguinity, was determined to recreate his grandfather's Hispanic empire by reuniting the two kingdoms. The pope, commenting that dissension among Christians encouraged the Muslims who would never leave Spain of their own volition, warned him to preserve the peace and to collaborate with Archbishop Rodrigo in his crusade against the Muslims. Early in 1218 Alfonso IX acknowledged his son as king of Castile and both men pledged to act in unison against all enemies. Fernando III promised, once his truce with the Muslims expired, to collaborate with his father against them. Meantime Castilians wishing to assist the king of León would be permitted to do so.[9]

Inasmuch as Archbishop Rodrigo and certain magnates had "assumed the living cross" and were determined "to rip from the hands of the Muslims the land they held to the injury of the Christian name," the pope on 15 March 1219 offered remission of sins to those personally participating in the crusade; those who paid the expenses of others or contributed financially would also receive the indulgence. Anyone taking "the sign of the cross" with the intention of going to the Holy Land, with the exception of magnates and knights, unless they were ill or poor, was authorized to fulfill his obligation in Spain. The archbishop was allowed to use half of the twentieth from the sees of Toledo and Segovia for his crusade and to distribute among the crusaders (*crucesignatos*) a third of the tithe collected in the province of Toledo for three years.[10]

Although Navarre did not have a contiguous boundary with al-Andalus, Sancho VII, "burning with zeal for the Christian faith . . . took the sign of the cross to set out against the Moors of Spain." The pope commanded Archbishop Rodrigo to protect Navarre against invasion by its neighbors and to admonish Sancho VII not to injure the kingdom of Aragón during his crusade. Quite possibly the king joined the archbishop in an expedition into the kingdom of Valencia in September 1219. Several castles were taken and Requena, about forty miles west of Valencia, was besieged; but after the loss of 2,000 men the siege was abandoned on 11 November.[11]

Pleased with Archbishop Rodrigo's success thus far, the pope now permitted him to appropriate the entire twentieth from the province of Toledo for use in his crusade during the next three years (4 February 1220). Within five months, however, Honorius III, irritated that conflicts among the Christians were diverting attention from the crusade, revoked his concession, insisting that the entire twentieth should now be used solely for the Fifth Crusade. Despite that, Rodrigo laid siege to Requena again in the summer of 1220, but with no better success. For all practical purposes his crusade had achieved little other than the seizure of several castles. Sancho VII of Navarre, who complained that while he was on the frontier, "having assumed the cross against the Moors," the Aragonese plundered his kingdom, may also have taken part in this crusade.[12]

Archbishop Rodrigo's crusade would seem to have been in violation of the truce with the Almohads, but a campaign in the kingdom of Valencia may have been construed as only an indirect threat to the caliph. Violations occurred on both sides, as an agreement between the masters of Calatrava and Santiago in August 1221 makes clear. Promising mutual assistance in case of Muslim attacks, they agreed to fight as a unit and to divide booty equally. For the time being, however, Fernando III was unprepared to break the truce, and renewed it in October.[13]

Meanwhile, in 1217, Alfonso IX, who had taken the crusader's vow, granted the recently conquered fortress of Alcántara on the Tagus River to the Order of Calatrava. In July of the following year Calatrava ceded Alcántara to the Leonese Order of San Julián del Pereiro, thereby satisfying the king's desire to create an autonomous branch of Calatrava in his kingdom. The presence on that occasion of the masters of Calatrava and the Temple, and the prior of the Hospital, suggests that a military campaign was discussed. In November the "friars of the Orders of Spain began a crusade" (*fizieron cruzada*), aided by men from Castile, León, Gascony, and other kingdoms, including Savaric de Mauléon, former castellan of Bedford. They besieged Cáceres, a long-time objective of Alfonso IX, but heavy rains and flooding forced them to withdraw by Christmastime.[14]

Two years later, Honorius III, reacting to a complaint by the master of Calatrava that the kings of Spain—he clearly meant Fernando III—prohibited the Order from responding in kind to Muslim attacks, warned the kings not to impede those wishing to assist the knights. To anyone who helped to defend the Order he extended the indulgence already granted to those combating the Muslims and especially to Alfonso IX, "who has assumed the cross." In the hope that Spanish Christians might achieve a success comparable to the capture of Damietta by the Fifth Crusade, Honorius III on 13 February 1221 granted absolution of sins to those who joined the king of León in the struggle against the Muslims. The same privilege was offered to financial contributors and to those paying the expenses of others.[15] It seems quite ironic that Alfonso IX, against whom Pope Celestine III had proclaimed a crusade in 1197, should now declare himself a crusader and thus profit from the spiritual benefits that that entailed. He may be the only figure of his time to be both the object of a crusade and the leader of a crusade.

Alfonso IX evidently convened his Curia at Zamora in November 1221 to organize a crusade against Cáceres for the following May. Expressing his desire to "exalt the Catholic faith and suppress the wickedness of the Moors," Bishop Martín Rodríguez of Zamora declared that "in this year we took care to sign ourselves in God with the sign of cross, so that we might obtain indulgence from Christ, as our sins require." The king told him to be prepared for war by 1 May. Although these documents are undated, the probability is that the bishop took the crusader's vow during the Curia of Zamora. A formulaic letter in which an unnamed bishop, perhaps the bishop of Zamora, requested 1,000 gold pieces from an abbot "because we will be with the king of León on 1 May to invade the frontier" is certainly related to this crusade. The same is true for a letter of the master of the Temple "in the whole of Spain" (Pedro Alvítiz), requiring his subordinates to provide him with money, because he intended to set out for Muslim territory around Eastertime (3 April 1222), and did not have the wherewithal to do so.[16] With the help of the Military Orders, Alfonso IX "made a crusade" (*fizo cruzada*), besieging Cáceres in the summer of 1222. The Christians knocked down towers and seemed on the verge of taking it when the caliph in Morocco offered to pay a substantial sum if Alfonso IX would withdraw; although he did so the caliph failed to fulfill his promise. Apparently Alfonso IX made another unsuccessful attack on Cáceres in the following year.[17]

The First Crusade of Fernando III

Thus far Fernando III remained aloof from the crusading efforts of Archbishop Rodrigo and Alfonso IX because he needed to establish himself firmly on the throne, but the crisis of the Almohad regime soon induced him to take up arms against the Muslims.[18] The death of Caliph al-Mustanṣir in January 1224 opened a power struggle among the Almohads in Morocco and encouraged Almohad governors in Spain to seek autonomy. The ensuing struggle over the office of caliph initiated an era of instability, resulting in the neglect of al-Andalus, where several petty kingdoms proliferated once again.[19]

Fernando III may have been spurred on by John of Brienne, the former king of Jerusalem and a leader of the Fifth Crusade, who, after a pilgrimage to Santiago de Compostela, visited the king at Toledo in April 1224 and married his sister, Infanta Berenguela, at Burgos in May. A comparison of the oriental and the occidental crusades surely must have taken place. After the wedding, in the presence of his mother and his court, Fernando III expressed his belief that it was time, unless he should seem weak and ineffectual,

to serve God against the enemies of the Christian faith. The gate is indeed open and the way is clear. There is peace in our kingdom while discord and capital hatreds, divisions, and quarrels are newly arisen among the Moors. Christ, God and Man, is on our side, but on the side of the Moors is the unfaithful and damned apostate, Muḥammad. What is there to do? I beseech you, most clement mother, to whom, after God, I hold whatever I have, that it may please you that I should go to war against the Moors.

After consulting the barons, Queen Berenguela agreed that it was time to abandon the truce and to make war. In the Curia of Carrión in July the decision was taken that all should be ready at the beginning of September. None of the sources mentions whether Fernando III and his barons took the crusader's vow, but it would seem to have been an appropriate time to do so. The phrase "in fulfillment of his vow" (*quasi uoti compos*) used by the author of the *Latin Chronicle* suggests that the king took the vow at this time. Archbishop Rodrigo's statement that the king "wished to dedicate the first fruits of his knighthood to the Lord" also suggests the taking of a vow. Perhaps it was at Carrión that the masters of Calatrava, Santiago, the Temple, and the prior of the Hospital promised to cooperate "against the enemies of the cross of Christ."[20]

The campaign in the fall of 1224 resulted in the capture of Quesada, about twenty miles southeast of Úbeda, but the Muslims soon reoccupied it. In March 1225 Abū Zayd, the governor of Valencia, kissed Fernando III's hand in vassalage and his brother, Abū Muḥammad, commonly called al-Bayāsī, the governor of Baeza, did so in June; he also promised to surrender Martos, Andújar, and Jaén, once he recovered them. Thus, while acknowledging the caliph, the two brothers hoped to maintain themselves in the midst of the general confusion. Meantime, Fernando III, "having a firm and irrevocable purpose of destroying that cursed race [the Muslims]," laid waste the region around Jaén and advanced toward Granada whose people, in return for his promise to depart, liberated 1,300 Christian captives. After the king's lieutenants inflicted a major defeat on Abū-l-ʿUlā, one of the claimants to the caliphal title, near Seville, Córdoba and many other towns acknowledged al-Bayāsī as their ruler.[21]

Among the magnates engaged in this war was Alfonso Téllez de Meneses. Commending him for struggling "manfully against the Saracens in the affair of the Christian faith in Spain," Honorius III allowed him to use the *tercias* or third of the tithe in the province of Toledo to defend Alburquerque, a fortress set on a rocky promontory in Extremadura about twenty-five miles northwest of Badajoz near the Portuguese frontier; the pope also commanded the Military Orders to aid Alfonso. Alburquerque was the likely setting for *Cantiga* 205 relating the siege of a frontier castle by the knights of Santiago and Calatrava, under Alfonso's command (see Figure 3). During the summer of 1225, Alfonso, the bishop of Cuenca, and the urban militias invaded the kingdom of Murcia, controlled by Abū Zayd of Valencia, who had repudiated his vassalage to Fernando III. Archbishop Rodrigo granted remission of sins to all those who helped for a month to fortify the castle of Aliaguilla about fifty miles southeast of Cuenca. Alfonso's brother, Bishop Tello of Palencia, "fired by zeal for the Christian faith," and inspired to participate in the "affair being carried out against the Saracens of Spain," received Honorius III's permission to use his diocesan *tercias* for that purpose. The pope also urged the clergy and people of Palencia to provide the bishop with "a moderate subsidy" for the war against the Muslims.[22]

Early in the fall, on 25 September, the pope congratulated Fernando III and remarked:

Although the affair begun against the Saracens of Spain is the business of all the faithful because it pertains to Christ and to the Christian faith, there is no doubt that it pertains especially to you and to the other kings of Spain because they [the Saracens] remain in occupation of your land, to the very grave injury to all Christendom.

As the king, "fired by zeal for the faith," had "begun to fight vigorously against the enemies of the cross," Pope Honorius, in response to the royal petition, conceded to everyone who, "having taken up the sign of the cross," participated in the Spanish wars the indulgence extended by the Fourth Lateran Council to crusaders going to the Holy Land. Designating Archbishop Rodrigo and Bishop Mauricio of Burgos as protectors of "the crusaders of the kingdom of Castile" (*crucesignatis regni Castelle*), he commanded them to

Figure 3. Alfonso Téllez and the Military Orders besiege a castle; Holy Mary saves a
Muslim woman and child who are then baptized. *Cantigas de Santa Maria,* F 5
(E 205). Biblioteca Nazionale, MS Banco Rari 20, Florence.

publicize the indulgence.[23] One would assume that if Fernando III had not taken the cross during the Curia of Carrión in 1224, then he certainly would have done so in response to this papal concession of crusading indulgences.

Around the feast of All Saints (1 November), despite the harshness of the weather, the king returned to the frontier, summoning al-Bayāsī to appear before him and to surrender Andújar, Martos, and other castles and to admit a Castilian garrison into the citadel of Baeza to guarantee the transfer of custody. In the following spring, while Fernando III besieged Capilla, about fifty-five miles west of Ciudad Real, the people of Córdoba assassinated al-Bayāsī; as a consequence the Castilians garrisoned in Baeza seized the entire town. The defenders of Capilla, seeing that they could expect no relief, capitulated and were allowed to depart, taking their movable goods with them. The archbishop of Toledo, the bishop of Palencia, and others cleansed the mosque of Capilla "of all the filthiness of the Muḥammadan superstition" and "dedicated the church . . . to Jesus Christ, celebrating mass and the divine office with great joy."[24] Fernando III then returned to Toledo and would not reappear on the frontier for several years.

Perhaps having agreed to act jointly with his son, Alfonso IX carried out an expedition in the vicinity of Badajoz on the Guadiana River in July 1226. In preparation for that campaign Martín Muñiz, known as Falcón, drew up his will in April, declaring: "I am crossed with the sign of the cross [*Cruciatus sum cum signo crucis*] in the name of our Lord Jesus Christ and for love of my lord the archbishop and I wish to go with him in the host against the Saracens to serve him and the lord king Alfonso and I wish everything to be in order if perchance I should die." The new king of Portugal, Sancho II (1223–48), also took the offensive, laying waste the area around Elvas, about twelve miles west of Badajoz, and destroying its walls.[25]

Rising hostility in Spain toward the Almohads, meanwhile, prompted Ibn Hūd (1228–38), descended from the former kings of Zaragoza, to rebel at Murcia. Condemning the Almohads as heretics, he declared that the caliph of Baghdad was Muḥammad's true successor. In order to contain the uprising, Caliph Abū-l-ʿUlā, probably in November, concluded a truce for one year with Castile promising to pay tribute, but his departure for Morocco in the following year left Islamic Spain to its own defenses.[26]

The new pope, Gregory IX (1227–41), continued his predecessor's policy of encouraging the crusade in Spain while also attempting to persuade the Spanish clergy and laity to lend financial support to the oriental crusade. When the Castilian clergy protested that Fernando III was taking the *tercias* for his campaigns, the pope initially ordered him to desist, but later praised his efforts to extend the Christian religion, and advised the bishops to provide the king with financial support.[27] It is also likely that the papal legate Jean Halgrin d'Abbeville, cardinal bishop of Santa Sabina, who convened several councils in all the Christian kingdoms in 1228–29 to promote the reforms of the Fourth Lateran Council, exhorted the Christian rulers to take up arms against the Muslims, as his contemporary, Lucas of Túy, indicated. Gregory IX had, in fact, authorized his legate to grant the usual indulgences to those who did so and to employ ecclesiastical censures against any Christian ruler who invaded the territory of his Christian neighbors.[28]

The Last Crusade of Alfonso IX of León

Indeed, Lucas stated that on that account Alfonso IX, aided by Castilian troops (chiefly knights of Calatrava) besieged and captured Cáceres in the summer of 1227. Nevertheless, the legate had not yet arrived in Spain, so the fall of Cáceres cannot be attributed to his encouragement. The settlement charter given to Cáceres declared that "our Lord Jesus Christ, who never refuses the prayers of the Christian people, gave Cáceres to the Christians. . . . The pagan people were expelled from it and it was restored to Christian society." No doubt like many others intending to join the king, Fernando Suárez, "wishing to go in the expedition against the Moors," made his will.[29]

After the knights of Santiago and others took Montánchez, about twenty-five miles southeast of Cáceres, the king in the spring of 1230 besieged Mérida on the Guadiana River, another twenty-five miles directly south. The defenders appealed to Ibn Hūd, who was now widely recognized as king by the Muslims of Seville, Córdoba, Jaén, and Granada. Determined to oppose further Leonese expansion, he advanced to Alange, about eight miles southeast of Mérida, where he was routed by Alfonso IX. According to Lucas of Túy "the blessed St. James visibly appeared in this battle with a host of white knights who valiantly overthrew the Moors." Once Mérida was taken in March 1230, the king of León moved against Badajoz, which quickly surrendered on Pentecost Sunday, 26 May. Deploring the loss of this region, the seventeenth-century historian al-Maqqarī expressed the pious hope, "may God restore it to the rule of Islam!"[30] Bishoprics were soon established in both Mérida and Badajoz, although the metropolitan status of the former see, dating to Visigothic times, was not restored, its rights having been transferred to Santiago de Compostela.[31]

News of the fall of Mérida prompted the Muslims of Elvas, about twelve

miles west of Badajoz, to flee. Portuguese knights, who had been campaigning with Alfonso IX, occupied the fortress and informed Sancho II, who took
possession of it, as well as Juromenha about twelve miles farther south. Alfonso IX's next goal was to move on Seville but he died on 24 September 1230
en route to Santiago de Compostela to give thanks for his triumph. The king
who had once been himself the object of a crusade died as a crusader and, no
longer excommunicated, was given the honors of Christian burial in the
cathedral of Santiago.[32]

Unaware of the king's death, Gregory IX authorized Archbishop Pedro
of Compostela to commute the vow of any Leonese crusaders (*crucesignati*)
planning to go to the Holy Land so that they might participate in the Spanish
crusade. Now that the Muslims were put to flight, the pope encouraged the
people to help retain the places conquered by giving their personal or financial support. Assuring them that this cause was a matter of eternal salvation,
he conferred the indulgence for a term of four years.[33]

Jaime I's Crusades to Peñíscola and Mallorca

While the other Christian rulers were crusading against the collapsing Almohad empire, a ten-year truce with the Almohads concluded in 1214 enabled
Jaime I of Aragón to survive a troubled minority.[34] Acknowledging that the
Muslims might attack the young king, Pope Honorius III in 1222 offered full
remission of sins to those who came to his aid. Still struggling to make himself master of his realm, Jaime I, however, made no move to undertake a crusade at that time. Indeed, he prohibited Gil García de Azagra, a knight of
Santiago, who wished to wage war against the Muslims, from purchasing
supplies in Aragón, though the pope admonished him to lift that ban.[35]

Once the truce expired Jaime I, then just seventeen, in April 1225 informed the Curia of Tortosa that "we have assumed the cross to attack the
barbarous nations." Proclaiming the Peace and Truce of God, he asked this
assembly of Catalan prelates, nobles, and townsmen to give him aid and
counsel "to promote the affair of the cross."[36] This was the first time that he
took the crusader's cross, but other than Honorius III's bull just cited, no
other concession of crusading indulgences appears to be extant. Although
the king did not name his immediate objective, he advanced on Peñíscola, a
coastal fortress about thirty miles below Tortosa, in the late summer of 1225.
The siege ended in failure, as did his plan to invade the kingdom of Valencia
in the following year.[37]

Nevertheless, the prospect of an invasion convinced Abū Zayd, the Muslim king of Valencia, to pay a fifth of his revenue as tribute. Probably hoping to preserve his independence of both Christians and Muslims, he informed the pope that he wished to convert to Christianity and to subject his kingdom to the Holy See. After being expelled from Valencia in 1229 by Zayyān ibn Sa'd ibn Mardanīsh, he met the papal legate, Jean d'Abbeville, and became a Christian; he also pledged homage to Jaime I, who agreed to collaborate against their common enemy, Zayyān. Despite that, Jaime I's first great military success would not lie in the south but rather in the Balearic Islands.[38]

As Almohad rule disintegrated, the islands, occupied by the Almohads in 1203, regained their independence in 1224. Both Alfonso II and Pedro II had contemplated the conquest of the islands, without, however, mounting an offensive. Catalans, who were just beginning to develop a merchant fleet, viewed the islands as a source of piratical raids on Christian shipping and urged Jaime I to take action against them. When Abū Yaḥyā, the king of Mallorca, rejected his demand for restitution of plunder taken from Catalan ships, Jaime I sought support for an assault from the Catalan *Curia generalis* of Barcelona in December 1228.[39] In response, Guillem de Montcada, viscount of Béarn, one of the most distinguished Catalan barons, agreed to raise 100 knights, as did Nunyo Sanç, count of Roselló, Cerdanya, and Conflent; the count of Empúries pledged sixty. Archbishop Aspàreg of Tarragona, while excusing himself because of his advanced age, promised 1,000 silver marks, 100 knights, and 1,000 sergeants. Bishop Berenguer de Palou of Barcelona and the bishop of Girona offered 100 knights and thirty knights respectively, while the Abbot of San Feliu de Guixols promised four knights and an armed galley. The towns of Barcelona, Tarragona, and Tortosa pledged to provide ships.[40] While the king proclaimed the Peace and Truce of God, the nobles granted an extraordinary tax, the *bovatge*, to finance the expedition. Although he had received a *bovatge* at his accession, as a matter of right, this new levy was freely given. He also acknowledged that the aid which the bishops granted "to subjugate the land and the perfidy of the pagans" was given of their own volition. In return he declared his intention to reward his collaborators.[41]

Gregory IX on 12 February 1229 authorized his legate, Jean d'Abbeville, "if an army shall be organized in that region against the Moors," to "grant the accustomed indulgences." In the Council of Lleida on 29 March, the legate prohibited the sale to the Muslims of arms and other materials essential to military operations, and condemned anyone who abetted the enemy.[42] He also conferred the crusader's cross on Jaime I, Bishop Berenguer of Barcelona, and other Catalan clerics and barons, but the Aragonese seem to have held back. They had asked the king to direct the crusade against Valencia, but he refused. The bishop of Barcelona subsequently gave the cross to Guillem de Montcada and other knights. The king renewed his pledge to allot a share in the lands conquered to those participating in the conquest. [43]

After hearing mass and receiving communion, the king and his army of about 800 knights and a few thousand footsoldiers (including prelates, nobles, Templars, Hospitallers, and townsmen) set sail, in a fleet of about 150 ships, from the Catalan ports of Salou, Cambrils, and Tarragona on 5 September. Enroute a great storm came up and the king was urged to turn back, but he declared:

We have undertaken this voyage with faith in God and in quest of those who do not believe in him; and we are going against them for two things: either to convert them or to destroy them, and then to restore that kingdom to the faith of our Lord. And since we are going in His name, we have confidence that He will guide us.

When they encountered another storm as they approached land, he appealed to God, saying: "I am going on this journey to exalt the faith that You have given us and to bring down and destroy those who do not believe in You."[44]

Three or four days later the fleet reached the bay of Palma; surprisingly the Muslim fleet made no attempt to impede the landing of the crusaders in the port of Santa Ponça, about ten miles from Palma. The bishop of Barcelona proclaimed that "this enterprise . . . is the work of God, not ours; and so those who die in it, die for our Lord and will gain paradise, where they will enjoy everlasting glory. Those who survive will also have glory and honor and will finally come to a good death." He urged them to "destroy those who deny the name of Jesus Christ," assuring them that God and his mother would be with them and lead them to victory. After some initial resistance at Monte de Pantaleu and Portopí (where Guillem de Montcada was killed) the crusaders overran much of the island and began the siege of Palma. The Dominican Fray Miguel de Fabra preached to the troops and absolved them of their sins. As the siege dragged on, initial enthusiasm seems to have waned and some apparently thought to return home. To provide continuing support, Gregory IX on 28 November proclaimed the crusade again, instructing the Dominican Ramon de Penyafort and the Dominican prior of Barcelona to preach the indulgence in the French ecclesiastical provinces of Arles and Narbonne.[45]

After attempts to negotiate a settlement failed, Jaime I ordered a full-scale

assault on 31 December. Once again the army heard mass and received communion before launching the attack to the cry of "Saint Mary, Saint Mary!"
The king reported that a white knight, believed to be St. George, was in the
midst of the Christian host. Ibn al-Abbār alleged that 24,000 inhabitants of
the town were massacred and that the king of Mallorca (as well as the king of
Almería) was captured and died soon after being subjected to torture.
Recording the fall of Mallorca, Ibn Abī Zarʿ exclaimed: "May Allāh return it
to Islam."[46]

By Palm Sunday, 31 May 1230, the conquest of Mallorca was completed,
although hostile bands were not subdued until two years later. Jaime I returned to the mainland late in the year, but revisited his recent conquest in
the following spring in order to repress holdouts in the mountains. Most
of the Muslims opted to depart, either for the other islands or North Africa.
The king granted franchises to those who would settle there, and inasmuch
as most were Catalans the *Usatges of Barcelona* was established as the fundamental law. The church was endowed, the city of Barcelona was granted
commercial rights, and Genoa, Pisa, and Marseille were rewarded with houses
and trading privileges. Infante Pedro of Portugal received Mallorca as a fief
to be held for life in exchange for his claims to the county of Urgell. During
the king's second visit to Mallorca the Muslims of Menorca recognized him
as their sovereign on 17 July 1231, promising an annual tribute and surrender-
ing several strategic castles; but the Catalans did not conquer the island until
1287. After returning to the mainland, Jaime I hastened to defend his conquest in spring of 1232 when he learned that the emir of Tunis was preparing
an attempt to recover Mallorca; but the expected assault did not materialize.[47]

Meanwhile, Guillem de Montgrí, the archbishop-elect of Tarragona,
and his brother, Berenguer de Santa Eugènia, asked the king to grant them
the islands of Ibiza and Formentera in fief; then, after obtaining a bull of crusade from Gregory IX on 24 April 1235, they occupied the islands. The conquest of Mallorca was the first significant step in the development of the
Catalan Mediterranean empire.[48]

The Castilian Crusade: Quesada and the Conquest of Córdoba

In the summer of 1229, while Jaime I was engaged in the Mallorcan crusade,
the Almohads in Morocco engaged in civil war and two competitors for leadership appeared in al-Andalus. Ibn Hūd, who acknowledged the ʿAbbāsid
caliph of Baghdad, and ruled Granada, Almería, Jaén, Córdoba, Málaga, and

Seville, seemed at first the stronger of the two; he did not control Valencia, where Zayyān seized power from Abū Zayd, nor Niebla in the Algarve where Ibn Maḥfūt asserted his independence. His great rival was Ibn al-Aḥmar (1232–73), the founder of the Naṣrid dynasty that ruled the kingdom of Granada until 1492. Proclaiming his independence at Arjona in 1232, he soon gained recognition in other towns and presented a serious challenge to Ibn Hūd.[49]

Taking advantage of this discord Fernando III seized several castles near Úbeda in 1229, and in the following summer unsuccessfully besieged Jaén, a formidable fortress in upper Andalucía. The death of his father, Alfonso IX, in September 1230 interrupted this campaign, though he was now able to acquire the kingdom of León, separated from Castile since 1157. With the combined resources of both kingdoms he would be able to push deep into the Guadalquivir valley before the middle of the thirteenth century.[50]

While the king was busy securing his new realm, Gregory IX, acknowledging that Archbishop Rodrigo girded himself to "to rip occupied land from the hands of the impious," in April 1231 conceded the indulgence authorized by the Fourth Lateran Council for the Holy Land to anyone who joined the archbishop or the king in an invasion of Saracen lands "to vindicate injury to the Crucified One;" those who helped to pay the expenses of the expedition would also gain the indulgence. Furthermore, the archbishop was empowered to absolve crusaders who incurred the penalty of excommunication by inadvertently striking clerics in battle. Shortly afterward Archbishop Rodrigo captured Quesada southeast of Úbeda as well as other castles, including Cazorla, about three miles to the north, which became the basis of an archiepiscopal administrative district. In June the pope reiterated his previous concession of the indulgence and the power of absolution. Inasmuch as the archbishop raised an army at his own expense and fortified numerous castles, Gregory IX in 1232 admonished the churches and monasteries of the archdiocese to assist him with an appropriate subsidy payable over three years. Recognizing the necessity of Christians settling in Quesada to trade with the nearby Muslims, the pope permitted them to do so, excepting strategic materials such as arms, horses, iron, and wood. At the king's request, Gregory IX, in 1234, again allowed the bishops to absolve anyone who set out "to spread Christianity" and accidentally laid violent hands on a cleric. He also permitted the knights of Santiago to use the *tercias* of their churches to defend the frontier and urged the bishops to support those "athletes of Christ" with victuals and not to cite them before civil tribunals during campaign.[51]

Besides the archbishop, Fernando III's brother, Alfonso de Molina, together with Álvar Pérez de Castro and the knights of Calatrava and Santiago, devastated the Andalusian countryside. When the master of Calatrava and the bishop of Plasencia attacked Trujillo, about twenty-five miles east of Cáceres, Ibn Hūd made a half-hearted effort to relieve it, but the defenders had to surrender on 25 January 1232. By then, Fernando III was ready to undertake a major offensive and besieged Úbeda, about thirty miles northeast of Jaén, whose possession was essential to the security of Baeza and Quesada. The Muslims surrendered in July 1233 on condition that they be allowed to leave with whatever goods they could carry. Soon after the king made a truce with Ibn Hūd, who promised to pay 1,000 dinars daily as tribute. The Castilian offensive, however, continued in other sectors. In the old Muslim kingdom of Badajoz the Military Orders captured Medellín, Alange, and Santa Cruz in 1234 and Magacela in February 1235. In the spring the king renewed the truce with Ibn Hūd, who, as a sign of vassalage, promised to pay over the next year a substantial tribute of 430,000 *maravedís*. That done, Fernando III ravaged the lands of Ibn al-Aḥmar, king of Jaén and Arjona, taking several castles north of Úbeda and Baeza.[52]

The Castilian advance reached an unexpected climax toward the end of 1235 when Christian soldiers, called *almogávares* (from Arabic, *al-maghāwīr*), abetted by Muslim traitors, broke into eastern quarter of Córdoba and sent an urgent summons to Fernando III to come to their aid. Álvar Pérez de Castro and other royal lieutenants on the frontier hastened to join them. The king was at Benavente in the kingdom of León when he received their message in January 1236. Some among his courtiers tried to dissuade him from taking action because it was mid-winter, when the roads would be impassable because of rain and snow, and it was feared that Ibn Hūd and the Moroccans would come to Córdoba's aid. "Placing his hope in the Lord Jesus Christ," Fernando III, a *miles Christi*, closed his ears to such talk, and resolved that he had to help those who had placed themselves at such great risk.

All the while summoning his vassals to join him, he rapidly moved southward, arriving at Córdoba on 7 February with only 100 knights in his company. To deny the defenders free egress from the city, the king, with 200 knights, occupied the area south of the Guadalquivir opposite the bridge of Alcolea on the road to Écija. Ibn Hūd gathered a force of reportedly 4,000 to 5,000 knights and 30,000 footsoldiers, as well as 200 Christian knights in his service, and came up to Écija, but inexplicably failed to challenge the Castilians and withdrew to Seville. After Easter reinforcements from Castile, León, and Galicia swelled the Christian ranks. As the siege tightened, the defenders perceived the hopelessness of their situation and negotiated a settlement.

However, when they learned that the Christians were short of food and that the Leonese towns intended to depart once their three months service was up, the Córdobans reneged on the agreement. To intimidate them, Fernando III made an alliance with Ibn al-Aḥmar, the king of Jaén, an enemy of Ibn Hūd and of Córdoba. As a consequence the defenders offered to surrender, provided that, taking their movable goods, they would have safe passage out of the city. Some counselled Fernando III to take the city by assault, but he opted to accept the conditions stated and Córdoba surrendered on 29 June 1236. A truce of six years was now concluded with Ibn Hūd, who again promised to pay an annual tribute of 156,000 *maravedís.*[53]

Thus "the famous city of Córdoba . . . which for such a long time had been held captive, that is, from the time of Rodrigo, king of the Goths, was now restored to the Christian cult." Abū Hazam, the governor of Córdoba, "delivered the keys to our lord the king and the lord king at once, as a *uir catolicus* gave thanks to our Savior." He ordered the standard of the cross and his own standard to be placed on the highest tower of the mosque. At vespers Bishop Juan of Osma, the royal chancellor, and Master Lope who had placed the standard of the cross on the tower, made preparations so "that the mosque should become a church . . . the superstition and filthiness of Muḥammad being expelled therefrom." When the king, his barons, and people entered the city on the next day, 30 June, the bishops of Osma, Cuenca, and Baeza, and all the clergy in solemn procession received them at the mosque now dedicated as the church of Saint Mary. After the bishop of Osma celebrated mass, the king entered the Muslim royal palace and sat on the throne of glory of the kingdom of Córdoba. Next he compelled Muslim captives to carry back to Compostela the bells that al-Manṣūr had seized nearly three hundred years before and, "to the distress of the Christian people, hung as lamps" in the mosque of Córdoba. Centuries later al-Maqqarī mourned that Córdoba, "that seat of the western Khalifate, repository of the theological sciences, and abode of Islam, passed into the hands of the accursed Christians."[54]

As the Muslims had evacuated Córdoba, and there was a shortage of food, most of the nobles elected to return home, leaving the king to provide the city with a Christian population. Each of the magnates and the masters of the Military Orders agreed to supply knights for defense of the city; the arrival of 150 knights from Segovia helped as well. Entrusting the defense to

Tello Alfonso and his brother Alfonso Téllez de Meneses, the king returned to Toledo. While he fell seriously ill, people unexpectedly began to flock to Córdoba by mid-November 1236.[55] The fall of Córdoba opened the whole of the Guadalquivir valley, where many adjacent towns and castles, including Écija, acknowledged his sovereignty and agreed to pay tribute.[56] The king soon realized, however, that in order to maintain Córdoba he would have to send substantial sums of money and other supplies. Returning to the city in 1240, he spent thirteen months there providing for its defense, organizing the municipal council, overseeing the restoration of the bishopric, and distributing property among those who had collaborated in the conquest. After establishing municipal boundaries, he granted the city a *fuero* based on that of Toledo, derived in turn from the old Visigothic Code, the *Forum Iudicum*; the king had commanded that it be translated into Castilian as the *Fuero Juzgo*.[57] He also renewed his truce with Ibn al-Aḥmar.

The financial drain represented by Córdoba prompted the king to appeal to Gregory IX, who in September 1236 praised him as an "athlete of Christ" and instructed the prelates to provide a subsidy of 20,000 gold pieces annually for three years from both the Castilian and Leonese churches and monasteries in support of the king's campaigns. On the same day he encouraged the bishops to exhort their people to enlist in the royal army for a year or to pay the expenses of others, in return for which they would receive the crusading indulgence granted by the Fourth Lateran Council. As a further measure of his esteem the pope took Fernando III under his protection and forbade anyone to excommunicate him without papal permission.[58]

While the king attended to matters of internal administration he entrusted the defense of the frontier and his new kingdom of Córdoba to his son Infante Alfonso, Alvar Pérez de Castro, Alfonso Téllez, and the Military Orders. In recognition of the ongoing crusade in which the Military Orders had played a prominent role, Gregory IX on 12 April 1238 granted an indulgence to all those who accompanied the knights of Alcántara on campaign and lost their lives in battle. Two years later, on 2 June, the pope acknowledged that because the knights of Calatrava

are placed near to Saracen territory, so that you may be seen as a sign placed for an arrow, it is necessary for you to fight often against them, in which fight many of the faithful following your standard are killed. . . . To those who for the defense of the Catholic faith fought the Saracens . . . we . . . grant to all the faithful who die in this way indulgence of all their sins which they have confessed and of which they are truly contrite.

He also allowed the ordination of persons of illegitimate birth in the province of Santiago de Compostela if they lived on the frontier and wished to take part in the defense of the faith. The wisdom of cooperation in campaigns against the Muslims, even to the extent of placing their Orders under a single command, was recognized by Gómez, master of Calatrava, and Pelay Pérez Correa, master of Santiago, in a pact concluded on 1 August 1243, after the latter's return from Murcia.[59]

The fall of Córdoba was a blow to the Spanish Muslims, who were unable to join forces in a common defense against the Christian advance, and seemed to foreshadow even worse things to come. Indeed the loss of the city and the increased burden of tribute paid to Fernando III cost Ibn Hūd, who witnessed a rapid decline in his popularity. His assassination by one of his own men at Almería in January 1238 illustrated the disarray of Spanish Islam. While his family was now confined to the kingdom of Murcia, his principal rival, Ibn al-Aḥmar, proclaimed as king in Málaga, Almería, Arjona, Jaén, and Granada, enjoyed an ascendancy over Andalucía.[60] The task facing Ibn al-Aḥmar and the other surviving Muslim lords in Spain, as we shall see in the following chapter, was how to avoid being swallowed up by advancing Christian armies.

In the quarter century following the Crusade of Las Navas de Tolosa, several crusades were undertaken as the Christian rulers broadened their frontiers at Muslim expense. Although Innocent III hoped to focus attention on the recovery of the Holy Land, Honorius III and Gregory IX frequently conceded crusading indulgences for the peninsular war against Islam. Once again crusaders intending to take part in the Fifth Crusade collaborated with the Portuguese in capturing Alcácer do Sal. The Portuguese bishops conferred the crusader's cross on numerous persons while at the same time Alfonso IX of León, Sancho VII of Navarre, and many bishops and nobles took the crusader's vow. The king of León achieved major goals with the conquest of Mérida and Badajoz which opened the way toward Seville.

Archbishop Rodrigo of Toledo, one of the more active crusaders, carried out military operations in the southeast at a time when Fernando III still maintained a truce with the Almohads. Jaime I of Aragón, as he tells us in his autobiography, took the crusader's cross, though his attempt to seize Peñíscola ended in failure. A few years later, however, he received the cross from the papal legate before embarking on the crusade that resulted in the conquest of Mallorca. Gregory IX supported that endeavor with crusading bulls on at least two occasions. About the same time Archbishop Rodrigo, aided by crusading indulgences, captured Quesada. Fernando III's subsequent conquest of

Córdoba must also be counted among the crusades because the pope in 1231 offered the indulgence to everyone who collaborated with the king or the archbishop. In 1238 Gregory IX conferred crusading indulgences on the Military Orders and those who joined forces with them. Another important note of these papal privileges is that persons contributing money could also gain the indulgence, though, unfortunately, there is no evidence of how much money was raised in that way.

Chapter 5

From Córdoba to Seville, 1236–1248

In the decade and a half following the fall of Córdoba, the Christian kings achieved exceptional success as they took advantage of continued rivalry among the Spanish Muslims, who could no longer expect any significant assistance from the Almohads of Morocco, preoccupied as they were by internal dissension. As a consequence, the Christians were able to subjugate the Muslim kingdom of Valencia, complete the conquest of the Alentejo and the Algarve, subject the Muslims of Murcia to tributary status, and conquer the kingdoms of Jaén and Seville. By the middle of the century Islamic Spain had been reduced to the kingdom of Granada in vassalage to Castile, while Portugal and Aragón had reached the geographical limits that they retained, with slight modifications, until the modern era.

Jaime I's Valencian Crusade

The conquest of the kingdom of Valencia, which had disintegrated into several parts, became the principal objective of Jaime I, once his hold on Mallorca was secure.[1] While Zayyān ibn Mardanīsh controlled the city of Valencia, Abū Zayd, whom he deposed in 1229, held Segorbe, about twenty-five miles farther north. Other Muslims dominated the lands around Játiva south of the river Júcar and acknowledged Ibn Hūd of Murcia as their lord. Dissension among them, however, afforded the Christians an opportunity for conquest. Thus, the king in 1226 granted Blasco de Alagón any castle or town that he might capture "in the land of the Saracens." Three years later, Abū Zayd, the ousted king of Valencia, became a vassal of Jaime I, promising him a fourth of the revenues of whatever places he might recover in the kingdom of Valencia; but, recognizing that previous treaties between Castile and Aragón reserved Valencia for Aragonese conquest, he ceded all claims to any lands that Jaime I might conquer. Assured of his suzerain's support, Abū

Zayd could now attempt to regain his former realm, but Jaime I's ultimate right of conquest and overriding jurisdiction were fully acknowledged.[2]

The Valencian crusade began in earnest toward the end of 1231 at Alcañiz when the king listened to a proposal put forward by Hug de Forcalquer, master of the Hospital, and Blasco de Alagón. They argued that, as God had favored the conquest of Mallorca, he would surely do the same for Valencia. Although there were forty or fifty fortresses throughout that kingdom, Blasco proposed that an attack be launched first against Borriana on the coast about thirty miles north of the city of Valencia, predicting that it could be taken in a month. Jaime I agreed, but he was unable to concentrate fully on the conquest because of problems in Mallorca. Early in the new year, however, Blasco seized Morella, about thirty miles southeast of Tortosa, while men from the frontier town of Teruel captured Ares, about eight miles south of Morella. In January of that year the king made a new pact with Abū Zayd, who yielded all his revenues from the city of Valencia and the surrounding region. Invigorated by the prospect of further conquest, the king revealed his future aspirations in March at Monzón, about sixty miles northeast of Zaragoza, by granting property in Valencia once the city was captured.[3]

Meanwhile Gregory IX, on 10 March, without explicitly referring to the projected crusade, consoled the king because he had not yet been able "to bring your desire to fulfillment." Zurita affirmed that a papal bull of crusade (which is not extant) was published at Monzón and the king and his vassals then assumed the cross. Whatever plans the king may have had for a crusade, however, had to be put on hold during the summer while he attended again to the defense of Mallorca. At the end of the year, on 17 December, according to Zurita, the Catalans, although they had already granted the *bovatge* at the time of the king's accession and again for the Mallorcan crusade, authorized still another levy of this extraordinary tax for the conquest of Valencia.[4]

In May of the following year, the royal army besieged Borriana, forcing it to surrender on 28 July. As a consequence Muslim lands to the north were now cut off. Realizing that they could not expect assistance from Valencia, the coastal towns of Peñiscola, Polpís, and Alcalá de Chivert submitted within the next two years; other towns, including Castelló de la Plana, Cervera, Coves de Vinromá, Villafamés, and Borriol also surrendered. The frontier was now pushed south of Castelló de la Plana and the road to Valencia was open.[5]

Whether Jaime I had obtained crusading indulgences in 1232 is problematical, but soon after the fall of Borriana, in response to his plea, the pope did issue a bull of crusade. Lauding the king's intention "to proceed with main force against the pagans for the exaltation of the Christian name," Gregory IX, on 9 August 1233, instructed the archbishops of Tarragona, Bordeaux, Auch, and Narbonne to encourage the faithful to join the king. If they served personally for three years they would gain the indulgence given to crusaders to the Holy Land.[6]

The Recovery of the Holy Land: Thibault I of Navarre

Nevertheless, other issues distracted Jaime I from the crusade. At the very time when he and other Christian kings were engaged in the struggle against Islam in Spain, Gregory IX, while he might applaud their efforts, hoped to enlist their participation in the recovery of the Holy Land. Proclaiming a crusade to the Holy Land in 1234, he took several steps intended to win Spanish support. First he recommended to the patriarch of Antioch the friars of Calatrava, who proposed to establish houses in Syria. He also permitted the bishops to lift the excommunication of the "great multitude" who sold arms to the Muslims, provided that they gave a subsidy for the Holy Land. Most importantly, he invited the Spanish rulers and bishops to aid Emperor Frederick II and offered a crusading indulgence to those giving three months service.[7] As both Fernando III and Jaime I were still contending with the Spanish Muslims, they were not likely to provide either troops or money for a crusade to the Holy Land. Nevertheless, the Genoese troubadour Lanfranc Cigala argued that the Spaniards ought not to be excused from the task of rescuing the holy places:

> If I were the admiral of the Germans
> all their knights would pass over
> nor would the Spaniards be excused,
> even though the wicked Saracens are nearby,
> because they were not the ones who destroyed
> the Sepulchre where God was laid and rose again.
> I marvel that one can make the sign of the cross,
> for no one has the courage to defend it.[8]

In actuality, the only real response to the papal plea came from the new king of Navarre, Thibault I (1234–53), whose kingdom was cut off from direct access to Muslim Spain. As a member of a crusading family from Champagne, he surely was drawn more to the Holy Land than to the reconquest. When his uncle Sancho VII died in 1234, naming him as his heir, both Jaime I and Fernando III were tempted to divide Navarre in accordance with treaties made by their predecessors. Gregory IX, however, strongly urged Fernando III, now secure in possession of Córdoba, to make no move against Navarre, and again admonished him when Thibault I took the crusader's vow in 1238. Later in the year the pope asked the Navarrese clergy to support Thibault I's crusade financially.[9] The Muslims temporarily occupied Jerusalem in 1239, but King Thibault's crusade, which took place between 1239 and 1240, achieved nothing of consequence.[10]

The Valencian Crusade Resumed

Aside from the Navarrese succession, Jaime I, despite his expressed desire "to fight, with God's help, against the barbarous infidel nations," had to contend with a restive nobility. Preparing to resume the Valencian crusade, he proclaimed the Peace and Truce of God in a Catalan *Curia generalis* at Tarragona in February 1235, and also endeavored to pacify Aragón by convening another *Curia generalis* at Zaragoza in March.[11] Gregory IX demanded that the nobles renew their oath of fidelity to the king, who "was entirely bent on prosecuting the war against the pagans, so that once their infidelity was uprooted from the land, the faith of Christ might be disseminated;" he also threatened them with excommunication, so that "the king may more freely execute the affair undertaken against the pagans." As Burns put it, the pope threatened a "crusade against the Christians hindering the crusade!"[12]

Once these obstacles were overcome the king turned again to the Valencian crusade. In May 1236 he renewed his alliance with Abū Zayd, who by now had become a Christian, taking the name Vicent. Then in October, intending "to make war against the Moors," Jaime I gathered the Catalans and Aragonese in a *Curia generalis* at Monzón, and "assumed the cross to conquer the kingdom of Valencia for the exaltation of the Christian faith." Adopting the title king of Valencia, which Abū Zayd had used, he renewed the Peace and Truce of God proclaimed in the previous curias of Barcelona, Tarragona, and Zaragoza, and assured crusaders that they could postpone payment of their debts until they returned home. Moreover, he pledged to endow the see of Valencia once it was reestablished and to distribute conquered lands among his vassals. In return for his confirmation of the

Aragonese coinage the towns granted him a subsidy of one *maravedí* from each household assessed at ten *maravedís*.[13]

Again he appealed to Gregory IX. Commenting that "the king has taken up the sign of the cross for the defense of the faith," the pope on 5 February 1237 asked that the crusade be preached in the provinces of Tarragona, Narbonne, Arles, Auch, and Aix, offering participants the indulgence for the Holy Land. Anyone could commute his vow to go to the Holy Land if he contributed money to the Valencian crusade. Arsonists, those who struck the clergy, and those who violated the ban on trafficking with the Muslims could gain absolution if they took the cross and remained until the fall of the city. A partial indulgence of thirty-one days was offered to those who helped by erecting buildings or digging ditches and fortifications. The pope also offered the viscount of Cardona a dispensation from the law of consanguinity if he provided forty knights for the crusade.[14]

Despite the sparse number of crusaders who assembled at Teruel in the following spring, the king decided to establish a base of operations in the abandoned fortress of Puig de Cebolla (renamed Puig de Santa Maria) about twelve miles away from the city of Valencia. While he was trying to recruit additional forces in Catalonia and Aragón, Zayyān, the king of Valencia, attempted to dislodge the crusaders, but they defeated him on 15 August. Even so some nobles urged the king to withdraw from Puig and abandon the attempt to take Valencia because of the cost; rejecting that advice, he declared that he would not leave until Valencia was taken.[15]

When he complained that some nobles were organizing leagues against him, thereby interfering with the "business of the faith," Gregory IX in 1238 authorized the use of ecclesiastical censures to bring about the dissolution of the leagues and to compel the nobles to return to their obedience. Remarking that Jaime I "gathered a great army against the Saracens," the pope extended his protection to the king and his kingdoms until the "business of the cross" was completed and threatened with excommunication and interdict those who impeded him.[16]

Seeing the Christian forces ensconced in Puig and poised for a final assault on Valencia, Zayyān offered to surrender numerous castles as well as a substantial portion of the city's revenues (amounting to 10,000 bezants annually), but Jaime I refused the offer. Soon afterward several coastal communities lying south of Borriana acknowledged his suzerainty under the guarantee of freedom of religion and the retention of their property. Then in April 1238 he began a formal siege of Valencia. Crusaders from France, including Archbishop Pierre of Narbonne, and others from England joined the host.[17] As their food supplies were intercepted the defenders in August sent Ibn al-Abbār, a native of Valencia, to plead for help from Abū Zakariyā', the Ḥafṣid emir of Tunis. Describing the woes of his city, he urged the emir:

> Start with your riders, God's riders, for Andalus:
> The road to its salvation is concealed now!
> Give it the mighty help which it expects, because
> powerful succor from you is still its hope![18]

Nevertheless, the Catalan fleet blockading Valencia turned away Tunisian ships sent in relief.

Realizing that he could not expect any further assistance, Zayyān capitulated on 28 September 1238.[19] A truce of seven years was agreed upon and the defenders, numbering about 50,000 and carrying their movable goods, were given safe conduct as far as Cullera and Denia, some twenty-five to sixty miles to the south. Zayyān also promised to cede all the castles and towns north of the Júcar river within twenty days, except Denia and Cullera. Seeing his banner raised on the ramparts, Jaime I exclaimed: "We dismounted from our horse and turned toward the east and tears fell from our eyes and we kissed the ground because of the great favor that God had done to us." He made his triumphal entrance into the city of Valencia on 9 October. The mosque was transformed into a cathedral and the archbishop of Tarragona celebrated a solemn mass of thanksgiving on 17 October. All the mosques and churches were transferred to the newly established bishopric, which was incorporated into the ecclesiastical province of Tarragona, though Archbishop Rodrigo of Toledo claimed jurisdiction over it.[20] While reserving an extensive domain for the crown, the king began to distribute houses and lands to his fellow crusaders.[21] He later estimated the number of Christians in Valencia, most of whom were Catalans, at 30,000, but they were long a minority among the large Muslim population remaining in the kingdom. In 1240 he published a law code, the *Forum regni Valentie*, for his new kingdom, and had it translated into Catalan in 1261.[22]

The fall of Valencia was a source of great sadness to the Muslims. Recalling the surrender of his native city, Abū-l-Muṭarrif ibn ʿAmīra lamented:

Like a bird of prey the enemy seized the city—elegant, beautiful, brilliant Valencia—by the throat. The call to prayer in the mosque was quickly reduced to silence. The life of the Muslim faith was ripped from its body. . . . The infidel has destroyed the Muslim faith there and the bell has replaced the call of the muezzin.[23]

On the other hand, Christians exulted. The Galician poet, Pero da Ponte, playing on the name of the city and the word *valença* or valor, celebrated the Christian triumph and hailed Jaime I as a valorous king of Aragón:

> The one who conquered Valencia
> always will be more valorous. . . .
> God gave him strength and wisdom
> to rule over Valencia
> and made him valorous
> with what valor was needed. . . .
> The King of Aragón is a king of good sense,
> a king of merit, a king of all good,
> a true king of Aragón.[24]

The English chronicler, Matthew Paris, spoke admiringly of the "most Christian king, magnificent and vigorous in arms," who had conquered the great city of Valencia. Many years later Louis IX of France, in recognition of Jaime I's achievement, sent him a thorn (still to be seen in the cathedral of Valencia) from the crown of thorns, which the French king had acquired in 1239 and housed in the Sainte Chapelle in Paris.[25] Gregory IX trumpeted to all the world that

the king, our most dear son in Christ . . . with many Catholic men, stirred by zeal for the faith and signed with the sign of the cross, after great labor and expense had ripped the kingdom [of Valencia] from the hands of the pagans, and after shedding much Christian blood, with heavenly assistance, restored it to the cult of the Christian faith.

Emphasizing the need to secure the new conquest the pope offered the crusading indulgence to all those who hastened to defend it.[26]

The Submission of the Kingdom of Murcia

After the fall of Valencia, Zayyān ibn Mardanīsh, the erstwhile ruler, took advantage of the confusion brought on by the murder of Ibn Hūd in 1238 to establish himself in Murcia, but three years later he was forced to retreat to the port of Alicante, about ninety miles south of his former capital. Although he offered to exchange Alicante for Mallorca, Jaime I refused, in part because Alicante, according to past treaties, was reserved for Castilian conquest. Nevertheless, by entitling himself "king of Murcia" in 1239, Jaime I indicated his ambitions there. Three years later he consolidated his control over the province of Castelló de la Plana through a series of surrender agreements with several towns west of Borriana.[27]

The Order of Santiago, meanwhile, was advancing into the southeast, seizing castles and towns in the sierras of Alcaraz and Segura about eighty to a hundred miles west of Murcia. Threatened by possible absorbtion by Ibn al-Aḥmar of Granada or by the emir of Tunis, the family of Ibn Hūd decided to acknowledge Fernando III as their overlord and so informed his son Infante Alfonso at Toledo in late February or early March 1243. At a subsequent meeting at Alcaraz, about ninety-five miles west of Murcia, a pact was concluded, probably in late April. Accompanied by Pelay Pérez Correa, master of the Order of Santiago, the infante entered Murcia about 1 May, where he received homage and fealty from the king, al-Mutawwakil ibn Hūd, and occupied the alcázar. Al-Mutawwakil also yielded a substantial portion of the public revenue to Fernando III, who allowed him to continue governing as in the past.[28]

Controversy concerning the delimitation of the frontier soon arose as Castilian forces attempted to take Alcira, about eighteen miles south of Valencia, as well as several dependencies of Játiva, about thirty miles to the south. Jaime I thwarted these attempts, occupying Alcira and Bairén in December 1243 and besieging Játiva, while the commander of Alcañiz seized Villena, Sax, and Bogarra on the border between Murcia and Valencia, about thirty miles northwest of Alicante, in the area reserved for Castile. Armed conflict between the Christians was averted, however, when Jaime I and Infante Alfonso negotiated a settlement at Almizra, about four miles east of Villena. The treaty of Almizra, signed on 26 March 1244, confirmed the essential points of the agreement reached at Cazola in 1179 by Alfonso VIII of Castile and Alfonso II of Aragón. The frontier was drawn on a line from the confluence of the rivers Júcar and Cabriel on the western edges of Valencia and Murcia through Biar, about twenty-five miles northwest of Alicante, to Denia on the coast. Alicante, about sixty miles south of Denia, remained for Castilian conquest, and Villena and other towns on the western frontier were handed over to Castile.[29]

Once peace was restored, both men resumed military operations. Játiva and Denia surrendered to Jaime I in May, and early in the following year Biar capitulated after a siege of three months.[30] With the fall of Biar, the Valencian reconquest was finished. The treaty of Almizra had the effect of ending further Aragonese expansion in the peninsula, inasmuch as its territory was no longer contiguous to that of the Muslims. The conquest of the remainder of Andalucía was left to Castile. For his part Infante Alfonso, between April and June, compelled the towns of Mula (about twenty miles west of Murcia) and Lorca (about forty miles southwest) to accept Castilian suzerainty. The port of Cartagena (about twenty-five miles southeast), blockaded by ships from the Bay of Biscay, also surrendered, probably in the spring of 1245, and a bishopric was soon established there. In the next year Alicante capitulated to the Castilians, and Zayyān withdrew to Tunis, leaving the peninsula for good.[31]

Jaime I and the Crusade Against al-Azraq

Although Valencia and Murcia were now under Christian rule, the population of both kingdoms was still heavily Muslim, and that was to be the cause of great difficulty in the future. Informing the Cortes of Huesca in 1247 that he "had completed the acquisition of our conquest from the Saracens and all that pertains to due limits of our conquest as far as the shores of the eastern sea," Jaime I was now open to proposals for extrapeninsular crusades and responded positively when Pope Innocent IV (1243–54) summoned him to the First Council of Lyon in 1245 to undertake a crusade to liberate Jerusalem, overrun by the Muslims in the preceding summer.[32] Although the king intended to aid the Latin Empire of Constantinople the pope on 18 March 1246 offered the crusade indulgence for the Holy Land.[33]

While the king was making his preparations a Muslim called Albacor (perhaps a Latinized version of al-Baqqār), rose in revolt around Alcoy, about sixty miles south of Valencia, but he was captured and executed when he attacked Alcira. Another leader, al-Azraq, who had pledged homage to Jaime I in 1244, sparked a more widespread revolt of the Muslims in the mountainous areas south of the city in the summer or fall of 1247. In reply Jaime I in December announced his intention to expel all the Muslims and also appealed to Rome for help.[34]

In response, Innocent IV on 13 November 1248 offered a plenary indulgence to all the faithful who assumed the cross and personally went to the king's assistance; those who contributed money according to their means would receive the crusading indulgence offered by the Fourth Lateran Council. The pope also instructed the bishops and clergy of the Crown of Aragón to offer an opportune subsidy to the king, who had distinguished himself among Catholic princes by his "desire to increase the cult of the divine name." As a further sign of his support for the crusade, Innocent IV ordered papal collectors of the twentieth destined for the Holy Land to suspend collection for three years, so that the bishops might aid their king in this hour of need. As the rebellion continued Archbishop Pere of Tarragona and the other bishops agreed to contribute the twentieth of ecclesiastical revenues for one year in support of the crusade against al-Azraq. Repeating the concession of indulgences in 1250, the pope encouraged enlistment in the crusade, and authorized the bishops to excommunicate Christians who lent aid to the Muslims.[35]

As al-Azraq's counter-crusade troubled the Crown of Aragón for many more years, extending well beyond the chronological limits of this book, its later history will not be addressed here, especially as Burns has studied it in detail. Suffice it to say that al-Azraq helped to curtail Jaime I's ambitions to lead a crusade to the orient.[36]

The Portuguese Crusade

While Fernando III and Jaime I were bringing about the fall of Córdoba and Valencia, the crusade in Portugal also proceeded inexorably, though the participation of Sancho II, preoccupied by conflicts with the prelates and nobles, remains problematical. As a stimulus to action, Gregory IX in 1232 forbade anyone to excommunicate the king while he was at war with the "infidels" and authorized his absolution should he incur excommunication by accidentally striking a cleric while on campaign. That, however, cannot be taken as proof that he was actually engaged in hostilities against the Muslims. Still, the pope persisted. Rejoicing that the king had girded himself for the defense of lands conquered and to be conquered, Gregory IX on 21 October 1234 granted the crusade indulgence for four years to all those participating in the struggle against the Muslims.[37]

Rather than the king, however, the Military Orders, especially the Order of Santiago, seem to have been chiefly responsible for gains made in the Alentejo and the Algarve. Sometime between 1232 and 1234, the Portuguese seized Moura, Serpa, and Beja, about sixty to seventy miles southwest of Badajoz, along the eastern banks of the Guadiana River. Aljustrel, about twenty miles southwest of Beja, fell to the knights of Santiago in 1234, and four years later they captured Mértola, about thirty miles south of Serpa, and

Alfajar de Pena. Sancho II seems to have become more actively involved and was present at the fall of Ayamonte at the mouth of the Guadiana on the Gulf of Cádiz, and Cacela about eight miles to the west in 1239 or 1240.[38]

About this time his younger brother, Infante Fernando, lord of Serpa, a turbulent warrior excommunicated for his outrages against the clergy, apparently felt the need for atonement and decided to release his warlike energy against the Muslims. He and Infante Alfonso de Molina, the son of Alfonso IX of León, and a brother of Fernando III, probably using Serpa as a base, planned a crusade.[39] As both men proposed "to assume the sign of the cross to combat the Saracens," Gregory IX, on 25 November 1239, placed them under papal protection. Three days later he granted the crusading indulgence to everyone who provided financial support. Anyone excommunicated for using violence against clerics could be absolved if he gave due satisfaction and "took the sign of the cross and hastened to the castle of Serpa to fight the Saracens." The bishops were commanded to encourage their people, in remission of their sins, to defend the castle. Moreover, "because it is proper that ecclesiastical persons who are especially sustained by the patrimony of Christ should try to support strongly those who expose themselves in the service of Jesus Christ," the pope required the clergy to make an appropriate donation to Infante Fernando. Two weeks later, the pope granted Fernando and others who took the cross the crusading indulgences and immunities established by the Fourth Lateran Council. Certain Portuguese knights who "had affixed the sign of the cross to their shoulders" but had neglected to fulfill their vow were obliged to do so, presumably in the infante's crusade. In order to defend Serpa and to ransom captives the pope permitted Fernando to allow the Muslims to repurchase any booty taken, except iron, horses, arms, and wood, which they might employ against Christians. The infante, who came to Rome to become a papal vassal, pledged to do public penance for the offenses he had committed.[40] Whether he carried out a crusade is unknown, but it seems reasonable to suppose that, armed with this sheaf of papal bulls, he made some effort to contribute to the conquest of the Algarve.

Two years later, on 18 February 1241, the pope, commending Sancho II's intention to take action against "the enemies of the cross of Christ," offered the crusading indulgence to everyone who aided the king in person or contributed financially for at least a year. Whether the king actually took part in the ensuing crusade cannot be determined with certainty, but several places were taken, probably through the efforts of the knights of Santiago.

Alvor, about ten miles southwest of Silves, fell in 1240 or 1241 and Tavira, about fifteen miles west of Ayamonte, and Paderne, about thirty miles farther west, were probably taken in 1242.[41] As a consequence the Muslims in the southwestern corner of Portugal were cut off from their fellows in Niebla and Seville.

These successes may have encouraged the king's brother, Afonso, Count of Boulogne, who had left Portugal years before, to participate in the crusade. Asked by Innocent IV in January 1245 to aid the Holy Land, he asserted that he planned to attack the "perfidy of the Saracens in Spain." Applauding his resolve, the pope on 8 April granted the crusading indulgence to him and all the Portuguese who joined him. One suspects, however, that the count had an ulterior motive for proclaiming his desire to become a crusader. The turmoil that had troubled Portugal for so many years reached a climax early in 1245 when the pope, instigated by the Portuguese bishops and perhaps by Count Afonso, charged Sancho II with allowing violence and disorder to lead to anarchy, and neglecting to defend the realm against the Muslims. During the Council of Lyon, on 25 July, the pope entrusted the responsibility of restoring order to Count Afonso, who would effectively exercise royal authority.[42] His arrival in Lisbon early in 1246 plunged Portugal into a civil war that ended when Sancho II withdrew to Castile, where he died two years later.

Now seated on the Portuguese throne, but wary of Castilian expansion westward, Afonso III (1248–79) moved quickly to complete the conquest of the Algarve. With the help of the Orders of Santiago and Avis he took Faro in March 1249 and in the next year received the submission of Albufeira, Porches, Silves, and other towns.[43] As a consequence, the Portuguese had pushed their frontier as far south as possible and Portugal was now complete.

The Castilian Crusade: The Siege of Jaén

While Innocent IV in the Council of Lyon proclaimed a crusade to deliver the Holy Places, Fernando III was intent on gaining control of the upper Guadalquivir about the hitherto impregnable city of Jaén. After capturing Arjona and several other towns in 1244, he set out to destroy Jaén's food supply and established a formal siege in August 1245. Unable to aid the beleaguered city and knowing that he could expect no help from Morocco or Tunis, Ibn al-Aḥmar, the king of Granada, decided to save himself by becoming Fernando III's vassal; not only did he promise to serve him in peace and war and to attend his cortes, but he also agreed to pay an annual tribute of 150,000 *maravedís* over twenty years. Left to their own resources with no expectation of relief, the Muslims of Jaén came to terms in March 1246 and evacuated the city. One resident lamented: "I give you my goodbyes, O Jaén, my city, and I shed my tears as though they were pearls. I did not want to leave you, but this cruel age compels me." Fernando III entered in triumphal procession and heard mass in the mosque which was transformed into a cathedral; the bishopric seated at Baeza was now transferred to Jaén. During the next eight months he busied himself with the repopulation and fortification of Jaén and its environs and granted it a *fuero*.[44]

Just as Jaén was capitulating, the pope on 22 March 1246 lauded Gutierre, bishop-elect of Córdoba, for dedicating himself "to ripping from the hands of the impious the land which they occupied after having profaned the sanctuaries." Anyone from Castile or León who joined in invading Saracen lands or supplied money for that purpose would receive the crusading indulgence. A month later, the pope offered the same indulgence to Infante Alfonso, the heir to the throne, but during the ensuing year he was busy defending Castilian claims to lands east of the Guadiana River against Count Afonso of Portugal. When his father began the siege of Seville in 1248, however, he had to abandon his intervention there.[45]

Until then continuation of the Castilian crusade seemed problematical as Spanish Christians were caught in a tug-of-war between a natural desire to prosecute the reconquest and the powerful attraction of the Holy Land. Papal ambivalence in this respect surely heightened the confusion. Within a few months of launching an oriental crusade, Innocent IV granted an indulgence to those who assisted the Order of Santiago financially, and allowed individuals to fulfill their vow to visit the Holy Land by entering the Order. Yet in the next year when he granted Bishop Gutierre the indulgence for the crusade in Spain, he also called on the Castilian clergy to provide a subsidy for the Holy Land. A Castilian poem entitled *Ay Jherusalem!* lamenting the fall of the Holy City echoed the papal and conciliar efforts to encourage a crusade, but most Spanish Christians likely preferred to expend their crusading energies in the peninsula.[46]

Pelay Pérez Correa, master of Santiago, who had made an exceptional contribution to the crusade both in Portugal and Castile, reflected that uncertainty. While attending the Council of Lyon he agreed to provide military support for Baldwin II, the Latin Emperor of Constantinople. In February 1246 the pope encouraged him to do so and in May Infante Alfonso, evidently thinking that the Castilian reconquest was temporarily in abeyance, authorized the Order to send troops to the Latin Empire. A contract between the knights and the emperor was drawn up in August 1246 at Valladolid, but Baldwin II's inability to raise the money needed to pay the knights and the beginning of Fernando III's campaign against Seville dashed any expectation that the Order might participate in the Empire's wars.[47]

The Castilian Crusade: The Conquest of Seville

After the fall of Jaén the only major cities in Muslim hands were Granada and Seville. The moderates in Seville decided that the city should follow the lead of Ibn al-Ahmar, the king of Granada, and a vassal of Fernando III, by paying an annual tribute; Jerez did likewise, probably in the spring of 1246. Nevertheless, a fanatical element in the city, opposed to any accommodation with the Christians, assassinated the moderate leader and gave their allegiance to the emir of Tunis, though there was little likelihood that he could assist them in any significant way.[48] Although Seville now stood alone, it presented several formidable obstacles to any potential conqueror. Not only was it protected by a ring of fortresses, but the Almohads in the late twelfth century had rebuilt its walls. A goodly supply of arms and machines of war was on hand and preachers spurred on the people to resist the "infidels."

Rather than expend time and money ravaging the countryside, Pelay Pérez Correa, master of Santiago, urged the king to besiege the city, arguing that once it was taken the rest of the region would submit. While the king agreed, he also recognized the need for a fleet to blockade the city and commissioned Ramón Bonifaz of Burgos to assemble the necessary ships. Until the fleet could be brought into action, the king proposed to plunder the surrounding area, destroying the city's means of sustenance. In the fall of 1246 Castilian troops laid waste the countryside around Carmona about twenty miles east of the city. Stricken with terror, the Muslims of Alcalá de Guadaira, about eight miles southeast of Seville, yielded to Ibn al-Ahmar, who promptly handed the town over to the Castilians. Meantime, the Christians devastated the Aljarafe or tableland of Seville, and the neighborhood of Jerez.[49]

At the same time the king dispatched Archbishop Rodrigo of Toledo (who died on his return journey) to Lyon to intercede with Innocent IV. Praising the king as a "special athlete of Christ" who had contended thus far against the Muslims and now proposed to attack Seville, the pope on 15 April 1247 commanded the bishops of Castile and León to cede half of the *tercias*, the third of the tithe destined for the maintenance of churches, to Fernando III for three years. Goñi Gaztambide commented that this was "the first clear and categorical concession" of the *tercias reales* to the crown.[50] Given the papal grant of crusading indulgences in the spring of 1246 to Bishop Gutierre of Córdoba and to Infante Alfonso and all who served with them against the Muslims, additional crusading bulls may have seemed superfluous at this time.

As the campaign of devastation continued into the summer of 1247, the Muslims of Carmona, rather than subject themselves to the horrors of an assault, made an agreement with Fernando III that if they received no aid within six months they would surrender; in the interim they would pay tribute. In the ensuing months Constantina, Reina, and Lora del Río, north of the Guadalquivir, acknowledged Fernando III's suzerainty but they had to admit Castilian garrisons into their alcazares. The Muslims of Cantillana (about fifteen miles north of Seville) opted to oppose the Christians, but the town was taken by assault and the vanquished were sold into slavery; given that example, Guillena and Gerena, just north of the city, capitulated, and nearby Alcalá del Río, after a brief siege, followed suit. As a consequence of these operations the Castilians effectively cut off Seville's lines of communications to the east and north and the time for the establishment of a formal siege was at hand. When Ramón Bonifaz's fleet of thirteen galleys and some smaller ships from the towns on the Bay of Biscay arrived at the mouth of the Guadalquivir, they scattered some forty Muslim ships attempting to prevent them from proceeding up river. The king now moved the bulk of his army to Tablada south of Seville while Pelay Pérez Correa, master of Santiago, crossed the river and positioned himself just below Aznalfarache. Thus by July 1247 a siege was established by land and by sea.

In the months that followed numerous skirmishes between Christians and Muslims took place. Lacking a fleet of their own, the defenders loaded a barge with Greek fire (*fuego de alquitran*) and floated it downstream against Ramón Bonifaz's ships, but without success. As reinforcements arrived, the besieging army, besides bishops, magnates, Military Orders, and town militias, now included some Catalans, Aragonese, and Portuguese. Infante Alfonso was stationed immediately to the east of the city near the Carmona gate, and the king took up a nearby position just south of the alcázar. Other troops occupied the area just north of the city near the Macarena and Córdoba gates while the master of Santiago and others completed the blockade on the east. The fleet, on 3 May 1248, broke the bridge of boats providing

communication between Seville and Triana on the western side of the Guadalquivir, which was now cut off from the city. Despite this success, the Christians discovered that their siege machines were ineffective and often broke
after being used once or twice.

While Seville had put up a good defense thus far, food supplies began to
dwindle because of too many mouths to feed. The population was already
swollen by refugees from other towns seeking shelter within the walls. Faced
with the specter of starvation and forced to eat leather, the defenders appealed to the emir of Tunis, who sent a relieving fleet, but Castilian ships
prevented them from entering the Guadalquivir. Giving up any hope of assistance from that quarter, the defenders vainly pleaded with the Almohads,
who were preoccupied with the threat posed by the rising power of the
Marīnid dynasty.

Isolated from their fellow Muslims, the people of Seville then began negotiations, offering first to admit a Christian garrison into the city and to
give Fernando III his revenues, while leaving the population in place. When
he rejected that they proposed handing over half of the city for Christian occupation, but he rebuffed them again. In the end they had to yield the city
and the Aljarafe (which the Christians had not yet occupied). Once the
documents of capitulation were signed the alcázar had to be surrendered
and by the end of a month the evacuation of the city and its territory had to
be complete. Fernando III promised to give the departing leaders al-Shaqaf
and Ibn Juib, Aznalfarache in the Aljarafe, Sanlúcar at the mouth of the
Guadalquivir, and Niebla, about forty miles west of the city, then held by Ibn
Maḥfūt, after it was conquered.

After a siege of sixteen months, Seville capitulated on 23 November
1248. Castilian troops occupied the alcázar immediately (see Figure 4), raising the king's standard on the tower of the mosque, as they cried out: "May
God help us!" In the course of the month the Muslims sold their property
and went into exile, carrying their movable goods, money, and arms. The
numbers of those departing given in the *Estoria de Espanna* are unbelievable,
but still the exodus must have been substantial. Some were given safe conduct to Jerez while others were carried to Ceuta in Morocco on five ships and
eight galleys. Most probably withdrew to Granada. As they departed they delivered the keys of the city to the king. Ibn Khaldūn, himself a descendant of
a Sevillan family, related that the heads of the principal Muslim families went
to Ifrīqīya and Tunis, because of the close relation with the Ḥafṣids during
the last days of the city's independence.[51]

Figure 4. Entrance to the Real Alcázar of Seville. Photograph by J. F. O'Callaghan.

Fernando III, "the tyrant, the accursed one" as one Muslim writer described him, made his triumphal entrance into Seville on 22 December 1248. The mosque was transformed into a cathedral and Remondo, bishop of Segovia, was consecrated as archbishop of the newly reestablished metropolitan see. In May 1250 Guillermo Pérez de Calzada, abbot of Sahagún, wrote a poem entitled *Rithmi de Iulia Romula seu ispalensi urbe* in honor of the fall of Seville and dedicated it to Infante Alfonso, the oldest son of Fernando III, "king of Spain."[52] Lauding this triumph, Pero da Ponte hailed

> The good king who conquered the frontier . . .
> this good and worthy king, is the valorous
> King Don Fernando, the good king who conquered
> the land of the Moors from sea to sea. . . .
> There is neither emperor nor king in the world
> who could achieve such a conquest. . . .
> I tell you, of all the conquests made by other kings
> of the three laws, all are nothing after Seville. . . .
> For the good king, whom God protects and guides . . .
> took Seville from Muḥammad and
> there endowed God and Holy Mary.[53]

Following the fall of Seville, the Muslims of Jerez, Sanlúcar at the mouth of the Guadalquivir, Cádiz and Santa María del Puerto on the Gulf of Cádiz, Lebrija, Trebujena, and Arcos, just north of Jerez, and Medina Sidonia, Alcalá de los Gazules, and Vejer, south of Jerez, all acknowledged Castilian suzerainty and promised to pay tribute. Ibn Maḥfūt, who ruled Niebla, also became Fernando III's vassal. The king granted the *fuero* of Toledo to Seville and commenced distributing property in the city and its district to the victors, but that task was largely carried out by his son, Alfonso X.[54]

Voicing the exultation felt by the Spaniards as they contemplated their achievements, the canonist Vincentius Hispanus (d. 1248) rejected the idea that all kingdoms were subject to the Holy Roman Empire and proudly asserted:

The Spaniards alone gained an empire by their valor. . . . The Spaniards rule Blessed Lady Spain; ruling by virtue of their audacity and probity, they are winning dominion over her and expanding it. . . . O Spain, who can count your praises? Spain, rich in horses, celebrated for food, shining with gold, steadfast and wise, the envy of all, skilled in law, stands high on sublime pillars.[55]

By contrast, Muslim poets and writers, forced to emigrate from their native country, for which they retained a deep affection, gave voice to feelings of despair, dejection, and resignation to the will of God. The poet al-Rundī summed up their sense of loss and ruin:

> Ask Valencia what became of Murcia,
> And where is Játiva and where is Jaén?
> Where is Córdoba, the seat of great learning,
> And how many scholars of high repute remain there?
> And where is Seville, the home of mirthful gatherings
> On its great river, cooling and brimful of water?
> These centers were the pillars of the country:
> Can a building remain when the pillars are missing?
> The white wells of ablution are weeping with sorrow,
> As a lover does when torn from his beloved;
> They weep over the remains of dwellings devoid of Muslims,
> Despoiled of Islam, now peopled by Infidels!
> Those mosques have now been changed into churches,
> Where the bells are ringing and crosses are standing. . . .
> This misfortune has surpassed all that has preceded,
> And as long as Time lasts, it can never be forgotten! . . .
> What an opprobrium, when once powerful people
> Have been humbled to dust by tyrants and injustice!
> Yesterday they were kings in their own palaces,
> Today they are slaves in the land of the Infidels![56]

The Projected Crusade to Morocco

The subjugation of Islamic Spain was nearly complete as a consequence of the fall of Seville. To be sure there were many Muslims still in the peninsula, but they were all subject in varying degrees to Christian rule. Even though Jaime I had direct control over the kingdom of Valencia, the substantial Muslim population there would be a source of continued trouble in the second half of the thirteenth century. Neither the Muslims in the kingdom of Murcia nor Ibn al-Aḥmar, the king of Granada, who recognized Castilian suzerainty, were an apparent threat. In the circumstances Fernando III could contemplate the possibility of extending his rule into Morocco, long considered part of the Visigothic inheritance of the kings of Spain. Aside from that ideological reason, strategic considerations encouraged the acquisition of the Moroccan ports of Tangier and Ceuta, from which Muslim armies had embarked when invading Spain.

For centuries there had been a Christian presence in Morocco, though most Christians were captives and slaves and likely to remain so unless they became Muslims or were ransomed by their families or by the Orders of the Trinity or La Merced, both recently founded for that purpose. In 1198 Innocent III asked the Almohad caliph to allow the Trinitarians to carry out their labors in his realm and two years later wrote a letter of consolation to Christian prisoners in Morocco.[57] Besides captives, in the twelfth and early thirteenth centuries disgruntled Castilian nobles and other adventurers went into exile in Morocco and often served the caliphs. Honorius III also appealed to the caliph to allow Christians in Morocco to freely exercise their religion, and absolved them from any violation of the canons that they might have committed out of fear of the caliph.[58]

Prior to the twelfth century very little effort to convert the Muslims of Spain or Morocco had been expended. Although Celestine III asked Archbishop Martín of Toledo to send a bilingual priest to attend to the needs of Christians in Morocco, Seville, and other cities, he said nothing about preaching to the Muslims. In 1213 Archbishop Rodrigo of Toledo commissioned one of his canons, Mark of Toledo, to make a new translation of the Qur'ān, but that did not result in any concerted missionary effort.[59]

St. Francis of Assisi (d. 1226) challenged traditional Christian attitudes toward the Islamic world by calling on Christians to preach the Gospel to the Muslims. For that purpose he sent his friars to Morocco in 1220, where they promptly lost their lives because proselytization was contrary to Islamic law. Though other friars were martyred in ensuing years, the missionary enterprise continued. In 1225 Pope Honorius III exhorted Bishop Domingo, "residing in the kingdom of Morocco," and Dominicans and Franciscans to carry out their mission with zeal. Early in the following year he instructed Archbishop Rodrigo to dispatch Franciscans to Morocco to attempt the conversion of the Muslims, and to consecrate one or two friars as bishops for the Moroccan mission. Ibn Abī Zarʿ, a Moroccan historian, reported that the Caliph Abū-l-ʿUlā acceded to Fernando III's demand to erect a church in Marrakech where the Christians could freely exercise their religion; although other aspects of this story are highly questionable it is possible that a church dedicated to the Virgin Mary was built. In 1233, in a letter exhorting the Caliph al-Rashīd to embrace the Christian religion, Gregory IX commended him for his kind treatment of Bishop Agnello who had established himself in Fez, the seat of the Almohad empire. Four years later the pope praised the strength of the Moroccan church and announced that he was dispatching another bishop.[60]

Castilian interest in Morocco took a somewhat different turn in 1245 when "Zeid Aazon, the illustrious king of Salé," expressed interest in becoming a Christian and offered to cede his kingdom to the Order of Santiago. He may be identified with the *sayyid* or prince, al-Ḥasan, one of the sons of Abū Zayd, the last king of Valencia, who had converted to Christianity. Acknowledging that the Order could use Salé, a port on the Atlantic coast of Morocco, as a base for subjecting the neighboring regions and thus "more freely and more efficaciously" aid the Christian faithful in the Holy Land, Innocent IV authorized the knights to accept. We know nothing further of al-Ḥasan's proposed conversion or the cession of Salé to the Order of Santiago, perhaps because his brother-in-law, the Almohad Caliph Abū-l-Ḥasan ʿAlī al-Saʿīd, discovered his intention and ordered his execution.[61]

The proposal may have stimulated Innocent IV to think not only about intensifying Christian missionary work in Morocco, but also about launching a crusade there. On the death of Bishop Agnello, he appointed Lope Fernández de Ain (1246–60) as bishop for Morocco and asked the emirs of Tunis, Ceuta, and Bugia to permit him and certain Franciscan friars to attend to the needs of Christians living there. Thanking the Caliph al-Saʿīd for the protection hitherto accorded to Moroccan Christians, the pope congratulated him on victories achieved over his enemies with Christian help, and urged him to accept Christianity. Most importantly he asked him to receive the new bishop and to grant to the Christians dwelling there certain fortresses in the interior of his realm and on the coast, to be subject to the caliph's sovereignty, where they could take refuge when their persons or property were threatened.[62]

Whereas these letters seem to contemplate friendly relations with the caliph, a flurry of other letters suggests that Innocent IV and Bishop Lope were contemplating more militant action in Morocco. Appealing to Fernando III, Jaime I, Afonso III, and Thibault I, the pope asked them, for remission of their sins, to support Bishop Lope and to lend him and his companions "counsel, aid, and favor" when he requested it. Other letters along the same lines were addressed to the knights of Santiago; the Franciscan authorities; all the Christians on the Spanish coast, as well as the archbishops and municipalities of Tarragona and Narbonne; the bishops and municipalities of Bayonne, Valencia, and Barcelona; the archbishop and people of Genoa; the bishop of Mantua; the bishop and council of Porto; the municipal councils of Santander, San Sebastián, Laredo, and Castrourdiales, a group of ports on the Bay of Biscay that eventually established the "brotherhood of the sea" to advance their mutual interests; and the bishop and people of Lisbon.[63]

Possibly all the pope meant was that general encouragement should be given to the missionaries in Morocco. On the other hand, the phrase *consilium, auxilium, et favorem* seems to imply military action on the part of the Christian rulers of Castile, Aragón, Portugal, and Navarre, the Order of Santiago, and the maritime towns along the coasts of the Bay of Biscay, the Atlantic, and the Mediterranean. Did the pope proclaim a crusade? No, but these letters seem to serve as an alert to that possibility. In the following year, although Innocent IV authorized Bishop Lope to grant to those laypersons who came to dwell with him in Africa the remission of sins given to those aiding the Holy Land, that does not seem to be a clarion call for military intervention in Morocco.[64]

In any case Fernando III's involvement in the conquest and repopulation of Seville precluded him from undertaking any action in Morocco at this time. Inasmuch as the Caliph al-Saʿīd had refused to provide the Christians in Morocco with coastal fortresses for their security, Innocent IV in 1251 repeated his appeal, arguing that many Christians serving in the caliph's army needed a place where their wives and children could be safe from attacks by hostile Muslims. Although the fortresses would remain under Almohad sovereignty, the caliph probably suspected that they could easily be turned into bases for a Christian invasion of Morocco, so it is not likely that the pope's plea met with any greater success than before. Should the caliph not consent, the pope authorized Bishop Lope to recall Christians from the caliph's service and to forbid others to enter Morocco for that purpose.[65]

Fernando III, meanwhile, reached an agreement, whose nature is unknown, with the Muslims of Africa, and the pope subsequently confirmed it. Whatever plans the king may have had for intervention in Morocco, however, were postponed by his death in Seville on 30 May 1252 (see Map 4). He was buried in the cathedral of Seville, near the *miḥrāb*, the niche in the *qibla* wall of the mosque facing Mecca, according to al-Ḥimyarī, who described him as a pleasant man, with good political sense. In the words of the *Chronicle of Cardeña* "he expelled the power of the Moors from all of Spain and gained all the land from Toledo as far as the sea." The *Estoria de Espanna* lauded his persistence in "serving God and destroying the unbelievers." The English historian Matthew Paris remarked that the people of England believed that Fernando III "alone has done more for the honor and profit of Christ's Church than the pope and all his crusaders . . . and all the Templars and Hospitallers." Lomax summed up his achievement by saying: "At a time when the crusading efforts of all the rest of Christendom hardly sufficed to

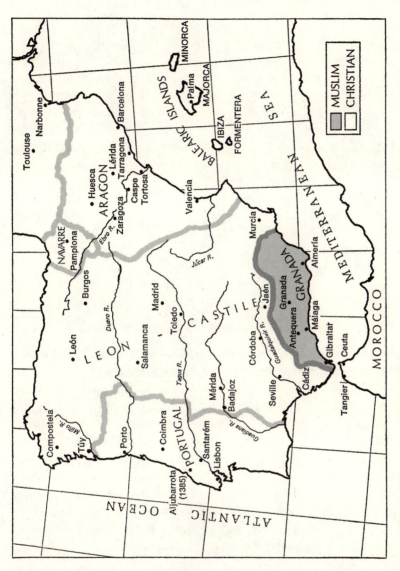

Map 4. Spain at the death of Fernando III, 1252.

maintain a foothold on the coast of the Holy Land, Fernando inflicted on medieval Islam its greatest defeat so far, and one equalled only by the Mongol sack of Baghdad ten years later."[66]

The thirteenth-century Christian kings of Spain conquered more land than all of their predecessors put together, but the problem of integrating it into their existing dominions proved to be extraordinarily difficult. Christian settlers had to be brought in to secure control of recently conquered lands, but the presence of a substantial Muslim population complicated the situation enormously. The rebellion of the Valencian Mudejars continued well into the second half of the thirteenth century and the revolt in 1264 of the Andalusian and Murcian Mudejars, abetted by the king of Granada, thwarted Castilian plans for a Moroccan crusade.[67] The Islamic problem in Spain was not resolved until the early modern era, when the Muslims were given the choice of conversion or expulsion.

Gregory IX and Innocent IV issued a plethora of crusading bulls during the second quarter of the century. Jaime I, who took the cross in 1236, received successive bulls in 1233, 1237, 1239, 1248, and 1250 for his Valencian crusade. The popes also granted the crusading indulgence to Sancho II of Portugal in 1234 and 1241, and to his brother, Infante Fernando de Serpa, though their role as crusaders is unclear. Afonso III, who eventually completed the Portuguese reconquest, also obtained a crusading bull in 1245. Although Fernando III had been the recipient of the indulgence in 1231, no other crusading bull was addressed to him; perhaps he concluded that the bull of 1231 was sufficient. Nevertheless, his brother, Infante Alfonso de Molina, took the crusader's vow in 1239 and his son and heir, Infante Alfonso, received the papal indulgence in 1246, as did Bishop-elect Gutierre of Córdoba. Innocent IV's concession of remission of sins in that year to those helping the bishop of Morocco was probably not issued at the king's request. Even so given the crusading tradition in the royal family as exemplified by the king's predecessors, his brother, and his son, there is every reason to believe that Fernando III saw himself as a crusader attempting to merit remission of his sins.

Innocent IV's concession of a portion of the *tercias* to fund Fernando III's wars against the Muslim was of great importance for crusading finance. Besides that and other levies on ecclesiastical income, taxes, such as the *bovatge*, the offerings of the faithful who gained the indulgence, and tributes paid by various Muslim leaders helped to pay the bills. Fleets from northern Europe, Genoa, and Pisa had contributed significantly to earlier crusades, but now the Catalans, Portuguese, and Castilians were able to provide their own ships. The withdrawal of the northern crusaders before Las Navas de Tolosa may have made Fernando III wary of them, but French and English crusaders assisted in the conquest of Valencia. In the chapters that follow the military organization, finance, and liturgy of reconquest and crusade will be the focus of our attention.

Chapter 6

Warfare in the Crusading Era

During the age of the crusades the organization and operations of Christian armies engaged in the reconquest developed significantly. Not only was the formation of armies improved, but there were frequent opportunities to consider strategic issues of defense and offense, including the relative wisdom of undertaking raids, sieges, or pitched battles. Whereas the focus of this chapter is on peninsular warfare, many will observe that its methods and operations were often typical of medieval warfare in general. Any attempt to distinguish between reconquest and crusade in this regard is meaningless. Whether an expedition had the formal character of a crusade or not, the military organization, strategy and tactics were the same. The ultimate military objective was the reconquest of lands once held by Christians and occupied, unjustly it was believed, by the Muslims, who, in the end, would be expelled from Spain.

Strategic planning to achieve that goal was usually determined by the king and his council. In the Curia of León in 1188 Alfonso IX voiced a principle reflecting ongoing practice: "I promised that I would not make war or peace or treaty without the counsel of the bishops, nobles, and good men by whose counsel I ought to rule." Strategic discussions surely took place during the Council of León in 1135, when Alfonso VII ordered his frontiersmen "to wage war assiduously against the Saracen infidels every year." Alfonso VIII, in consultation with his court, developed the plan for the Crusade of Las Navas, and Fernando III, prior to embarking on his initial campaign, took counsel with his mother, his nobles, the Military Orders, and others. Jaime I, who recorded numerous instances when he took counsel, planned the Crusades of Mallorca and Valencia after consulting military experts.[1]

The first line of defense was castles and towns strategically situated along the frontier to provide maximum protection and to delay, if not to prevent, enemy penetration into the heart of the realm. About 1,500 to 2,000 castles in various states of repair still exist. Most were erected on promontories enabling the garrison to see for miles in every direction and to prepare for an approaching enemy. At times a moat was dug as a further protection.[2] Many castles originated as a simple tower around which towns gradually developed. The walls of Ávila, still intact, were likely typical of most frontier towns. Maintenance of the walls was a continuing responsibility. The *alcaide* (Ar., *al-qāʾid*) or castellan, who rendered homage to the king, assumed the obligation "to make peace and war" at the king's command and received a certain sum to provide castle guard, as well as sufficient food, water, and arms. Castles had to be given up to the king on demand, but could not be surrendered to the enemy without his consent.[3]

The Formation of Armies

As there was no standing army, all military operations were essentially ad hoc, usually planned in the winter or early spring to be executed in the late spring, summer, and early fall. If the prince alerted his people by letter, messenger, or lighted fires, according to the *Usatges of Barcelona*, all men of appropriate age and capacity had to go his aid. A time (about three to four weeks) and a place was usually fixed when the army would assemble with suitable equipment and supplies. The principal ecclesiastical and secular lords were likely summoned individually and in writing.[4] Royal messengers also publicly proclaimed the summons. Everyone summoned had to appear or give a suitable excuse. Failure to respond could result in fines, confiscation, and excommunication.[5] Nobles usually had to serve for three months, in return for a monetary stipend, or tenancy. Towns had a similar obligation. After the expiration of that term troops might be persuaded to remain if their expenses were paid or they were assured of substantial booty. The Muslims of Córdoba, for example, were about to surrender in 1236, but on learning that the Christians were short of food and that the Leonese militias did not wish to remain beyond their three months, they opted to hold out longer.[6]

The Latin sources usually employed the word *exercitus* for an army, but *fonsado* and *hueste* were also used to refer to any military expedition. As a medieval king was expected to lead troops in battle, princes of the royal family were trained to the military life from an early age. Besides his brothers and sons, the king was accompanied by his *mesnada*, an elite corps of knights acting as his bodyguard. Reilly estimated that about fifty mounted warriors, each supported by a squire and a groom, or about 150 men, attended Alfonso VII. Thirty-five *caualleros de mesnada* of Fernando III and thirty-three of Alfonso X received land in Seville after its conquest. Jaime I remarked at one point that he was escorted by fifty knights of his *maynada*.[7]

Prelates and other clerics were often an integral part of the army. While the primary role of the nearly fifty bishops was to provide spiritual sustenance, they were also expected to provide a certain number of troops. Some, such as Jerome, bishop of Valencia, whom the *Poem of the Cid* depicted as equally adept at liturgical celebration and the use of a lance, may be described as warrior bishops. Both Martín of Pisuerga and Rodrigo Jiménez de Rada, archbishops of Toledo, led armies against the Muslims. Gregory IX acknowledged that Rodrigo raised 1,000 men-at-arms and 400 *jinetes* or light cavalry, and fortified thirty-five castles at his own expense. Bishops Gutierre of Córdoba and Sancho of Coria participated in the siege of Seville "with their company of horse and foot."[8]

Prior to the Mallorcan Crusade, the bishops and other clergy pledged military support as follows:

Prelates	Knights	Sergeants
Archbishop of Tarragona	100 knights	1,000 sergeants
Bishop of Barcelona	100 knights	1,000 sergeants
Bishop of Girona	30 knights	300 sergeants
Abbot of San Feliu de Guixols	4 knights	
Archdeacon of Barcelona	10 knights	200 sergeants
Sacristan of Barcelona	15 knights	
Sacristan of Girona	10 knights	
	269 knights	2,500 sergeants

Other clerics and monks promised undetermined numbers of knights, sergeants, and food supplies.[9] The clerical contribution of 269 knights and 2,500 sergeants (*servientes, sirvens*)—2,769 men in all—was quite substantial. The proportion of sergeants to knights appears to be ten to one, or in the case of the archdeacon of Barcelona twenty to one.

During the Crusade of Lisbon Bishop Pedro of Porto and Archbishop João of Braga played prominent roles as preachers and negotiators. Sancho I subsequently exempted the Portuguese clergy from military service except when the Muslims "invade our kingdom." Although Bishops Sueiro of Lisbon and Sueiro of Évora took an active role in the Crusade of Alcácer, evidence concerning later participation by Portuguese prelates in the reconquest is minimal. The bishop of Porto, who held the city in lordship, strongly objected when Sancho II demanded military service from the clergy and laity of the city; Gregory IX twice ordered the king to desist.[10]

As royal vassals receiving estates in full ownership from the king or else as benefices, the magnates (*ricos hombres, barones*) were a major component of the army. From the eleventh century onward as the flow of tribute from the petty Muslim kings increased, kings were able to pay their vassals a cash stipend (*stipendium, soldadas*). Many a noble enriched himself by plunder and was rewarded for faithful service to the king by the concession of additional estates. As feudalism was more fully developed in Catalonia, nobles retained their fiefs and castles so long as they remained loyal and fulfilled their feudal obligations.[11]

The nobility gradually developed an awareness of their distinctive character formed by the common bond of knighthood or chivalry. Young nobles were trained to war from childhood under the direction of a master soldier and served their elders as squires. A young man who distinguished himself on the battlefield might be knighted at once, though it became customary for an aspirant to undertake the vigil of arms and to receive the accolade the next day from an older knight or from the king. Kings such as Afonso I, who, at fourteen, took his arms from the altar on Pentecost Sunday, knighted themselves.[12] Knights were expected to be courageous, experienced in military matters, endowed with good judgment and a sense of loyalty, and capable of evaluating horses and arms. The number of magnates probably was no more than a dozen or two at any given time. Each one was usually accompanied by his own retinue of vassals, responding to a similar obligation to serve. González suggested that the minimum number of knights in the *mesnada* of a Castilian magnate was 100, but some were able to maintain 200 or 300. At least fifteen magnates and 200 knights received a share in the partition of Seville.[13]

Various magnates pledged a certain number of knights to the Mallorcan Crusade, as well as an indefinite number of archers, and sergeants, and agreed to provide them with food, drink, arms, armor, and horses.

Nobles	Knights
Nunyo Sanç, count of Roselló	100 knights
Hug, count of Empúries	70 knights
Guillem de Montcada, viscount of Béarn	100 knights
Ferran de San Martín	100 knights
Guerau de Cervelló	100 knights
Ramon de Montcada, lord of Tortosa	25 knights

Ramon Berenguer d'Ager	25 knights
Bernat de Santa Eugénia	30 knights
Gilabert de Croyles	30 knights
	580 knights

If a ratio of sergeants to knights similar to that of the prelates is assumed, that is, ten or twenty to one, then the number of sergeants might approach 5,800 or 11,600. That would give a total of either 6,380 or 12,180 men, but it is impossible to say whether these figures are reasonably accurate or not.[14]

The Military Orders comprised the first line of defense, but the number of friars ready for battle at any given moment is difficult to determine. There were perhaps no more than fifty to a hundred, depending on the Order. The Templar commander of Miravet, for example, pledged thirty knights, twenty mounted crossbowmen, and other troops for the Mallorcan Crusade. When Pelay Pérez Correa, master of Santiago, agreed in 1246 to provide Baldwin II of Constantinople with 1,500 men, that included 300 knights, but not all were members of the Order. Nor is it likely that the 200 archers (100 horse and 100 foot), and 1,000 sergeants or footsoldiers belonged to the Order.[15]

Perhaps aware that rivalry between the Templars and Hospitallers had contributed to the downfall of the Latin Kingdom of Jerusalem, the peninsular Orders several times promised mutual support and collaboration. In 1221 the masters of Calatrava and Santiago concluded a pact of brotherhood, stipulating that their knights would march together, fight side by side under one commander, and share booty equally. Three years later, the masters of Calatrava, Santiago, the Temple, and the Hospital in León and Castile pledged concerted action in battle. In 1239 the masters of Calatrava and Santiago confirmed all previous agreements between their Orders, and four years later they again emphasised the need for cooperation under a single commander.[16]

The municipalities also were required to respond to the summons to war.[17] As the population of most Christian towns probably ranged between 1,500 to 3,000 persons, the number of adult males eligible for military service likely was no more than 600 to 1,200. Sentinels or lookouts were posted to warn of an approaching enemy so that the summons to defend the town could be given. The walls provided a secure haven for both urban residents and those living within the district. Towns also raided enemy territory in the hope of bringing back booty. Indeed, Dufourcq and Gautier-Dalché spoke of "war as an industry" during this era.[18]

The nature and extent of municipal military obligations were spelled out in royal charters, such as the *Fueros* of Jaca, Teruel, Cuenca, and Coria.[19] While in theory all able-bodied men, organized by districts or parishes, were required to serve, only a limited number might have to do so. Kings often granted exemption from military service in exchange for a tax called *fonsadera*. Before setting out, a muster (*alarde*, Ar., *al-ʿarḍ*) was held in the town square to determine whether the soldiers were properly equipped. Knights, who were a prominent element in the municipal militia, came to enjoy both political and social ascendancy in their towns. After the conquest of Seville, as the towns allowed their military skills and equipment to deteriorate, Alfonso X in 1256 and 1264 assured municipal mounted warriors of significant tax advantages, provided that they were suitably equipped for war. The urban militias were commanded by the *juez* or chief administrator of the town, but the *alcaldes* or magistrates organized the troops from each district. Scouts, lookouts, a chaplain, a surgeon, and notaries or scribes responsible for supplies and the distribution of booty, accompanied the militia.[20]

Almogávers or *almogávares* (Ar., *al-maghāwīr*, raiders), men wearing rough garments, armed with daggers, short lances, and darts, and often living in forests, engaged in daily raids against the Muslims. In Catalonia they were usually footsoldiers, but in Castile they might also be horsemen. Light infantry carrying lances, knives, and daggers, perhaps the most numerous element of the army, included archers (*arqueros*) and crossbowmen (*ballesteros*); some ninety-five *ballesteros* received lands in the partition of Seville. While the cavalry was more mobile, the infantry was valued because it could go where cavalry could not.[21]

Once an army was organized obedience and prompt execution of orders were essential for discipline. Disobedience, fomenting discord, quarreling, wounding, killing, stealing, desertion, and aiding and abetting the enemy were punished severely. Penalties included fines, exile, shaving the head and face, mutilation of the ears or hands, and execution.[22] Trading with the enemy during wartime, especially in wheat, horses, weapons, iron, and wood, was condemned as treason, although the popes occasionally permitted people on the frontier to purchase necessities from neighboring Muslims.[23]

Arms and Armor

In order to acquit themselves effectively soldiers were required to bring a sword, a lance, a javelin, a bow and arrows, or a crossbow and darts. Knights ordinarily carried an iron sword, usually about three feet long, doublesided and with a hilt. The sword was primarily used for striking an enemy in the hope of cutting through his coat of mail, rather than piercing his body. Both knights and footsoldiers used wooden or iron lances about six or seven feet long, and tipped with a long iron point. Footsoldiers also wielded a shorter javelin. Although the bow and arrow enjoyed some popularity, the crossbow became the most important projectile weapon, employed by both knights and footsoldiers.[24]

Protective armor included the coat of mail, worn over a quilted jacket, and reaching the knees or even below; the helmet or iron cap, sometimes fitted with a nose guard, and worn over a cloth cap; and metal or leather braces protecting the arms and thighs. Shields or bucklers made of wood covered with leather or iron bands, were either round, or triangular, similar to a kite. The coats of arms of kings and knights were painted on their shields. Almoravid shields were made from hippopotamus hides.[25] Body armor and arms varied greatly depending on the warrior's status. Magnates may have adorned their helmets with precious stones, as visual testimony of their triumphs.[26]

Several codices illustrate various types of weapons and protective gear. A twelfth-century miniature in Beatus's *Commentary* depicts soldiers on horseback and on foot, wearing conical iron caps and chain mail covering the body including the head and reaching to the knees; they carried swords, lances, and round shields. A battle scene in *Cantiga* 63 displays Christian knights wearing chain mail covered with surcoats, gloves, and bowled or square helmets shielding the entire face; their kite shields have distinctive markings such as a zig-zag pattern in black and white (a Muslim shield has gold half moons on red); they carry lances with triangular pennons, and a red flag (see Figure 5). Around 1300 murals in the royal palace of Barcelona portrayed knights in chain mail with pot helmets, footsoldiers bearing lances and swords, and archers equipped with swords, as well as crossbows and darts in quivers.[27]

Knights sometimes imitated the Muslim riding style, known as *a la jineta*; with a short stirrup strap and bended knees the knight was able to control his horse and to move swiftly. The French practice, known as *a la brida*, also gained popularity. A long stirrup strap extended the warrior's legs giving him greater security, though somewhat sacrificing maneuverability. Horses were sometimes protected by a coat of mail. Given their great cost and the expense of maintaining them, the number of mounted warriors likely was small in comparison with infantrymen. Thirteenth-century laws

Figure 5. Count García of Castile fights al-Manṣūr in the Battle of San Esteban de Gormaz. *Cantigas de Santa Maria*, 63. Escorial, MS T.1.j.

prohibiting the export of horses attested to their scarcity. After losing eighty-six horses, Jaime I purchased replacements but admitted that he probably paid more than they were worth. The Almoravids brought camels to Spain, causing consternation among the Christians, but neither Muslims nor Christians used them regularly.[28]

Armies probably employed trumpets or other horns to summon one another. The sound of Almoravid war drums covered with elephant hides reportedly terrified the Christians who had never heard them before. *Cantiga* 165 illustrates a Muslim army equipped with standards, trumpets, and drums.[29]

Supply was a major concern of any army. It has been estimated that each man required about two and a half pounds of grain and two quarts of water per day; horses needed eight gallons of water and twenty-eight pounds of fodder. Beasts of burden, rather than wheeled carts, ordinarily were used to transport supplies. Mules, needing less food and water and able to cover as many as twenty-five miles a day with loads of 200 pounds or more, were preferred to horses. Municipal *fueros* often specified the obligation to provide beasts of burden. Jaime I employed 2,000 pack animals capable of carrying 400,000 pounds of supplies to relieve Puig, while the king of Granada sent 1,500 animals to Fernando III's siege of Jaén. An army on the move usually followed river routes and marched through areas that might yield forage and plunder.[30]

Military Standards and Leadership

The military standard was a sign whereby kings, magnates, Military Orders, and town militias identified themselves; it also acted as a rallying point. Guillem de Montcada, who led the van in the battle of Portopí, commanded his men: "let no one separate himself from my standard" and Alfonso VIII ordered his standardbearer to advance into the midst of the battle of Las Navas to hearten his troops.[31] Standards varied in size and shape in accordance with a person's rank. Royal standards more than likely were similar to royal seals. Castles were probably depicted on the Castilian standard and lions on the Leonese; after the union of the realms, the two were combined. Innocent III permitted Pedro II and his successors to use a banner bearing their arms, four red stripes on a yellow shield. The royal murals of Barcelona show knights carrying standards with distinctive arms and some have similar identifying signs on their helmets.[32] Standards bearing religious symbols will be discussed in a later chapter.

Town militias gathered for prayer and for the blessing of their standards before setting out on campaign. In the Cortes of Seville in 1250 Fernando III stipulated that a town's standard must be borne not by an artisan, but by the *juez* or judge, a person of knightly rank, who would not bring shame on the town in time of danger, presumably by fleeing. Standards given to towns by the king were destroyed after his death and replaced by others presented by his successor. Soldiers were expected to defend the standard, and suffered dire punishments if they fled with it, thereby disrupting the army, or abandoned it, an act tantamount to treason. Rewards were given to those who defended the standard or recovered one taken by the enemy, or raised up one that had fallen, or captured an enemy standard.[33]

The success of any military undertaking depended largely on the quality of leadership. Although the king was the natural commander, he was not necessarily a good general, and so relied on the counsel of his vassals, who brought their own experience into play. Afonso I and Sancho I of Portugal and Alfonso I and Jaime I of Aragón appear to have been more than competent commanders, while the Cid and Pelay Pérez Correa, master of Santiago, stand out as notable generals. The *alférez* (Ar., *al-fāris*, knight) or *signifer*, a prominent noble who bore the royal standard, commanded the army during the king's absence. The Cid, named as *alférez* by Sancho II of Castile, was the most famous person to hold that position.[34]

Below the magnates, each of whom commanded his own vassals, there were many other commanders and the law prescribed harsh penalties for those who killed, wounded, or dishonored them. In its most limited sense *adalid* (Ar., *al-dalīl*, guide) meant one whose knowledge of roads and passages was such that he could lead troops safely through difficult terrain, and knew where to place lookouts. Sponsored by twelve of his fellows, he was appointed by the king to command a mounted troop; after swearing an oath to defend the realm, he received a standard from the king as a sign of his office. At least twenty *adalides* shared in the partition of Seville. If someone were to be promoted to the post of *almocadén* (Ar., *al-muqaddam*, commander) or infantry commander, twelve others had to swear that he was brave and loyal, knowledgeable in war, capable of command and of protecting his men. The king conferred on him a lance with a small pennant by which he could be recognized. His twelve sponsors then raised him high four times on two lances; pointing his lance toward each of the four corners of the world, he swore the same oath as the *adalid*. Fifty-one *almocadenes*, each with a company of foot, were given property in the partition of Seville.[35]

Wars of Pillage and Devastation

Offensive warfare most often took the form of cavalcades or raids of shorter or longer duration into enemy territory. Both Christian and Muslim raiding parties of lightly armed cavalry tried to profit by a rapid strike, seizing livestock and whatever other booty they could in a day or two. Perhaps numbering only 50 to 300 men, raiders usually were familiar with the land and tried to conceal their movements as long as possible. They had to move swiftly so the enemy would not have time to retaliate and so that they could regain the safety of their town. The best guarantee of that was surprise. When Jaime I carried out a raid with 130 knights, 150 *almogàvers*, and 700 footsoldiers, they traveled by night, but the Muslims of Valencia alerted their people by bonfires.[36]

Raids lasting several weeks or even months and reaching deep into enemy territory often involved thousands of knights and footsoldiers and had to be planned well in advance. They were usually undertaken during the summer and fall when the harvest was ripe for destruction or could provide sustenance for the raiders. The purpose of these raids was devastation: to destroy the enemy's crops; trees and vineyards were burned and cut down; livestock was seized; villages were pillaged; fortifications were wrecked; and persons having the misfortune of being in the way were captured. The raiders hoped to undermine the enemy's morale and his will to resist. Once an enemy had been softened up in this way, it was possible to besiege a stronghold in the expectation that the defenders would have insufficient supplies and manpower to maintain themselves for any length of time.

As the element of surprise was missing in a large cavalcade acting in broad daylight, the army had to be well organized and disciplined, moving in a column, ready to defend itself at any moment. The army ordinarily was divided into a vanguard, a rearguard, and flanking detachments. Defensible places adjacent to water and food supplies were chosen for encampments. Tents were set in a circle or a square with the king's tent in the center. Sometimes defensive barriers were established. In 1231 Jaime I ordered 300 campfires lit so the Muslims would conclude that his army was much larger than in actuality. From a base camp smaller raiding parties were detached to plunder the surrounding area. Alfonso I, departing from Zaragoza in September

1125 and ending about a year later, carried out a notable cavalcade through Andalucía. Once the decision was taken to return home, the army was vulnerable to reprisals because of the burden of captives and livestock seized as booty.[37]

Siege Warfare

Sooner or later, if the king wished to take possession of any area, he had to seize the enemy's strongholds and the territory dependent on them. Some fortresses were taken by surprise, usually because the garrison was small and unprepared. Taking advantage of the dark of night, the twelfth-century Portuguese adventurer Geraldo the Fearless scaled the walls of several towns but few of his conquests were permanent. Other places were captured when the attackers overwhelmed the defenders. When the crusaders enroute to Las Navas seized Malagón in a few hours, other nearby fortresses, after offering minimal resistance, soon capitulated. After breaking into the suburbs of Córdoba by surprise, the Castilians soon established a full-blown siege.[38]

A siege was a long and costly operation of uncertain outcome (see Figure 6). The approaches to a fortress were often difficult to traverse, especially if it stood on a mountain, or if it were protected by a moat or a palisade. The Genoese closed the moat of Tortosa, reportedly about 126 feet wide by 96 deep, by filling it with stones. The Muslims defending Calatrava la vieja in 1212 set iron spikes in the Guadiana River to impede the crusaders. Stone walls several feet thick protected the defenders while holding off the enemy; sometimes an outer wall encircling the original walls presented an additional barrier. The last bastion of defense was the citadel within the walls and often on a height overlooking a town. Sieges such as those of Toledo (1085), Zaragoza (1118), Lisbon (1147), Almería (1147), Tortosa (1148), Silves (1189), Alcácer do Sal (1217), Mallorca (1229), Córdoba (1236), Valencia (1238), Jaén (1245), and Seville (1248) occupy a significant place in contemporary narratives. The besieging army attempted to sever the enemy's lines of communication and to deprive the defenders of sustenance by ravaging the surrounding countryside. Care had to be taken, however, not to destroy the army's own food supply. While the work of pillage continued, the defenders often made sorties, skirmishing with their opponents, and then retreating hastily to safety.[39]

Arms and armor as well as water, wheat, and other food supplies were stockpiled in preparation for a siege. The defenders of Lisbon eventually were reduced to eating cats and dogs—to the horror of the crusaders—as

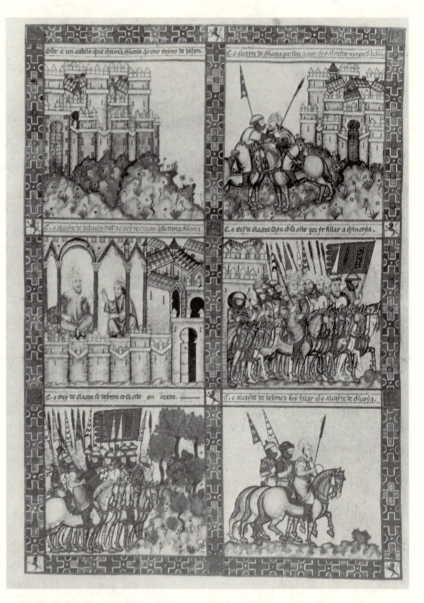

Figure 6. The king of Granada attempts to capture Chincoya Castle. *Cantigas de Santa Maria*, 187. Escorial, MS T.1.j.

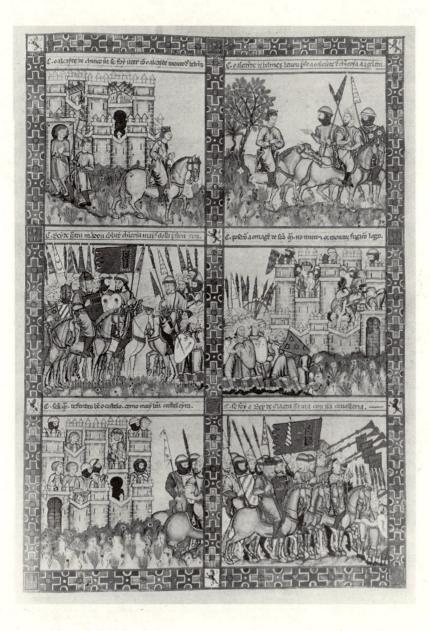

well as garbage thrown from crusader ships and washed up under the walls. Although the food supply supposedly had rotted, when the crusaders occupied the city they discovered 8,000 seams of wheat and 12,000 sextars of oil, which they found quite acceptable. Failure to cut off the food supply or to reduce the defenders to starvation often forced a siege to be abandoned. Limitations on military service also hampered besieging armies, as knights or townsmen opted to depart once their term was up.[40]

A blockade was established so supplies and reinforcements could not be introduced and the defenders could not escape. Attempts were made to breach the walls by sapping or battering them. Mantlets made of hides and osier protected sappers trying to dig under the walls and others using a battering ram from being pummeled from above by stones. If a castle were built on rock, mining would be time-consuming and costly and ultimately unsuccessful. Within a month the crusaders at Lisbon dug a mine with five entrances, extending about sixty feet; when inflammable material was placed in the mine about forty-five feet of the wall fell down. Crusaders mining the walls of Alcácer do Sal caused one tower to collapse. The Muslims thwarted an attempt during the siege of Seville to undermine Triana.[41]

While mining was in progress, wooden towers were constructed and moved up against the walls, sometimes on wheels, sometimes over greased wooden rollers. Standing on top of the towers, archers and crossbowmen shot arrows and other missiles down on the defenders; eventually an assault might be launched across a bridge from the tower to the walls. Two movable towers, one eighty-three feet high and another ninety-five feet, were built during the siege of Lisbon. Mats, penthouses, and mantlets made of interwoven branches protected the towers against fire and stones; however, the defenders dumped burning oil on one tower, reducing it to ashes. During the siege of Almería the Muslims used Greek fire to burn wooden castles built by the Christians.[42]

Siege engines previously used were sometimes transported to the current site, while at other times they were built on the spot. While bombardment might continue by day and night, walls were not easily destroyed. The defenders often had siege engines of their own to hurl missiles at their tormentors. Chevedden argued that all siege machines were essentially variations of the trebuchet, a wooden beam on a rotating axle fixed on a single pole or on a trestle. Attached to the long narrow end of the beam was a sling containing a projectile; ropes tied to the other, wider end, when pulled by a crew, propelled the projectile through the air. Three types were used: the traction trebuchet driven by a crew pulling ropes; the counterweight trebuchet powered by a counterweight placed opposite the sling; and the hybrid trebuchet employing both the counterweight and the pulling crew.[43]

Among the siege engines in which the beam was fixed on a single pole were the mangonel, probably a traction trebuchet; the *fundibulum*; and the *algarrade* (Ar. *'arrādah*). Heavier machines set on a trestle included the *al-manjanech* (Ar. *al-manjanīq*), probably a hybrid trebuchet; and the *brigola*, a counterweight trebuchet. Stones were often transported to the siege, but at other times were gathered on site. The maximum size that could be fired by a traction trebuchet was 200 pounds for a maximum distance of about 120 meters or 390 feet. A counterweight trebuchet could launch even heavier missiles. Two Balearic mangonels, hybrid trebuchets used by the crusaders at Lisbon with alternating crews of 100 men, were able to fire 5,000 stones in ten hours, or 250 an hour, or approximately four every minute. One can imagine the destruction that might be done and the fear raised among the population.[44]

Both sides also practiced a form of pscyhological warfare. Jaime I, for example, shot the head of a Muslim captive over the walls of Palma. While the crusaders at Lisbon impaled the heads of eighty Muslim captives so the defenders could see them, the Muslims taunted them, objecting to their worship of Jesus, abusing the cross, and suggesting that their wives were producing bastards at home. When the Almoravids threatened Toledo in 1148, Queen Berenguela called their manhood into question for attacking a woman and told them to seek out her husband, Alfonso VII, who would readily take them on. Shamed, they withdrew.[45]

Persistence eventually brought the besieged to their knees. As supplies were exhausted, starvation loomed; people died; rotting corpses raised a stench, and disease began to spread. In the circumstances the defenders might appeal to their coreligionists for help, promising that if that proved fruitless within a specified period they would surrender. After an army coming to relieve Alcácer do Sal was defeated, the defenders capitulated a month later. When Alfonso IX routed Ibn Hūd at Alange, Mérida surrendered; nearby Badajoz apparently put up little resistance, and the Muslims abandoned Elvas. Fernando III allowed Carmona to seek help in 1247, but when it was not forthcoming, the town yielded.[46]

Although no surrender pacts for Castile-León and Portugal are extant, the chroniclers often reported the terms of surrender. Some Aragonese pacts do survive and are likely representative of the genre. Alfonso VI allowed the Muslims of Toledo to remain, retaining their property, worshipping freely, and living in accordance with Islamic law; those who wished to depart with their movable goods could do so, but they could return later if they wished. Alfonso I gave similar guarantees to the Muslims of Zaragoza. Although the Muslims of Lisbon were permitted to leave, provided that they gave up their arms, money, animals, and clothing, the crusaders sacked the city, killing many. Sancho I agreed to allow the Muslims of Silves to depart with their movable goods, but his crusading allies insisted on their right to plunder the city, even though he offered them 10,000 *maravedís* as compensation.[47]

Fernando III's general policy in Andalucía was to require the Muslims to evacuate the principal urban centers capitulating after a siege. Thus the Muslims of Capilla, Baeza, Úbeda, Córdoba, Jaén, and Seville were allowed to depart, taking their movable goods under safeconduct to Muslim territory. The Muslims similarly evacuated Palma, Borriana, and Valencia, but a significant number remained in Jaime I's dominions, assured of religious liberty and the observance of Islamic law. The fall of a city usually resulted in the capitulation of smaller towns in the vicinity. Thus when Toledo surrendered, other towns in the Tagus valley acknowledged Alfonso VI's sovereignty. After the surrender of Córdoba, several adjacent towns offered tribute to Fernando III. Many towns in the countryside surrounding Seville, including Jerez and Medina Sidonia, acknowledged his suzerainty, while retaining their property, law, and religion.[48]

While many sieges ended with capitulation, some towns were taken by assault. This was the bloodiest outcome of a siege and in some respects the least desirable. Men, women, and children were slaughtered indiscriminately, and survivors were reduced to slavery. Although the defenders at Almería offered Alfonso VII 100,000 *maravedís* if he would lift the siege, the Genoese refused to agree and took the city by assault. Some 20,000 Muslims were said to have been killed and another 30,000 taken captive; 10,000 women and children were transported to Genoa, where they were likely sold as slaves or ransomed. Following Las Navas the Muslims of Úbeda offered Alfonso VIII 1,000,000 *maravedís* to pass them by, but he refused and assaulted the city, enslaving the survivors. Jaime I reported that 24,000 inhabitants were massacred during the assault of Palma.[49]

Battles

Numerous battles resulted when a relieving army attempted to drive off besiegers or to intercept a raiding expedition, but only rarely did kings risk the possibility of a great victory or a terrible defeat by deliberately engaging in a pitched battle. The Cid, besieged in Valencia, repulsed the Almoravids at Cuart de Poblet in 1094, and two years later Pedro I triumphed at Alcoraz over the Muslims coming to relieve Huesca. The Almoravids, in turn, overwhelmed a Christian army trying to succor Uclés in 1108. Alfonso I gained three notable victories on the battlefield, first over the king of Zaragoza who made a sortie from his beleaguered city in 1118; then at Cutanda in 1120 over the Almoravids; and at Lucena in 1126 during his march through Andalucía. He was not so fortunate, however, at Fraga in 1134, when he was defeated and killed by the Almoravids. There is little information about it, but at Ourique in 1139 Afonso I defeated the Muslims attempting to halt incursions into the Alentejo. A century later, as noted above, at Alange in 1230 Alfonso IX bested Ibn Hūd attempting to relieve Mérida. Muslim troops stationed on a height at Portopí overlooking the shore attempted to halt Jaime I's invasion of Mallorca in 1229, but the Christians forced them to flee. When Zayyān, the king of Valencia, attacked Jaime I's base at Puig de la Cebolla in 1237, he was driven off. The victory undermined the morale of the Valencian Muslims and stiffened the king's determination to have the city.[50]

The classic battles of the reconquest, however, were Zallāqa, Alarcos, and Las Navas de Tolosa. Alfonso VI and Yūsuf ibn Tashufīn fought the battle of Zallāqa on 23 October 1086, on a broad plain in a place now called Sagrajas, near the juncture of the Guadiana and the Gevora Rivers, about eight to ten miles north of Badajoz. A description by a contemporary author, Abū Bakr al-Turṭūshī, probably reflects the tactics employed by the Almoravids at Zallāqa:

This is the battle order that we use . . . and which seems most efficacious in our battles with our enemies. The infantry with their shields, lances, and iron-tipped and penetrating javelins are formed in several ranks. Their lances rest obliquely on their shoulders, the shaft touching the ground, the point aimed at the enemy. Each one kneels . . . on his left knee and holds his shield in the air. Behind the infantry are the elite archers, whose arrows can pierce coats of mail. Behind the archers are the cavalry. . . . When the enemy comes near, the archers let fly against them a shower of arrows, while the infantry throw their javelins and receive the charge on the points of their lances. Then infantry and archers . . . open their ranks to right and left and the Muslim cavalry, charging through the open space, routs the enemy, if Allāh so decides.[51]

Alfonso VI, possibly expecting a quick victory over forces assumed to be as ineffective as the *reyes de taifas*, charged and drove back the *taifa* contingents, but superior Almoravid numbers halted his advance. Their first line of defense consisted of soldiers equipped with long lances, and the second line threw javelins at the enemy. At this point Yūsuf carried out a flanking movement and surrounded the Christians; many were killed as they attempted to escape, but some apparently died from the labors of the day. Though wounded, Alfonso VI escaped under cover of night. Despite his victory, Yūsuf advanced no further, perhaps reasoning that it was late in the year and that greater success could be achieved in the spring. Thus he gained no significant territory at Christian expense, though the subjugation of Andalucía to Almoravid rule put the Christians on the defensive for many years to come. Another consequence was to attract French knights to the war against Islam in Spain.[52]

A century later Alfonso VIII chanced the future of his kingdom on a pitched battle at Alarcos on 19 July 1195. There, a few miles south of Toledo, a castle, still unfinished, was situated on a small hill adjacent to the Guadiana River and overlooked a broad plain. Thinking that the Almohads were weakened by rebellions in Morocco and elsewhere, he evidently concluded that he could defeat them on the battlefield and refused to await reinforcements from Alfonso IX. The Caliph al-Manṣūr had the advantage in numbers and also opted to give his men a day of rest rather than accept the challenge offered by the Christians. On the following morning the Almohads, well-rested and organized in tribal groups each with its own standard, initiated the combat. The Christians, disconcerted, charged in a disorderly manner, dispersing some of the volunteers who had come to participate in the holy war; but the main Almohad lines held firm and executed a flanking movement that encircled the Christians. To rescue the situation Alfonso VIII brought up his reserves, but the caliph responded with the full force of his army. In the ensuing mêlée the Christians were driven back and the king had to flee. Those seeking refuge in the castle of Alarcos were shortly forced to surrender. The battle had raged from early morning until sundown. Many other nearby castles surrendered or were abandoned by the Christians, but the caliph did not press his advantage, returning instead to Seville. In the next two years, however, Almohad forces ravaged the Tagus River valley.[53]

The battle of Alarcos was an ignominious defeat for Alfonso VIII, but on 16 July 1212 at Las Navas de Tolosa he redeemed himself with a glorious triumph. Marching southward from Toledo the crusaders seized most of the fortresses lost as a result of Alarcos. As they passed through the Puerto del Muradal they encountered the Almohad army. The battle likely occurred about seven or eight miles north of Las Navas between Santa Elena and Miranda del Rey. The Christians were grouped in three ranks, each organized in a vanguard and a rearguard. Alfonso VIII held the center, while Pedro II occupied the left and Sancho VII of Navarre the right. Lightly armed cavalry, including volunteers dedicated to the holy war, formed the first rank of the Almohad army. The main force consisted of troops from both Morocco and Andalucía. Combat commenced when the crusader vanguard broke through the first enemy lines but the Almohad van stiffened, prompting some of the urban militiamen to flee. Fearing disaster, Alfonso VIII moved up with his rearguard while Pedro II and Sancho VII also joined the attack. At that point the Caliph al-Nāṣir fled, leaving his army to be cut to pieces. In the ensuing days Alfonso VIII temporarily occupied Baeza and Úbeda, but exhaustion and fear of famine forced him to return to Toledo. Although it was not apparent at the time, his victory at Las Navas de Tolosa opened the entire Guadalquivir valley to Christian conquest.[54]

In the three battles just described several factors had a paramouint influence on the outcome. The Muslims appear to have had numerical superiority at Zallāqa and Alarcos, whereas at Las Navas the forces seem to have been evenly matched. Secondly, Yūsuf ibn Tashufīn and al-Manṣūr, the victors at Zallāqa and Alarcos, exercised more effective generalship. Both Alfonso VI and Alfonso VIII underestimated their opponents, and overconfidence probably led them into battles that they should have avoided. The Muslim tactic of giving way and feigning retreat evidently fooled the Christians at Zallāqa and Alarcos, who were then surrounded as the enemy swept around their flanks. Alfonso VIII probably learned something from his experience at Alarcos and put it to good use at Las Navas; the caliph, however, seems to have remained passive during the battle until he fled in disgrace. The terrain at Zallāqa and Alarcos apparently did not favor one side over the other, though at Zallāqa the Almoravids had the river Guadiana at their back; that could have slowed their retreat to Badajoz, if that had been necessary. The battlefield of Las Navas was much hillier than at either of the other sites but the Christians were able to overcome the obstacles posed. Although the chroniclers tend to emphasize the action of the cavalry in all these battles, infantry forces were present as well (see Figure 7).[55]

The Question of Numbers

Any attempt to determine the number of troops engaged in any given campaign is a frustrating task. Documents recording numbers are generally lacking, and chroniclers' statements are often exaggerated and must be viewed with great scepticism. Numbers varied considerably depending on whether

the military action was a raid, a seige, or a battle. Some raiding parties probably counted no more than 50 to 100 or 200 to 300, while others were substan-
tially larger, approaching the size of armies. The number of soldiers involved
in a siege probably changed over the course of the operation. Some contingents likely did not arrive at the outset, perhaps in accordance with a precon-
ceived plan, while others left early, citing foral limitations on their service.
During the several months of the siege of Seville Fernando III commanded
perhaps 5,000 to 7,000 men.[56]

Numbers given by the sources of soldiers engaged in pitched battles are
generally unacceptable. Muslim authors related that at Zallāqa the Almoravids had 500, or 12,000, or 20,000 light cavalry, and estimated the Christians
at 40,000, 60,000, or 80,000 horse and 200,000 foot; the number killed
ranged from 10,000 to 54,000, or 300,000. Reilly, however, estimated the
Christian army at about 2,500 men, consisting of perhaps 750 heavily armed
and 750 lightly armed knights, and about 1,000 squires and footsoldiers.
Muslim sources, all of a later date, recorded the death of 30,000 Christians at
Alarcos, and the capture of 5,000, while only 500 Muslims were killed; according to al-Maqqarī there were 146,000 dead Christians, and 30,000 prisoners; the booty consisted of 150,000 tents, 80,000 horses, 100,000 mules,
and 400,000 asses. Prior to Las Navas, Alfonso VIII estimated that 2,000
knights with their squires, 10,000 sergeants on horseback and up to 50,000
sergeants on foot came to Toledo. Archbishop Rodrigo stated that the Almohads had 185,000 knights and an incalculable number of infantry, and that
their losses amounted to 200,000 men. Muslim sources related that only 600
out of 600,000 Almohad soldiers survived the battle. Such figures are wholly
unreliable.[57]

The numbers for Jaime I's crusades are also difficult to calculate because of discrepancies in the sources. According to the number of knights
and sergeants pledged by prelates and nobles for the Mallorcan Crusade,
cited above, the king may have had anywhere from 9,000 to 13,000 men.
While he noted that he embarked 1,000 men in his ships, the *Latin Chronicle*
reported that his letters stated that he had scarcely seventy knights and
13,000 foot when he took Mallorca. At Portopí, according to the king, 2,000
Muslims attempted to prevent the landing of 4,000 to 5,000 men, and the
Muslims trying to dislodge the Christians from Puig de la Cebolla numbered
600 knights and 11,000 foot. Whether the size of the Muslim army was as
great as reported cannot be ascertained.[58]

Without detailed records it is impossible to determine the size of armies
clashing in pitched battles. The number on each side might fall between

Figure 7. Christian knights bearing the banner of Holy Mary defeat the Marīnids in Morocco. *Cantigas de Santa Maria*, 181. Escorial T.1.j.

1,000 and 10,000 men, and perhaps no more than 3,000 to 5,000 were involved in any one of the battles mentioned. Exaggerating the number of enemy soldiers or those killed, of course, was one way of exalting the triumph of one's coreligionists or explaining away a terrible defeat.

The Distribution of the Spoils

Booty taken in the innumerable raids typical of frontier warfare was a means of enriching oneself or of attaining higher status. A footsoldier who captured a horse and became a mounted warrior, for example, altered his situation permanently. The capture of enemy arms also replenished the store of weapons. The spoils of war contributed mightily to the economic growth of frontier towns. Nevertheless, the evidence can hardly be quantified, as the chronicles speak in general terms of booty taken. The Toledan militia, after routing the kings of Córdoba and Seville, "took a lot of gold and silver, royal standards, precious vestments, excellent arms, chain mail, helmets, shields, excellent horses with their saddles, and mules and camels laden with great riches."[59] The day before Las Navas Archbishop Rodrigo threatened with excommunication anyone who abandoned pursuit of the enemy to gather booty. The Almohads left behind "gold, silver, precious garments, silk hangings, and many other precious ornaments, as well as a lot of money and precious vases," besides camels and other animals, and tents; Alfonso VIII sent the caliph's tent to the pope and the tent flap to Las Huelgas de Burgos.[60]

Quarrels inevitably erupted concerning the disposal of booty. The municipal *fueros*, however, stipulated that booty was communal property and prescribed an elaborate process for distribution. Everything was gathered and recorded under the supervision of *quadrilleros* representing municipal parishes. An auction was held, usually in the town square, under the presidency of the principal magistrate, and the money realized was apportioned among the victors. First, however, families were compensated for the loss of a relative, a horse, another animal, or equipment. Next, muncipal officials who had served with the militia were paid, and those who had distinguished themselves in combat were rewarded. A fifth of all booty, owed to the king as a sign of sovereignty, was in effect a form of taxation that enabled him to execute his functions. At times he consigned a portion to the Military Orders. Once these claims were satisfied the remainder was distributed among the rank and file. People who provided animals or equipment, archers, commanders, surgeons, chaplains, and clerks received additional shares because of their special contributions. The *mayordomo mayor* had the responsibility for supervising the distribution of booty taken by a royal army; each man was compensated according to the number of men, arms, and animals that he brought to the campaign.[61]

The greatest form of booty was plunder seized when a fortress surrendered. Aside from people, animals, and movable goods, there was also real estate to be distributed. In the twelfth century *quadrilleros* or municipal company commanders apportioned land among the soldiers planning to settle in the new community. In the thirteenth century royal partitioners assigned houses, shops, farmland, vineyards, and orchards to the conquerors in accordance with their status and contribution to victory. The most comprehensive *repartimientos* or books recording this distribution of property are those for Mallorca, Valencia, and Seville.[62]

Casualties and Ransoming Captives

Casualties were a consequence of all military actions. Numbers were sometimes reasonably stated, but Alfonso VIII's assertion that 100,000 Muslims died at Las Navas was a gross exaggeration; equally absurd is his statement that only twenty-five or thirty Christians were killed.[63] Physicians and surgeons often accompanied militia forces and were paid specific fees for treating the wounded. The latter were compensated for injuries and were often cared for in hospitals. In 1225 Jaime I placed all the hospitals in his realms under royal protection. The Military Orders maintained hospitals to care for their wounded. Calatrava, for example, had hospitals at Guadalerzas, Évora, Cogolludo, El Collado de Berninches, and Santa Olalla. The commander of Santa Olalla was obliged to accompany royal armies "to provide for knights and footsoldiers, both the wounded and the poor, the ill and the sick, and to take a chaplain with him to offer *viaticum* to the wounded, if necessary, and a master of surgery to give medicine to the wounded." The hospitals of the Order of Santiago were situated at Toledo, Cuenca, Alarcón, Moya, Huete, Talavera, Uclés, Castrotoraf, and Salamanca.[64]

The king and the most powerful magnates had their own physicians, but only three kings seem to have been injured or wounded: Alfonso VI was wounded at Zallāqa; Afonso I broke his leg attempting to escape from Badajoz; and during the siege of Valencia, a bolt from a crossbow creased Jaime I's forehead. The primitive character of medieval surgery is illustrated in *Cantiga* 126. A bolt fired from a crossbow lodged in a Christian's neck, but the surgeon's initial attempt to extract it was unsuccessful; he then vainly attached the bolt to a crossbow, hoping to fire it. Happily for the wounded man the Virgin Mary, so we are told, was able to pull it out.[65]

One of the hazards of war, both for soldiers and civilians, was the possibility of being captured. The loss of "liberty which is the most precious thing that people can have in this world" was sufficient cause for grief, especially because captivity, aside from the separation from family and friends, was usually quite harsh. Some captives never returned home and others were subjected to torture to force their conversion to Islam. Dominican and Franciscan friars were sent to attend to the spiritual needs of captives in Morocco so they would not apostasize. Sometimes prisoners escaped or were liberated by victorious armies. Both Santo Domingo de la Calzada and Santo Domingo de Silos came to be known as wonderworkers who could break chains and set captives free.[66]

Family members often sought to ransom captured relatives but not every family could raise the money. Catalan confraternities received bequests for that purpose, and municipal *fueros* regularized the redemption of captives, allowing families to purchase Muslim slaves to be exchanged for Christian captives. Merchants functioning as professional ransomers often turned over ransom money or executed the exchange. The ransomer, called an *exea* (Ar., *shī'a*, guide), or later, *alfaqueque* (Ar., *al-fakkāk*, redeemer) was paid a commission of 10 percent for each captive ransomed or a gold *maravedí* for every prisoner exchanged. The *alfaqueque*, appointed by a municipality or the king, was expected to be honest and to know Arabic.[67] The hospitals of the Military Orders, such as the Holy Redeemer at Teruel in Aragón, not only cared for the wounded, but also coordinated the process of raising ransom money, and welcomed captives after their release. The hospitals maintained by Calatrava and Santiago, mentioned above, also ransomed captives, but as the need declined by the middle of the thirteenth century, they began to disappear.[68]

The French Order of the Trinity and the Order of La Merced were specifically dedicated to the redemption of captives. St. Jean de Mathe (d. 1213), a Provençal, the founder of the Trinitarians, received Innocent III's approbation and planned to devote a third of the Order's revenues to ransom. Trinitarian hospitals were situated at Toledo, Valencia, and other towns. The Order also benefited from the partition of Seville.[69] The origins of the Order of La Merced can be traced to 1230 when a citizen of Barcelona made a bequest to St. Pere Nolasc for ransoming captives. Within a few years the house of Santa Eulalia of Barcelona and others in Mallorca and Girona were established; Gregory IX confirmed the Order in 1235. Ten years later Innocent IV cited the Order's sixteen houses in the Crown of Aragón and three in Castile. The Mercedarians began by collecting alms to pay ransom but in time they journeyed to Muslim lands to attempt to secure the liberation of captives.[70]

Naval Forces

Naval forces facilitated the capture of some of the most important Muslim ports. Fleets of sailing ships, or *naves*, and galleys transported troops, horses, and supplies, broke up naval defenses, and blockaded towns under siege. A triangular lateen sail, fixed on a long yard extending down almost to the forward deck and reaching high above the masthead, enabled a sailing ship to maneuver more skillfully. Round ships with high prows and even higher sterns, and a castle or superstructure for cabins set in the stern, are illustrated in the *Cantigas de Santa Maria*; there were two masts with lateen sails with a crow's nest atop each mast, and a side paddle rudder for steering. A row boat seems to have been essential for getting to land or rescuing the crew if the ship began to sink. Many of the other sailing ships mentioned in the sources are likely variations of this basic model. The galley, lightly built and propelled by oarsmen, was also equipped with a mast and sail to take advantage of the wind. Noted for its speed and maneuverability, it was preferred for naval warfare. The *Cantigas* depicts several galleys with one tier of oarsmen, usually twelve on each side.[71]

Although Bishop Diego Gelmírez recruited Genoese and Pisan shipbuilders who built at least two galleys to repel Saracen pirates, the consistent use of naval power on the Galician coast was in the future. The first Christian naval forces deployed against the Muslims came not from the peninsula, but from Italy. In 1113 the Pisans provided most, if not all, of the 200 to 300 ships used in the Mallorcan Crusade. A Genoese fleet of sixty-three galleys and 163 other ships collaborated in the siege of Almería (the count of Barcelona contributed one ship) and later in conquering Tortosa. About 164 to 200 crusading ships participated in the conquest of Lisbon, while some fifty-five to seventy-four northern ships aided the capture of Silves; about 180 northern ships joined in the siege of Alcácer do Sal.[72]

Only in the thirteenth century did the Christian rulers develop their own naval power. The necessity to defend the Catalan coast against pirates encouraged shipbuilding, and during the reign of Jaime I shipyards were constructed at Barcelona. Two years before setting out for Mallorca, he prohibited the use of foreign ships to carry goods from Barcelona when Catalan ships were available. In 1229 he could rely almost entirely on ships from Barcelona, Tarragona, and Tortosa, and an armed galley provided by the abbot of San Feliu de Guixols. All told there were, by his reckoning, "150 capital ships" and many smaller boats, including twenty-five *naus*, eighteen *tarides*, twelve galleys, and 100 others. After the conquest of Mallorca he appointed an admiral named Carroz. During the Valencian Crusade ships transported supplies and siege engines along the coast. When the emir of Tunis in 1238 dispatched a relieving fleet of eighteen ships the king assembled three armed galleys and seven other vessels to repel them.[73]

A Castilian fleet of about thirteen *naves* and galleys from the Bay of Biscay, organized by Ramón Bonifaz of Burgos, collaborated in the siege of Seville. Near the mouth of the Guadalquivir they defeated thirty Muslim vessels. The Muslims vainly attempted to block the river by means of a large raft, full of jars loaded with Greek fire. As the Christians moved up river they broke the chain linking a bridge of boats stretching from the city to the suburb of Triana on the west bank. After the fall of Seville Alfonso X, taking up the project for an African Crusade, reconstructed the old Muslim shipyards, and contracted with twenty-one ship captains, each of whom pledged to maintain a galley manned by 100 armed men. Afonso III also employed a Portuguese fleet to thwart any attempt by Muslim galleys to relieve Faro.[74]

In conclusion, the general strategy of reconquest, now overlaid with the crusading indulgence, aimed first at the devastation of enemy territory by raids carried out by small or large forces. Next, castles, cities, and towns were taken through sieges, or after victory on the battlefield. Although truces were often set, the Christians had to be ready to resume hostilities at any moment. Castles had to be garrisoned and supplied; troops had to be alert to the summons to war and prepared to pass muster with appropriate arms and armor. Warfare involved everyone: kings, nobles, clerics, Military Orders, and town militias, though it is almost impossible to estimate the size of any given army. Fines or other heavy punishments helped to maintain military discipline and both kings and popes enacted laws prohibiting the sale of goods that Muslims might eventually use against Christians. The outcome of war might be victory or defeat, and surely resulted in death, wounding, or capture for many, whose number cannot be calculated. Booty, one of the rewards of victory and a means of personal enrichment, was closely regulated by royal and municipal law. Care of the wounded and redemption of captives were characteristic functions of hospitals established for that purpose. Crusading fleets played a significant role in the capture of coastal towns, but in the thirteenth century the peninsular rulers were able to organize their own fleets.

The business of financing these military and naval operations is the subject of the following chapter.

Chapter 7

Financing Reconquest and Crusade

Warfare in the crusading era placed a heavy strain on the resources of Christian Spain and required extraordinary financial support. The
almost total lack of official documentation, however, renders any financial
study exceptionally difficult. Although Bisson edited Catalan fiscal accounts
for the late twelfth and very early thirteenth centuries, similar records concerning the middle and later years of the reign of Jaime I, if they are extant,
have still to see the light. Whatever records may have been kept in the kingdoms of Castile, León, and Portugal have long since disappeared. There are
bits and pieces of evidence, but without any extensive statement of income
and expenditures, we cannot know how much money was spent on any given
campaign.[1]

Inasmuch as different currencies will be cited below, it is best to explain
the variety of coins used in the Christian states during the twelfth and thirteenth centuries. The old Roman terminology, *libra, solidus,* and *denarius*
was still employed, but Arabic terms also came into use. In imitation of the
gold dinar of the Caliphate, the petty Muslim kings issued their own currency, much of which passed into Christian hands in the form of tribute or
plunder. Count Ramon Berenguer I of Barcelona, duplicating the coins of
Málaga, was the first Christian to mint a gold coin, the *mancus.* Alfonso VI
issued a billon *denarius* or penny, an alloy of silver and copper. In Aragón
Sancho I Ramírez originated the *moneta iaccensis* or *jaqueses,* the silver
coinage of Jaca.

The Almoravid gold dinar was copied by Ibn Mardanīsh of Murcia, but
his overthrow in 1172 interrupted the flow of gold to the Christian north,
prompting Alfonso VIII to issue his own gold coinage, the *morabetinus* or
maravedí, essentially a copy of the Muslim coin; weighing about 3.89 grams,
it was quickly accepted in the western states. Both Enrique I and Fernando III
maintained it without change; although the latter minted a gold coin it did
not differ from that of his grandfather. Fernando II and Alfonso IX of León
as well as Sancho I of Portugal also issued their own gold *maravedís.* While

the *maravedí* or *morabetino alfonsín* was both a coin and a money of account, the coin in everyday use was a billon penny called a *denarius* or *dinero*. In Fernando III's reign these penny coins were described as *burgaleses* (minted in Burgos) or *leoneses* (minted in León).

In Catalonia the *solidus* or *sou*, rather than the *libra*, was the usual money of account, while the *diner* or penny served for everyday transactions. Coins from southern France also circulated in the peninsula as did the Almohad gold dinar. Known to the Christians as the *mazmudina* or *media dobla* (in contrast to the *dobla* or double dinar, weighing about 4.60 grams), it weighed 2.32 grams.[2]

Military Expenses and Ordinary Royal Revenues

How did kings raise the funds needed to maintain significant military forces in the field for months at a time year in and year out? Nobles and townsmen traditionally were obliged to serve three months annually. Armies also sustained themselves in part from forage and booty, though the evidence is generally anecdotal and cannot be quantified. The expectation of a share in the distribution of lands after a fortress was captured assured the king of military support, but he still had to come up with additional sums of money. Aside from the upkeep of his court, his expenses included stipends for his vassals; the maintenance and fortification of castles; the acquisition and maintenance of arms, armor, horses, mules, and other necessary animals; food for men and animals; building and transporting siege machinery; requisitioning ships and their crews when necessary; caring for the wounded, and burying the dead.

Stipends (*stipendia, soldadas*) owed to royal vassals were among his principal expenditures. The custom of paying vassals, rather than granting them fiefs, as in northern Europe, probably developed in the twelfth century, especially in the reign of Alfonso VII, and was facilitated by tribute exacted from the Muslim rulers. Grassotti argued that royal vassals received annual stipends for their maintenance and others for specific campaigns, but we do not know the number of recipients nor the amount of each stipend. The usual stipend in the thirteenth century, according to González, was 300 to 400 *maravedís*; nobles of lesser rank could expect about 67 *maravedís*. If a magnate maintained a *mesnada* of 100 knights, then stipends would amount to 30,000 to 40,000 *maravedís*. If Fernando III paid 300 to 400 *maravedís* to each of the 200 knights in his *mesnada* during the Córdoban campaign, his expense would have totalled 60,000 to 80,000 *maravedís*. If each of the six-teen to eighteen magnates who confirmed his charters before the fall of Se-ville received a similar stipend the cost would have been between 4,800–5,600 and 6,400–7,200 *maravedís*.[3]

Although records of disbursements for specific campaigns are usually lacking, Alfonso VII, preparing for his expedition to Almería, in addition to expenses sustained in raising his own forces, contracted to pay the Genoese 10,000 *morabetinos* by the end of September 1146 and another 10,000 by the following Easter. Before Las Navas, Alfonso VIII offered twenty *solidi* daily to each knight and five to each footsoldier. Archbishop Rodrigo's estimate of 10,000 knights and 100,000 footsoldiers is fantastic and would imply pay-ment of unheard of sums;[4] but if the daily wage of twenty *solidi* per knight and five per footsoldier is accurate, and it probably is, over sixty days (from 20 June to 10 August) each knight would have received 1,200 *solidi* or 160 *maravedís* (7.5 *solidi* or *sueldos* to the *maravedí*), and each footsoldier 300 *solidi* or 40 *maravedís*. If there were 500 knights and 5,000 footsoldiers, the expense would have been 80,000 *maravedís* for the knights and 200,000 for the footsoldiers. Nevertheless, as it is impossible to say how many men participated in the campaign, one cannot determine the amount of money expended.

A contract of 1246 requiring Pelay Pérez Correa, master of Santiago, to provide 1,500 men for two years service in defense of the Latin Empire of Constantinople suggests something of the costs involved. He agreed to bring 300 knights, 200 archers, and 1,000 sergeants or footsoldiers, as well as 300 war horses and 300 other pack horses. In turn, Emperor Baldwin II promised to pay 40,000 marks sterling, calculated at the rate of 13 *solidi* and 4 *denarii* per mark. The cost per man (including the horses) would be 13.33 marks per year or 26.66 for two years. According to Todesca the silver mark or mark sterling was equivalent approximately to ten *maravedís*; therefore the cost of an army of 1,500 men per year would be 400,000 *maravedís* or 800,000 for two years. By the same reckoning an army of perhaps 5,000 men in the siege of Seville in 1248 would have cost about 1,333,000 *maravedís* for one year.[5]

In order to meet the expenses of war the Christian rulers had at their disposal an indeterminate amount of money derived from traditional sources. Crown lands, including those added through reconquest, were a major source of income. Revenues derived from the royal domain included an annual trib-ute known by various names, hospitality, and provisions for the king and his court during annual visitations. *Fonsadera*, a payment made in lieu of military service, was also important, even though exemptions were often granted. With the development of transhumance and commercial enterprise, income from pasturage tolls, tolls on goods, and market tolls probably increased; again there were numerous exemptions. Income also came from the royal monopoly on saltpits and iron and mercury mines, royal mills, baths, ovens, shops, houses, orchards, vineyards, granaries, and wheat fields. Other resources included chancery fees, judicial fines, the royal fifth of booty, and tributes paid by Jewish and Mudejar communities.[6]

Fernando III's ordinary income, according to González, amounted to about 1,000,000 *maravedís*; but given the number of exemptions, expenses, especially those incurred in the reconquest, could not be met. That was likely true for the other Christian monarchs, who had to finance military operations from several exceptional sources, namely, the *tercias* or third of the tithe, as well as other ecclesiastical subsidies; *moneta*, a payment made in return for the king's pledge to maintain the coinage unchanged; the tribute or *parias* paid by petty Muslim rulers; loans from bankers; and forced loans from towns. Royal needs, however, had to compete with papal requirements of financial assistance for the Crusader Kingdom of Jerusalem.

Papal Levies to Finance Crusades to the Holy Land

Extraordinary taxation made its appearance when the popes authorized kings to take a portion of ecclesiastical revenues to finance crusades to the Holy Land. Once that was done, it was only a matter of time before the Christian kings of Spain also laid hands on church funds.

The papacy already collected monies from Spain under various headings; these included a census paid by churches in return for papal protection, and a census due as a sign of vassalage. Declaring himself a papal vassal in 1068, Sancho I Ramírez of Aragón promised an annual census and reportedly paid 500 *mancusos* from Gregory VII's time until his own death in 1094. His son, Pedro I, in 1098 sent 1,000 *mancusos* as payment for two years. Seeking papal protection, Count Ramon Berenguer III of Barcelona in 1116 also promised an annual census of 30 *maravedís*. Nearly a century later, in 1204, Pedro II pledged a yearly tribute of 250 gold *mazmudinas*, but apparently neglected payment because Honorius III in 1218 demanded that Jaime I pay arrears of 960 marks of silver.[7] When Afonso I pledged homage to the papacy in 1143 he indicated that he would pay four ounces of gold annually, though there is little reason to believe that he did so. In return for papal recognition as king in 1179 he agreed to pay two gold marks, and apparently made a gift of 1,000 *maravedís* to Alexander III. Nevertheless, the annual tribute was probably not paid until 1198 when Sancho I, stipulating that the amount was four ounces of gold, paid 504 *maravedís*, probably the arrears of twenty years. However, he objected to Innocent III's demand for any additional sum such as his father's gift of 1,000 *maravedís*. In 1213 Afonso II paid 3,360 *maravedís*, equivalent to 56 gold marks, covering the twenty-eight years from Sancho I's accession, but Honorius III in 1218 had to remind him to pay the annual tribute.[8] Though paid erratically, these sums represented a drain on the financial resources of the rulers of Aragón and Portugal.

Although the census was a voluntary contribution, papal taxation for the crusade was not. Here the burden fell directly on the clergy. In order to support the Third Crusade Gregory VIII required the clergy to donate a portion of their income. Clement III extended this to Spain, ordering the clergy of each diocese to contribute according to their means. Laypersons were also encouraged to provide financial aid. In 1199 Innocent III amplified this new mode of crusading taxation when he proposed that a fortieth of all ecclesiastical income for one year should be given to crusaders journeying to the east. Then in preparation for the Fifth Crusade, the Fourth Lateran Council introduced a tax of a twentieth on ecclesiastical income for three years. The master of the Temple and the prior of the Hospital in Spain, with the help of the cantor and archdeacon of Zamora, were responsible for collection.[9]

The Spanish clergy, who had already contributed heavily to the Crusade of Las Navas, were unhappy at the prospect of losing five per cent of their income in this way and responded with fraud and deception. After receiving a report from the papal tax collectors, Honorius III reprimanded Archbishops Rodrigo of Toledo, Pedro of Compostela, and Estevão of Braga and their suffragans for failing to pay the twentieth by All Saints Day (1 November 1216), the date set by his predecessor. Not only had they neglected to convene synods to announce the twentieth, but they also questioned whether the money was to be paid in cash; and by gathering foodstuffs and other offerings in kind they guaranteed that collection would drag on forever. The pope insisted that, without further delay, they collect the twentieth in cash and deposit it in three places named by the collectors, and inform him of the amount raised. He also authorized the absolution of clerics who committed fraud in order to escape payment. Given the inadequate measures taken thus far, in 1218 he dispatched Subdeacon Huguccio and Master Cintius to supervise the collection, recording amounts received, and depositing the money securely before sending it on to Rome.[10] His faith in his subordinates, however, was badly misplaced.

Meanwhile the Portuguese participating in the Crusade of Alcácer do Sal asked that the twentieth be used for that war. Although Honorius III failed to address that question, he did cede half of the twentieth from the sees of Toledo and Segovia to Archbishop Rodrigo for his crusade; the remainder would still go to the Holy Land. In 1219 a deposit was made in Toledo of 600 gold *maravedís* and 1,500 *dineros burgaleses*. In the next year the pope authorized the archbishop to use money from the province of Toledo for the next three years for his crusade, and he encouraged Archbishop Aspàreg of Tarragona and other bishops to assist their confrère.[11]

A few months later, however, the pope complained that Archbishop Rodrigo was not pressing his crusade, and demanded that the twentieth granted for that purpose should be diverted to the Holy Land. Accusing his own tax collector, Huguccio, of "seeking his own gain," Honorius III ordered Archbishop Aspàreg to conduct an inquiry and to forward the twentieth collected in his own province to Archbishop Rodrigo. The pope blamed Rodrigo for countenancing Huguccio's "many enormities and abuses," and promising him various benefices. The archbishop, as Lomax put it, bribed Huguccio in order to obtain additional money for his crusade. It would seem, therefore, that the pope's own tax collectors had had no more success than those initially appointed to the task. In 1221 4,706 *aurei* as well as an unspecified number of *burgaleses* and *pepiones* were deposited at the nunnery of Las Huelgas de Burgos. In 1222 the pope authorized the Hospitaller Gonzalo García to collect the twentieth and to absolve from excommunication, under certain conditions, those who had failed to pay. Archbishop Aspàreg and his suffragans were required to hand over to Brother Gonzalo the remainder of the twentieth and other tributes owed to Rome. Three years later the pope sent Pelagius, bishop-elect of Lod (Lydda) in Palestine, to collect the twentieth intended for the Holy Land. Inasmuch as the Fifth Crusade had come to an ignominious end with the fall of Damietta in 1221, there was little reason to believe that the Spanish clergy would have been any more inclined to contribute than before.[12]

Gregory IX and Innocent IV, although both were staunch supporters of the Latin Kingdom of Jerusalem, had little to say about the twentieth. When Thibault I of Navarre set out for the Holy Land, Gregory IX asked the Navarrese clergy to provide the king with a subsidy. In order to encourage Jaime I's crusade against al-Azraq, Innocent IV suspended collection of the twentieth for three years. Some years later, the pope sent Falco Pererius to Spain to collect the *decima*, an impost of 10 percent on the revenues of ecclesiastical benefices, to support the crusades to the Holy Land. This first levy of the *decima* amounted to 35,411 florins of Aragón, but there are no detailed accounts of it.[13]

It would seem that papal efforts to collect a twentieth of clerical income to support the crusades in the Holy Land were decidedly less than successful. Given the threat of Islam in Spain itself, even in times of truce, the Spanish clergy, resistant as they might well be to any form of taxation, had good reason to protest a levy that would not be utilized for the defense of Christendom in the Iberian peninsula.

The *Tercias* and other Royal Levies on Ecclesiastical Income

The Christian rulers, like the popes, soon discovered that the church was a convenient source of extraordinary income. In addition to seizing the goods of deceased bishops, or usurping church property without consent, kings and princes also attempted to levy tribute on the church.[14] Although kings were expected to "live off your own tributes and your rightful revenues," they felt no compunction in seizing church property when they deemed it necessary. Some said that Alfonso I's death at Fraga was the consequence of his having plundered the churches of León and Castile in order to pay stipends to his vassals. Indeed in his last will, he ordered restitution of whatever he or his predecessors had taken unjustly from the churches.[15]

Alfonso VIII's pledge in the Curia of Nájera in 1180 that he would not seize the property of deceased bishops, nor take anything from the clergy by force, "but only with their love and good will," suggests that he had indeed done so. The same may be said for Alfonso IX, who assured the clergy of Orense that he would never demand anything from them without their consent. Some years later, with episcopal permission, he exacted tribute from the people of Orense. Promising to make appropriate recompense, he affirmed that neither he nor any of his successors would ever demand tribute without the bishop's consent, as lord of the city. Honorius III reprimanded Fernando III for demanding an annual procuration of 1,000 *maravedís* from the see of Segovia; quite possibly the king made similar demands on other churches.[16]

The question whether the clergy were bound to contribute to royal levies arose in 1180 when Alfonso II demanded money from Zaragoza. Although the people agreed to pay, they insisted, rather forcibly, that the clergy should also do so. Often without asking consent, Pedro II attempted to tax ecclesiastical property, but the prelates assembled at Lleida in 1211 compelled him to declare that they would not incur any future prejudice on account of current contributions. From time to time, however, the clergy made voluntary donations. During the siege of Zaragoza Bishop Esteban of Huesca used his cathedral treasure to save the besiegers from hunger. In 1211, following the fall of Salvatierra, Alfonso VIII asked the clergy to pledge half their yearly income for the campaign that climaxed at Las Navas. Similarly, Abbot Fernando of Alcobaça, the Military Orders, and magnates offered to provide food and expenses for northern crusaders collaborating in the attack on Alcácer do Sal. Several years later Archbishop Aspàreg, unable to participate on account of age and infirmity, pledged 1,000 silver marks to the Mallorcan Crusade. In the Curia of Barcelona in 1228 Jaime I acknowledged that aid granted by the Catalan bishops "to attack the land and perfidy of the pagans" was given of their own free will and would not entail any future obligation.[17]

Whereas the *decima* was intended for the relief of the Holy Land, the traditonal tithe (*diezmo*), a tenth of every Christian's income, was directed to the support of the church in each kingdom. The Christian rulers soon found ways to lay hands on the *tercias* or third of the tithe reserved for the upkeep of churches. The decrees of the Councils of Palencia in 1129 and Valladolid in 1143 forbidding laymen to seize the *tercias* imply that they had done so.[18] Alfonso VIII, apparently forgetting his promise in 1180, seized the *tercias*, prompting Innocent III to demand restitution. Enrique I, acknowledging that he had sinned in taking the *tercias*, pledged not to do so in the future. That suggests that the seizure of the *tercias* was likely an ongoing practice.[19]

During the thirteenth century successive popes permitted kings and others to utilize the *tercias* for the reconquest. In 1219 Honorius III allowed participants in Archbishop Rodrigo's crusade to share in the *tercias* of the province of Toledo for three years. Six years later the pope authorized Alfonso Téllez de Meneses to apply the *tercias* of Toledo for two years to the defense of Alburquerque. Later in that year Alfonso's brother, Bishop Tello of Palencia, obtained papal permission to use his diocesan *tercias* for the crusade and to impose a charitable contribution on the clergy. The pope also exhorted the clergy and people of the diocese to provide their bishop with "a moderate subsidy" for the war against the Muslims.[20]

In view of these precedents it is not surprising that once Fernando III determined to take up arms against the Muslims he would use the *tercias* to finance his operations. When the clergy complained, Gregory IX in 1228 instructed Archbishop Rodrigo and the other bishops to compel the king to desist, but he evidently ignored this admonition. In responding to a further complaint, the pope praised the king's efforts to extend the Christian religion, which required continued support by the faithful. He urged the bishops to find a means of providing financial aid to the king that would not impinge on the liberties of the church so that his holy enterprise would not be interrupted for lack of funds. The bishops' reaction is unknown, but in view of the vagueness of the pope's bull, it is likely that Fernando III continued taking the *tercias*. He surely could do so without expecting papal opposition because he knew that Gregory IX allowed the diversion of ecclesiastical revenues to the campaigns against the Muslims of Archbishop Rodrigo and the Order of Santiago. The pope, for example, required the suffragan bishops of the province of Toledo to pay an annual subsidy for three years for the archbishop's expenses incurred in the conquest of Quesada. The knights of Santiago, with papal authorization, similarly used the *tercias* of their churches to defend their frontier positions.[21]

After the fall of Córdoba Fernando III appealed to Gregory IX to provide financial support for the continuing conquest of Andalucía. Praising the king as an *athleta Christi*, the pope instructed the Castilian and Leonese bishops to provide a subsidy of 20,000 gold pieces annually for three years from each kingdom. Thus the king could expect 40,000 gold pieces each year from the two kingdoms, or 120,000 over three years. Many years later, in 1267, Archdeacon Rodrigo of León alleged that the king had taken 60,000 *maravedís* each year for the three year period, or 180,000 all told.[22] Gregory IX's concession was not a confirmation of the royal right to the *tercias*, but a direct levy on ecclesiastical income. One wonders whether the king, once he received the money, continued to demand it thereafter. If he collected 40,000 gold pieces each year for the twelve years from 1236 to 1248, the total would be 424,000.

Fernando III's ongoing military success enabled him to appeal to Innocent IV for additional financial aid. Hailing the king as a *specialis atleta Christi* who proposed to launch an attack on the Muslims of Seville, the pope declared it right and just that those engaged in Christ's service should be supported by the faithful, and he authorized a subsidy of half the *tercias* of Castile and León. Mansilla and Goñi Gaztambide pointed out that this was the first categorical papal concession of the *tercias*. Rodríguez López affirmed, however, that "the appropriation of the *tercias* by the crown was a fact that had already occurred during this reign." The term of three years set by Innocent IV would have ended on 15 April 1250, and it may be his response to a royal request for renewal was to authorize Infante Alfonso on 30 April to take the *tercias* of the diocese of Cuenca.[23]

The *tercias* seem to have provided Fernando III with a fairly steady income from mid-April 1247 and thus contributed directly to the siege of Seville, but there is reason to believe that he had been taking them intermittently at least from 1228. Once he got his hands on ecclesiastical revenues, whether the *tercias*, or the subsidy authorized by Gregory IX in 1236, he probably did not easily let go and continued to collect half of the *tercias* until his death. Alfonso X's announcement during the Cortes of Seville in 1252, that, until he could resolve the matter, the *tercias* would be dealt with as in the time of his predecessors, Alfonso VII and Alfonso VIII, seems to imply a long-standing custom of using the *tercias* for royal needs.[24]

Sancho II of Portugal also appears to have taken ecclesiastical revenues without consent. The bishop of Porto, as lord of the city, complained that the king extorted money from the citizens, and made "improper exactions," demanding procurations from the bishop and the clergy, and despoiling them of their rights, especially over the tithes. They also accused him of seizing the revenues of vacant sees and of exercising the right of patronage over churches against the bishop's will. Although Gregory IX ordered the king to desist, he obviously ignored the papal directive, so that in 1233 the pope commanded him to restore whatever tithes and other property he had seized. In spite of these difficulties Gregory IX urged the faithful to aid the king who was girding himself to "retain lands recently acquired and to acquire others" in the cause of eternal salvation. As protests against Sancho II's conduct continued, the pope, though he might applaud the king's crusading ambitions, excommunicated him in January 1238. A few months later the king promised to cease violating the immunities of the church, but his eventual deposition by Innocent IV revealed that not much had changed.[25] Sancho II's conflict with the bishops was due in large measure to his demand for financial aid from the churches, but whether he used the money for the war against the "infidels" is problematical.

While safeguarding the church from what it perceived to be unjustified royal demands for money, the papacy nevertheless encouraged those who were unable to serve personally in the crusade to provide financial support; if they did so they would receive the crusading indulgence. Thus Honorius III in 1218 allowed the archbishop of Toledo to release from their vow persons judged *inutiles* for the crusade, provided that they contributed according to their means. A year later he extended the indulgence to those who paid the expenses of others or otherwise financially assisted Archbishop Rodrigo's crusade. In the following year he made a similar concession to persons aiding Alfonso IX's crusade. Gregory IX also offered the indulgence to anyone providing financial aid for the crusade, or contributing to pay a substitute's expenses. As a practical form of assistance the pope also exhorted the bishops to supply the Order of Santiago with victuals.[26] Although voluntary contributions probably were a not inconsiderable source of support for the Spanish crusades, totals cannot be ascertained.

Extraordinary Levies: *Petitum, Bovaticum*, and *Monetaticum*

As it became clear that ordinary revenues were insufficient to sustain the struggle against Spanish Islam, kings had to turn to extraordinary taxation. However great the need, kings could not simply take extraordinary taxes, but had to ask consent; from the late twelfth century onward such requests were made in an assembly of prelates, magnates, and municipal representatives, variously described as a *curia plena, curia generalis*, cortes, or corts.[27]

The first levy of an exceptional nature was imposed because of the threat represented by the Almoravids. In 1090 Alfonso VI asked the lower nobility and townsmen of the kingdom of León to pay two *solidi* in the current year. Though he stipulated that neither he nor his successors would again make this demand, he did so in the following year. The *petitum* as it was called seems to have evolved into a tax collected regularly without the necessity of asking consent, but as it tended to be rather low, and numerous exemptions were granted to ecclesiastical institutions, it was not very productive. During the Curia of León in 1208, Alfonso IX, while guaranteeing ecclesiastical property against confiscation, specifically renounced any right to impose the *petitum* on cathedral clergy. He admitted, however, that the bishops were accustomed "joyfully to underwrite our necessities."[28]

The origins of the *bovaticum* or *bovatge*, an extraordinary tax imposed on livestock in Catalonia, can be traced to Count Ramon Berenguer III, who, in 1118, pledged not to alter the coinage during his lifetime; in return he received twelve *diners* for each yoke of oxen, six for each cow, and three for each plow. During the Curia of Fondarella in 1173, when confirming the Peace and Truce of God, Alfonso II levied the *bovaticum*, a general tax payable for each cow. Nevertheless, this was a novelty and was so unpopular that he promised in the Curia of Girona in 1188 never again to impose it. However, Pedro II, on ascending the throne, collected it, and, according to Zurita, did so again when setting out for Las Navas. Receipts from the *bovaticum* in the diocese of Vic in 1200 amounted to 19,000 *sous*; according to Bisson this was the "earliest extant collector's account of an extraordinary tax in the Crown of Aragon." He also suggested that this was "the first attempt to collect the peace tax systematically throughout Catalonia." Jaime I received the *bovaticum* early in his reign during a *Curia generalis* held at Monzón in 1217, and again during the Curia of Barcelona in 1228 for the Mallorcan Crusade. Some years later, when he was preparing for the Valencian Crusade, the Catalans in the Curia of Monzón in 1236 authorized an additional *bovaticum*.[29]

Extraordinary revenue was also obtained from the *monetaticum* (*monedatge, moneda forera*), a tax levied every seven years in return for the royal pledge to maintain the coinage intact. Profits from mints were a valuable source of revenue; for example, whenever the king issued new coinage, he benefited by discounting the old money. Eventually rulers learned that they could also make a profit by coining new money with an increased alloy, but with the same—or perhaps even greater—exchange value as the old coinage. Such alterations, however, were upsetting to consumers and led to protests.[30]

Todesca emphasized that there is no evidence of a systematic debasement of the coinage of León and Castile in the twelfth century nor of consequent inflation. For the most part, as Bisson pointed out, the coinage of Aragón and Catalonia also remained relatively stable until the last quarter of the twelfth century. Nevertheless, as royal expenses increased Alfonso II manipulated the silver coinage of Barcelona and Jaca for his own benefit. Although he had confirmed his new coinage of Barcelona in 1174, he debased the money of Jaca around 1180–81. In response to protest he confirmed it for life, but realizing that he could not do without the profits that an alteration would bring, he appealed to the pope to release him from his oath. In return for his promise to give a tenth of the profits to the Templars for the Holy Land, he obtained Celestine III's permission in 1191 to alter the coinage of Jaca. Though he agreed to maintain it intact thereafter, he appears to have debased it at the end of his reign.[31]

In 1197 Pedro II confirmed his father's coinage but shortly obtained "a redemption of the money" from the Catalan town of Vic (and probably from others) because of the Muslim menace; the Almohad armies in alliance with Alfonso IX were ravaging Castile after the disaster at Alarcos. At that time King Pedro pledged that if a similar situation should arise in the future neither he nor his successors would renew this demand. He soon appealed to Innocent III, however, alleging that, while he was preparing to join Alfonso VIII against the Muslims, his counselors deceitfully persuaded him, without the consent of the people, to promise never to change his father's coinage; but now that the money had lessened in value he asked the pope to absolve him from his oath, which he did.[32]

In the neighboring kingdom of León Alfonso IX was equally preoccupied by the quest for exceptional income. In the Curia of Benavente in 1202 he promised not to alter his coinage for seven years, in exchange for one *maravedí* payable by each non-noble freeman. If *moneta* or *moneda forera* (as it came to be called) was levied every seven years thereafter, it should have been collected in 1209, 1216, 1223, 1230, 1237, 1244, and 1251. Alfonso VIII also seems to have collected *moneta*, but it is difficult to determine the starting date. As it was first mentioned in 1215 Enrique I may have promised to maintain his father's coinage intact. If it were paid in recognition of sovereignty at the outset of each reign, then Fernando III should have been able to levy it in Castile in 1217 and in León in 1230, and every seven years thereafter, in return for preserving the coinage unaltered. Indeed, he seems to have maintained the *maravedí* issued by his Castilian grandfather and by his Leonese father.[33]

Not long after Alfonso IX began to collect *moneta*, Pedro II did likewise. Although he pledged in 1205 to maintain the coinage of Barcelona without change throughout his lifetime and not to require any payment for doing so, there is some question whether this charter was promulgated. Yet he found it impossible to live off his customary revenues, especially after he promised to pay the pope an annual tribute of 250 gold *maravedís* as a sign of vassalage. Thus he appears to have introduced the *monetaticum* at Huesca in November 1205 to help defray that cost, among others. The Templars, Hospitallers, and knights of Aragón and Catalonia were exempted, but the levy of twelve *dineros* for every *libra* of value of movable and immovable property at the rate of 4.16 percent was considered heavy. Given the opposition he agreed four years later that he would not alter the coinage for as long as he lived.[34]

Jaime I confirmed the coinage of Jaca for ten years in the Curia of Lleida in 1218 and again during the Curia of Huesca three years later. Despite that, he apparently coined new money, but under pressure had to abandon it at Daroca in 1223; in exchange for confirming his father's coinage for ten years, he received three *monetatica*, which he promised to use to pay off royal debts. Later in the year he stipulated that his confirmation of the coinage would extend for seven years from Michaelmas next, that is, from 29 September 1223. Thus the next time he would be entitled to alter his coinage would be in 1230, but there is no evidence that he attempted to do so. During the Curia of Monzón in 1236, indeed in order to finance the Valencian Crusade, he confirmed for life the coinage of Jaca, receiving in return every seven years a *monetaticum* of one *maravedí* from each household worth ten gold pieces or more; that was a rate of about 3.33 percent. He remarked that he levied tribute in all the towns of Aragón and Catalonia. Inasmuch as the *monetaticum* was granted to him and his successors, it probably was collected every seven years without seeking consent.[35]

Afonso III may have levied *monetaticum* to assist him in completing the Portuguese reconquest, but without initially asking consent. The bishop of Porto complained in the Curia of Guimaraes in 1250 that the king compelled "the clergy to purchase our coinage contrary to the custom of other kings." The king replied that he had done so on account of "the utility of the whole realm" and with the consent of all the bishops. It may well be that his predecessors, while exempting the clergy, had attempted to collect *monetaticum* every seven years, and he may have taken it in 1247, as a law of 1253 refers to a seven-year period. The Cortes of Leiria in 1254 conceded *monetaticum* for seven years in exchange for confirming the coinage. Early in the following year, however, he was again demanding the tax on the threat of altering the coinage; but the negative reaction of the nobles and bishops forced him to abandon the plan and to swear to maintain the coinage intact until seven years had elapsed. The Cortes of Coimbra in 1261 in return for his oath to preserve the coinage granted him a subsidy.[36]

How well and efficiently these taxes were collected is not at all clear. Not only were the king's revenues reduced by the increasing number of exemptions, but the lack of any surviving records of income and expenditures thwarts every effort to determine exactly what money the king had in his treasury at any given time. Moroever, it is impossible to determine the number of persons or households who were obligated to contribute to such imposts as *bovaticum* or *monetaticum*. Even so, one may assume that over the years each of the rulers in question accumulated substantial financial resources. In the instances cited above the imposition of this tax was not necessarily linked to the financial necessities of the reconquest, but one can surely suppose that the burden of the war against the Muslims weighed heavily in the budgetary calculations of the Christian rulers.

The *Parias* of the Eleventh Century

Tribute or *parias* (a word apparently of Arabic origin) levied on Muslim vassals by their Christian overlords, though intermittent, was perhaps the most valuable source of extraordinary income. With it one could acquire castles, endow churches, pay stipends to vassals, or enrich one's heirs.[37] Although it is impossible to ascertain the total amount owed by any one of the Muslim rulers, the profit to the Christians appears to have been immense. As the Caliphate collapsed, the petty kings who came to power discovered that they could keep the Christians at bay only by paying tribute, a process that MacKay aptly described as protection rackets.[38]

The Catalan counts seem to have been the first to profit in this way. Counts Ramon Berenguer I of Barcelona (1035–76) and Ermengol III of Urgell in 1058 agreed to share the *parias* of Zaragoza, two-thirds to the former and one third to the latter. In return for 10,000 dinars, Ramon Berenguer II (1076–82) agreed to join the Muslims of Seville in conquering Murcia, but when the deal fell through he demanded 30,000 as compensation. Berenguer Ramon II (1076–97), who collected tribute from Zaragoza and Lleida, promised 50,000 gold coins (payable at the rate of 5,000 a year) from the *parias* of Tortosa for the restoration of Tarragona.[39] Sancho IV of Navarre (1054–76) also received 12,000 dinars annually from Zaragoza. The annual census that Sancho I Ramírez promised to the papacy, as well as other gifts to churches and monasteries, was derived from *parias*.[40]

The western rulers, Fernando I and Alfonso VI, also collected tribute. An anonymous Muslim poet commented: "The *Rūm* [the Christians] make incursions into the country and seize good booty; what remains to the people, the Arabs and the treasury take. All the money of the country goes to Castile." When the people of Toledo complained that they could not raise the tribute, Fernando I suggested that they withdraw to Morocco and abandon the land to the Christians to whom it had once belonged. Bishko estimated that he gathered an annual tribute of about 10,000 to 12,000 gold dinars, chiefly from Zaragoza, Toledo, Seville, Badajoz, and Valencia. *Parias* made it possible for him, about 1055, to promise an annual census of 1,000 gold *aurei* to Cluny, the largest gift the monastery received from anyone. Before he died he allotted the *parias* to his three sons.[41]

After acquiring his brothers' realms by 1072 Alfonso VI demanded tribute from each of the Muslim states. One Muslim author described the circumstances in this way:

Not only were the different independent chieftains at that time waging unrelenting war against each other, but they would not unfrequently avail themselves of the arms of the Christians to attack and destroy their own countrymen . . . lavishing on Alfonso costly presents, and giving him as many treasures as he chose to have, in order to conciliate his good wishes, and to obtain security for themselves and assistance against their enemies. The Christians, perceiving the state of corruption into which the Moslems had fallen, rejoiced extremely. . . . Those among the Moslem rulers who did not actually submit to Alfonso, consented to pay him an annual tribute, thus becoming collectors in their own dominions of the revenues of the Christian monarch![42]

These enormous sums enabled Alfonso VI in 1077 to double the annual tribute of 1,000 *aurei* promised by his father to Cluny and to confirm it in 1090. In addition, between 1088 and 1090 he gave Cluny 10,000 "talents commonly called *mencales*" for construction of the new monastery.[43]

'Abd Allāh, king of Granada, initially rejected Leonese demands for tribute, declaring that he could not raise the required 50,000 dinars without exposing his realm to conquest by the king of Seville. Thus Alfonso VI agreed to accept 25,000 dinars, as well as tapestries, clothes, and vases, and an additional 5,000, or a total of 30,000 in all. In addition, 'Abd Allāh also consented to pay an annual tribute of 10,000 dinars thereafter; if he did so over the thirteen years from 1074 to 1086, then his outlay would have amounted to 130,000 dinars. Al-Mu'tamid of Seville (1069–91) offered Alfonso VI 50,000 dinars and all the booty he could take if he would join in an assault on Granada. In 1082, when al-Mu'tamid brought out coins and ingots to pay the customary annual tribute, Alfonso VI's envoy, the Jew Ibn Shālib, insisted on minted gold, rejecting the ingots because they would have to be weighed, and the coins because they were debased. His insolence caused al-Mu'tamid to execute him.[44]

After al-Qādir had been deposed as king of Toledo, Alfonso VI restored him to power, demanding a heavy tribute. The consequent imposition of heavy taxes impelled the people of Toledo to seek aid from their coreligionists, but when Alfonso VI accepted with disdain rich gifts from envoys of other Muslim lords, the Toledans realized that they could expect no assistance and surrendered their city in 1085. Dispossessed, al-Qādir, was established at Valencia under Alfonso VI's protection. 'Uthmān, who had been ejected from the Valencian throne, also sought Leonese protection, promising an annual tribute of 30,000 dinars.[45]

Alfonso VI also obtained great sums of money from al-Muqtadir of Zaragoza and al-Mutawwakil of Badajoz (1068–94), though the amounts are unknown. Payment of tribute evoked protest from such distinguished personages as Ibn Ḥazm of Córdoba (d. 1064), who described the practice as "an infamous scandal contrary to the laws of Islam." Until the fall of Toledo the Muslim princes had been prepared to offer tribute if it would stave off hostile action against them, but at last al-Mu'tamid of Seville, commenting that he preferred to herd camels for the Almoravids than to tend the pigsty of Alfonso VI, appealed to the Moroccans. After Alfonso VI's defeat at Zallāqa, however, al-Mu'tamid and 'Abd Allāh, hoping that he would rid them of the Almoravid intruders, resumed payment; the king of Granada had to pay 30,000 dinars, the arrears of three years.[46] The Almoravids used the payment of tribute to justify their dispossession of the petty princes.

Meanwhile the Cid exacted 105,200 dinars annually from al-Qādir in Valencia and neighboring Muslim lords, as follows: Valencia, 12,000, plus another 1,200 for the bishop; Denia, Játiva, and Tortosa, 50,000; Albarracín and Alpuente, 10,000 each; Murviedro, 8,000; Segorbe, 6,000; Jérica and Almenar, 3,000 each; and 2,000 from Liria. After the assassination of al-Qādir in 1092 the Cid took control of Valencia until his death in 1099. Fearful of being swallowed up by the Almoravids, Ḥusām ibn Razīn, king of Albarracín, sent great gifts to Alfonso VI, but he was ousted from his kingdom in 1104. al-Musta'īn of Zaragoza also probably paid tribute to Alfonso VI for protection but the Almoravids captured the city in 1110, thereby consolidating their hold on Islamic Spain.[47]

The *Parias* of the Twelfth and Thirteenth Centuries

As the Almoravids overwhelmed the *taifas* the payment of tribute to the Christians ceased. Nevertheless, when the Almoravid regime declined, the Christians levied tribute on the second generation of *reyes de taifas*. One of them, Sayf al-Dawla (whom the Christians called Zafadola), pledged homage to Alfonso VII, offering him many gifts. In 1133 the people of Seville appealed to Sayf al-Dawla to persuade Alfonso VII to deliver them from the Almoravids, promising him "royal tributes greater than our fathers gave to his fathers"; but nothing came of it. After Alfonso VII ravaged widely in 1145 the Muslims offered to pay "royal tributes just as our fathers had paid his," and they accepted Sayf al-Dawla as their ruler in Córdoba. Later in the year when Baeza and Úbeda refused to obey Sayf al-Dawla and denied *parias* to Alfonso VII, his armies again compelled them to pay. Sayf al-Dawla quarreled, however, with the king's lieutenants who killed him.[48]

Ramon Berenguer IV, count of Barcelona and prince of Aragón, also exacted tribute from the Muslims. In 1149 Ibn Mardanīsh, who dominated Valencia and Murcia, agreed to pay an enormous annual tribute of 100,000 gold dinars. When he failed to fulfill his pledge in 1158 a show of force encouraged him to do so, but he again refused payment when Alfonso II succeeded his father. By 1168, however, he was forced to pay 25,000 *maravedís*, a reduction probably reflecting the shrinkage of his lordship before the Almohad advance. When the kings of Castile and Aragón met in 1170 they agreed that Ibn Mardanīsh would pay Alfonso II 40,000 gold *maravedís* for five years or more, but such expectations were doomed when Ibn Mardanīsh died in 1172. Although his son promised to pay tribute, his submission to the Almohads shut down that source of revenue.[49]

During the Almohad ascendancy from the last quarter of the twelfth century to the first quarter of the thirteenth, the Christian rulers were unable to levy tribute, but as the Almohad empire fragmented the possibility arose again. When Abū Zayd, king of Valencia, and his brother al-Bayāsī, king of Baeza, became vassals of Fernando III in 1224 and 1225, they probably agreed to pay tribute. Sometime in 1225 Abū Zayd, hoping to forestall an attack by Jaime I, agreed to pay him a fifth of his revenue as tribute. Six years later the Muslims of Menorca recognized Jaime I as their sovereign and pledged to pay a yearly tribute of ninety measures of barley and 100 of wheat; 100 head of cattle; 300 head of goats; 200 head of sheep; and two measures of lard or butter.[50]

Fernando III collected *parias* from four Muslim kings: Abū-l-ʿUlā of Seville, Ibn Hūd of Murcia, Ibn Maḥfūt of Niebla, and Ibn al-Aḥmar of Granada. When Abū-l-ʿUlā, who proclaimed himself caliph in 1227, realized that he lacked wide support, he asked Fernando III for a truce, pledging to pay tribute. The *Crónica de Castilla*, written during the reign of Alfonso X, reported that both in 1228 and 1229 he paid 300,000 silver *maravedís*, the coinage of Alfonso X, for a total of 600,000. In terms of Fernando III's gold *maravedís* that would be 150,000 each year, or 300,000 all told. Nevertheless, Abū-l-ʿUlā's departure for Morocco not only facilitated the collapse of Almohad rule in Spain but also terminated his payments.[51]

One of his rivals, Ibn Hūd, made a truce with Fernando III around 1233, promising to pay 1,000 dinars every day, or 365,000 dinars at least for that year. Two years later, according to the royal chancellor, Bishop Juan of Osma, the likely author of the *Latin Chronicle*, Ibn Hūd, after further hostilities, pledged to pay 430,000 *maravedís* by May of the following year, 1236; about a third of that (about 143,000) was paid immediately; another third (143,000) was due at the end of September, and the final third (143,000) at the end of January. Ibn ʿIdhārī stated that the sum was 133,000 dinars payable over three years, 50,000 at once, and the remainder in equal amounts in the next two years. If these figures are accurate, then one dinar would be worth approximately 3.23 *maravedís*, and the total tribute would be 429,590 *maravedís*, essentially the same as the figure given by the royal chancellor. Quite possibly Ibn Hūd paid the second installment in September 1235, but payment likely ceased after the Castilians broke into Córdoba two months later. Thus, at most Fernando III received 286,000 *maravedís* as a result of the truce concluded in May 1235. Meantime, Ibn Maḥfūt of Niebla also maintained a truce, probably paying *parias* from 1235 to 1261 when the Castilians besieged Niebla. He likely paid less than Ibn Hūd and Ibn al-Aḥmar, whose kingdoms were more extensive.[52]

After the fall of Córdoba, Ibn Hūd, concluding another truce for six years, promised to pay every quarter 40,000 *maravedís* plus 12,000, for a total of 52,000. A certain portion of that (perhaps 12,000 as González suggested) would be given to his rival, Ibn al-Aḥmar, currently in alliance with Castile. The annual tribute would be 208,000 *maravedís*, of which 48,000 may have been turned over to Ibn al-Aḥmar, in that case netting Fernando III 160,000. The Moroccan author, Ibn Abī Zar', writing at the close of the thirteenth century, however, stipulated that the truce was for four years and the tribute was fixed at 400,000 dinars annually, a figure that seems quite erroneous. Once again, I think the figures given by the royal chancellor are preferable.[53] The total of 208,000 *maravedís*, however, was considerably less than the 430,000 promised by Ibn Hūd in 1235. The difference of 222,000 *maravedís* may have resulted from the fact that Ibn Hūd no longer ruled Córdoba. Fernando III probably received a total of 208,000 *maravedís* in 1236 and 1237, or 416,000 all told, minus 24,000 (12,000 each year) given to Ibn al-Aḥmar, for a net of 392,000 *maravedís*. That fount of income was ended by Ibn Hūd's assassination in 1238.

When the Bānū Hūd, the lords of Murcia, submitted to Fernando III's son Infante Alfonso in 1243, they pledged to surrender their revenues, with certain exceptions. Though specific information is lacking, González suggested that Castile received at least half of the Murcian annual revenue.[54]

After the fall of Jaén in 1246, Fernando III concluded a truce for twenty years with Ibn al-Aḥmar, king of Granada, who became his vassal, guaranteeing an annual tribute of 150,000 *maravedís*. Assuming that that amount was paid in 1246, 1247, and 1248, Fernando III would have had 450,000 *maravedís* at his disposal for the siege of Seville. The *Chronicle of Alfonso X* reported that the Muslim king agreed to pay half his revenues, estimated at 600,000 *maravedís*, or 300,000. The value of the tribute was probably expressed in terms of the later *maravedí* of Alfonso X, and so the figure of 150,000 *maravedís* given by the *Estoria de Espanna* is more exact.[55]

The king also obtained money from other Muslims. For example, when

Priego surrendered in 1225 the Muslims purchased their liberty for 40,000 *maravedís*. Ten years later San Esteban yielded and handed over money, horses, and mules. Around 1246, Jerez also pledged to pay a fixed annual tribute each year, but the amount is unknown. The Muslims of Carmona in 1247 pledged "a certain tribute" for six months; if, during that time, they received no help from their fellow Muslims they would surrender.[56] Other towns likely made similar pledges. Whenever Muslims came under Christian rule they were expected to pay their customary tributes to the Christians.

Loans

In addition to all the other types of income mentioned above, the Christian rulers frequently borrowed money to meet their needs. Soldiers may also have mortgaged their property to churches and monasteries in order to raise money. Not every loan was specifically tied to the necessities of the reconquest, but it obviously loomed large in the budgets of all the Christian princes. Ramon Berenguer IV, for example, "laboring in the siege of Tortosa for the honor of God and the increase of holy Christendom," borrowed 50 *libras* of silver from the cathedral of Barcelona, and also obtained a loan of 7,700 *solidi* from the burghers of the city. In the aftermath of the battle of Alarcos Sancho VII of Navarre borrowed 70,000 *sueldos* from the bishop of Pamplona to defend his realm against invasion by Castile and Aragón.[57]

In his will of 1204 Alfonso VIII stipulated that all his creditors should be paid up to the amount of 90,000 *maravedís*; his executors would have to authorize any expenditure above that. He also ordered payment of the balance of 12,000 *maravedís* on a debt of 18,000 owed to his *almojarife*, the Jew Abū 'Umar ibn Shushan, an official responsible for overseeing his accounts, as well as a loan of an unspecified amount made by Esteban Illán, *alcalde* of Toledo. Acknowledging that the Jews of Zorita "served my father well with money, because it happened that he had many needs during his time," Enrique I exempted them from tribute. Although Afonso II of Portugal ordered payment of his debts before any bequests were distributed, there is little evidence that he actively engaged in the reconquest, so it is difficult to attribute his indebtedness to that reason. The same may be said about a similar clause in Sancho II's will.[58]

Alfonso II of Aragón borrowed frequently, especially from the Templars, and in his will of 1194 provided for the payment of his outstanding debts. His son, Pedro II, was an inveterate borrower, whose total indebtedness often exceeded 200,000 *sous* annually for the Crown of Aragón; in 1209 he owed at least 271,411 *sous* in Catalonia, and about 100,000 annually from about 1209–13. Included in those debts were 20,000 *maravedis* borrowed from Sancho VII of Navarre in 1209. A few months before Las Navas Sancho VII lent him 10,000 silver *mazmudíes.* As many of Pedro II's debts were unpaid at the time of his death, Innocent III ordered the collection of subsidies from the Catalan and Aragonese towns to redeem lands pledged by the king.[59]

Jaime I also borrowed continuously and in his will of 1232 ordered his executors to pay all his debts, some of which obviously arose from the Mallorcan and Valencian crusades. During the siege of Mallorca in 1229 he borrowed 60,000 *libras* from merchants accompanying the host, with a promise of payment once the city was taken. During the siege of Borriana, the Templars and Hospitallers guaranteed a loan of 60,000 *sous* to enable him to retain two ships supplying his army. After seizing Puig de la Cebolla, he estimated that he required wheat for three months, wine for six, and salt meat and barley for two; in order to pay his suppliers he borrowed 60,000 *sous* from the chief men of Lleida. He turned to Montpellier for help in covering his expenses in conquering Valencia, but whether he obtained a loan or an outright grant is unknown.[60] He likely borrowed other sums to finance further stages of the conquest.

Many persons of lesser rank also turned to the moneylenders for help in dealing with expenses incurred in the reconquest. Honorius III, for example, asked the Templars in 1223 to excuse Pedro Alvítiz, master of the Templars in Spain, of debts contracted in the struggle against the Muslims. Bishops and Military Orders frequently entered financial arrangements with Tuscan or Lombard bankers. In 1238 the Order of Santiago settled debts of 830 and 30 *maravedís* contracted with bankers in Siena. During the Council of Lyon in September 1245, Pelay Pérez Correa, master of Santiago, borrowed 1,000 marks sterling, payable at Paris in the following June. However, he failed to meet that date and was reprimanded by Innocent IV three years later; he also had to pay another 200 *livres tournois* borrowed by the Order's procurator in Rome. In 1253 the pope authorized the procurator to obtain loans up to a maximum of 100 *livres tournois.* Meantime, papal judges-delegate threatened to excommunicate the master for non-payment; in 1258 Alexander IV lifted the ban.[61]

Given the extent to which other kings, bishops, and Military Orders borrowed, it seems reasonable to suppose that Fernando III did so as well, most likely from the Jews of his own realm, especially those in Toledo. Nevertheless, records indicating such loans are lacking. On several occasions he obtained money by means of a *manlieva*, that is, a loan. Early in 1238 he raised 25,000 *maravedís* in Toledo to sustain the people of Córdoba, and an equal amount to distribute among frontier castles. Continued reports of misery prompted him to obtain another *manlieva* in Toledo, probably in April; again in the summer he had to provide additional support for the settlers in Córdoba and the defense of the frontier. In July 1243 he procured another *manlieva* at Toledo to succor Córdoba and also to assist his son, then accepting the submission of Murcia.[62]

In these three instances it seems likely that Fernando III borrowed from the Jews of Toledo, perhaps from the Ibn Shushan family, who served the crown as *almojarifes* and tax collectors. The royal chancellor, Bishop Juan of Osma, in his own name or in that of the king, borrowed from them, including 3,000 *maravedís* owed to the royal *almojarifes* "by the king," and 2,148 *maravedís* "as a forced loan." Other debts included 2,500 *maravedís* due to Abulafia; 200 *maravedís* (plus 60) owed to Don David, and 500 to the wife of the *alfaquí* Don Yucef and his children. Perhaps too, Don Zulema, the king's envoy sent to collect *parias* from the king of Granada, was among the royal creditors. Many of the Jews (most were from Toledo) mentioned in the distribution of lands in Seville in 1252 and settled in Paterna, renamed Aldea de los Judíos del Rey, were likely rewarded for having lent money to the king. They included: Zag, the *almojarife*; his sons Mose, Zag, Abraham, and Jucef; the *alfaquí* Jucef and his son Jucef; Ziza, the *alfaquí*; and Zulema, the father of Zag de la Maleha, the tax collector in the reign of Alfonso X.[63]

Empréstitos

Aside from these advances, Fernando III also demanded forced loans from the towns to finance the conquest of Seville. During the siege, on 21 June 1248, he requested an extraordinary aid or *empréstito* from all the Galician towns. Twenty-two towns were named individually, including Santiago de Compostela, Orense, Lugo, Túy, and Mondoñedo, all held in lordship by their bishops, and several others dependent directly on the king. Declaring that in laboring for the "exaltation of Christendom," he incurred greater expenses than any king in Spain, he asked the towns to lend him money at the rate of 5 percent of each individual's income. Anyone worth 1,000 *maravedís* would lend 50; the rate on 500 *maravedís* was 25, and on 300 it would be 15. Nothing was asked of those whose wealth was less than 300 *maravedís*. He acknowledged that he could not demand this aid as a matter of right.[64]

He described this as an *emprestido* or loan, which he promised to repay when he next levied *moneda*. If *moneda forera* had been levied in the kingdom of León every seven years from 1202, then it would be collected again in 1251. Consequently, those who lent money in 1248 would have to wait at least three years before being repaid, and the king said nothing about paying interest. Should there be any dispute about anyone's worth, the municipal council was authorized to elect six jurors from each parish to make the assessment. Anyone refusing to pay would be fined 100 *maravedís* and his body and goods would be at the king's mercy. The king's *portero*, Domingo Pérez de Toro, was entrusted with the task of collecting the money.[65]

One cannot ascertain the number of Galician townspeople wealthy enough to contribute. To put this in perspective, the salary of the dean of Astorga was set at 500 gold *aurei*; the archdeacon received 400; the treasurer and cantor 300 each; the *maestrescuela* 250, and each canon 100. Two years after his father's death, Alfonso X fixed professorial salaries in the University of Salamanca as follows: master of civil laws, 500 *maravedís*; master of decretals, 200; masters of logic, grammar, and medicine, 200 each; a stationer 100; and two conservators, 200 each. The impact that a tax of 50, 25, or 15 *maravedís* had on an individual can be assessed if those sums are compared with prices set in the Cortes of Seville in 1252, just four years after Fernando III's demand for an *empréstito*. The price of arms, saddle, and iron cap was set at 20 *maravedís*; a saddle, bridle, and breastplate for a warhorse, at 35. The price of a good horse could be 200 *maravedís*; the toll on livestock was two cows out of every 1,000, each worth 4 *maravedís*; a woman's silk headdress was 3 *maravedís*.[66]

The royal demand made of the Galician towns in 1248 should not be thought of as an isolated instance. Grassotti argued that the precedent for it was set by Alfonso IX in 1204, when, with the consent of the bishop of Orense, he asked the canons and citizens of Orense for certain sums. Promising repayment, he assured them that neither he nor his successors would be entitled to such an exaction in the future without the bishop's consent. Unlike his father, Fernando III made no reference to episcopal authorization. Although there is no documentary evidence, it seems reasonable to suppose that Alfonso IX made similar demands on other occasions and that Fernando III did so before 1248. One could also argue that he required other towns of León and Castile, north of the Duero, who were not providing military or naval contingents to the war effort, to make similar contributions. Some may have been asked to provide funds for Ramón Bonifaz's fleet. In 1258, for example, Oviedo promised Alfonso X 1,200 *maravedís* for his fleet. However, Castilian and Extremaduran towns whose militias went to the frontier were not also required to contribute money.[67]

Even after 1248 the king seems to have asked for *empréstitos*, as several of his son's charters suggest. Alfonso X's pledge to Burgos in 1255 that he would not demand "any forced loan without your consent" implies that the practice continued and probably was more frequent during Fernando III's reign than the one example from 1248 indicates. The representatives of Ledesma, Valladolid, Salamanca, and Ribadavia, moreover, complained that merchants suffered because of Fernando III's *empréstitos*. In 1255–56 Alfonso X declared that in the future no *empréstito* would be taken without consent. Thus, one can conclude that Fernando III demanded *empréstitos* at least from some of the towns of Galicia, Leonese Extremadura, and Old Castile, that did not participate directly in the war.[68]

The sums collected from the Galician *empréstito* were probably included in the accounts rendered by Domingo Pérez de Toro at Seville in 1251. His collections from 1245 to 1251 totalled 141,442 *maravedís* and a *sueldo* of León. That included the twentieth; forced loans; *fonsadera*; *moneda* from Salamanca; tribute from the royal domain; payments in lieu of providing beasts of burden; the *tercias*; and exactions on the Jews.[69] If his total were apportioned equally over six years, it would amount to about 23,500 *maravedís* annually. As it is unlikely that he was the only royal tax collector, the king's Leonese income in any given year would have been much more than that. Moreover, royal income from Castile, more extensive and populous, was probably greater still.

Any attempt to assess the means of financing the wars of reconquest and crusade can only be frustrating, as the preceding presentation makes clear. Without detailed financial records, even for a year or two, we will never satisfactorily understand royal finances in the twelfth and thirteenth centuries. That being said, there are a few conclusions that one can draw. The costs of warfare were tremendous and were not likely to be covered by ordinary revenues, forage, or booty. Engaged in a nearly continuous struggle against Islam, the Christian kings of Spain needed a steady flow of extraordinary income. Indeed, a royal budget would likely show that the bulk of the revenue was expended on war. The Catalans granted the *bovaticum* to assist the king in meeting the costs of war against the Muslims. In return for a pledge not to alter the coinage the Christian kings obtained *monedatge* or *moneda forera* every seven years; they exacted *empréstitos* and borrowed extensively, more often than the documentary evidence reveals. The papacy, acknowledging their role as crusaders, permitted them to tap ecclesiastical revenues in the form of the *tercias* and occasional subsidies by the church. Above all they exacted *parias*, surely one of the largest parts of the royal budget, from the *reyes de taifas* during periods of disintegration in Islamic Spain. Without much exaggeration, one could conclude that the petty Muslim kings financed their own destruction.

Chapter 8
The Liturgy of Reconquest and Crusade

The religious rituals or liturgy associated with the war against Islam were equally as important as considerations of strategy. Soldiers then as now needed a reason to go to war and to expose themselves to the possibility of being maimed or slaughtered. Christian warriors were exhorted to regain land, once theirs, but now wrongfully occupied by Muslim intruders who were charged with oppressing Christianity and despoiling churches. Seeking to exalt the Christian name and suppress that of Muḥammad, the Christians, certain that their cause was just and that God was on their side, faced the enemy.

Preaching the Crusade

Ideas such as these likely formed the stock themes of preachers rousing men to combat. Papal crusading bulls offering remission of sins often provided a framework for preaching. Bishops, instructed to preach the crusade, likely designated preachers in each diocese. Papal legates such as Cardinal Hyacinth, as well as Archbishops Diego Gelmírez of Compostela, Raimundo, Juan, and Rodrigo of Toledo, Oleguer and Aspàreg of Tarragona, and many other ecclesiastics actively stimulated the faithful to participate in the crusades. When Fernando III informed Honorius III that he intended to undertake a crusade the pope ordered Archbishop Rodrigo and Bishop Mauricio of Burgos to "publicly announce this indulgence so as to animate the faithful to undertake this affair."[1]

When exhorting the people to take up arms against "the infidels, the enemies of the cross of Christ," a habitual description of Muslims, preachers certainly stressed the principal spiritual reward, namely, the indulgence or remission of sins conceded to those participating personally or financially. As we have seen Paschal II extended to the people of Spain Urban II's grant of remission of sins to those doing penance by making the journey to the

Holy Land. Thereafter popes consistently emphasized that this indulgence was equivalent to that of the oriental crusades. When Archbishop Juan of Toledo in 1158 "had it preached that all those who went to the aid of Calatrava would merit remission of all their sins," the response was enthusiastic. "Such a great commotion was made in the city that there was hardly anyone who did not go in his own person or send horses, arms or money." Besides spiritual benefits preachers would certainly mention, as Urban II did at Clermont, the possibility of booty. Archbishop Raimundo of Toledo and Bishop Pedro of León, for example, while absolving soldiers at the siege of Almería, also promised them gold and silver aplenty. Lastly, preachers would proclaim that anyone killed in battle would receive eternal recompense in heaven and would be accounted among the martyrs.[2]

The sermon given by Bishop Pedro Pitões of Porto to northern crusaders on their way to the Holy Land and recorded in the *De Expugnatione Lyxbonensi* is one of the fullest examples of preaching in Spain. The sermon reflects common themes, but it also touches on the specific nature of the peninsular war against Islam. Lauding the crusaders for undertaking a pilgrimage in order to gain an eternal reward, Bishop Pedro lamented that God had punished Spanish Christians by subjecting them to Muslim rule. Just seven years before, the Muslims had plundered the church of Santa María in Porto, stealing liturgical vestments and vessels, and killing or enslaving the clergy. He pleaded with the crusaders to take vengeance on the "heathens" and to lift up the church.

Acting in self-defense, he assured them that their conduct was in accordance with law. Whereas the biblical admonition "all who take the sword will perish by the sword" (Matt. 26: 52) referred to persons acting without proper authorization, he remarked that those who defended the fatherland, repulsed enemies, and protected their fellows from robbers acted justly and in good conscience. They had no reason to fear being charged with murder or other crimes. He cited St. Isidore: "a war is just which is carried on after a declaration to recover property or to repel enemies." In language reminiscent of St. Bernard, the chief preacher of the Second Crusade, Bishop Pedro implored the crusaders: "Act like good soldiers; for it is not a sin to wage war, but it is a sin to wage war for the sake of plunder. . . . When a war is undertaken at God's direction, one cannot doubt that it is rightly undertaken."[3]

An anonymous priest, perhaps the author of the *De Expugnatione Lyxbonensi*, also preached during the siege of Lisbon. After Archbishop João of Braga blessed an assault tower, the priest, holding a piece of the "holy wood of the cross," began to preach. He recalled that the Muslims, who were thieves and robbers, taunted the Christians for believing that God would choose to be born of a woman and suffer the travails of human existence. Earlier the author related that the Muslims chastised the Christians for venerating Jesus as though he were God, rather than a prophet. The Muslims violated the cross by spitting on it and wiping it "with the filth of their posteriors." The preacher reminded the crusaders that they had put on Christ and asked them to look on the cross, to kneel, and to strike their breasts in repentance. Recalling Constantine's vision, he assured them that "in this sign, if you do not hesitate, you will conquer. For if it should befall anyone signed with it to die, we do not believe that life has been taken from him, for we do not doubt that it is changed for the better. Here, therefore, to live is glory and to die is gain."[4] Proclaiming that they would triumph and win eternal glory, he commanded them to arise and blessed them with the sign of the cross. Then he urged them to attack.

Folquet de Marselha, a troubadour, then a Cistercian monk, and finally archbishop of Toulouse (1205–31), left a sermon both in prose and in poetry, commenting on the disaster of Alarcos and preparations for Las Navas. A great sadness, he remarked, fell over Spain when King Alfonso was defeated by Miramamolín (the Christian form of the caliphal title, *amīr al-mu'minīn*), the king of Morocco, who seized Calatrava, Salvatierra, and Castel de Dueñas, and, after ravaging the kingdom, besieged Toledo, thereby dishonoring Christendom. King Alfonso then asked the pope to encourage the French and English barons, the king of Aragón, and the count of Toulouse to help. Folquet roused the crusaders by pointing out that besides divine pardon, honor and booty were to be gained. Not requiring ships to make the journey to Jerusalem, they would have no fear of wind or sea. If they aided the king of Castile they would receive riches enough from God. Then in a bit of convoluted theology, he argued that God displayed greater love by allowing Spain to be lost than if he had come again to die, because he offered pardon and salvation to crusaders in Spain. In his poetic sermon, Folquet declared that his hearers could not excuse themselves from serving God, who offered his favor, first through the loss of the Holy Sepulchre, and now in Spain. Arguing that any effort undertaken without God was vain, he urged the king to accept God as his companion, and thereby gain merit hundredfold.[5]

During mass before the battle of Las Navas the anonymous homilist may well have exhorted the troops in words similar to those recorded in the *Latin Chronicle*. Perhaps taking as his text the Easter hymn, *Aurora lucis rutilat*—"the dawn of the sun shone brightly"—he assured Alfonso VIII that whatever opprobrium he and his kingdom had incurred at Alarcos "would be purged on that day by the power of our Lord Jesus Christ and his most victorious cross, against which the king of Morocco had blasphemed from his filthy mouth." On hearing that King Alfonso had sent Archbishop Rodrigo and others to France and elsewhere to seek help, the caliph "said that he was powerful enough to fight against all those who adored the sign of the cross." The homilist concluded with the prayer: "O Lord, Jesus Christ, you have cast him down while he was exalted, for such ones are raised up on high by unrestrained pride, so that they may fall down more quickly."[6]

As the Catalan crusaders prepared to encounter the enemy at Portopí, mass was celebrated in the king's tent and Bishop Berenguer of Barcelona preached, saying "this enterprise . . . is the work of God, not ours. . . . Those who die in this affair, will die for our Lord and will gain paradise, where they will enjoy everlasting glory. Those who survive will also have honor and esteem while they live and at death a good end." He urged them to "destroy those who deny the faith and the name of Jesus Christ," assuring them that God and his mother would lead them to victory. During the siege of Palma the Dominican Miguel de Fabra preached and, with episcopal authorization, granted pardon for sins. Before the final assault on Palma, a bishop reminded the crusaders that they had come "to serve God and to destroy the enemies of Jesus Christ." Just as Jesus had willingly died for them, "each one should be willing to die for Jesus Christ if it were necessary . . . and they should not fear to die for him."[7]

The Crusader's Vow and the Wearing of the Cross

Preaching likely preceded the taking of the crusader's vow and the adoption of the cross. Urban II urged his listeners at Clermont to make a vow to go on pilgrimage to Jerusalem and, in imitation of Christ, to take up the cross, wearing it on the breast. Once the vow was fulfilled the crusader customarily placed the cross on his back. Whereas crusaders to the Holy Land were described as *peregrini* or pilgrims, following the Third Crusade canonists began to refer to them by the technical term *cruce signati* (signed with the cross). A ceremony for taking the cross developed in the later twelfth century as an extension of the rite for conferral of the pilgrim's scrip and staff. As various prayers were said the cross was blessed and delivered to the crusader. In some instances mass was celebrated.[8] The votive masses for pilgrims in the eleventh-century Catalan Sacramentaries of Vich and Ripoll contain similar prayers. Prayers for taking the cross are included in a sacramentary, perhaps from the Catalan abbey of San Miguel de Cuxà. A review of Spanish sacramentaries, most of which have not been edited, may reveal additional texts of this sort.[9]

The people of Spain were long familiar with monastic vows and vows taken by pilgrims making the journey to Jerusalem or to Santiago de Compostela.[10] Many Spaniards, such as Archbishop Bernard of Toledo, vowed to participate in the First Crusade; when he appeared in Rome "signed with the sign of the cross," Urban II absolved him of his vow and sent him home. Pedro I also "accepted the cross," but changed his mind and directed his warlike energy at home. The phrase "accepted the cross" suggests that he had taken the crusader's vow and wore the cross as a sign of his determination. The description of the king as *crucifer* or crossbearer "with the standard of Christ" before Zaragoza in 1101 implies that he may have been wearing the cross on his clothing as a symbol of his intentions. His erection of a castle opposite Zaragoza called *Juslibol* (*Deus le veult*—"God wills it") reflects the influence of crusading ideology.[11]

Prior to the Mallorcan Crusade, Count Ramon Berenguer III, probably while taking the crusader's vow, "received on his shoulder the sign of the most holy cross" from Archbishop Pietro of Pisa. When granting remission of sins for the war against the Muslims in Spain Calixtus II reminded those who "place the sign of the cross on their garments on this account" that if they neglected to "fulfill their vow" within a year they would be excommunicated. It seems likely that Archbishops Oleguer of Tarragona, whom the pope named as his legate, and Diego Gelmírez of Compostela took the crusader's vow about that time, as each of them offered remission of sins to the defenders of Spanish Christianity. No source mentions that Alfonso I took the vow or the cross during the Crusade of Zaragoza, but if anyone could be described as a crusader, he certainly should be. Ordericus Vitalis stated that the king and his men at Fraga were "signed with the cross of Christ." Although the king fell in battle, the rumor spread that, out of shame, he went on pilgrimage to Jerusalem. In repentance for his sins, Munio Alfonso, *alcaide* of Toledo, vowed to go to the Holy Land, but the bishops ordered him to do penance by engaging the Spanish Muslims. The Council of Valladolid in 1143 stipulated that arsonists ought to be required to do penance for a year "in the service of God against the pagans."[12]

By the time Eugenius III proclaimed the Second Crusade and acknowledged that the war against Spanish Islam was on a par with the oriental crusade it is likely that the Spaniards were quite familiar with the ideas and practices of crusading. As the ceremony of taking a vow and placing the cross on one's clothing as an outward manifestation of one's intent was a powerful means of arousing support for a projected military campaign, it is plausible to believe that the Christian rulers did just that. Thus, despite the silence of the sources, one might expect that when the northern crusaders besieged Lisbon, Afonso I and his troops took the crusader's vow and assumed the cross. Knowing that the pope had granted remission of sins for the struggle against the Muslims, Alfonso VII may also have taken the vow and the crusader's cross during the siege of Almería. As the pope granted a crusading bull for the assault on Tortosa, it also seems reasonable to conclude that Count Ramon Berenguer IV took the vow; in 1152, after receiving still another bull of crusade, he probably did so again. When Cardinal Hyacinth proclaimed a crusade in the Council of Valladolid in 1155 he emphasized that he placed the sign of the cross on his breast at the urging of the kings, princes, clergy, and people of the Spains. That being so, one might be justified in believing that Alfonso VII and the archbishops of Toledo and Santiago and others followed his lead.[13]

Despite the lack of papal bulls authorizing crusades in Spain during the third quarter of the twelfth century, the crusading spirit was very much alive in the Military Orders. Commending the knights of Santiago as athletes of Christ vowed to the defense of Christendom, Alexander III remarked that they wore "on the breast the sign" of Christ. Recognition that one could atone for one's sins in Spain as well as in the Holy Land was made explicit when the papal legates in 1172 required Henry II of England to expiate the assassination of Thomas à Becket either by going to Jerusalem or "to Spain to liberate that land from the infidel." In fact, he did neither. Three years later Alexander III published a crusading bull for Spain, but whether any of the Christian kings took the vow is unknown. After the fall of Jerusalem Clement III offered Spanish Christians the same remission of sins, but again sources say nothing of the taking of vows, probably because of the bitter rivalries among the Christian princes.[14]

Nevertheless, when a northern fleet participating in the Third Crusade joined Sancho I in the conquest of Silves, it is likely, despite the silence of the sources, that he took the crusader's vow and adopted the cross. Nor is it stated that Alfonso VIII did so prior to Alarcos, although Celestine III in 1193 praised him for taking up arms against the Muslims, and granted remission of sins. Perhaps feeling remorse over his failure at Alarcos, Diego López de Haro pledged to go to the Holy Land, but the pope absolved him from his vow provided that he engage the Muslims in Spain. The prior of Santa Cruz in Coimbra was also authorized to absolve those who assumed the cross to combat the "pagans." It seems reasonable to believe that Alfonso VIII, Pedro II, and Sancho I of Portugal took the crusader's vow after the pope proclaimed a crusade against Alfonso IX, who allied himself with the Muslims following Alarcos. Celestine III also released the people of southern France, "signed with the sign of salvation," from their obligation to go to the Holy Land if they helped to deliver Spain from the "ferocity of perfidious men," presumably Alfonso IX.[15]

As the Christian rulers settled their internecine quarrels they began to think about taking action against the Muslims. When Pedro II in 1204 "accepted the material sword to punish evildoers" who "wished to abolish the memory of the Christian name," he perhaps took a vow, but Innocent III dissuaded him for the time being. Six years later, however, when Infante Fernando of Castile announced that he intended "to dedicate the first fruits of his knighthood to Almighty God by driving the enemies of the Christian name from the bounds of his inheritance which they impiously occupied," it would seem that he took the crusading vow. Although none of the sources underscored the point, it is probable that prior to the Crusade of Las Navas, Alfonso VIII and his forces, as well as the other peninsular monarchs and the French crusaders took the vow and adopted the cross. While Archbishop Rodrigo preached, offering "remission of sins," he exhorted his French hearers to "fortify themselves with the sign of the cross." As crusaders arrived at Toledo, he commented that "the number of those bearing the stigmata of the Lord [presumably the cross] on their bodies increased every day." Both he and Archbishop Arnald Amaury of Narbonne affirmed that the crusaders wore the sign of the cross on their garments. When the French abandoned the Crusade after the capture of Calatrava, they "removed the sign of the cross" as they made their way home.[16]

A fleet of northern crusaders (*multitudo crucesignatorum*) participating in the Fifth Crusade collaborated in taking Alcácer do Sal. Bishops Sueiro of Lisbon and Sueiro of Évora preached and "imposed the sign of the cross on almost everyone in our dioceses and indeed in the dioceses of the whole realm" and asked the pope to grant the crusading indulgence both to the "army of pilgrims" from the north and to Portuguese crusaders (*crucesignati*) as well as to those to be signed with the cross (*signandi*). Both Alfonso IX and Sancho VII of Navarre, as well as others, "took the sign of cross against the Saracens of Spain." The pope himself confirmed that both monarchs had "assumed the cross." Among those joining the Leonese *cruzada* was Bishop Martín Rodríguez of Zamora who announced that "in this year [1221] we took care to sign ourselves in God with the sign of cross."[17]

About the same time Archbishop Rodrigo and certain magnates "assumed the living cross" and carried out a crusade on the Castilian frontier. Preparing to join the crusade, Martín Muñiz described himself as "crossed [*cruciatus*] with the sign of the cross." The language of the *Poem of Fernán González*, written after the middle of the thirteenth century, also suggests that crusading language had gained currency. Describing the defeat of the Visigothic king, Rodrigo, at the Guadalete in 711 and the campaigns of the tenth-century count of Castile, Fernán González, the poet anachronistically spoke of "*pueblo cruzado*" or "*gente cruzada*," that is, people signed with the sign of the cross. The poet Gonzalo de Berceo (d. c. 1250) also used the word *cruzada*.[18]

When he announced his desire to engage the Muslims during the Curia of Burgos in May 1224, Fernando III may have taken the crusader's vow or perhaps in the Curia of Carrión in July. Archbishop Rodrigo's comment that the king "wished to dedicate the first fruits of his knighthood to the Lord" and the *Latin Chronicle*'s reference to the "fulfillment of his vow" suggest that he did so. On the king's request, Honorius III granted remission of sins to everyone who accepted "the sign of the cross," and placed "the crusaders of the kingdom of Castile" (*crucesignatis regni Castelle*) under papal protection. Papal bulls granting indulgences in subsequent years to Archbishop Rodrigo's or Fernando III's collaborators evidently were an inducement to taking the crusader's vow. Several bulls suggest that the king and others renewed their vow in preparation for the assault on Seville. Both Gutierre, bishop-elect of Córdoba, and Infante Alfonso of Castile obtained crusading bulls from Innocent IV in 1246. In the following year the pope encouraged Fernando III as a "special athlete of Christ" in his plan to attack Seville.[19]

Inspired by a similar zeal, Jaime I during the Curia of Tortosa in 1225 proclaimed that "we have assumed the cross to attack the barbarous nations" and requested aid and counsel "to promote the affair of the cross." Before embarking on the conquest of Mallorca four years later he and his bishops and magnates received the cross from the papal legate, Cardinal Jean d'Abbeville, during the Council of Lleida. According to Zurita Jaime I took the crusader's vow again at Monzón in 1232 in preparation for the Valencian Crusade. During the Curia of Monzón in 1236 he "assumed the cross to conquer the kingdom of Valencia for the exaltation of the Christian faith." Gregory IX lauded him for having taken up the cross and encouraged others to do so. Many years later Innocent IV urged the faithful to accept the cross to assist the king in suppressing al-Azraq's rebellion.[20]

Sancho II may have taken the crusader's vow when he occupied Elvas in 1226 and again in 1234 and 1241 when Gregory IX issued crusading bulls and praised him for having "girded himself" for the war against Islam. The pope noted in 1239 that the king's brother, Infante Fernando de Serpa, and Infante Alfonso de Molina, Fernando III's brother, also intended "to assume the sign of the cross to combat the Saracens." Another brother of the Portuguese king, Count Afonso of Boulogne, apparently vowed to go to the Holy Land in 1245 but decided instead to attack the Muslims in Spain and received a crusading bull from Innocent IV.[21]

In discussing these instances the sources ordinarily do not use the words *uouere*, to take a vow, or *uotum*, a vow. Most often the act of taking the cross is mentioned and that probably followed a public declaration of intention or a vow. Although the evidence is not clear, except perhaps in the case of Jaime I, I am inclined to believe that every time a monarch set out on a major campaign supported by crusading bulls he renewed his vow and the act of taking the cross. Papal documents stating that a king, fired with zeal for the exaltation of the Christian faith, had girded himself for the struggle against Islam, can be interpreted, I think, as evidence that the king had taken a vow announcing his intention for everyone to hear.

Liturgical Preparations for Battle

Once the army was ready, the clergy reminded the troops that they were fulfilling a religious duty in the service of Christendom. After blessing the soldiers' arms, priests absolved them from their sins, celebrated mass, and, calling on divine assistance, accompanied them into battle.

The liturgy celebrated on the occasion of the king's departure for war in Visigothic Spain and also in Asturias-León prior to the twelfth century imitated the ceremony followed by Christian Roman emperors. According to the Visigothic *Liber ordinum* the clergy welcomed the king to the church with incense; entering, he prostrated himself before the altar. The verse "May God be on your journey and may his Angel accompany you" (Tob. 5: 21) was followed by a prayer asking the God of battles to protect him and make him a *triumphator*. After a blessing, a deacon took from the altar a golden cross containing a relic of the true cross, and gave it to the bishop who presented it to the king; he in turn gave it to a priest to carry into battle before him. The gold cross of Oviedo made by Alfonso III in 908 may have been just such a cross. Following an antiphon and versicle, a priest presented banners to the royal standardbearers. After the Gloria, the bishop gave his blessing, asking that the cross of Christ always attend upon the king and enable him to achieve victory. A final request assumed a royal triumph: "Through the victory of the holy cross, may you successfully complete the journey begun here and bring back to us flourishing signs of your triumphs. Amen." Then as the deacon said "go in peace" the king left the church and the antiphon "Lord God, the strength of my salvation, cover my head on the day of battle" was sung.[22]

In the second half of the eleventh century, the Roman liturgy displaced the Mozarabic, so it is likely that the prayers in the older liturgical books fell into desuetude and newer texts of general European origin came into use. The eleventh-century Catalan Sacramentaries of Vich and Ripoll, reflecting the Gregorian and Gelasian Sacramentaries, contain prayers for a *Missa in tempore belli*. An alternative opening prayer asked God "to repress the enemies of the Christian name," and another prayer, nearly identical to that in the modern Roman Missal, appealed to divine mercy "so that, once the ferocity of the gentiles has been repressed and exhausted, we may give praise in thanksgiving."[23]

The thirteenth-century *Ceremonial of Cardeña* contains prayers to be recited in time of war against the Muslims, probably after the celebration of the votive mass of the cross when the king departed for war and was presented with the cross. The Offertory prayer reads in part: "Protect your people, O Lord, by the sign of the holy Cross from all the wickedness of every enemy." The Communion prayer says: "By the sign of the Cross deliver us, our God, from our enemies." After mass and the plea, "may your right hand destroy enemies," a series of verses and responses ask God to "scatter your enemies," to safeguard the king and his people "against the face of the enemy." There followed a concluding appeal to Jesus:

Look favorably on your servant our king, and on his army. . . . Grant that, by the power of your name and the most victorious Cross, the people of the Moors, who everywhere always humiliate it, may powerfully be conquered. And grant that, when the barbaric ferocity is trampled under foot, he may return home with honor and joy.[24]

The likelihood that the Visigothic custom of presenting the king with a cross before embarking on a campaign continued into the age of the crusades is suggested by the description of Pedro I as *crucifer* before Zaragoza and by Alfonso VIII's statement that "the sign of the Lord's cross" preceded his army at Las Navas. The cross was also carried before the kings of Castile-León and Portugal at Salado in the fourteenth century.[25]

Apart from the battlefield, prayers were frequently offered asking God to grant victory or to protect the weak and the innocent. When the Almoravids ravaged the Tagus valley, Archbishop Bernard and his people begged God and Holy Mary to disregard their sins, so that they would not be put to the sword, or enslaved, and Toledo destroyed and "the holy law of God" held in opprobrium. A merciful God, according to the chronicler, sent the Archangel Michael to protect the city and to comfort them.[26]

Processions were often undertaken to welcome monarchs and to ask for divine aid before battle. Thus when Pedro II arrived in Toledo just before Las Navas he was greeted by the archbishop and clergy in procession. At the same time Innocent III ordered processions in Rome on 16 May to pray for the success of the Crusade. The basilicas of Santa Maria Maggore, the Twelve Apostles, and Santa Anastasia served as gathering places respectively for women, clergy, and laymen. As church bells pealed, each company, preceded by a cross, set out. The pope, accompanied by cardinals and bishops, carried a relic of the True Cross from the basilica of Sancta Sanctorum to the palace of the cardinal-bishop of Albano, where a bishop preached. The women processed to the basilica of Santa Croce de Gerusalemme, and, after a cardinal-priest celebrated mass, returned home. Meantime, the pope, cardinals, bishops, clergy, and laymen went to St. John Lateran, where mass was celebrated. After processing in bare feet to Santa Croce the clergy and laity went home. While praying for a Christian triumph, everyone, except those who were ill, was expected to fast on bread and water and to give alms. In France "litanies and prayers" were offered for the crusaders and the same was likely true in Spain itself.[27]

The usual liturgical preparations for battle were the celebration of mass, absolution of sins, and reception of the eucharist. In the circumstances, it is likely that general absolution was given. Muslim sources relate a similar practice of asking pardon for sin before entering combat. Summoning crusaders in 1125, Bishop Diego Gelmírez of Compostela called for true confession and sincere repentance. When the Lisbon crusaders first set out on their journey to Jerusalem they pledged to make weekly confession and to receive the eucharist. The bishop of Porto, at their first meeting, said mass, giving them absolution, as he did again when they prepared to engage the enemy.[28]

En route to Las Navas, the kings of Castile, Aragón, and Navarre "received the episcopal blessing and the grace of the sacrament" on Saturday and on Sunday the bishops visited the soldiers' tents and "propounded the word of exhortation and indulgence most devoutly." Then about midnight "the voice of exultation and confession sounded in the Christian tents and the voice of the herald summoned all to arm themselves for the Lord's battle. After celebrating the mystery of the Lord's passion, and making confession, and receiving the sacraments, they took up arms and advanced to the field of battle." Forming their ranks, they raised their hands and eyes to God, and, their hearts stirred with thoughts of martyrdom, unfurled the standards of the faith, invoked the name of the Lord, and set out to do battle. The *Latin Chronicle* tells us that "after hearing the solemnities of mass and being born again by the life-giving sacraments of the Body and Blood of our God, Jesus Christ, fortifying themselves with the sign of the cross, they quickly took up the arms of war and joyfully hastened to battle . . . prepared to die or to conquer." This passage suggests the ideology that surrounded the crusade. After hearing mass and receiving the eucharist, the troops took up their weapons but likely also placed the sign of the cross on their bodies. The celerity with which they rushed into battle suggests that they believed that if they were killed they would receive the reward of paradise. "To conquer or to die" is language reminiscent of St. Bernard's exhortation to the Templars.[29]

In preparation for his Mallorcan Crusade, Jaime I heard mass on Christmas Eve 1228 in the cathedral of Santa Creu in Barcelona. Before the battle of Portopí, he assured his troops that "God is with us and we will defeat them. Each one should think about confessing and doing penance for his sins." Then on Christmas Day, and again on New Year's Eve, the king and his army heard mass, confessed their sins, and received communion. During the siege of Borriana and again while laying siege to Peñíscola he heard the mass of the Holy Spirit and the office of the Virgin Mary "so that He and his Mother might direct us in this affair and in all the others that we undertake." Just before the battle of Puig de la Cebolla, the crusaders "heard mass and those who had not received the body of Jesus Christ did so . . . and commended themselves to our Lord."[30]

The literary texts written in the crusading era transposed these liturgical practices to an earlier epoch. The early thirteenth-century *Poem of the Cid*, for example, related that before battling the Muslims, the Cid promised his men that "God will aid us," and announced that "Bishop Jerome will give us absolution; he will say mass for us." On the following morning the bishop said: "Whoever dies fighting here, I take away his sins and God will have his soul." Then he asked the Cid to allow him to strike the first blows. In several other passages Bishop Jerome celebrated mass and gave absolution. The later-thirteenth-century *Poem of Fernán González* described how the Castilians, rising from sleep, "went to hear mass, to confess themselves to God. . . . All men, both great and small . . . repented of the evil that they had done, all received the consecrated host, and from the heart all asked God's mercy."[31]

The custom of giving blessed bread to the faithful after mass was a very old one and was evidently observed during the Spanish crusades. In 1138 the leaders of the Toledan militia urged their followers: "confess your sins to one another, pray, and receive the blessed bread that you have with you, and God will have mercy on your souls." During the siege of Lisbon, after mass, a Flemish priest noticed that the bread blessed for distribution was bloody. When cleansed with a knife the bread was suffused with blood just as flesh would bleed when cut. After the blessed bread was broken into fragments, the blood remained and continued to be seen for many days after the fall of the city. Some witnesses, in a seeming condemnation of some of crusaders, saw it as a sign that although they were on a pilgrimage, some people "had not yet given up their thirst for human blood." Another contemporary recording this portent stated that "the people about to go to battle, after the solemnities of mass were completed, wished to be fortified with blessed bread or *eulogiae*."[32]

In addition to the exhortations of bishops and priests, military leaders also appealed for God's help. Before the battle of Cuart the Cid "manfully comforted and encouraged his men and unceasingly and devoutly entreated the Lord Jesus Christ to lend divine aid to his troops." When attacking Bairén, he assured his men that "today Our Lord Jesus Christ will deliver them [the Muslims] into our hands." In like manner, Munio Alfonso, the *alcaide* of Toledo, before engaging the Muslims at Montiel, went down on bended knee and prayed:

O great Virgin of Virgins, intercede for us before your son our Lord Jesus Christ and, if you will deliver us, we will faithfully give to your church in Toledo a tenth of all that you gave us or will give us. O St. James, apostle of Christ, defend us in battle, lest we perish in the great judgment of the Saracens.[33]

The dialogue between Alfonso VIII of Castile and Archbishop Rodrigo at Las Navas de Tolosa was probably typical of many such encounters:

"Archbishop, you and I will die here." He replied: "never, for you will overcome your enemies here." The king, unconquered in spirit, then said: "Let us hasten to aid those first put in danger." . . . Then the king said again: "Archbishop here we will die. . . . A death in such circumstances is not worthy." . . . But he said: "If it please God, let it be not death but the crown of victory; but if it should please God otherwise, we are all prepared to die together with you."[34]

When the crusaders en route to Mallorca encountered a great storm, they wanted to turn back, but Jaime I declared that he was undertaking this journey "with faith in God to convert them [those who did not believe in God] or to destroy them, and to restore that kingdom to the faith of Our Lord." During another storm he prayed: "Lord, my Creator, help me, if it pleases you, in this great peril . . . for I am going on this voyage to exalt the faith that you have given us and to humiliate and to destroy those who do not believe in you." During the battle of Portopí Ramon de Montcada declared that "the Saracens are great people, but God will be with us; let each one be strong of heart and with good hope in God and we will bravely fight them." As they prepared to enter the fray, Guillem de Montcada urged the crusaders to "combat the enemies of Jesus Christ. . . . Stirred by the love of God and determined to die for Him, if necessary, they were very happy."[35]

At times pagan superstition intruded, as, for example, when the militia of Ávila, after hearing mass and doing penance, armed themselves and consulted the flight of birds about the possibilities of victory. The *Poem of the Cid* mentioned that he also consulted the flight of birds. The practice may have been fairly common.[36]

The Use of Religious Banners

The religious character of the military enterprise was exemplified by banners carried by troops both as a form of identification and as a rallying point, but also as a symbol of the cause for which they were fighting. As we have seen when the Visigothic monarch went to war the bishop presented him with a golden cross, which, together with the army's standards, was carried from the church. That custom probably continued into the age of the crusades.[37]

By the end of the first millennium the use of religious banners had become commonplace. Although Alexander II supposedly sent a banner to the crusaders attacking Barbastro, that seems to be an erroneous interpretation of Ibn Ḥayyān's remarks. There is no evidence that the popes ever sent banners to the Spanish kings. Nevertheless, it seems reasonable to surmise that the bishops, like their Visigothic counterparts, blessed banners before battle. When Pedro I appeared before Zaragoza "with Christ's standard" he presumably carried a banner with a representation of Christ on it. The church of San Isidoro in León conserves the so-called *pendón de Baeza*, a banner said to date from Alfonso VII's victory at Baeza in 1147, but more likely from the early thirteenth century (see Figure 8). The king, attributing his triumph to St. Isidore, had a silk standard embroidered in his honor. Portrayed on a red background, the figure of the mitred saint, dressed in gold and mounted on horseback, carries a cross in his left hand and a sword in his right. On the right side of the banner an arm bearing a sword, reported to be that of St. James, reaches down from the clouds, nearly touching a star. Castles and lions, the royal arms of Castile and León, are quartered on a shield and are also depicted separately across the top of the banner. Fernando II of León's description of himself as "the standardbearer of Saint James" suggests that he carried a standard bearing the saint's image.[38]

A standard portraying the Virgin Mary, protector and patron of Toledo and of Spain, was borne at Las Navas de Tolosa. The figures of Mary and her Son were superimposed on the king's standards. Alberic of Trois Fontaines related that the Virgin appeared to a sacristan at the French Marian shrine of Rocamadour instructing him to take a banner depicting the Virgin and Child to the king; at Mary's feet was the sign, probably a castle, that appeared customarily on the royal standard. The banners were carried "joyfully" to the enemy camp. The archiepiscopal banner on which "the cross of the Lord" and the image of Holy Mary were represented was usually carried before the archbishop by a canon of Toledo; but, according to Rodrigo, the banner miraculously passed over the Muslim lines and remained there, unharmed, until the end of the battle. Alfonso VIII informed the pope that the Muslims "threw stones and arrows at [the cross and the standard bearing Mary's image]" but turned in flight.[39]

After the battle Alfonso VIII ordered the erection of a church at Las Navas where the archiepiscopal cross and other trophies (including a royal scepter) could be displayed. The royal standard was kept by a confraternity of Santa Cruz at Vilches, and later in the nearby church of Santa Elena; it was returned to Vilches around 1654 and placed in the parish church of San Miguel. The spread of Marian devotion lay behind the decision to depict her on the royal standards. Fernando III's standard, representing the Virgin, was preserved in the cathedral of Seville. The banner illustrated in *Cantiga* 181, showing the seated Virgin Mary holding the Infant Jesus in her arms, was likely the same type carried at Las Navas and in Fernando III's campaigns.[40]

Whereas banners portraying Mary and the saints were commonplace, kings often wanted to have more tangible evidence of saintly assistance.

Figure 8. The pendón of Baeza. Iglesia Colegiata de San Isidoro, León.

Thus, Alfonso I always carried with him "an ark made of pure gold, adorned within and without with precious stones," containing "the wood of the cross of salvation." He also had "ivory caskets covered with gold and silver and precious stones containing the relics of Holy Mary, the cross of the Lord, of the apostles, martyrs, confessors, virgins, patriarchs and prophets." Priests celebrated daily mass over these relics guarded in the chapel next to the king's tent. During the siege of Fraga he "ordered the holy relics of his chapel to be brought out," and swore not to abandon the siege. At the same time, Robert Burdet, count of Tarragona, and his men struck many blows against the Muslims, "shouting on high the name of Jesus." The king's defeat at Fraga regrettably resulted not only in his death but also in the loss of the golden ark, the other caskets, and the royal chapel.[41]

Invocation of the Saints and Saintly Intervention in Battle

In the heat of battle soldiers were wont to cry out words of encouragement to one another and to call on the saints for help. Before the battle of Fraga, for example, priests and people beseeched God "to rip them from the hands of the Saracens and not to be mindful of the sins of the king nor of his relatives and those who were with him." Christian soldiers facing the Almoravids "cried out to the God of the heavens and the earth and to Holy Mary and to St. James in prayer to aid and defend them." In an engagement outside Seville, the Muslims called on Muḥammad, while the Christians "cried out to the Lord God, to Holy Mary, and St. James to have mercy on them and to forgive the sins of their kings, of themselves, and of their relations." The leaders of the Toledan militia, after appealing to Jesus and Mary, pleaded: "O St. James, Apostle of Christ, defend us in battle lest we perish in a great judgment with the Saracens."[42]

The crusaders besieging Alcácer do Sal called on Santiago and São Vicente, "the patron of that region." Jaime I and the Catalans at Portopí and again during the assault on Palma invoked the Virgin Mary. During the siege of Seville Pelay Pérez Correa, master of Santiago, and his knights "in manly voice called God and Santiago to their aid." The thirteenth-century literary texts also reflect the habits of the real world of combat. The *Poem of the Cid* reported that "the Moors call on Muḥammad and the Christians on Santiago." In another passage the Cid exhorted his knights: "In the name of the Creator and the Apostle Santiago, strike them." The *Poem of Fernán González* also commented that "they began the struggle . . . calling on Santiago, the honored Apostle." While war cries of a religious nature were used, the *Chronicle of Ávila* reported that the urban cavalry shouted, "Ávila, knights!" More than likely commanders also urged their soldiers onward by proclaiming the name of their town or kingdom. In the battle of Jerez in 1231 the Christians cried out "Santiago, and at times, Castile."[43]

The invocation of God and the saints unfortunately did not always have a positive outcome. Although the Christians prayed for victory at Fraga, "their prayers were not heard before God, on account of their sins, because the Archangel Gabriel, the chief messenger of God did not take them before Christ's tribunal, nor was Michael, the commander of the heavenly militia, sent by God to aid them in battle." From the eleventh century onward western Europe had become familiar with the cult of the warrior St. Michael the Archangel, who assured triumph in battle to his adherents.[44]

Appeals to the saints for help were sometimes answered, or so it was said, by the direct intervention in various battles from the ninth century to the early thirteenth of such celestial visitors as St. James, St. Isidore of Seville, San Millán de la Cogolla, and St. George.

The tomb of the Apostle James (usually identified with James the Great rather than James the Less), whom late medieval legend described as Santiago Matamoros—Saint James the Moorslayer—reportedly was discovered in the ninth century at the site later known as Santiago de Compostela; but three centuries passed before there was any mention of his appearance in battle. Writing about 1118, the anonymous monk of Silos related that prior to attacking Coimbra Fernando I made a pilgrimage to Compostela to implore "the Apostle to intercede for him before the divine majesty, so that his campaign would have a happy and successful outcome." While the king "assaulted Coimbra with the material sword, James, the knight of Christ, did not cease to intercede" before God for victory. During the siege, a Greek pilgrim, hearing people speaking of Santiago as a "good knight," noted that he was not a knight and had never mounted a horse, but that night while the pilgrim was at prayer, the Apostle appeared and rebuked him. Indeed there appeared "a most splendid horse of great stature" whose "snowy brilliance illuminated the whole church through the open doors." Mounting the horse, St. James showed the pilgrim the keys that on the morrow would open Coimbra to the king. In this instance the Apostle did not appear in battle nor did he use any weapon, though he did carry the keys to open the city gates.[45]

St. James supposedly first appeared in the battle of Clavijo in the ninth century. According to a privilege dated in 844, on the eve of battle he told King Ramiro I of Asturias (842–850) that "eternal rest is already prepared for many of your people, for they are about to receive the crown of martyrdom." He also said: "I will come to your aid and on the morrow by the hand of God you will overcome the countless multitude of Saracens.... You and the Saracens will see me on a white horse ... bearing a great white banner." On the next day after the troops had confessed their sins, heard mass, and received communion, the Apostle appeared in their midst. As he commanded, they shouted, "May God and St. James help us!" We are told that this was the first recorded usage of this war cry.[46] Again, Santiago was not armed nor did he engage in combat, but he did encourage the Christians. The image of the warrior clothed in white and mounted on a white horse is reminiscent of the Apocalyptic horseman described in Revelation 19: 11.

In gratitude for his victory Ramiro I reportedly granted the church of Compostela certain tributes from the entire people. The so-called Privilege of the Vows of Santiago recording this marvelous occurrence is universally acknowledged today as a twelfth-century forgery. Even so, Archbishop Rodrigo, who usually displayed balanced judgment, could not bring himself to repudiate this tale outright; he somewhat sceptically reported that St. James "was said to have appeared on a white horse bearing a standard in his hand" and that the Christians thereafter used the war cry, "O God and St. James, help us!"[47]

About the middle of the twelfth century a tympanum over one of the doors on the south side of the cathedral of Santiago depicted a bearded St. James mounted on a horse and bearing a sword in his right hand and a standard in his left with the inscription *Sanctus Iacobus Apostolus Christi*.[48] This is the oldest portrayal of the Apostle on horseback, but while he carries a sword aloft—the first recorded instance of his wielding a sword—he is surrounded not by Muslims, but by persons kneeling in prayer with their hands clasped in supplication.

St. James sometimes had helpers. Among them was St. Emilian or San Millán de la Cogolla (d. 574). The thirteenth-century priest-poet Gonzalo de Berceo described the wondrous intervention of the two saints in the battle of Simancas in 939. Refusing to bow to the caliph's demand for a tribute of one hundred maidens, King Ramiro II (930–51) promised an annual tribute to Saint James if he would assure him of victory. Not to be outdone, Count Fernán González pledged a similar tribute to San Millán. During the battle the troops saw "two heavenly knights mounted on white horses, armed and ready for battle." The Christians looked to the sky and "saw two handsome and shining persons, whiter than the recent snows, coming on two horses whiter than crystal, bearing arms that no mortal man had ever seen. The one held a crozier and a pontifical miter, and the other, a cross, such that man had never seen." As the Christians threw themselves on their knees, promising to atone for their sins, the heavenly horsemen descended with swords in hand, striking and routing the Muslims. The two warriors were believed to be St. James, with the miter and crozier, and San Millán, with the cross.[49] On the distribution of the spoils, the king and the count paid the tributes promised to their respective saintly patrons. Just as the Privilege of the Vows of Santiago was falsified, so also the Privilege of the Vows of San Millán, Berceo's source, was forged early in the thirteenth century.[50]

The chroniclers are inexplicably silent on the failure of St. James to appear in any subsequent battles until the thirteenth century. Nevertheless Lucas of Túy, seemingly willing to believe almost anything, stated that during Alfonso IX's victory at Alange "the blessed St. James visibly appeared in this battle with a host of white knights, who valiantly overthrew the Moors." The Apostle was not described as a warrior participating in the battle or wielding any weapons. In the battle of Jerez in 1231, according to the *Estoria de Espanna*, the Christians, shouting "Santiago" or "Castiella," waded into the enemy. "They say, and the Moors themselves later affirmed this, that St. James appeared on a white horse with a white banner in his hand and a sword in the other and there was with him a legion of white knights; they also say that they saw angels above them in the air, and it seemed to them that these white knights, more than any others, destroyed them [the enemy]."[51]

After obtaining the remains of St. Isidore of Seville from the Muslim king of Seville, Fernando I interred them in the newly-built church of San Isidro in León. Lucas of Túy recorded that during the siege of Baeza while Alfonso VII slept, the "blessed confessor" appeared to him, saying that "he himself had been given to him and to his people as defender." Urging the king to attack vigorously, Isidore declared that the enemy would disappear like smoke. After routing his opponents Alfonso VII established in León a confraternity in memory of the saint's miraculous intervention. Even more fanciful is the version of this story given in Lucas's *Liber de miraculis Sancti Isidori*, incorporated into the Spanish translation of his chronicle. In this account a white-haired man, dressed in episcopal garments, with a face shining like the sun, and accompanied by a right hand brandishing a fiery sword, appeared to the king in a dream. When the king inquired the apparition's identity, the reply was "I am Isidore, doctor of the Spains, successor in grace and preaching to the fortunate Apostle James. This right hand is that of the Apostle James, defender of Spain." When Alfonso VII related this vision, his followers proposed to establish a confraternity in Isidore's honor. They also agreed that when the battle was joined they would call upon both saints. While the king slept before the battle, Isidore appeared again, saying that he would take the confraternity under his protection and promised that both Muslim and Christian princes would be subject to his dominion. The *pendón de Baeza*, described above, commemorates this event.[52]

There are still other stories of Isidore's intervention. When Fernán Rodríguez, *el Castellano*, and the Muslims attacked Ciudad Rodrigo, St. Isidore supposedly revealed their coming so that Fernando II could save the city. Lucas also related that Isidore, in a vision, affirmed that he would be in the saintly host to assure victory to Alfonso IX at Alange. Lucas's continuator stated that Fernando III, with the help of Santiago "the patron and defender of all Spain," triumphed in several skirmishes during the siege of Seville. Once the city surrendered the king visited San Isidro at León and prayed to St. Isidore, who had "always shown [himself] to be the helper and defender of the kings of Spain," and promised to give him a share in the spoils of his conquest.[53] St. James was the patron of León, but St. Isidore provided some competition. In addition, the Castilian Berceo endeavored to exalt a Castilian saint, San Millán, to near equal status.

Nevertheless, none of these saints cut much of a figure in Aragón and Catalonia, although Jaime I related that he received the name of the Apostle James. Despite that, the great warrior saint of the Crown of Aragón was St. George whose cult began to develop in the west in the eleventh century. The participants in the First Crusade claimed that St. George and other saints, and an army of angels, mounted on white chargers with white banners, appeared during the battle of Antioch. A fourteenth-century Aragonese chronicler fabricated the fantastic story that a German knight, seated behind St. George on his horse, was transported unknowingly from Antioch to Alcoraz outside Huesca. There, with St. George's help, Pedro I defeated the king of Zaragoza and dedicated the church of San Jorge de las Boqueras in the saint's honor. The fact that the siege of Antioch occurred in 1098 while the battle of Alcoraz was fought in 1096 points up the absurdity of this tale.[54]

It is more likely, although the source of the story is also late, that Pedro I sought the intercession of the martyr St. Victorian, whose remains were honored at the monastery of Montearagón; indeed, after the death of Sancho I at Huesca, the new king brought his father's body to Montearagón prior to eventual burial at San Juan de la Peña. "Comforted by the martyr's prayer," Pedro I repulsed the enemy. However that may be, devotion to St. George had likely taken root and prompted the king to dedicate a church in his honor. Zurita added that Pedro I adopted the cross of St. George on a silver field. The Military Order of San Jorge de Alfama founded by Pedro II in 1201 on the Valencian frontier also expressed devotion to this saintly patron of Aragón and Catalonia.[55]

Jaime I, a lover of a good story, seems to have indulged in wishful thinking when he recorded St. George's appearance during the assault on Palma. "As the Saracens told us," said the king, "the first to enter on horseback was a white knight with white arms, and we believe that he was St. George since we find in histories that Christians and Saracens saw him in other battles." The king's evidence was hearsay, because he did not claim to have seen St. George. Burns described the king as "neither credulous nor agnostic." Jaime I made no further mention of the saint's appearance, but a fourteenth-century chronicle reported that he was seen in the battle of Puig. Many years later a Franciscan reported that an angel dressed in white had appeared to him in a vision and told him that "a king of Aragón named James" would save Spain from the Mudejar uprising of 1264. In spite of his scepticism Jaime I could not resist recounting this story.[56]

Two other examples of miraculous interventions should be noted. As the crusaders advanced toward Las Navas they were unable to find a passage through the mountains and "decided to ask divine assistance. . . . God sent a certain person in the guise of a shepherd who spoke secretly to the glorious king, promising to show, to whomever he should designate, a place quite nearby through which the whole army could cross the highest mountains without danger." According to the *Latin Chronicle*, "it was believed by those who know rightly that that was not an ordinary man but some divine power that came to the aid of the Christian people in such difficulty, because even though so many military commanders, so many shepherds, so many friars of Calatrava had often crossed through those places, none of them knew anything about that place; nor did the shepherd appear afterward." Archbishop Rodrigo described the shepherd as a "messenger from God."[57]

During the Crusade of Alcácer do Sal onlookers declared that the standard of the cross appeared in the sky as a sign of a future Christian victory. Furthermore, a heavenly host of knights all clad in white showered their arrows, blinding the Muslims who turned in flight. Unlike St. James and the other saints mentioned above, knights from heaven actively participated in this battle, wounding and killing the enemy. The cross in the sky, of course, is reminiscent of Constantine's victory at the Milvian Bridge. The appearance of the heavenly host here probably encouraged the author of the thirteenth-century *Poem of Fernán González* to announce that angels in white armor would appear in battle; "each one will bear the cross on his banner."[58]

In assessing this one ought to emphasize that there is no mention in any chronicle or authentic document written before the twelfth century of saintly participation in battle. The documents concerning the vows of Santiago and San Millán are outright forgeries. When recording tales of saintly intervention the chroniclers made no claim to be eyewitnesses. The stories told do not usually present their heroes as warrior saints striking deadly blows at the Muslims, but rather as assuring victory on the eve of battle to an anxious king or military leader. On occasion the saint may appear in the battle, but his brilliant presence, usually dressed in white garments and mounted on a white steed, rather than his warlike skill seems to have been sufficient to guarantee victory. Only on the tympanum of Santiago de Compostela and the banner of Baeza are St. James and St. Isidore respectively depicted with sword in hand. Of course, those who saw the saint wielding a sword had every reason to believe that it was not borne in vain. The stories also suggest difficulties in establishing one of the saints as the overall patron of Spain. Although the Apostle James could claim a higher rank and was venerated especially in Galicia and León, regional loyalties suggested that St. Isidore in León, San Millán in Castile, and St. George in the Crown of Aragón were equally efficacious protectors of Spain. Despite all that, when the crusaders reported wondrous occurrences in the heat of battle they took them as signs of God's favor and assurance of victory.

The Idea of Martyrdom

Twelfth-century crusading ideology expressed the belief that those who confessed their sins and received absolution would gain eternal life if they were killed in battle; they would also be accounted as martyrs. Delaruelle argued that it was natural that the ancient doctrine of martyrdom should be extended to Christians who fell combatting the Muslims, for they were witnesses to Christ, suffering death for his sake. St. Bernard elaborated this idea in his crusade preaching.[59]

There is ample evidence that those who died fighting the Muslims in Spain were considered martyrs. During the siege of Almería Bishop Arnaldo of Astorga urged the troops to confess their sins and promised that the gates of paradise would be open before them. While he did not use the word martyr, the concept is there in that the warrior giving his life for God is rewarded with eternal life. His hearers would not have been wrong if they assumed that they would be reckoned as martyrs. After the conquest of Lisbon the northern crusaders buried "the bodies of our martyrs" in the "sepulchre of the martyrs" outside the walls; two persons, hitherto mute, reportedly regained their speech, presumably through the martyrs' intercession. The *Latin Chronicle* stated that at Alarcos, God "sent the Moors to hell, but the Christians to eternal palaces." A hermitage dedicated to Santa María de los Martyres was erected outside the walls of Calatrava to honor those killed when the Muslims seized the fortress.[60]

Innocent III not only promised absolution to those who died at Las Navas, but also assured them of entrance into paradise. Encouraged by battlefield preachers, the troops, "their hearts stirred to martyrdom, unfurling the banners of the faith, and invoking the name of God, all advanced to the field of battle." Recounting his victory, Alfonso VIII lamented "that so few martyrs from such a great army went to Christ in martyrdom!" Archbishop Rodrigo proudly commented that the crusaders desired nothing "other than to suffer martyrdom or to win." The expectation of martyrdom was no doubt quite real. Preparing to take Puig de la Cebolla, Jaime I advised one noble: "if you should die in the service of God and ourself, there can be no doubt that you will gain paradise." About the same time Diego Pérez de Vargas exhorted the Christians defending Martos: "Those of us who . . . will die here today will save our souls and will go to the glory of Paradise." The Portuguese described as martyrs the knights who "shed their blood for the honor of the faith of Jesus Christ" at Tavira. A few years later Pelay Pérez Correa, master of Santiago, urged Afonso III not to be distressed over the loss of so many knights, "because they died in the service of God and for the salvation of their souls."[61]

The idea of eternal life in paradise if one were killed fighting the "infidels" also appears in literary and legal sources. In the *Poem of Fernán González*, the count declared that "all my vassals who died here will be avenged this day by their lord and all gathered with me in paradise." Alfonso X emphasized that "it is a sure thing that the one who dies in the service of God and for the faith passes from this life to paradise." His nephew, Juan Manuel, writing early in the fourteenth century, summarized the evolution of this idea:

Good Christians hold that the reason why God consented that Christians should receive so much harm from the Moors is so that they would have a reason to make war with them rightfully, and so that those who died in it, having fulfilled the commandments of Holy Church, should be martyrs, or that their souls should be released, by martyrdom, from the sins that they committed. . . . Sinners who die and who are killed by the Moors, if they die in defense and exaltation of the holy Catholic faith, have a greater hope of salvation than other sinners. . . . It is certain that all those who go to war against the Moors in true repentance and with a right intention . . . and die are without any doubt holy and rightful martyrs, and they have no other punishment than the death they suffer.

He also argued that Fernando III should be accounted a martyr because, although he did not die on the battlefield, he expended great energy in God's service.[62] Language such as this must have served as a powerful incentive, especially as preachers proclaimed to the troops that their cause was just, and that a heavenly reward awaited them if they fell in combat.

Whether victorious or not the survivors had to attend to the mournful task of burying their dead. After the death of Alfonso I the people of Zaragoza lamented: "O best defender, who have you named to defend us? For the Almoravids will now invade the kingdom that by royal power you ripped from the hands of the Saracens, and we will be captured without a defender." Men shaved their heads and tore their clothing while women scratched their faces, crying out: "the wrath of God has fallen on us for our sins." When it came time to bury those who had fallen at Portopí, Jaime I affirmed that they "have died in the service of God and of ourselves, and if we can redeem them, their death can be turned to life." After the fall of Tavira in 1242 six knights of the Order of Santiago and a merchant who had guided them were interred with great reverence in a tomb adorned with seven shields like the scallop shells of Santiago. Proper burial of one's comrades was a Christian duty, whereas the disposal of the bodies of the enemy was an unwelcome, though necessary, burden. The stench of dead bodies in Valencia after its capture was such that the bishops offered "1,000 days of pardon [indulgence] to each man who would remove one body from the city." Wood was gathered and the bodies were burned.[63]

The Providential Character of the Reconquest

The custom of attributing victory or defeat to God was an ancient one. God was thought to decide the outcome of battle, sometimes by miraculous means; in any case the divine decision was a judgment on the guilt or innocence of the contenders. Victory was gained because the people were pleasing to God and did God's will; conversely, defeat was a divine punishment for sin. From the earliest times the chroniclers, emphasizing that divine providence would restore liberty to the Christians, routinely referred victory or defeat to divine favor or displeasure. The twelfth-century *History of Rodrigo* declared that Alfonso VI, "by divine clemency," captured Toledo. The Cid, described as an "invincible warrior trusting in the Lord and in his mercy," reportedly prayed for divine aid before the battle of Cuart outside Valencia, and his subsequent triumph was declared to be a gift from God. After capturing Bairén he and his men "with all the devotion of their souls glorified God for the victory that God had given them . . . and returned to Valencia praising God."[64]

The affliction that could occur by ignoring God's will could be overcome by repentance, as the men of Salamanca discovered. Failing to trust in God, they suffered, but when they repented, God endowed them with the military skill and bravery needed to triumph over their enemies. Alfonso VIII's defeat at Alarcos was a sign that "the Lord God seemed to be angry with the Christian people," who "ignored the way of the Most High." And yet it was "by virtue of the cross of Christ [that] the king of Morocco was conquered" at Las Navas. Alfonso IX's victory at Alange similarly was attributed to "the aid of our Lord Jesus Christ" and Jaime I believed that, when he conquered Mallorca, God granted him a grace given to no other king of Spain.[65]

The heroes of the literary sources also appealed to God before battle and expressed gratitude for victories achieved through divine assistance. The Cid declared "With God's help I must begin this battle," and Fernán González appealed to Christ, saying "May Christendom be exalted by you today." After his victory at Valencia, the Cid stated: "I thank God who is on high that we have gained such a battle." When the Muslims routed the Visigoths at the Guadalete, according to the *Poem of Fernán González,* "the affair was . . . determined by God so that the people of Spain would be put to the sword." The defeated Christians recognized that "God has abandoned us who abandoned him, and what others won we have lost by abandoning God who has abandoned us." On the other hand, when the count of Castile defeated al-Manṣūr "the power of the Messiah was demonstrated there, and the count was David and Almanzor Goliath."[66]

This kind of language appears throughout the twelfth- and thirteenth-century sources and testifies to Christian awareness of a mortal struggle against Islam. Internecine conflicts among the Muslims prompted a Portuguese annalist to remark that God "had withdrawn his wrath" from the Christians which "he had directed against them in the time of King Rodrigo because of their sins . . . but now the Lord was pleased with his Christian people and averted his indignation from them and put a sword between the Ishmaelites and the Moabites, that is, the Andalusians against the Arabs."[67]

The Celebration of Victory

Once the battle was won the clergy intoned the Christian hymn of victory and thanksgiving, *Te Deum laudamus, Te Dominum confitemur.* The militia of Toledo, returned home in triumph, "praising and blessing the Lord." After still another victory, they returned to the city "with great joy and happiness, singing: '*Te Deum laudamus.*'" The bishops and the clergy similarly "raised their hands to heaven and sang the *Te Deum*" after the capture of Oreja. In the same manner the Genoese "rendered thanks to God for having given them such a great victory" at Almería.[68]

Following the triumph at Las Navas, Archbishop Rodrigo said to the king: "Be mindful of God's grace which supplied all your defects and lifted today the opprobrium tolerated for so long. Be mindful also of your knights with whose help you achieved such great glory." Then the prelates, with tears of devotion, raised their voices in the canticle of praise, *Te Deum laudamus.* The *Latin Chronicle* proclaimed that "the Christians can sing with the psalmist: 'Lord, Lord, my God, who train my hands for battle and my fingers for war, my compassion and my refuge, my safeguard and my liberator'" (Ps. 144: 1–2). When the Muslims handed the keys of Córdoba to Fernando III, he "gave thanks to our Savior and acknowledged that by his special mercy he had received such a great favor." Jaime I related that when he heard of the Christian victory at Puig de la Cebolla "we went to the cathedral . . . and with the bishop and the canons we sang *Te Deum laudamus.*"[69]

The literary sources also offer several examples of prayers of thanksgiving. Speaking of his victory over the Almoravids, the Cid announced that "God and all his saints wished this." Similarly, after defeating al-Manṣūr, Fernán González "gave thanks to God and to Holy Mary because he revealed to them such a great miracle."[70]

When a town or fortress was taken the victors often placed their banners on the walls in witness of their triumph. Placing the royal standards on the highest tower of Oreja, Alfonso VII's troops cried out in a loud voice: "Long Live Alfonso, Emperor of León and Toledo." Archbishop João of Braga and the other bishops bearing the sign of the cross, accompanied by Afonso I and the leaders of the crusade, made their solemn entrance into Lisbon and placed the cross on the highest tower. The clergy chanted the *Te Deum,* and the *Asperges me,* an antiphon of purification. In a symbolic act of possession the king traversed the walls on foot. When Jaime I saw his standard mounted on the highest tower of Valencia, he dismounted, turned to the east, and wept, kissing the ground in thanksgiving for God's great favor. The next day mass was celebrated there. Not many years before the author of the *Poem of the Cid* described the placement of Rodrigo's banner on the walls of Valencia.[71]

After the Muslims surrendered Córdoba, Fernando III ordered the cross to be carried before his own standard and placed on the highest tower of the mosque. "When the standard of the eternal king, accompanied by the standard of King Fernando, appeared for the first time on the tower, it caused confusion and ineffable lamentation among the Saracens and, on the contrary, ineffable joy to the Christians." Archbishop Rodrigo reported that when "the wood of the living cross" was raised on the main tower, everyone shouted with tears of joy, "God help us!" When the royal standard was placed next to the cross the clergy intoned the *Te Deum*. In like manner when the king's standard was raised on the tower of the alcázar of Seville, "all the Christians cried out 'God help us' and gave thanks to Our Lord."[72] Fernando III seems to have initiated the custom of placing the image of the Virgin Mary on the walls of conquered cities, including Toledo, Córdoba, and Seville.

Cleansing of Mosques and Consecration of Churches

While the victors customarily guaranteed religious freedom to the vanquished, they also took over the principal mosques and transformed them into churches. The cleansing of mosques of "the filthiness" of the Prophet Muḥammad and the celebration of Christian services was a manifestation of Christian possession and power. The ceremony of purification probably involved sprinkling of holy water while the clergy intoned the hymn, *Asperges me*: "Cleanse me with hyssop that I may be pure; wash me, make me whiter than snow" (Ps. 51: 9), as at Lisbon mentioned above. The Muslims had similarly purified captured towns and churches "from the filth of idolatry and . . . from the stains of infidelity and polytheism." Emotions attributed to the Visigoths by the *Poem of Fernán González* following their defeat at the Guadalete were likely similar to those of thirteenth-century Christians: "The churches were turned into stables, many wild follies were committed on the altars, treasures were robbed from sacristies, and Christians wept by night and day." Muslims no doubt had similar reasons for lamentation when in 1138 Alfonso VII ravaging upper Andalucía, "destroyed their synagogues [mosques] and burned the books of Muḥammad's law with fire. All the learned men of the law, wherever they were found, were put to the sword."[73]

After occupying Toledo Alfonso VI permitted the Muslims to retain their mosques, but the new Archbishop Bernard, a Frenchman, found that unacceptable; occupying the chief mosque during the king's absence, he cleansed it "of the filthiness of Muḥammad" and consecrated it as a church. The king was said to be annoyed, but did not alter the archbishop's action. Archbishop Amat of Bordeaux, after the fall of Huesca, similarly "consecrated the city and the synagogue of the pagans to the work of the Lord;" together with the bishops of Oloron and Lescar he cleansed the mosque and dedicated it as a church. After Tudela fell the chief mosque was dedicated in honor of Saint Mary. On occasions such as this the mass for the dedication of a church found in the Sacramentaries of Vich or Ripoll or others derived from the Gregorian Sacramentary was probably said.[74]

In Valencia, "in the house of the Saracens which they call a mosque," the Cid constructed a church in honor of the Virgin Mary. The "uncleanness of the barbarian people and the contamination of Muḥammad was swept" from the town of Coria after its capture in 1141 and "once all the filthiness of the pagans was erased from the city and its temple, they dedicated the church in honor of Holy Mary, ever Virgin, and of all the saints." After the fall of Lisbon on All Saints Day the mosque was cleansed by Archbishop João of Braga and four other bishops. When Alfonso VIII captured Alcaraz, "he was received in the town on the feast of the Ascension . . . with a solemn procession by the archbishop of Toledo, after the filth of the Moors was purged and they had left the town." In like manner after Fernando III seized Capilla, Archbishop Rodrigo, Bishop Tello of Palencia, and other clerics "cleansed the mosque of the Moors of all the filthiness of Muḥammadan superstition by the power of our Lord Jesus Christ and his most triumphant cross. They dedicated the church to the Lord Jesus Christ and celebrated mass and the divine offices with great joy." Jaime I, once he captured Palma, built a church there in honor of the Virgin Mary. The Portuguese transformed the mosque of Tavira into a church dedicated to Saint Mary of the Martyrs.[75]

After seizing Córdoba, Fernando III took possession of the great mosque that had been built on the site of a Christian church, which in turn was founded on the remains of a pagan temple. On a Sunday, around vespers, Bishop Juan of Osma and Master Lope, who had placed the cross on the tower of the mosque, entered the city. "After eradicating Muḥammadan superstition and filthiness, they sanctified the place by sprinkling holy water with salt so that what had formerly been a cubicle of the devil was made a church of Jesus Christ under the invocation of his glorious mother." On the next day, the king entered the city and went to the church, where the bishops of Osma, Cuenca, and Baeza, and all the clergy in a solemn procession received him honorably. After the bishop of Osma celebrated mass, the king occupied the palace of the Muslim kings. A decade later, accompanied by the clergy in procession, he entered the mosque of Jaén, now consecrated as a church in honor of Saint Mary. There, Gutierre, bishop of Córdoba, celebrated mass. Making a similar entrance into Seville two years later, the king was received by a great procession of bishops, clergy and people, giving thanks to God and praising the king's deeds. Gutierre, now archbishop-elect of Toledo, celebrated mass.[76]

The Triumphal Return from Battle

Once the campaign was concluded soldiers, whether victors or vanquished, their emotions varying widely depending on the outcome of the battle, returned home. The Visigothic *Liber ordinum* mentioned above contained a ceremony for the king's return from war, paralleling that for his departure. After a prayer asking God to protect the king, there followed a blessing, and other prayers, beseeching God to assure peaceful times, so that the king might rule in peace and justice.[77]

Reception of the king by a procession of ecclesiastics chanting psalms or other hymns seems to have been customary throughout Christian Spain even in peacetime during the era of the crusades. In 1134 the bishop and the clergy greeted Alfonso VII in the main square of Zaragoza and conducted him to the church of Saint Mary, singing "Fear God and keep His commandments" (Eccles. 12: 13). After the bishop gave a blessing, "according to royal custom," they repaired to the royal palace. His departure was also marked by a blessing and other hymns of praise. When he returned to Toledo after seizing Oreja the whole population, Christians, Muslims, and Jews alike, came out to meet him with drums, zithers, psalteries, and other instruments, praising and glorifying God: " 'Blessed is he who comes in the name of the Lord' (Matt. 21: 9) and blessed are you and your wife and your children and the kingdom of your fathers and blessed be your mercy and patience." Leading him through the Alcántara gate, Archbishop Raimundo and the clergy in procession received him in the plaza and accompanied him to the cathedral, chanting, "Fear God and keep His commandments."[78]

After routing the Muslims at Montiel in 1143 the militia of Toledo, singing a hymn and accompanied by captives in chains, entered by the Alcántara gate with the royal standards held on high and the heads of defeated

Muslim captains fixed on their lances. Queen Berenguela, Archbishop Raimundo, and the clergy and people received them at the cathedral, singing the *Te Deum*. There the archbishop blessed them and the king gave thanks to God "who delivered you from the sword of those kings and from the hands of the Saracens." The heads of the Muslims, put on public display as a sign of divine aid to the Christians, were taken down on the queen's orders, anointed with myrrh and aloes and wrapped in precious cloth, and, as a gesture of compassion, were sent to the widows in Córdoba. By contrast, Alfonso VIII, on returning to Toledo from Alarcos, "lamented and bemoaned that he had suffered such a grave disaster." When he entered the city after the triumph of Las Navas, however, "he was received with exultation and joy by all the people, who cried out and said: 'Blessed is he who comes in the name of the Lord.' " Fernando III similarly returned to Toledo "with great joy and honor" after taking Capilla and Córdoba.[79]

In thanksgiving for their success returning warriors often pledged a portion of the booty to the church. The militia of Toledo, victorious at Montiel, gave a tenth of the booty to the cathedral, as they had promised. The king received the royal fifth, but enemy standards, horses, mules, and other objects were sent to Santiago de Compostela. In 1148 Ramon Berenguer IV endowed a Christian church in newly conquered Tortosa, giving it all the goods pertaining to the chief mosque of the city. Following Las Navas, Alfonso VIII sent the caliph's tent to Innocent III, and the tent flap to Las Huelgas de Burgos. After the surrender of Córdoba Fernando III ordered the bells that al-Manṣūr had carried off from Santiago de Compostela in 997 and hung as lamps in the mosque of the city to be taken back to the Apostle's shrine.[80]

The literary sources again reflect traditional practices of the crusading era. In an act reminiscent of al-Manṣūr's display of the bells of Santiago, the Cid ordered Bishop Jerome to hang captured Almoravid drums in the cathedral of Valencia. Asking that a thousand masses be said, Rodrigo also sent gold and silver to the cathedral of Burgos. Fernán González lavished booty on the monastery of San Pedro de Arlanza, depositing tents, cups, gold vases, swords, shields, harnesses, and ivory boxes on the altar: "all with one voice gave thanks to God, and each one offered his jewels on the altar."[81]

As we have just seen, every effort was made to surround the military enterprise with liturgical rituals intended to encourage and to justify the actions to be undertaken. Not only did preachers assure the troops that God was on their side, aiding and protecting them, but they also assured them that they were taking part in a just war, pleasing to God. At times preachers also proclaimed the remission of sins given to crusaders. Before setting off to war, men, in expectation of death, made their wills and undoubtedly said their private prayers.[82] Communal prayers and hymns marked the departure of the army. Before engaging the enemy, soldiers confessed their sins and received absolution from the priests who celebrated mass for them and offered them the eucharist. During battle they cried out to God and the saints for help, and probably were willing to believe any rumor of saintly intervention on their side. Once victory was gained hymns of joy and celebration were sung, while the gruesome task of burying the dead was carried out. Sad though it might be, those who had fallen were now believed to have been received into heaven as martyrs.

Christian customs and practices characteristic of the wars of the crusading era were mirrored in the Islamic world. If one were to study in detail the Muslim chronicles and other sources one would discover that Muslim soldiers also believed that God was on their side; they too asked divine pardon before battle, and believed that if they were killed they would be admitted to paradise as martyrs.[83] Whether the Christians borrowed these habits from the Muslims misses the point that all of this arises from human nature, especially when strong religious belief is entirely integrated into the daily life of a community. A community concerned intensely with the service of God will always see the divine hand in all of its affairs.

Chapter 9
Epilogue

In contrast to the dismal failure of the oriental crusades to secure enduring Christian control over the Holy Land, crusading Spain expanded successfully in the twelfth and thirteenth centuries. By the middle of the thirteenth century the Christian reconquest was nearly complete, as only the kingdom of Granada, in feudal dependence on Castile, survived. That last semblance of Islamic rule was erased in 1492. Thus, whereas the crusades to the Holy Land ultimately failed, in part because of the difficulty of implanting an alien power and culture in a region far distant from western Europe, the home of the crusaders, the crusades in Spain were triumphant, depriving the Muslims of control of the Iberian peninsula and the Balearic Islands.

Christian success in Spain owed much to papal encouragement. Alexander II granted participants in a projected expedition into Spain a remission of sins comparable to later crusading indulgences. From then on Gregory VII, Urban II, Paschal II, and their successors took great interest in the struggle to drive the Muslims out of Spain, declaring that effort to be tantamount to the crusades to the Holy Land. Crusading bulls liberally sprinkled throughout the twelfth and thirteenth centuries give strong witness to papal recognition of the importance of the conflict between Christianity and Islam in the peninsula and helped to implant there the idea of the crusade. Not only did the popes grant plenary remission of sins to those taking part in the Spanish crusades, but they also gave partial remission to those who, unable to participate in person, made it possible for others to do so by contributing money. Furthermore, the popes helped to finance the Spanish crusades by conceding to the Christian rulers a portion of the twentieth intended for the Holy Land, the *tercias*, the *decima*, and other ecclesiastical subsidies. For the general European population the Christian conquest of the greater part of Spain did not have the emotional significance of the crusades simultaneously aimed at liberation of the Holy Places in Palestine. Nevertheless, while the existence of the crusader states in the east proved ephemeral, the Christian conquest of Spain, effected with the help of papal bulls of crusade, was permanent.

Given their success in conquering Muslim lands, it is not surprising that Christian authors adopted a triumphant tone, exalting the achievements of their fellow countrymen. In the thirteenth century Vincentius Hispanus boasted that "the Spaniards rule over Blessed Lady Spain," and a century later Álvaro Pelayo announced that the kings of Spain, unlike other kings, were not subject to the emperor, "because they have ripped their kingdoms out of the jaws of the enemy." Echoing the language of many papal bulls, Alfonso de Cartagena at the Council of Basel in 1435 emphasized that the kings of Spain "gained and seized their kingdoms from the teeth of their enemies."[1]

The Struggle for the Strait of Gibraltar

In the century following the fall of Seville the kings of Castile, the only Christian rulers whose frontiers were contiguous with Islamic Spain, attempted to gain control of the Strait of Gibraltar by securing possession of the peninsular ports that had given access to Moroccan invaders for many centuries. Indeed, from the third quarter of the thirteenth century until the middle of the fourteenth the Marīnids, a Muslim dynasty that rose to power on the ruins of the Almohad empire, invaded Spain and gave substantial support to the rebellious attitude of the kings of Granada, who were emboldened from time to time to repudiate their vassalage to Castile and to refuse payment of tribute.

Alfonso X initiated the effort to control the Strait by constructing shipyards at Seville, developing naval bases at Cádiz and El Puerto de Santa María on the Gulf of Cádiz, and obtaining crusade indulgences for a projected invasion of North Africa. The temporary seizure of Salé in 1260 on the Atlantic coast of Morocco was the only result of his *fecho de Africa*, but the capture of Niebla in 1262 on the Atlantic coast west of Seville strengthened his position near the Strait. The revolt of the Mudejars in 1264 interrupted his plans, and the invasions of the Marīnids after 1275 put him on the defensive for the rest of his reign. Four years later his attempt to take Algeciras ended in failure.[2] His son Sancho IV (1284–95) seized Tarifa, directly opposite Morocco, in 1292, and his men successfully defended it two years later. In the meantime the possibility of exploiting Africa was not forgotten as Sancho IV and Jaime II of Aragón (1291–1327) signed a treaty at Monteagudo on 29 November 1291 marking out spheres of influence and possible conquest there. The river Muluia was the line of demarcation between Morocco, reserved for Castile, and Tunis, where Aragón had a paramount interest.[3]

As the Crown of Aragón no longer bordered Islamic Spain, further expansion within the peninsula seemed precluded. Thus, Jaime I prepared for a crusade to the orient but never completed it, and, though he attended the Second Council of Lyon in 1274, he did not participate in the crusade then projected. After his son Pedro III (1276–85) seized Sicily and had to turn back a papal crusade launched against him, a long struggle for possession ended with the establishment of an independent kingdom there. Determined to gain further territory in Spain, Jaime II concluded a treaty with Fernando IV of Castile (1295–1312) at Alcalá on 18 December 1308, which assigned a sixth of the kingdom of Granada, including Almería, to Aragonese conquest. In the ensuing campaign, though aided by crusading indulgences, Jaime II's efforts to take Almería were unavailing, but Fernando IV captured Gibraltar in 1309. That proved to be a temporary success as the Muslims regained possession in 1333. Fernando IV's subsequent efforts to take Algeciras were unsuccessful.[4]

An old Muslim, forced to abandon his home as a result of the fall of Gibraltar, poignantly expressed the plight of his people to Fernando IV:

My lord, why do you drive me hence? When your great-grandfather King Fernando took Seville, he drove me out, and I went to live at Jerez; but when your grandfather [Alfonso X] took Jerez, he drove me out, and I went to live at Tarifa, thinking that I was in a safe place. Your father King Sancho came and took Tarifa and drove me out, and I went to live here at Gibraltar, thinking that I would not be in any safer place in the whole land of the Moors . . . but now I see that I cannot remain in any of these places, so I will go beyond the sea and settle in a place where I can live in safety and end my days.[5]

The inexorability of the Christian advance into Muslim territory was given explicit expression by Alfonso X's nephew, Juan Manuel, politician, warrior, and litterateur:

There is war between Christians and Moors and there will be until the Christians have recovered the lands that the Moors have taken from them by force. There would not be war between them on account of religion or sect, because Jesus Christ never ordered that anyone should be killed or forced to accept his religion.[6]

The last significant Muslim attempt to invade the peninsula was halted by Alfonso XI (1312–50), who, supported by a papal crusading bull and aided by Portuguese troops and Catalan ships, defeated the Marīnids at the battle of Salado on 30 October 1340. His success prompted Álvaro Pelayo to urge the king to expel the Muslims from Spain and to conquer Africa:

Africa, where the name of Christ was revered, but where Muḥammad is exalted today, belongs to you by right. The kings of the Goths, from whom you descend, subjected Africa to the faith. . . . Take it, as the other western lands, for it is yours by hereditary right. Because it is yours, subject it to the faith and take it in the name of Christ.[7]

Perhaps reflecting that counsel, the king wrote to Pope Clement IV in 1345 stating that "the acquisition of the kingdom of Africa, as is well known, belongs to us and to our royal right and to no one else."[8] Although the old Muslim mentioned above on leaving Gibraltar thought that he would be safe in Morocco, there is no doubt that the Castilians ultimately intended to occupy Moroccan seaports. In the second half of the thirteenth century, Juan Gil de Zamora remarked that "Africa was a province that belonged to the dominion of the Goths" and he prophesied that the kings of Spain "would acquire [lands] not only from sea to sea, but happily, also beyond." Before undertaking any action in Africa, however, Alfonso XI besieged Algeciras, capturing it in 1344. He then turned against Gibraltar on the opposite shore of the Bay of Algeciras but his death in 1350 brought the siege to an end, and it was not until 1462 that the Christians finally seized that great fortress.[9]

The Neglect of the Reconquest

The death of Alfonso XI interrupted the reconquest for nearly a century and a half. As a consequence of his victory at Salado and the subsequent decline of the Marīnids, the kingdom of Granada could no longer count on Moroccan assistance and so constituted no real danger to Christian rule. The Christian monarchs, therefore, failed to press the reconquest with any vigor until the close of the Middle Ages. Despite the distractions of civil and dynastic wars, however, Spanish Christians never accepted the idea that the kingdom of Granada should be allowed to exist forever. Remarking sadly that when "the Christians are at war [among themselves], the Moors are happy," Pedro López de Ayala, in the late fourteenth century, complained that knights, waging war every day to enrich themselves, "have forgotten to make their wars against the Moors, because in other broad lands they find enough to eat."[10] If the Muslims retained part of Spain, that, according to the fifteenth-century *Libro de la consolación de España*, was because of God's will and the sins of the Christians:

On account of our sins our Spain was held captive in the power of the Moors in the time of King Rodrigo, and not long ago the mercy of God delivered us from their power, although a small part still remains to them, and God consents to that because of our wicked life.[11]

Prior to the last years of the fifteenth century, only intermittent efforts were made to conquer the kingdom of Granada. Infante Fernando, the uncle and regent for Juan II (1406–54) of Castile, achieved the conquest of Antequera in 1410, but his election as king of Aragón two years later removed him from the Granadan frontier. Commenting on this, Fernán Pérez de Guzmán assured his readers that if the infante had not become king of Aragón he would have pressed the war against Granada and "would, without doubt, have conquered it." He remarked further that

if the sins of Castile had not provoked the indignation of our Lord . . . this noble infante undoubtedly would have put an end to the said war and would have returned Spain to her ancient possession, expelling the Moors from it and restoring it to the Christians.[12]

The poet Alfonso Álvarez de Villasandino called for the completion of the reconquest, urging Castilians "to conquer or to die in this very just, very holy, very worthy war"; he voiced the hope that Juan II would "bring down and destroy the vile dog, the sect of the false Muḥammad." Perhaps with the Castilian victory over the Muslims at La Higueruela in 1431 in mind, Alfonso de Cartagena, bishop of Burgos, proclaimed to the Council of Basel in 1435 that the king of Castile rendered greater services to the church than other monarchs precisely because he waged war against the "infidels." The king was engaged in extending the boundaries of Christendom, exalting the Catholic faith, and destroying the "cursed sect" of Muḥammad. This said the bishop, conformed to the church's desire "that the pagans and the barbarous nations and the infidels should be converted to the faith or destroyed."[13] This last remark introduced a hostile note that had not been heard before, but reflected an opinion increasingly held by highly placed Christian personages. Ironically, the monarch held up as a model Christian warrior, Juan II, was the most indolent of men, preoccupied with rivalries among the aristocracy and, with the exception of the campaign of La Higueruela, entirely neglectful of the war against Islam.

Thus when Ferdinand (1479–1516) and Isabella (1474–1504) restored internal peace to Castile and Aragón, the poets encouraged them to subjugate the kingdom of Granada as alien to Christian Spain. Diego de Valera urged them to prosecute "this holy and necessary war," so that "the enemies of our holy faith may be diminished and the land that they have usurped may be taken, and where God is now condemned, blasphemed and despised, he may be praised, adored, and loved." When the king and queen asked the pope in 1485 to grant the bull of crusade for the war against Granada, they declared that they hoped that "the holy Catholic faith would be increased and Christendom would be delivered from this continued threat at the gates [and] these infidels of the kingdom of Granada [will be] ejected and expelled from Spain." They also recalled that previous pontiffs had accepted "this war against Granada as no less just and necessary as that of the Holy Land."[14] Embarking on the final stage of the reconquest, they received the surrender of Muḥammad XII (Boabdil), the last king of Granada, in January 1492 and made their triumphal entrance into the city. Announcing their victory to the pope they proclaimed:

It pleased our Lord to give us a complete victory over the king and the Moors of Granada, enemies of our holy Catholic faith. . . . After so much labor, expense, death, and shedding of blood, this kingdom of Granada which was occupied for over seven hundred and eight years by the infidels . . . [has been conquered]."[15]

With that the territorial reconquest of Spain was concluded and the last great crusade of the Middle Ages was also finished.

Expansion into Africa

Fifteenth-century Spanish publicists called not only for the completion of the reconquest, but also for the extension of Spanish rule into North Africa. In the second quarter of the fourteenth century both Castile and Portugal had exhibited interest in the Canary Islands off the west African coast, but it was not until 1402 that a band of Norman adventurers established a colony there, with the support of Enrique III of Castile (1390–1406). Despite that, Portugal asserted its own claims and the issue continued to trouble relations between the two realms nearly to the end of the century. Alfonso de Cartagena, defending Castilian rights there, declared that "the conquest of that region of Africa beyond the sea formerly called Tingitana . . . and of the adjacent islands . . . usually called the Canary Islands" pertained to the king of Castile.[16]

Emphasizing Spanish pretensions in Africa, supposedly dating from

Visigothic times, Rodrigo Sánchez de Arévalo expressed the hope that the name and power of Enrique IV (1454–74) would resound there and that "those broad provinces which the famous King Theodoric and your progenitors peacefully held under the great monarchy of Spain, would be recovered." Similarly Diego de Valera affirmed that King Ferdinand had been chosen by God not only to rule the Spains, but also "to subjugate the lands beyond the sea to the glory and exaltation of our Redeemer, the increase of the Christian religion, and to the great honor and excellence of your royal crown."[17]

The ideal of restoring the Visigothic monarchy in its fullest extent demanded this, but on a more practical level the seizure of North African ports used by Muslim armies to invade Spain had long been a Christian objective. Portugal, having completed its territorial expansion in the peninsula in the thirteenth century, gained control of the eastern and western ends of the Strait of Gibraltar by the conquest of Ceuta in 1415 and Tangier in 1471. The Spaniards, supported by crusading benefits, occupied Melilla in 1497, Mazalquivir in 1505, and Oran in 1507. Subsequent efforts to expand that hold on the North African coast met with only partial success, however, and other considerations distracted the Christian monarchs from this enterprise.[18]

By that time the reconquest of Spain, an ideal affirmed so many times in the past, had been achieved, but Spanish ambitions in Africa were far less successful. In the meantime, the idea of crusade, forgotten perhaps in other parts of Europe, had become firmly embedded in the mentality of the people of Spain and Portugal, who were long accustomed to spiritual benefits given in exchange for monetary contributions. Given the fact that the peninsular struggle between Christians and Muslims was a thing of the past, the popes of the sixteenth, seventeenth, and eighteenth centuries attempted unsuccessfully to terminate the bull of crusade, which now served primarily as a source of royal revenue. Finally, in the Concordat of 1851 between Spain and the Papacy the contributions of the faithful were directed to the Church, rather than to the Crown, and were to be expended on works of charity. The most characteristic spiritual benefit extended by Pope Pius VI in 1778 to anyone making a small donation in support of the crusade was a dispensation from the requirement to abstain from meat during Lent.[19] That concession was finally abolished after the reforms of the rules of fasting and abstinence by the Second Vatican Council. With that bulls of crusade and crusading wars in Spain came to an end.

Abbreviations

AC—Archivo catedralicio

ACA—Arxiu de la Corona d'Aragó, Barcelona

AEM—Anuario de Estudios Medievales

AHDE—Anuario de Historia del Derecho Español

BA—Bullarium Ordinis Militiae de Alcantara. Ed. Ignacio José Ortega y Cotes et al. Madrid: Antonio Marín, 1759.

BAE—Biblioteca de Autores Españoles, 203 vols. thus far. Madrid: Real Academia Española, 1846–.

BC—Bullarium Ordinis Militiae de Calatrava. Ed. Ignacio José Ortega y Cotes. Madrid: Antonio Marín, 1761; reprint Barcelona: El Albir, 1981.

BRAH—Boletín de la Real Academia de la Historia

BS—Bullarium Equestris Ordinis Militiae Sancti Iacobi de Spatha. Ed. José López Agurleta. Madrid: Juan de Ariztia, 1719.

CAI—Chronica Adefonsi Imperatoris. Ed. Antonio Maya Sánchez. *Chronica hispana Saeculi XII,* Pars I. Ed. Emma Falque, Juan Gil, and Antonio Maya. *Corpus Christianorum. Continuatio Mediaevalis* 71. Turnhout: Brepols, 1990.

CAVC—Cortes de los antiguos Reinos de Aragón y de Valencia y Principado de Cataluña. 25 vols. Madrid: Real Academia de la Historia, 1896–1919.

CDACA—Colección de documentos inéditos de la Corona de Aragón. Ed. Prosper Bofarull et al. 41 vols. Barcelona: Imprenta del Archivo, 1847–1910.

CEM—Cuadernos de Estudiós Medievales

CGPIII—Crònica general de Pere III el Cerimoniós dita comunament Crònica de Sant Joan de la Penya. Ed. Amadeu-J. Soberanas Lleó. Barcelona: Alpha, 1961.

CHE—Cuadernos de Historia de España

CHR—Catholic Historical Review

CJI—Crònica de Jaume I. 9 vols. Ed. Joseph M. de Cascuberta and Enric Bagüe. Barcelona: Editorial Barcino, 1926–1962.

*CSI-AII—*Antonio Brandão. *Crónicas de Sancho I e Afonso II.* Ed. A. de Magalhâes Basto. Porto: Livraria Civilização, 1945.

CSII-AIII—Antonio Brandão. *Crónicas de Sancho II e Afonso III*. Ed. A. de Magalhâes Basto. Porto: Livraria Civilização, 1945.

CSJP—Crónica de San Juan de la Peña. Ed. Antonio Ubieto Arteta. Valencia: Anubar, 1961.

CSJP (tr)—*The Chronicle of San Juan de la Peña: A Fourteenth-Century Official History of the Crown of Aragón*. Tr. Lynn H. Nelson. Philadelphia: University of Pennsylvania Press, 1991.

CSM—*Cantigas de Santa Maria*. Ed. Walter Mettmann. 4 vols. Coimbra: Universidade de Coimbra, 1959–72; reprint 2 vols. Vigo: Edicions Xerais de Galicia, 1981.

DJI—Ambrosio Huici Miranda and María Desamparados Cabanes Pecourt. *Documentos de Jaime I de Aragón*, 2 vols. Valencia: Anubar, 1976.

DMP DR—*Documentos Medievais Portugueses: Documentos régios*, 1 vol. thus far. Lisbon: Academia Portuguesa de História, 1958.

DP—Demetrio Mansilla. *La documentación pontificia hasta Inocencio III (963–1216)*. Rome: Instituto Español de Estudios eclesiásticos, 1955.

EEMCA—*Estudios de la edad media de la Corona de Aragón*

ES—*España Sagrada*, 52 vols. Ed. Enrique Flórez et al. Madrid: Antonio Marín et al., 1754–1918.

HC—*Historia Compostellana*. Ed. Emma Falque Rey. *Corpus Christianorum. Continuatio Mediaevalis* 70. Turnhout: Brepols, 1988.

LFM—*Liber Feudorum Maior. Cartulario real que se conserva en el Archivo de la Corona de Aragón*. Ed. Francisco Miquel Rosell, 2 vols. Barcelona: CSIC, 1945–47.

MFIII—Miguel de Manuel Rodríguez, *Memorias para la vida del santo rey don Fernando III*. Madrid, 1800; reprint Barcelona: El Albir, 1974.

MGH SS—*Monumenta Germaniae Historica, Scriptores*. Ed. Georg H. Pertz et al. Hannover and Berlin: Hahn et al. 1826–.

MH—*Monumenta Henricina*. 15 vols. Coimbra: Commissão executiva das Conmemoraes do V Centenario do Morte do Infante D. Henrique, 1960–74.

PC—*Poem of the Cid*. Spanish Text by Ramón Menéndez Pidal. English Verse Translation by W. S. Merwin. New York: Meridian, 1975.

PCG—*Primera Crónica General*. Ed. Ramón Menéndez Pidal. 2 vols. Madrid: Gredos, 1955.

PFG—*Poema de Fernán González*. Ed. A. Zamora Vicente. Madrid: Espasa-Calpe, 1946.

PL—*Patrologiae Cursus Completus. Series Latina*. Ed. Jacques Paul Migne. 221 vols. Paris: Garnier, 1844–64.

PMH SS—*Portugalliae Monumenta Historica. Scriptores,* Ed. Alexandre Herculano and Joaquim da Silva Mendes Leal. 1 vol. in 3 parts. Lisbon: Academia Real das Ciencias de Lisboa, 1856–61.

QBS—Reinhold Röhricht. *Quinti Belli Sacri Scriptores minores.* Geneva: J. Fick, 1879.

RHGF—*Recueil des Historiens des Gaules et de la France.* Ed. Martin Bouquet et al. 24 vols. Paris: Academie des Inscriptions et Belles Lettres, 1738–1904.

Notes

Chapter 1

1. Roger Collins, *The Arab Conquest of Spain, 710–797* (Oxford: Blackwell, 1989); Évariste Lévi-Provençal, *Histoire de l'Espagne musulmane*, 3 vols. (Leiden: E.J. Brill, 1950); Richard Fletcher, *Moorish Spain* (Berkeley: University of California Press, 1992), 1–78; Hugh Kennedy, *Muslim Spain and Portugal: A Political History* (London: Longman, 1996).

2. Joseph F. O'Callaghan, *A History of Medieval Spain* (Ithaca, N.Y.: Cornell University, 1975); Bernard F. Reilly, *The Medieval Spains* (Cambridge: Cambridge University Press, 1993); Roger Collins, *Early Medieval Spain: Unity in Diversity, 400–1000* (New York: St. Martin's Press, 1983); Angus MacKay, *Spain in the Middle Ages: From Frontier to Empire, 1000–1500* (New York: St. Martin's Press, 1977).

3. See the classic exposition of the idea of reconquest in Ramón Menéndez Pidal, *The Spaniards in Their History*, tr. Walter Starkie (New York: W.W. Norton, 1950); Claudio Sánchez Albornoz, *España, un enigma histórico*, 2nd ed., 2 vols. (Buenos Aires: Editorial Sudamericana, 1962); José Antonio Maravall, *El concepto de España en la edad media*, 2nd ed. (Madrid: Instituto de Estudios Políticos, 1964), 249–341.

4. José Ángel García de Cortázar et al., *Organización social del espacio en la España medieval: La Corona de Castilla en los siglos VIII a XV* (Madrid: Ariel, 1985), 12–14; Jocelyn N. Hillgarth, *The Spanish Kingdoms, 1250–1516*, 2 vols. (Oxford: Clarendon Press, 1976), 1: 20, 105, 107, 109, 186, 248, 287, 316; Thomas N. Bisson, *The Medieval Crown of Aragon: A Short History* (Oxford: Clarendon Press, 1986), 10, 15–16, 18, 28, 160.

5. Derek W. Lomax, *The Reconquest of Spain* (London: Longman, 1978), 1–2, 173; Peter Linehan, *History and the Historians of Medieval Spain* (Oxford: Clarendon Press, 1993), 103, and ch. 4.

6. I use the editions of the *Chronique prophétique*, the *Chronique d'Albelda*, and the *Chronique d'Alphonse III* by Yves Bonnaz, *Chroniques asturiennes (fin IXe siècle)* (Paris: CNRS, 1987). Kenneth Baxter Wolf, *Conquerors and Chroniclers of Early Medieval Spain* (Liverpool: Liverpool University Press, 1990), 81–110, 158–77, includes translations of Isidore's *History of the Kings of the Goths* and of the *Chronicle of Alfonso III*. Collins, *Early Medieval Spain*, 225–27.

7. Justo Pérez de Urbel, *Sampiro, su Crónica y la Monarquía leonesa en el siglo X* (Madrid: CSIC, 1952); *Crónica del Obispo Don Pelayo*, ed. Benito Sánchez Alonso (Madrid: Sucesores de Hernando, 1924); *Historia Silense*, ed. Justo Pérez de Urbel and Atilano González Ruiz-Zorrilla (Madrid: CSIC, 1959).

8. Isidore of Seville, *Historia de regibus Gotorum, Wandalorum et Suevorum*, *MGH Auctores Antiquissimi* XI, *Chronica Minora*, 2: 267–303.

9. *Chronique d'Albelda*, 10–11; *Historia Silense*, 118, ch. 6; Juan Gil de Zamora, *Liber de preconiis Hispaniae*, ed. Manuel de Castro (Madrid: Universidad de Madrid, 1955), 21–22, 75, 235.

10. Álvaro Pelayo, *Espelho dos reis*, ed. Miguel Pinto de Meneses, 2 vols. (Lisbon: Universidade de Lisboa, 1956), 12; Antonio Rumeu de Armas, *España en el Africa atlántica*, 2 vols. (Madrid: CSIC, 1956–57), 2: 1–2, no. 1 (13 March 1345); Joseph F. O'Callaghan, "Castile, Portugal, and the Canary Islands: Claims and Counterclaims, 1344–1479," *Viator* 24 (1993): 291, 300–303.

11. *Primera Crónica General*, ed. Ramón Menéndez Pidal, 2 vols. (Madrid: Editorial Gredos, 1955), 2: 494, ch. 813.

12. The *Chronicle of 754* is edited as the *Continuatio Hispania*, MGH Auctores Antiquissimi XI, *Chronica Minora*, 2: 323–68, esp. 352–53, ch. 72; Wolf, *Conquerors*, 111–58; Linehan, *History*, 12–13.

13. *Chronique prophétique*, 7, ch. 5; *Chronique d'Alphonse III*, 37, ch. 5; *Chronique d'Albelda*, 18, ch. 6; *Historia Silense*, 118, ch. 6; *Crónica de San Juan de la Peña*, ed. Antonio Ubieto Arteta (Valencia: Anubar, 1961), 24–25; Rodrigo Jiménez de Rada, *Historia de rebus Hispaniae sive Historia Gothica*, ed. Juan Fernández Valverde, *Corpus Christianorum, Continuatio Mediaevalis* 72 (Turnhout: Brepols, 1987), 124–25, Bk. 4, ch. 8; the *De rebus Hispaniae* is also found in Rodericus Ximenius de Rada, *Opera*, ed. Francisco de Lorenzana (Madrid, 1793; reprint Valencia: Anubar, 1968), 1–208; *Chronica latina regum Castellae*, ed. Luis Charlo Brea, in *Corpus Christianorum, Continuatio Mediaevalis* 73, *Chronica Hispana Saeculi XIII* (Turnhout: Brepols, 1997), 35, ch. 1. There are three other editions of this chronicle: *Chronique latine des rois de Castille jusqu'en 1236*, ed. Georges Cirot (Bordeaux: Feret et Fils, 1913); *Crónica latina de los reyes de Castilla*, ed. Luis Charlo Brea (Cádiz: Universidad de Cádiz, 1984); *Crónica latina de los reyes de Castilla*, ed. Maria de los Desamparados Cabanes Pecourt (Valencia: Anubar, 1964). See also *The Latin Chronicle of the Kings of Castile*, tr. Joseph F. O'Callaghan (Tempe, Ariz.: ACMRS, 2002); Juan Gil de Zamora, *Liber de preconiis Hispaniae*, 181; *PCG*, 1: 558, ch. 312.

14. *Chronique d'Alphonse III*, 38–42, ch. 6.1, 6.2; *Chronique d'Albelda*, 23, ch. 36; Linehan, *History*, 102–3.

15. *Chronique d'Albelda*, 23, ch. 35; MS A of *Chronique prophétique*, 4, ch. 3.

16. *Chronique prophétique*, 3, ch. 2.1; ibid., 2, ch. 1–2. Isidore of Seville, *Historia*, 268, ch. 1d, identified the Goths with Gog; *Poema de Fernán González*, ed. A. Zamora Vicente (Madrid: Espasa-Calpe, 1946), 5, v. 15; *Crónica de 1344 que ordenó el Conde de Barcelos don Pedro Afonso*, ed. Diego Catalán and María Soledad (Madrid: Gredos, 1977), 197, ch. 127, and ibid., 302.

17. The *Chronique d'Albelda*, 24, ch. 44.1; ibid., 23, ch. 36, beginning with Pelayo, recorded the "*ordo regum gothorum*" of Oviedo; *Chronique d' Alphonse III*, 31; Linehan, *History*, 88–93.

18. *Historia Silense*, 119, ch. 8; Álvaro Pelayo, *Espelho*, 4; *Poema de Alfonso XI*, ed. Yo Ten Cate (Madrid: CSIC, 1956), 481, v. 146; Pedro López de Ayala, *Crónica del rey don Pedro*, BAE 66: 555–56, n. 2.

19. Fernán Pérez de Guzmán, *Generaciones y Semblanzas*, ed. J. Domínguez Bordona (Madrid: Espasa-Calpe, 1965), 11; Diego Enríquez del Castillo, *Crónica de*

Enrique IV, BAE 70: 104, ch. 6, and 123, ch. 43; Diego de Valera, *Doctrinal de Principes,* in *Prosistas castellanos del siglo XV,* ed. Mario Penna and Fernando Rubio, 2 vols. *BAE* 116, 171 (Madrid: Real Academia Española, 1959–64), 116: 173, prologue; Alfonso de Cartagena, *Discurso,* ibid., 116: 208; Maravall, *Concepto,* 299–341.

20. *Memorial Histórico Español,* 50 vols. (Madrid: Real Academia de la Historia, 1851–1963), 3: 456 (29 November 1291).

21. *Chronique d'Albelda,* 24–26, ch. 38, 46–47; *Historia Roderici* in *Chronica Hispana Saeculi XII,* ed. Emma Falque, Juan Gil, and Antonio Maya, *Corpus Christianorum, Continuatio Mediaevalis* 71 (Turnhout: Brepols, 1990), 50, ch. 10; *Chronica latina,* 35–36, ch. 2, and 39, ch,. 5; Juan Gil de Zamora, *Liber de preconiis Hispaniae,* 125, ch. 32, and 232–34, ch. 6.

22. *PCG,* 2: 772–73, ch. 1132.

23. José Salarrullana and Eduardo Ibarra, *Documentos correspondientes al reinado de Sancho Ramírez,* 2 vols. (Zaragoza: M. Escar, 1904–13), 1: 187–89, no. 48 (1192).

24. Demetrio Mansilla, *La documentación pontificia hasta Inocencio III (965–1216)* (Rome: Instituto Español de Estudios eclesiásticos, 1955), 40, 43, 46, 50, 59, 65, nos. 24 (10 October 1088), 27 (15 October), 29 (1 July 1089), 32 (1 July 1091), 45 (6 March 1101). See also ibid., 21–25, 61, 65, 67, 76, 79, 80, 89, 92, 97, nos. 13 (28 June 1077), 42 (26 April 1100), 47 (3 November 1109), 59 (3 November 1121), 62 (2 April 1121–1124), 63 (23 June 1124), 72 (13 May 1144), 76 (27 May 1146), 80 (6 January 1150); Damian J. Smith, "¿'Soli Hispani'? Innocent III and Las Navas de Tolosa," *Hispania Sacra* 51 (1999): 500.

25. *The Tibyān: Memoirs of ʿAbd Allāh b. Buluggīn, last Zīrid Emir of Granada,* tr. Amin T. Tibi (Leiden: E.J. Brill, 1986), 103, ch. 6.

26. Ibn ʿIdhārī, *Al-Bayān al-Mugrib,* 4 vols., ed. Évariste Lévi-Provençal, Georges Colin, and I. ʿAbbās (Paris: P. Geuthner, 1930; Leiden: E.J. Brill, 1948; Beirut: Dar al-Thaqafair, 1967), 3: 282; the translation is by David Wasserstein, *The Rise and Fall of the Party Kings: Politics and Society in Islamic Spain, 1003–1086* (Princeton, N.J.: Princeton University Press, 1985), 250.

27. Ramón Menéndez Pidal, *La España del Cid,* 4th ed. 2 vols. (Madrid: Espasa-Calpe, 1947), 2: 822; Claudio Sánchez Albornoz, "La potestad real y los señoríos en Asturias, León y Castilla," in his *Estudios sobre las instituciones medievales españolas* (México: Universidad Autónoma de México, 1965), 799, 802, and *España,* 1: 301–10; Vicente Cantarino, "The Spanish Reconquest: A Cluniac Holy War Against Islam?" in *Islam and the Medieval West,* ed. Khalil I. Semaan (Albany: State University of New York Press, 1980), 82–109.

28. James Turner Johnson, *The Holy War Idea in Western and Islamic Traditions* (University Park: Pennsylvania State University Press, 1997); Peter Partner, *God of Battles: Holy Wars of Christianity and Islam* (Princeton, N.J.: Princeton University Press, 1997); Thomas Patrick Murphy, ed., *The Holy War* (Columbus: Ohio State University Press, 1974); Jean Flori, *La Guerre sainte: La formation de l'idée de Croisade dans l'Occident chrétien* (Paris: Presses Universitaires de France, 2001).

29. Janina M. Safran, "Identity and Differentiation in Ninth-Century al-Andalus," *Speculum* 76 (2001): 573–98; Jessica A. Coope, *The Martyrs of Córdoba: Community and Family Conflict in an Age of Mass Conversion* (Lincoln: University of Nebraska

Press, 1995); Kenneth B. Wolf, *Christian Martyrs in Muslim Spain* (Cambridge: Cambridge University Press, 1988); Edward Colbert, *The Martyrs of Córdoba (850–859): A Study of the Sources* (Washington, D.C.: Catholic University of America Press, 1962); Thomas E. Burman, *Religious Polemic and the Intellectual History of the Mozarabs, c. 1050–1200* (Leiden: E.J. Brill, 1994).

30. *Vita S. Anastasii, PL* 149: 429. D. M. Dunlop, "A Christian Mission to Muslim Spain in the Eleventh Century," *Al-Andalus* 17 (1952): 263–290; Benjamin Kedar, *Crusade and Mission: European Approaches Toward the Muslims* (Princeton, N.J.: Princeton University Press, 1984), 42–43, 45.

31. James Kritzeck, *Peter the Venerable and Islam* (Princeton, N.J.: Princeton University Press, 1964); Charles J. Bishko, "Peter the Venerable's Journey to Spain," in *Petrus Venerabilis, 1156–1956: Studies and Texts Commemorating the Eighth Centenary of His Death*, ed. Giles Constable and James Kritzeck (Rome: Herder, 1956), 163–76; Marie-Thérèse d'Alverny, "Deux traductions latines du Coran au Moyen Âge," *Archives d'histoire doctrinale et littéraire du Moyen Âge* 16 (1947): 69–131; Marie-Thérèse d'Alverny and Georg Vajda, "Marc de Tolède, traducteur d'Ibn Tūmart," *Al-Andalus* 16 (1951): 99–140, 249–307; 17 (1952): 1–56.

32. Pérez de Urbel, *Sampiro*, 346, ch. 30; *Crónica de Juan II, BAE* 68: 281, Año 1, ch. 11; ibid, 314, Año 3, ch. 5; Diego de Valera, *Memorial de diversas hazañas, BAE* 70: 4, ch. 3, and *Cancionero castellano del siglo XV*, ed. R. Foulché-Delbosc 2 vols. (Madrid: Bailly-Bailliére, 1912–15), 2: 332; Hernando del Pulgar, *Crónica de los señores reyes católicos Don Fernando y Doña Isabel de Castilla y Aragón, BAE* 70: 390, ch. 23. In the early thirteenth century Rodrigo, *Historia*, 270, Bk. 8, ch. 9, spoke of a *bellum Domini*.

33. Jaime Oliver Asín. "Orígen árabe de 'rebato,' 'arrobda,' y sus homónimos," *Boletín de la Real Academia Española* 15 (1928): 542; Américo Castro, *La realidad histórica de España*, new ed. (México: Porrua, 1962), 419–20.

34. W. Montgomery Watt, "Islamic Conceptions of the Holy War," in Murphy, *Holy War*, 141–56; W. Madelung, "Jihād," *Dictionary of the Middle Ages* 7 (1986): 110–11; D. B. Macdonald, "Djihād," *Encyclopedia of Islam* 1 (1934): 1041–42, and "Djihād," *Shorter Encyclopedia of Islam*, ed. H.A.R. Gibb and J. H. Kramers (Ithaca, N.Y.: Cornell University Press, 1974), 89; Gustave von Grunebaum, *Medieval Islam: A Study in Cultural Orientation* (Chicago: University of Chicago Press, 1961), 9–10.

35. Al-Ḥimyarī, *Kitāb ar-Rawd al-Mi'ṭar*, tr. Mª Pilar Maestro González (Valencia: Anubar, 1963), 17; 'Īsā ibn Ahmad al-Rāzī, *Anales palatinos del Califa de Córdoba al-Hakam II*, tr. Emilio García Gómez (Madrid: Sociedad de Estudios y Publicaciones, 1967), 267, ch. 230; Georges Marçais, "Ribāṭ," *Encyclopedia of Islam* 3 (1936): 1150–53, and "Ribāṭ," *Shorter Encyclopedia of Islam*, 473–75; Oliver Asin, "Orígen," 540–42; Castro, *Realidad*, 408.

36. Lucas of Túy, *Crónica de España*, ed. Julio Puyol (Madrid: Revista de Archivos, Bibliotecas y Museos, 1926), 445–46, ch. 101.

37. Louis J. Swift, *The Early Fathers on War and Military Service* (Wilmington, Del.: Michael Glazier, 1983); C. John Cadoux, *The Early Christian Attitude to War* (New York: Seabury, 1982); Ron Musto, *The Catholic Peace Tradition* (Maryknoll, N.Y.: Orbis, 1986).

38. *Contra Faustum*, 22: 75, *PL* 42: 448; *Ad Optatum*, Ep. 189, *PL* 33: 855–56; *De*

civitate Dei, 4: 6, *PL* 41: 116–17; R. Hartigan, "Saint Augustine on War and Killing," *Journal of the History of Ideas* 27 (1966): 195–204; Robert A. Markus, "Saint Augustine's Views on the Just War," *Studies in Church History* 20 (1983): 1–13.

39. Frederick Russell, *The Just War in the Middle Ages* (Cambridge: Cambridge University Press, 1975); Étienne Delaruelle, "Essai sur la formation de l'idée de croisade," *Bulletin de litterature ecclésiastique publié par l'Institut catholique de Toulouse* 42 (1941): 24–45, 86–103. See the reprint: *L'idée de croisade au Moyen Âge* (Turin: Bottega d'Erasmo, 1980).

40. John Gilchrist, "The Papacy and War Against the 'Saracens,' 795–1216," *International History Review* 10 (1988): 174–97; H. E. J. Cowdrey, "The Genesis of the Crusades: The Springs of Western Ideas of Holy War," in Murphy, *Holy War*, 9–32, especially 19; James A. Brundage, "Holy War and the Medieval Lawyers," ibid., 99–140; I. S. Robinson, "Gregory VII and the Soldiers of Christ," *History* 58 (1973): 169–92.

41. Joseph F. O'Callaghan, "The Mudejars of Castile and Portugal in the Twelfth and Thirteenth Centuries," and Robert I. Burns, "Muslims in the Thirteenth-Century Realms of Aragon: Interaction and Reaction," in *Muslims Under Latin Rule, 1100–1300*, ed. James M. Powell (Princeton, N.J.: Princeton University Press, 1990), 11–56, 57–102.

42. Ron Barkai, *Cristianos y musulmanes en la España medieval (El enemigo en el espejo)* (Madrid: Rialp, 1984); Eva Lapiedra Gutiérrez, *Cómo los musulmanes llamaban a los cristianos hispánicos* (Alicante: Instituto de Cultura Juan Gil Albert, 1997); Aziz al-Azmeh, "Mortal Enemies, Invisible Neighbors: Northerners in Andalusi eyes," in *The Legacy of Muslim Spain*, ed. Salma Khadra Jayyusi, 2 vols. (Leiden: E.J. Brill, 1994), 259–72. For the general Western European view of the Muslims see Norman Daniel, *Islam and the West: The Making of an Image* (Edinburgh: University of Edinburgh Press, 1960).

43. Ibn ʿAbd al-Ḥakam, *Conquista de Africa del Norte y de España*, tr. Eliseo Vidal Beltrán (Valencia: Anubar, 1966), 38–39; *Crónica anónima de ʿAbd al-Raḥmān III al-Nāṣir*, ed. E. Lévi-Provençal and Emilio García Gómez (Madrid-Granada: CSIC, 1950), 111, 121, 129, 131, 134, ch. 9, 22, 30, 34, 36; Ibn Ṣāḥib al-Salā, *Al-Mann bil-Imāma*, tr. Ambrosio Huici Miranda (Valencia: Anubar, 1969), 12; al-Marrākushī, *Kitāb al-Muʾyib fî Taljīṣ Ajbār al-Magrib*, tr. Ambrosio Huici Miranda (Tetuán: Editora Marroquí, 1955), 6, 9; Lapiedra Gutiérrez, *Cómo los musulmanes*, 67–285; 316–20, 326–35; Barkai, *Cristianos y musulmanes*, 62, 68–69, 72–74; Cristina Grandá Gallego, "Otra imagen del guerrero cristiano (su valoración positiva en testimonios del Islam)," *En la España medieval* 5, 1 (1986): 471–80.

44. *Chronique prophétique*, 3–5, ch. 3; Kenneth B. Wolf, "The Earliest Spanish Christian Views of Islam," *Church History* 55 (1986): 281–93, and "Christian Views of Islam in Early Medieval Spain," in John Victor Tolan, ed., *Medieval Christian Perceptions of Islam: A Book of Essays* (New York: Garland, 1995); Barkai, *Cristianos y musulmanes*, 19–53.

45. Pérez de Urbel, *Sampiro*, 322, ch. 22; *Historia Compostellana*, ed. Emma Falque; *Corpus Christianorum, Continuatio Mediaevalis* 70 (Turnhout: Brepols, 1988); *Gesta comitum Barchinonensium*, ed. L. Barrau Dihigo and J. Massó Torrents (Barcelona: Fundació Concepció Rabell i Cibils and Institut d'Estudis Catalans, 1924), 5: ch. 2; Rodrigo, *Historia*, 234, Bk. 7, ch. 14, and *Historia arabum*, in *Opera*, 242–83; PFG,

226 226 Notes to Pages 16–19

24, vv. 82–83; *Libro de Alexandre,* in *Poetas castellanos anteriores al siglo XV,* ed. Tomás Antonio Sánchez, Pedro José Pidal, and Francisco Janer (Madrid: M. Rivadeneyra, 1864), line 2346.

46. *PFG,* 70, 77, vv. 231, 250–52; *Historia Roderici,* 84, ch. 53–54. The expression *inimici crucis Christi* comes from St. Paul's Letter to the Philippians, 3: 18.

47. *Continuatio Hispana,* 344, 359; Pérez de Urbel, *Sampiro,* 376, ch. 22; Fernán Pérez de Guzmán, *Generaciones,* 93–94.

48 *Chronica Byzantina-Arabica, MGH Auctores Antiquissimi* XI. *Chronica Minora,* 2: 338. See Kenneth B. Wolf, "The Earliest Latin Lives of Muḥammad," in *Conversion and Continuity: Indigenous Christian Communities in Islamic Lands, Eighth to Eighteenth Centuries,* ed. Michael Gervers and Ramzi Jibran Bikhazi (Toronto: Pontifical Institute of Mediaeval Studies, 1990), 89–101. Wolf edited the eleventh-century *Istoria de Mahomet.* See the works cited in n. 32 above and Barkai, *Cristianos y musulmanes,* 22–27, 35–38.

49. *Chronique d'Albelda,* 21, ch. 24; *Chronique prophétique,* 4–6, ch. 3–4. This life of Muḥammad was also used by Eulogius of Córdoba, *Liber apologeticus martyrum,* ch. 16; Colbert, *Martyrs,* 336–38. The life of Muḥammad attributed to Joannes Minimus in Alvarus of Córdoba, *Epistolae,* 6, *PL* 121: 460–61, described Muḥammad as prince of the Arabs, a heretic, a pseudo-prophet, and the precursor of Anti-Christ.

50. Rodrigo Jimenez de Rada, *Historia arabum,* 242–48, ch. 1–6. Lucas, *Crónica de España,* 202–5, Bk. 3, ch. 5. Juan Gil de Zamora, *Liber de preconiis Hispaniae,* 73, ch. 5: 10.

51. *Chronica Naierensis,* ed. Juan A. Estévez Sola, in *Chronica Hispania Saeculi XII, Pars II, Corpus Christianorum, Continuatio Mediaevalis 71 A* (Turnhout: Brepols, 1995), 111, Bk. 2, ch. 17; *PFG,* 80, vv. 267–68; *Libro de Alexandre,* l. 2346; *Crónica de 1344,* 84, ch. 71; *Poema de Alfonso XI,* 481, vv. 138, 140, 147; Fray Martín de Córdoba, *Jardín de las doncellas,* proemio, in Penna and Rubio, eds., *Prosistas, BAE* 171: 68.

52. *Historia Silense,* 176, ch. 71; Gonzalo de Berceo, *La Vida de San Millán de la Cogolla,* ed. Brian Dutton (London: Tamesis, 1967), v. 369. Bishop Sampiro dismissed al-Manṣūr's title, meaning victorious, as a false name, remarking that he had not been victorious in the past nor would he be in the future. Pérez de Urbel, *Sampiro,* 344, ch. 30. The *Song of Roland,* vv. 68, 73, employed Almanzor (al-Manṣūr) as a generic name for Muslim warriors.

53. Abilio Barbero and Marcelo Vigil, *Sobre los orígenes sociales de la Reconquista* (Barcelona: Ariel, 1974); Yves Bonnaz, "Divers aspects de la continuité wisigothique dans la monarchie asturienne," *Mélanges de la Casa de Velázquez* 12 (1976): 81–99; Isabel Montenegro y Arcadio del Castillo, "Don Pelayo y los orígenes de la reconquista," *Hispania* 180 (1992): 5–32. See additional studies cited by Manuel González Jiménez, "¿Re-conquista? Un estado de la cuestión," in Eloy Benito Ruano, *Tópicos y realidades de la Edad Media* (Madrid: Real Academia de la Historia, 2000), 155–78.

54. Richard Fletcher, "Reconquest and Crusade in Spain, c. 1050–1150," *Transactions of the Royal Historical Society* 5th ser., 37 (1987): 34.

55. Charles Julian Bishko, "The Spanish and Portuguese Reconquest, 1095–1492," in Kenneth Setton, ed., *A History of the Crusades,* 5 vols. (Philadelphia and Madison:

University of Pennsylvania Press and University of Wisconsin Press, 1955–85), 3: 396–97; Collins, *Early Medieval Spain*, 268; Lomax, *Reconquest*, 1–2, 173; Linehan, *History*, 103.

56. MacKay, *Spain*, 1–3; Claudio Sánchez Albornoz, "The Frontier and Castilian Liberties," in A. R. Lewis and T. F. McGann, eds., *The New World Looks at Its History* (Austin: University of Texas Press, 1965), 26–46.

57. Joaquín Arrarás, ed., *Historia de la cruzada española*, 35 vols. (Madrid: Ediciones españolas, 1939–43); Peter Linehan, "Religion, Nationalism, and National Identity in Medieval Spain and Portugal," *Studies in Church History* 18 (1982): 161–99, and *History*, 205–7.

58. José Goñi Gaztambide, *Historia de la bula de la cruzada en España* (Vitoria: Editorial del Seminario, 1958), ch. 3, esp. p. 46. Luis García Guijarro, *Papado, Cruzadas, Órdenes Militares, Siglos XI–XIII* (Madrid: Cátedra, 1995), ch. 4, discussed the evolution of the concept of crusade without reference to Spain. James F. Powers, "The Early Reconquest Episcopate at Cuenca, 1177–1284," *CHR* 87 (2001): 1 remarked: "The Christian Iberian Reconquest is often assumed by scholars outside of the peninsula (and sometimes by those within it) to be a part of the crusading movement."

59. Robert I. Burns, "The Many Crusades of Valencia's Conquest (1225–1280): An Historiographical Labyrinth," in *On the Social Origins of Medieval Institutions: Essays in Honor of Joseph F. O'Callaghan*, ed. Donald J. Kagay and Theresa M. Vann (Leiden: E.J. Brill, 1998), 167–78.

60. Paul Rousset, *Histoire des croisades* (Paris: Payot, 1957), 33–34; Hans Eberhard Mayer, *The Crusades*, tr. John Gillingham (New York: Oxford University Press, 1972), 19–20.

61. Setton, ed., *A History of the Crusades;* Bishko, "The Spanish and Portuguese Reconquest, 1095–1492," ibid., 3: 396–456.

62. Steven Runciman, *A History of the Crusades*, 3 vols. (Cambridge: Cambridge University Press, 1953); James A. Brundage, *Medieval Canon Law and the Crusader* (Madison: University of Wisconsin Press, 1969).

63. Jonathan Riley-Smith, *What Were the Crusades?* (London: Macmillan, 1977), 15, and *The Crusades: A Short History* (New Haven, Conn.: Yale University Press, 1987); Christopher Tyerman, *The Invention of the Crusades* (Toronto: University of Toronto Press, 1998).

Chapter 2

1. Bernard F. Reilly, *The Contest of Christian and Muslim Spain, 1031–1157* (Cambridge: Blackwell, 1992), 1–73; David Wasserstein, *The Rise and Fall of the Party Kings: Politics and Society in Islamic Spain, 1003–1086* (Princeton, N.J.: Princeton University Press, 1985).

2. Richard Fletcher, *The Quest for El Cid* (New York: Alfred Knopf, 1990).

3. *Gesta comitum*, 6, ch. 3 (rp = *redacció primitiva*), and 32, ch. 11 (rd = *redacció definitiva*); *CSJP*, 52; *CSJP(tr)*, 16–17, 47–48, chs. 6, 29; *Crònica general de Pere III el Cerimoniós dita comunament Crònica de Sant Joan de la Penya*, ed. Amadeu-J. Soberanas

Lleó (Barcelona: Alpha, 1961), 31, 57–59, 91–93, ch. 6, 16, 29; *Chronicon Conimbricense, Chronicon Complutense sive Alcobacense, Chronicon Lamecense*, and *Chronicon Laurbanense, PMH SS* 1: 2, 18–20; *Historia Silense*, 183–209, chs. 80–106; *Chronica Naierensis*, 153–70, Bk. 3, ch. 4–12; Rodrigo, *Historia*, 184–94, Bk. 6, ch. 6–13; Pilar Blanco Lozano, *Colección diplomática de Fernando I (1037–1065)* (León: CSIC, 1987).

4. *Historia Silense*, 119, ch. 7, and 193, ch. 90; *Chronica Naierensis*, 160, Bk. 3, ch. 7; Bernard F. Reilly, *The Kingdom of León-Castilla Under King Alfonso VI, 1065–1109* (Princeton, N.J.: Princeton University Press, 1988); Andrés Gambra, *Alfonso VI: Cancillería, Curia e Impero*, 2 vols. (León: Centro de Estudios e Investigación "San Isidoro," 1997).

5. Charles Julian Bishko, "Fernando I and the Origins of the Leonese-Castilian Alliance with Cluny," in his *Studies in Medieval Spanish Frontier History* (London: Variorum, 1980), No. II, and "Liturgical Intercession at Cluny for the King-Emperors of León," *Studia Monastica* 3 (1961): 53–76.

6. Samuel Loewenfeld, ed., *Epistolae pontificum Romanorum ineditae* (Leipzig: Veit, 1885), 43, no. 82; Erdmann, *Origin*, 138–39; Rousset, *Histoire*, 30; Marcel Villey, *La Croisade: Essai sur la formation d'une théorie juridique* (Paris: J. Vrin, 1942), 69; Goñi Gaztambide, *Historia*, 49–52.

7. Cowdrey, "The Genesis of the Crusades: The Springs of Christian Ideas of the Holy War," in Murphy, *Holy War*, 9–32; Goñi Gaztambide, *Historia*, 50–51; Brundage, *Canon Law and the Crusader*, 24–25, 145–46; Jean Flori, "Reforme, *reconquista*, croisade (L'idée de reconquête dans la correspondance pontificale d'Alexandre II à Urbain II), in his *Croisade et Chevalerie (XIe–XIIe siécles)* (Paris: De Boeck & Larcier, 1998), 51–80.

8. Alexander II, *Epistolae, PL* 146: 1386–87. Goñi Gaztambide, *Historia*, dated the letter about May 1064 when the Catalan assembly banned the killing of Jews. The pope's letter was later included in Gratian's *Decretum*, C. 23, q. 8, c. 11; Norman Zacour, *Jews and Saracens in the Consilia of Oldradus de Ponte* (Toronto: Pontifical Institute of Mediaeval Studies, 1990), 16–19, 47–53; Loewenfeld, *Epistolae*, 43, no. 83.

9. Goñi Gaztambide, *Historia*, 51; Menéndez Pidal, *España*, 1: 147; Marcelin Dufourneaux, *Les français en Espagne aux XIe et XIIe siècles* (Paris: Presses Universitaires de France, 1949), 131–35; Reilly, *Contest*, 69; Mayer, *Crusades*, 19; Runciman, *Crusades*, 1: 91.

10. Paul Kehr, *Papsturkunden in Spanien: Vorarbeiten zur Hispania Pontificia*, 2 vols. (Berlin: Weidmannsche Buchhandlung, 1926), 1: 267–69, no. 11 (17 April 1063); Ferran Soldevila, *Història de Catalunya*, 3 vols. (Barcelona: Alpha, 1962), 1: 101.

11. Federico Balaguer, "Los límites del obispado de Aragón y el concilium de Jaca de 1063," *EEMCA* 4 (1950): 68–138, appendix 135–38; Jaime Villanueva, *Viage literario a las iglesias de España*, 22 vols. (Madrid: Imprenta Real, 1803–52), 6: 308–9, no. 31; Fidel Fita, "Cortes y usages de Barcelona en 1064: Textos inéditos," *BRAH* 17 (1890): 385–428; Jerónimo Zurita, *Anales de la Corona de Aragón*, ed. Ángel Canellas López, 9 vols. (Zaragoza: CSIC, 1967–85), 1: 69–72; *Historia Silense*, 189–91, chs. 86–87.

12. Alberto Ferreiro, "The Siege of Barbastro, 1064–65: A Reassessment," *Journal of Medieval History* 9 (1983): 129–44, esp. 133–35; Pierre Boissonade "Cluny, la papauté et la première grande croisade internationale contre les sarrasins d'Espagne," *Revue*

des questions historiques 60 (1932): 257–301, and "Les prémiers croisades françaises en Espagne," *Bulletin Hispanique* 36 (1934): 5–28. Erdmann, *Origin*, 136–40; H. E. J. Cowdrey, "Cluny and the First Crusade," *Revue bénédictine* 83 (1973): 289, 291–300.

13. Ibn Ḥayyān, quoted by al-Maqqarī, *The History of the Mohammedan Dynasties in Spain*, tr. Pascual de Gayangos, 2 vols. (London: W.H. Allen, 1840–43), 2: 265–70, Bk. 7, ch. 5; Reinhart Dozy, *Recherches sur l'histoire et la littérature de l'Espagne pendant le moyen âge*, 3rd ed., 2 vols. (Paris, Maisonneuve, 1881), 2: 335–53; Jacinto Bosch Vila, "Al-Bakri: Dos fragmentos sobre Barbastro," *EEMCA* 3 (1947–48): 242–61; *Gesta comitum*, 12, ch. 8 (rp) and 33, ch. 12 (rd). I am indebted to Professor Chevedden for reviewing the variant Arabic texts of Ibn Ḥayyān. He concluded that the correct translation is "commander of the cavalry of Rome," and not "cavalry of the Romans" or "the Christians;" that would require insertion of the definite article: "*al-rūm or al-rūmiyah*." Chevedden thinks that Al-Bakrī's reference to the commander as "*al-Biyuṭbīn*" is a corruption of Crispin.

14. Amato of Montecassino, *Storia de' Normanni*, ed. Vincenzo de Bartholomaeis, *Fonti per la Storia d'Italia* 76 (Rome: Tipografia del Senato, 1935), 13–15, Bk. 1, ch. 5–7; *La Chronique de Saint-Maixent, 751–1140*, ed. Jean Verdon (Paris: Société de l'Édition Les Belles Lettres, 1979), 136; *Chronicon Turonensis*, RHGF 11: 160–62; *Historiae Francicae fragmentum* and Hugh of Fleury, *Historia*, RHGF, 12: 461, 796; Jean Verdon, "Une source de la reconquête d'Espagne: La Chronique de Saint-Maixent," *Mélanges offerts á René Crozet*, 2 vols. (Poitiers: Société d'Études Médiévales, 1966), 1: 273–82; Menéndez Pidal, *España*, 1: 147–51.

15. Salarrullana, *Sancho Ramírez*, 1: 7–8, no. 3 (February 1068); Paul F. Kehr, "El papado y los reinos de Navarra y Aragón hasta medios del siglo XII," *EEMCA* 2 (1946): 14–21, and "Cómo y cuándo se hizo Aragón feudatario de la Santa Sede," *EEMCA* 1 (1945): 285–326; Antonio Durán Gudiol, *La iglesia de Aragón durante los reinados de Sancho Ramírez y Pedro I, 1062–1104* (Rome: Iglesia Nacional Española, 1962), 21–26, 52–54; I. S. Robinson, "Gregory VII and the Soldiers of Christ," *History* 58 (1973): 169–92.

16. *DP*, 10–13, nos. 5–6 (30 April 1073).

17. Suger, *Vita Ludovici Grossi*, ch. 5, PL 186: 1260; *Historiae Francicae Fragmentum*, RHGF, 12: 1–2; José María Lacarra, *Alfonso el Batallador* (Zaragoza: Guara Editorial, 1978), 15; Erdmann, *Origin*, 155–56; Defourneaux, *Les français*, 138–39; Menéndez Pidal, *España*, 1: 230–33.

18. *DP*, 21–25, no. 13 (28 June 1077); Joseph F. O'Callaghan, "The Integration of Christian Spain into Europe: The Role of Alfonso VI of León-Castile," in *Santiago, Saint-Denis, and Saint Peter: The Reception of the Roman Liturgy in León-Castile in 1080*, ed. Bernard F. Reilly (New York: Fordham University Press, 1985), 102–4.

19. *The Tibyān*, 90, ch. 5; 'Abd Allāh, *El Siglo XI en 1ª Persona: Las "Memorias" de 'Abd Allāh, último rey Zirī de Granada destronado por los Almorávides (1090)*, tr. Evariste Lévi-Provençal and Emilio García Gómez (Madrid: Alianza, 1980), 153–62, and "Les Mémoires de 'Abd Allāh, dernier roi Ziride de Grenade," tr. Evariste Lévi-Provençal, *Al Andalus* 3 (1935): 233–344; 4 (1936–39): 29–143; 6 (1941): 1–63.

20. *Crónica del Obispo Don Pelayo*, ed. Benito Sánchez Alonso (Madrid: Sucesores de Hernando, 1924), 81–82; *Chronica Naierensis*, 177–78, Bk. 3, ch. 20; *Historia*

Silense, 120, ch. 9; *Chronicon Conimbricense, Chronicon Complutense sive Alcobacense,* and *Chronicon Lamecense, PMH SS* 1: 2, 18–19; Rodrigo, *Historia,* 203–5, Bk. 6, ch. 22–23; *Chronicon Turonensis, RHGF,* 12: 464; al-Maqqarī, *History,* 2: 262–64, Bk. 7, ch. 5, and Ibn al-Kardabūs, *Kitábu-l-iktifá,* ibid., 2: xxvii–xxxi.

21. Gambra, *Alfonso VI,* 2: 224–29, 264–66, nos. 86 (18 December 1086), 101 (9 November 1089); *DP,* 43–45, 64–66, nos. 27 (15 October 1088), 45 (6 March 1101).

22. *Crónica del Obispo don Pelayo,* 83; *Chronica Naierensis,* 178, Bk. 3, ch. 2; *Chronicon Lusitanum, ES* 14: 416–18; *Chronicon Conimbricense, Chronicon Complutense sive Alcobacense,* and *Chronicon Lamecense, PMH SS* 1: 2, 18–19; *Historiae Francicae fragmentum, Chronicon Sancti Petri Vivi Senonensis,* and Hugh of Fleury, *Historia, RHGF* 12: 2–3, 279, 797; *Chronique de Saint-Maixent,* 148; *The Tibyān,* 114–17, ch. 7; Ibn Abī Zarʿ, *Rawd al-Qirtas,* tr. Ambrosio Huici Miranda, 2 vols. (Valencia: Anubar, 1964), 1: 281–93; *Al-Ḥulal al-Mawshiyya, Crónica árabe de las dinastías almorávide, almohade, y benimerín,* tr. Ambrosio Huici Miranda (Tetuán: Editora Marroquí, 1951), 51–76; al-Marrākushī, *Kitāb,* 101–6; Ibn Khaldūn, *Histoire des Berbères et des dynasties musulmanes de l'Afrique septentrionale,* tr. Baron de Slane, 4 vols. (Paris: P. Guenther, 1852–56), 2: 59–64, 67–85, 154–56; al-Maqqarī, *History,* 2: 270–303, Bk. 7, ch. 5–6, Bk. 8, ch. 1, and Ibn al-Kardabūs, *Kitábu-l-iktifá,* ibid., 2: xxxii–xxxvii; Ambrosio Huici Miranda, *Las grandes batallas de la reconquista durante las invasiones africanas (Almorávides, Almohades y Benimerines)* (Madrid: CSIC, 1956), 19–83.

23. *CSJP,* 52–60; *CGPIII,* 62–63, ch. 17; *CSJP (tr),* 19–21, ch. 17; *Historia Roderici,* 69–98, ch. 37–77; al-Maqqarī, *History,* 2: 333–34, Bk. 8, ch. 4, and Ibn al-Kardabūs, *Kitábu-l-iktifá,* ibid., 2: xxxviii–xliv.

24. *Annales Complutenses* and *Annales Compostellani, ES* 23: 314, 321; *CSJP,* 60–64; *CGPIII,* 65–66, ch,. 18; *CSJP (tr),* 21–25, ch. 18; *Chronique de Saint-Maixent,* 154–56, 172; Ibn ʿIdhārī, *Al-Bayān al-Mugrib: Nuevos fragmentos almorávides y almohades,* tr. Ambrosio Huici Miranda (Valencia: Anubar, 1963), 65–102; Antonio Ubieto Arteta, *Colección diplomática de Pedro I de Aragón y Navarra* (Zaragoza: CSIC, 1951), 83–100, 103–10, 241–45, 251–52, 333–35, 345–47, nos. 24–25 (17 December 1096), 30 (5 April 1097), 89 (October 1100), 96 (5 May 1101).

25. Guibert de Nogent, *Dei gesta per Francos et cinq autres textes,* ed. R. B. C. Huygens (Turnhout: Brepols, 1996), 107, Bk. 2, ch. 1; *DP,* 39–45, nos. 24–26 (10 October 1088), 27 (15 October).

26. Lawrence J. McCrank, "La restauración y la reconquista abortiva de Tarragona, 1076–1108," *CHE* 61–62 (1979): 145–245; Paul H. Freedman, *The Diocese of Vic: Tradition and Regeneration in Medieval Catalonia* (New Brunswick, N.J.: Rutgers University Press, 1983), 29–34, and "Archbishop Berenguer Seniofred de Lluça and the Gregorian Reform in Catalonia," in his *Church, Law and Society in Catalonia, 900–1500* (Aldershot: Variorum, 1994), No. III.

27. *DP,* 46–53, nos. 29 (1 July 1089), 30 (August), 31 (1090), 32 (1 July 1091), 33 (25 April 1092); Paul F. Kehr, *Das Papsttum und der katalanische Prinzipat bis zur Vereinigung mit Aragon* (Berlin: Preussische Akademie der Wissenschaften, 1926), 1: 44, n. 2.

28. *DP,* 50–53, nos. 32 (1 July 1091), 33 (25 April 1092); Kehr, *Papsturkunden,* 1: 286–87, no. 22 (1 July 1091).

29. Lawrence J. McCrank, "The Foundation of the Confraternity of Tarragona

by Archbishop Oleguer Bonestruga, 1126–1129," in his *Medieval Frontier History in New Catalonia* (Aldershot: Variorum, 1996), No. III.

30. Rodrigo, *Historia*, 202, 209, Bk. 6, ch. 20, 26; Jonathan Riley-Smith, *The First Crusade and the Idea of Crusading* (Philadelphia: University of Pennsylvania Press, 1986), and *The Crusades: A Short History* (New Haven, Conn.: Yale University Press, 1987).

31. Kehr, *Papsturkunden*, 1: 287–88, no. 23 dated this between 1089–91 but it probably was issued in 1096; Goñi Gaztambide, *Historia*, 56–61; Erdmann, *Origin*, 317–18.

32. *Chronicon Burgense, Annales Complutenses, Annales Compostellani, Chronicon de Cardeña*, and *Anales Toledanos I*, in *ES* 23: 310, 315, 322, 372, 379, 386. *Chronicon Dertusense I*, in Villanueva, *Viage*, 5: 233; Rodrigo, *Historia*, 202, Bk. 6, ch. 20.

33. *DP*, 53–54, 58–59, nos. 34 (16 March 1095), 39 (May–December 1098); Ubieto Arteta, *Pedro I*, 235–36, no. 21 (1095).

34. Ubieto Arteta, *Pedro I*, 113, n. 6, and 115, n. 9; Fidel Fita, "El Concilio nacional de Palencia en el año 1100 y el de Gerona en 1101," *BRAH* 24 (1894): 231–32; *CDACA*, 4: 294–97, no. 119 (July 1160).

35. *CSJP*, 120; *CGPIII*, 98–99, ch. 31; *CSJO (tr)*, 50, ch. 31; Antonio Ubieto Arteta, "La participación navarro-aragonesa en la primera cruzada," *Príncipe de Viana* 8 (1947): 357–83, and 370, nn. 8, 30; *Gesta comitum*, 7, ch. 4 (rp) and 37, ch. 16 (rd); Luciano Serrano, *El obispado de Burgos y Castilla primitiva desde el Siglo V al XIII*, 3 vols. (Madrid: Impresa de E. Maestre, 1935), 1: 353; Fita, "El Concilio nacional de Palencia," 230, 232; Fray Juan Gil de Zamora, "Liber de preconiis numantine," ed. Fidel Fita, "Dos libros inéditos de Gil de Zamora," *BRAH* 5 (1884): 188; Alfonso Sánchez Candeira, "Las cruzadas en la historiografía española de la época," *Hispania* 20 (1960): 327–30, 338–67 (a late thirteenth-century translation entitled *Anales de Tierra Santa*); Miguel Fernández de Navarrete, "Disertación histórica sobre la parte que tuvieron los españoles en las guerras de ultramar o de las cruzadas," *Memorias de la Real Academia de la Historia* 5 (Madrid: Real Academia de la Historia, 1817).

36. Rodrigo, *Historia*, 209–10, Bk. 6, ch. 26; Guibert de Nogent, *Dei gesta*, 107, Bk. 2, ch.1, William of Malmesbury, *Historia novella*, ed. William Stubbs, 2 vols. (London: Longman, 1887–89), 2: 395; Alexandre Herculano, *História de Portugal desde o começo da monarquia até o fim do reinado de D. Afonso III*, 9th ed., 8 vols. (Lisbon: Bertrand, n.d.), 2: 23–26; Luiz Gonzaga de Azevedo, *História de Portugal*, 6 vols. (Lisbon: Biblion, 1940–42), 3: 52–60; *La Gran Conquista de Ultramar*, ed. Pascual de Gayangos, *BAE* 44: 16; Goñi Gaztambide, *Historia*, 60, 64–67.

37. *Historia Compostellana*, ed. Emma Falque Rey, *Corpus Christianorum, Continuatio Mediaevalis* 70 (Turnhout: Brepols, 1988), 25–26, Bk. 1, ch. 9 (14 October 1100).

38. *HC*, 77–78, Bk. 1, ch. 39 (25 March 1101); Ibn 'Idhārī, *Nuevos fragmentos*, 117–18; Ibn Abī Zar', *Rawd al-Qirtas*, 1: 311; Rodrigo, *Historia*, 216–17, Bk. 6, ch. 32.

39. *La Chronique de Saint-Pierre-le-Vif de Sens dite de Clarius: Chronicon Sancti Petri Vivi Senonensis*, ed. Robert Henri Bautier and Monique Gilles (Paris: CNRS, 1979), 148; Defourneaux, *Les français*, 148–49, 151–52.

40. Snorre Sturlason, *Heimskringla*, tr. Erling Monsen and A. H. Smith (Cambridge: W. Heffer, 1932), 612; Jaime Ferreiro Alemparte, *Arribadas de Normandos y Cruzados a las Costas de la Península Ibérica* (Madrid: Sociedad Española de Estudios

Medievales, 1999), 19–72; Nelly Egger, "El paso por Galicia de un Rey de Noruega en el siglo XII," *Estudios en Homenaje a Don Claudio Sánchez Albornoz en sus 90 años*, 3 vols. (Buenos Aires: Instituto de Historia de España, 1983), 2: 267–74.

41. *Liber Maiolichinus de gestis Pisanorum illustribus*, ed. Carlo Calisse, *Fonti per la storia d'Italia* 29 (Rome: Istituto Storico Italiano, 1904), 8–9, vv. 71–81; *Vita Paschali II*, in *Liber Pontificalis*, 2nd ed. Louis Duchesne, 3 vols. (Paris: E. de Boccard, 1955–57), 2: 301; Bernardo Maragone, *Gli Annales Pisani*, ed. Michele Lupo Gentile, *Raccolta degli Storici Italiani* 6, Parts 2–3 (Bologna: N. Zanichelli, 1936), 4, 8.

42. *Liber Maiolichinus*, 137–42, nos. 1 (7 September 1113), 2–3 (1114); ibid., 17–22, vv. 250–424; *Vita Sancti Olegarii, ES* 29: 474; *Gesta triumphalia per Pisanos facta de captione Hierusalem et civitatis Maioricarum et aliarum civitatum et de triumpho habito contra Ianuenses*, ed. Michele Lupo Gentile, *Raccolta degli Storici Italiani* 6, Part 2 (Bologna: N. Zanichelli, 1936), 90–94; Bernardo Maragone, *Annales*, 8; Ibn Khaldūn, *Histoire*, 2: 83; Ibn al-Kardabūs, *Kitábu-l-iktifá*, in al-Maqqarī, *History*, 2: xxxviii–xlviii; *Chronicon Durtusense I* and *Chronicon Durtusense II*, in Villanueva, *Viage*, 5: 233, 237; *Gesta comitum*, 8, ch. 4 (rp) and 37, ch. 16 (rd); Soldevila, *Història*, 1: 132–34; Defourneaux, *Les français*, 155–56; Randall Rogers, *Latin Siege Warfare in the Twelfth Century* (Oxford: Clarendon Press, 1997), 165–69.

43. *DP*, 69–70, no. 50 (23 May 1116); *Liber Maiolichinus*, 144, no. 8 (26 June 1116); *Gesta comitum*, 8, ch. 4 (rp) and 38, ch. 16 (rd); Vita *Sancti Olegarii, ES* 29: 476–77; Kehr, *Das Papsttum und der Katalanische Prinzipat*, 56–57.

44. *CDACA*, 4: 373–74, no. 154.

45. Ibn 'Idhārī, *Nuevos fragmentos*, 126; Clay Stalls, *Possessing the Land: Aragon's Expansion into Islam's Ebro Frontier Under Alfonso the Battler, 1104–1134* (Leiden: E.J. Brill, 1995), 1–59, and "The Relationship Between Conquest and Settlement on the Aragonese Frontier of Alfonso I," in *Iberia and the Mediterranean World of the Middle Ages: Studies in Honor of Robert I. Burns, S.J.*, ed. Larry Simon (Leiden: E.J. Brill, 1995), 1: 216–31.

46. *The Ecclesiastical History of Ordericus Vitalis*, ed. and tr. Marjorie Chibnall (Oxford: Clarendon Press, 1978), 396–402, Bk. 13, ch. 2–4; *Chronique de Saint-Maixent*, 186; Lynn Nelson, "Rotrou of Perche and the Aragonese Reconquest," *Traditio* 26 (1970): 113–33; José María Lacarra, *Alfonso el Batallador*, 65–82, and "La conquista de Zaragoza por Alfonso I, 18 diciembre 1118," *Al-Andalus* 12 (1947): 65–96.

47. Gelasius II, *Epistolae, PL* 163: 508 (10 December 1118); José María Lacarra, *Documentos para el estudio de la reconquista y repoblación del valle del Ebro*, 2 vols. (Valencia: Anubar, 1982), 1: 67–69, no. 54.

48 *CSJP*, 71–73, 79–80; *CGPIII*, 67, ch. 19; *CSJP (tr)*, 25–27, 30–31, ch. 19; *Chronicon Durtusense II*, in Villanueva, *Viage*, 5: 327; *Annales Compostellani, ES* 23: 321; *Chronique de Saint-Maixent*, 188–90; Ordericus, *History*, 404–7, Bk. 13, ch. 6; Ibn Abī Zarʿ, *Rawd al-Qirtas*, 1: 316–18; Ibn Khaldūn, *Histoire*, 2: 83; al-Maqqarī, *History*, 2: 303–4, Bk. 8, ch. 1; Ibn 'Idhārī, *Nuevos fragmentos*, 160–68; al-Ḥulal, 108–15; José Ángel Lema Pueyo, ed., *Colección diplomática de Alfonso I de Aragón y Pamplona (1104–1134)* (San Sebastián: Eusko-Ikaskuntza, 1990), 138–40, no. 90 (1119); Zurita, *Anales*, 1: 138–45; Goñi Gaztambide, *Historia*, 71–76.

49. *Conciliorum oecumenicorum decreta*, ed. Giuseppe Alberigo et al., 2nd ed

(Freiburg im Breisgau: Herder 1962), 167–68; Fidel Fita, "Actas del Concilio de Clermont (18 nov. 1130). Revisión crítica," *BRAH* 4 (1884): 360–66; Goñi Gaztambide, *Historia*, 76–77.

50. *DP*, 79–80, no. 62 (2 April [1121–24]); *Vita Sancti Olegarii, ES* 29: 498; Brundage, *Canon Law and the Crusader*, 129; Goñi Gaztambide, *Historia*, 76–78; Juan Francisco Rivera Recio, *La Iglesia de Toledo en el siglo XII (1086–1208)*, 2 vols. (Rome: Instituto Español de Historia ecclesiástica, 1966), 1: 214–16.

51. *Chronicon Durtusense II*, in Villanueva, *Viage*, 5: 237, and ibid., 6: 338–39, no. 46 (14 April 1129); *Ordericus, History*, 402–4, Bk. 13, ch. 5; Loewenfeld, *Epistolae*, 95, no. 187 (25 March 1144); Lawrence McCrank, "Norman Crusaders in the Catalan Reconquest: Robert Burdet and the Principality of Tarragona, 1129–55," in his *Medieval Frontier History*, No. IV, and "Confraternity of Tarragona," 157–77.

52. *HC*, 379, Bk. 2, ch. 78; Goñi Gaztambide, *Historia*, 79–80; Richard Fletcher, *Saint James' Catapult: The Life and Times of Diego Gelmírez of Santiago de Compostela* (Oxford: Clarendon Press, 1984), 298–99.

53. Bernard F. Reilly, *The Kingdom of León-Castile Under Queen Urraca, 1109–1126* (Princeton, N.J.: Princeton Univesity Press, 1982).

54. Peter Rassow, "La cofradía de Belchite," *AHDE* 3 (1926): 200–226; Antonio Ubieto Arteta, "La creación de la cofradía militar de Belchite," *EEMCA* 5 (1952): 427–34; Elena Lourie, "The Confraternity of Belchite, the Ribāt, and the Temple," in her *Crusade and Colonisation: Muslims, Christians and Jews in Medieval Aragon* (London: Variorum, 1990), No. II; Goñi Gaztambide, *Historia*, 73–76 (n. 40), 80–82.

55. Lema Pueyo, *Alfonso I*, 194–96, 206–8, nos. 130–31, 141 (circa 1124); Lacarra, *Documentos*, 1: 182–84, no. 173; *ES* 46: 285–87 (5 June 1138); Villanueva, *Viage*, 15: 377–79; Zurita, *Anales*, 1: 150–51.

56. *CSJP*, 80–81; *CGPIII*, 67, ch. 19; *CSJP (tr)*, 30–31, ch. 19; Ordericus, *History*, 408–19, Bk. 13, ch. 8–9; Ibn 'Idhārī, *Nuevos fragmentos*, 209–10, 212, 216; al-Maqqarī, *History*, 2: 304–9, Bk. 8, ch. 1–2; Lacarra, *Alfonso el Batallador*, 83–92, 123–36; Zurita, *Anales*, 1: 154–67.

57. Lema Pueyo, *Alfonso I*, 356–68, 446-48, nos. 241–42 (October 1131), 284 (4 September 1134); *CDACA*, 4: 9–12; *Liber Feudorum Maior: Cartulario real que se conserva en el Archivo de la Corona de Aragón*, ed. Francisco Miquel Rosell, 2 vols. (Barcelona: CSIC, 1945–47), 1: 10–12, no. 6; A. J. Forey, "The Will of Alfonso I of Aragón and Navarre," *Durham University Journal* 73 (1980): 59–65; Elena Lourie, "The Will of Alfonso I, el Batallador, King of Aragon and Navarre: A Reassessment," and "The Will of Alfonso I of Aragon and Navarre: A Reply to Dr. Forey," in her *Crusade and Colonisation*, Nos. III–IV.

58. Kehr, *Papsturkunden*, 1: 318, 364–65, nos. 50 (10 June 1135/1136), 81 (24 June 1158); *CDACA*, 4: 70–73, 78–81, 93–99, 236–37, 325–26, nos. 32 (16 September 1140), 36 (29 August 1141), 43 (27 November 1143), 90 (6 April 1156), 137 (1141); *LFM*, 1: 15–19, nos. 10–12; .*Gesta comitum*, 38, ch. 16 (rd); *CSJP*, 81–99, 121; *CGPIII*, 69–71, 98–99, ch. 20, 31; *CSJP (tr)*, 31–40, 50, ch. 20, 31; Rodrigo, *Historia*, 179–80, Bk.6, ch. 2–3.

59. Ibn Khaldūn, *Histoire*, 2: 84–86, 161–83; Rodrigo, *Historia*, 231–32, Bk. 7, ch. 10; Ambrosio Huici, *Historia política del imperio almohade*, 2 vols. (Tetuán: Editora Marroquí, 1956).

60. The *Annales D. Alfonsi Portugallensium regis*, ed. Monica Blöcker-Walter, *Alfons I. von Portugal: Studien zu Geschichte und Sage des Begründers der Portugiesischen Unabhängigkeit* (Zurich: Fretz und Wasmuth, 1966), 155–56, form part of the *Chronica Gothorum, PMH SS* 1: 11–17.

61. The principal narrative source, ending in 1145, is the *Chronica Adefonsi Imperatoris*, in *Chronica Hispana Saeculi XII, Corpus Christianorum, Continuatio Mediaevalis* 71, ed. Emma Falque, Juan Gil, and Antonio Maya (Turnhout: Brepols, 1990), 162–64, 165–69, 179, 181–84, Bk. 1, ch. 27–29, 33–41, 63, 67–72. There is an older edition, *Chronica Adefonsi Imperatoris*, ed. Luis Sánchez Belda (Madrid: CSIC, 1950). Bernard F. Reilly, *The Kingdom of León-Castilla Under King Alfonso VII, 1126–1157* (Philadelphia: University of Pennsylvania Press, 1998); Peter Rassow, "Die Urkunden Kaiser Alfons VII von Spanien," *Archiv für Urkundenforschung* 10 (1928): 327–468, and 11 (1930): 66–137.

62. Soldevila, *Historia*, 1: 147–161; *Annales D. Alfonsi*, 151, 153–54; *Chronica Gothorum, PMH SS* 1: 11–13; *Chronicon Conimbricense, ES* 23: 331, and *PMH SS* 1: 2; *Chronicon Lamecense, Chronicon Alcobacense, Crónica Breve*, and *Vita S. Theotonii* (ch. 27), *PMH SS* 1: 20–21, 24; 86; *DMP DR*, 1: 233–34, no. 189 (1142), José Mattoso and Armindo de Sousa, *A Monarquia feudal (1096–1480)* vol. 2 of José Mattoso, ed., *História de Portugal*, 8 vols. (Lisbon: Editorial Estampa, 1997–99), 25–64.

63. *DMP DR*, 1: 250, no. 202 (13 December 1143); *Monumenta Henricina*, 15 vols. (Coimbra: Commissão executiva das Conmemoraes do V Centenario do Morte do Infante D. Henrique, 1960–74), 1: 1–2, no. 1; Lucius II, *Epistolae, PL* 179: 860–61, no. 26 (1 May 1144); Rodrigo, *Historia*, 227–28, Bk. 7, ch. 6; Herculano, *História*, 2: 192–94, 294–308, Ap. 19; Gonzaga de Azevedo, *História*, 4: 27–35.

64. *DP*, 90–92, nos. 74–75 (9 May 1145).

65. *Annales D. Alfonsi*, 155; *Chronica Gothorum*, 13–14; *De Expugnatione Lyxbonensi: The Conquest of Lisbon*, ed. and tr. Charles W. David (New York: Columbia University Press, 1936); see the reprint with a foreword by Jonathan Phillips, *The Conquest of Lisbon: De Expugnatione Lyxbonensi* (New York: Columbia University Press, 2001), 100–105; Ibn ʿIdhārī, *Nuevos fragmentos*, 236; Carl Erdmann, "Der Kreuzzugsgedanken in Portugal," *Historische Zeitschrift* 141 (1930): 23–53.

66. *Annales D. Alfonsi*, 156–57; *Chronica Gothorum, PMH SS*, 1: 14–15; *Cronicon Conimbricense, ES* 23: 331, and *PMH SS* 1: 2; *Chronicon Complutense sive Alcobacense, Chronicon Lamecense, Chronicon Alcobacense*, and *De expugnatione Scalabis, PMH SS* 1: 18, 20–21, 93–95; *CAI*, 187–89, Bk. 1, ch. 79–80, 84; Roger de Hoveden, *Chronica*, ed. William Stubbs, 4 vols., Rolls Series 51 (London: Longmans, 1868–71), 3: 333; Herculano, *História*, 2: 216–23; Gonzaga de Azevedo, *História*, 4: 46–55.

67. Bernard of Clairvaux, *Epistolae*, in *Opera*, ed. Jean Leclercq and Henri Rochais, 8 vols. (Rome: Editiones Cistercienses, 1955–77), 8: 228, no. 308; Harold Livermore, "The 'Conquest of Lisbon' and Its Author," *Portuguese Studies* 6 (1990): 116; Jonathan Phillips, "Saint Bernard of Clairvaux, the Low Countries and the Lisbon Letter of the Second Crusade," *Journal of Ecclesiastical History* 48 (1997): 485–97.

68. The *De Expugnatione Lyxbonensi* cited in n. 65 above is the principal source. Livermore (n. 67 above) proved that the author was Raol, an Anglo-Flemish priest.

Three brief letters, apparently copies of one another, also discuss the siege of Lisbon: Duodechin, a priest of Lahnstein, to Abbot Cuno of Disibodenberg, in *Annales Sancti Disibodi, MGH SS* 17: 27–28; Arnulf, a Flemish priest, to Milo, bishop of Thérouanne, *PMH SS* 1: 406–7, and *RGHF* 14: 325–27; and Winand, a priest of Cologne, in Susan Edgington, "The Lisbon Letter of the Second Crusade," *Historical Research* 69 (1996): 336–39; Virginia G. Berry, "The Second Crusade," in Setton, *Crusades,* 1: 481–82; Giles Constable, "A Note on the Route of the Anglo-Flemish Crusaders," *Speculum* 28 (1953): 525–26.

69. *De Expugnatione Lyxbonensi,* 80–82, 90–96, 110–15; see 70–85 for the text of the sermon. See Jonathan Phillips, "Ideas of Crusade and Holy War in *De expugnatione Lyxbonensi (The Conquest of Lisbon),*" in *Holy Land, Holy Lands, and Christian History,* ed. Robert Swanson, *Studies in Church History* 36 (2000): 123–41.

70. *De Expugnatione Lyxbonensi,* 114, 116, 120–23.

71. Letters of Duodechin, *MGH SS* 17: 27–28, and Arnulf, *RGHF* 14: 326; *De Expugnatione Lyxbonensi,* 136–39, 176–80; *Annales D. Alfonsi,* 157; *Chronica Gothorum, PMH SS* 1: 15; *Cronicon Conimbricense, ES* 23: 331 and *PMH SS* 1: 2; *Chronicon Complutense sive Alcobacense, Chronicon Lamecense,* and *Chronicon Alcobacense, PMH SS* 1: 18, 20–21; Herculano, *História,* 3: 7–51; Gonzaga de Azevedo, *História,* 4: 55–92; Rogers, *Latin Siege Warfare,* 182–88; Matthew Bennett, "Military Aspects of the Conquest of Lisbon, 1147," in *The Second Crusade: Scope and Consequences,* ed. Jonathan Phillips and Martin Hoch (Manchester: Manchester University Press, 2001), 71–89.

72. "Fragmento de los *Annales Ianuenses* de Caffaro" and Caffaro, *De captione Almerie et Tortuose,* ed. Antonio Ubieto Arteta (Valencia: Anubar, 1973), 17–18, 21; Caffaro di Caschifellone, *Ystoria de captione Almarie et Tortose,* in *Annali genovesi,* 1, ed. Luigi T. Belgrano and Cesare Imperiale (Genoa, 1890), *Fonti per la storia d'Italia,* 11: 79–89; *CAI,* 218–25, 240–48, Bk. 2, ch. 50–66, 94–111; *Annales Compostellani,* and *Anales Toledanos I, ES* 23: 323, 389; Rodrigo, *Historia,* 225, 229–30, Bk. 7, ch. 4, 8; *Chronica latina,* 39, ch. 5; Ibn Khaldūn, *Histoire,* 2: 187; Ibn Abī Zarʿ, *Rawd al-Qirtas,* 2: 509.

73. Cesare Imperiale di Sant'Angelo, ed., *Codice diplomatico della Repubblica di Genova,* 2 vols. (Rome: Tipografia del Senato, 1936–42), 1: 204–17, nos. 166–69; Emilio Sáez and Carlos Sáez, eds., *El fondo español del Archivo de la Academia de las Ciencias de San Petersburgo* (Alcalá de Henares: Universidad de Alcalá, 1993), 67–70; *CDACA,* 4: 332–34, 337–39, nos. 141, 144; John Bryan Williams, "The Making of a Crusade: The Genoese Anti-Muslim Attacks in Spain, 1146–1148," *Journal of Medieval History* 23 (1997): 29–53.

74. *Anales Toledanos I, ES* 23: 389; Alberic of Troisfontaines, *Chronicon, MGH SS* 23: 837; Eugenius III, *Epistolae, PL* 180: 1203 (13 April 1147); *DP,* 94–96, no. 78 (27 April 1148); Helmold, *Chronica Slavorum,* Bk. 1, ch. 50, *MGH SS* 21: 27; *Poema de Almería,* or *Prefatio de Almaria* in *CAI,* 256, 258, lines 38–48, 95–98; Giles Constable, "The Second Crusade as Seen by Contemporaries," *Traditio* 9 (1953): 213–79.

75. *Poema de Almería,* 264–65, lines 295–317; Caffaro, *De captione,* 21–24 and 24, n. 1 (7 September 1147). *CSJP,* 122–23; *CGPIII,* 101–2, ch. 32; *CSJP (tr),* 51, ch. 32; Reilly, *Alfonso VII,* 365, no. 562 (18 August 1147).

76. *Poema de Almería*, 267, lines 381–82. The *Poema* ends abruptly at this point. Caffaro, *De captione*, 25–30; *Cronicon Barcinonense I, Cronicon Barcinonense II, Cronicon Massiliense, Annales Compostellani*, and *Anales Toledanos I, ES* 23: 322–23, 328, 338, 390; *Cronicon Ulianense, ES* 28: 334; *Cronicon Durtusense I, Cronicon Durtusense II*, and *Cronicon Rivipullense*, in Villanueva, *Viage*, 5: 233, 238, 247; *CSJP*, 122; *CGPIII*, 101–2, ch. 32; *CSJP (tr)*, 51, ch.32; *Gesta comitum*, 8, ch. 5 (rp) and 39, ch. 17.1 (rd); Rodrigo, *Historia*, 232, Bk. 7, ch. 11; al-Maqqarī, *History*, 2: 311–12, Bk. 8, ch. 2; Ibn Khaldūn, *Histoire*, 2: 192–93; Imperiale di Sant'Angelo, *Genova*, 1: 228–30, nos. 182–83 (5 November 1147).

77. *ES* 36: 192–94 (17 February 1148); *DP*, 94–96, no. 78 (27 April 1148); *Anales Toledanos I, ES* 23: 389; Ibn Khaldūn, *Histoire*, 2: 187–88; Simon Barton, "A Forgotten Crusade: Alfonso VII and the Campaign for Jaén (1148)," *Historical Research* 73 (2000): 312–20..

78. *CDACA*, 4: 314–15, 332–34, 337–39, nos. 128 (22 June 1148), 141, 144 (n.d.); see ibid., 4: 113–25, 347–55, 371–72, nos. 51 (3 August 1146),147 (n.d.), 154 (n.d.); *DP*, 92–93, no. 76 (27 May 1146); Goñi Gaztambide, *Historia*, 86.

79. *CDACA*, 4: 130–35, no. 56 (31 December 1148); Caffaro, *De captione*, 30–35; *Cronicon Durtusense I, Cronicon Durtusense II, Cronicon Barcinonense I, Cronicon Barcinonense II*, and *Cronicon Rivipullense*, in Villanueva, *Viage*, 5: 234, 238, 247, 323, 329, and *Cronicon Rotense*, ibid., 15: 335; *CSJP*, 122–23; *CGPIII*, 101–2, ch. 32; *CSJP (tr)*, 51, ch. 32; *Gesta comitum*, 8, 12, ch. 5, 8 (rp) and 34, 39, ch. 12, 17.1 (rd); Nikolas Jaspert, "Capta est Dertosa, clavis christianorum: Tortosa and the Crusades," in Phillips and Hoch, *The Second Crusade*, 90–110.

80. Imperiale di Sant'Angelo, *Genova*, 1: 236–40, 244–45, 254–57, 266–67, 291–95, nos. 190 (November 1148), 191 (January 1148), 194 (April 1149), 202 (1149), 203 (January 1150), 215 (December 1150), 216 (1150), 243–44 (November 1153).

81. Carlos Alvar, *Textos trovadorescos sobre España y Portugal* (Madrid: Cupsa, 1978), 206–10, 212–15; M. Mila y Fontanals, *De los trovadores de España: Estudio de lengua y poesia provenzal. Obras completas* 2 (Barcelona, 1889), 73–81; Frederick Goldin, *Lyrics of the Troubadours and Trouvères: Original Texts with Translations and Introductions* (Garden City, N.Y.: Doubleday Anchor, 1973), 76–81, no. 15.

82. Fidel Fita, "Primera legación del Cardenal Jacinto en España: Bulas inéditas de Anastasio IV. Nuevas luces sobre el Concilio nacional de Valladolid (1155) y otros datos inéditos," *BRAH* 14 (1889): 544 (21 April 1150); John of Hexham, *Historia*, in Simeon of Durham, *Opera Omnia*, ed. Thomas Arnold, 2 vols. (London: Longmans, Green, 1882–85), 2: 324; *Annales D. Alfonsi*, 157–58; *Chronica Gothorum, PMH SS* 1: 15; *Chronicon Conimbricense, ES* 23: 332 and *PMH SS* 1: 2.

83. Francisco J. Hernández, *Los cartularios de Toledo: Catálogo documental* (Madrid: Fundación Ramón Areces, 1985), 81, no. 81 (24 August 1151); Reilly, *Alfonso VII*, 376, nos. 702–8 (11 July–27 August 1151); *CDACA*, 4: 168–70, 239–41, nos. 62 (27 January 1151), 91 (May 1156); al-Maqqarī, *History*, 2: 313, Bk. 8, ch. 2.

84. *CDACA*, 4: 314–15, 320–21, nos. 128 (22 June 1152), 133 (24 September 1153); Kehr, *Papsturkunden*, 1: 373–77, no. 70 (24 September 1153); Michele Amari, *I diplomi arabi del Real Archivio fiorentino*, 2 vols. (Florence: Felice LeMonnier, 1863), 1: 239–40, no. 1 (27 January 1149); Imperiale di Sant'Angelo, *Genova*, 1: 247–49, no. 196 (June 1149).

85. Carl Erdmann, *Das Papsttum und Portugal im ersten Jahrhundert der portugiesische Geschichte* (Berlin: Weidmannsche Buchhandlung, 1928), 55; Fidel Fita, "Primera legación del Cardenal Jacinto en España: Bulas inéditas de Anastasio IV. Nuevas luces sobre el Concilio nacional de Valladolid (1155) y otros datos inéditos," *BRAH* 14 (1889): 530–55, and "Concilios nacionales de Salamanca en 1154 y Valladolid en 1155," *BRAH* 24 (1894): 467–75.

86. *DP*, 116–17, no. 98; Goñi Gaztambide, *Historia*, 93–94, 643, appendix 1. The text is undated; Mansilla believes it relates to the Council of 1155, while Goñi Gaztambide favors 1172. Inasmuch as the letter mentions Robertus, "karissimum clericum et notarium nostrum" and another letter of the legate fully dated 3 March 1155 at Nájera was written "per manum Roberti, cappellani domini Jacinti diaconi Cardenalis atque legati" the first letter should be dated in 1155.

87. Ibn ʿIdhārī, *Nuevos fragmentos*, 302–5, 311–12; Évariste Lévi-Provençal, "Un recueil des lettres officielles almohades," *Hesperis* 28 (1941): 39, no. 16 (8–17 September 1157); al-Maqqarī, *History*, 2: 313–14, Bk. 8, ch. 2; Ibn Khaldūn, *Histoire*, 2: 192–93; Alvar, *Textos*, 224–25.

Chapter 3

1. *CAI*, 181–84, ch. 69–72; *Chrónicon de Cardeña*, ES 23: 379; Lucas, *Chronicon*, 4:104–5; Rodrigo, *Historia*, 228–29, Bk. 7, ch. 7; *Chronica latina*, 41, ch. 7–8.

2. *DP*, 122–23, no. 103 (18 February 1159); *CAI*, 247, Bk. 2, ch. 109; Rodrigo, *Historia*, 230, Bk. 7, ch. 9; Lucas, *Chronicon*, 4: 104–5, and *Crónica*, 398–400, ch. 81; Robert of Torigny, *Chronica*, MGH SS 6: 504; Marcelin Defourneaux, "Louis VII et les souverains espagnols," *Estudios dedicados a Menéndez Pidal*, 7 vols. (Madrid: Patronato Marcelino Menéndez Pelayo, 1950–62), 6: 647–61; Gonzaga de Azevedo, *História*, 4: 98, 262–63.

3. Julio González, *Regesta de Fernando II* (Madrid: CSIC, 1943), 241–43, no. 1 (23 May 1158), and *El reino de Castilla en la época de Alfonso VIII*, 3 vols. (Madrid: CSIC, 1960), 2: 79–82, no. 44.

4. Peter Linehan, "The Synod of Segovia (1166)," *Bulletin of Medieval Canon Law* 10 (1980): 31–44.

5. Ibn Ṣāḥīb al-Salā, *Al-Mann bil-Imāma*, tr. Ambrosio Huici Miranda (Valencia: Anubar, 1969), is the principal source for Almohad expansion. See also Évariste Lévi-Provençal, *Documents inédits d'histoire almohade: Fragments manuscrits du legajo 1919 du fonds arabe de l'Escorial* (Paris: P. Geuthner, 1928), 127, 216, and "Recueil," 31, 51, nos. 10 (9 September 1153), 25 (29 May 1169); Ibn ʿIdhārī, *Nuevos fragmentos*, 330–34, 338–39, 343–57, 377–83, 401–10, 414, 417, 420–21, and *Al-Bayān al-Mugrib fi Ijtiṣār ajbār Muluk al-Andalus wa al-Magrib*, tr. Ambrosio Huici, 2 vols. (Tetuán: Editora Marroquí, 1954), 1: 13–14; Ibn Khaldūn, *Histoire*, 2: 193–99; al-Maqqarī, *History*, 2: 313–16, Bk. 8, ch. 2; *Annales D. Alfonsi*, 158; *Chronica Gothorum*, PMH SS 1: 15; *Chronicon Conimbricense*, ES 23: 331 and PMH SS 1: 2; Rodrigo, *Historia*, 236–46, Bk. 7, ch. 17–23; *Chronica latina*, 41–43 ch. 9–10; Lucas, *Chronicon*, 4: 104–6, and

Crónica, 402–6, ch. 83; Roger de Hoveden, *Chronica*, 2: 334; *CDACA*, 4: 315–16, no. 129 (23 June 1158).

6. Ana Isabel Sánchez Casabón, *Alfonso II, Rey de Aragón, Conde de Barcelona y Marqués de Provenza. Documentos (1162–1196)* (Zaragoza: CSIC, 1995), 94–99, 147–49, nos. 56 (5 November 1168), 58 (19 December 1168), 90 (4 June 1170); Miguel Gual Camarena, "Precedentes de la Reconquista valenciana," *Estudios medievales* 1 (1952): 222–24, nos. 24–25; *Gesta comitum*, 9, 12–13, ch. 5, 9 (rd) and 45–47, ch. 24; *CSJP*, 125–26; *CGPIII*, 105–6, ch. 33; *CSJP (tr)*, 53–54, ch. 33; Ibn Ṣāḥib al-Salā, *Al-Mann*, 146–51, 154–62. 193–95; Ibn ʿIdhārī, *Nuevos fragmentos*, 411–12, 418–19, 421–26, 439–42; al-Marrākushī, *Kitāb*, 170–71; al-Maqqarī, *History*, 2: 318–19, Bk.8, ch. 3; Ibn Khaldūn, *Histoire*, 2: 200–202; *Anales Toledanos I, ES* 23: 392; González, *Alfonso VIII*, 2: 239–42, no. 140; Zurita, *Anales*, 1: 238–40, 245–48; 259–61, 268; Jordi Ventura, *Alfons el Cast: El primer comte rei* (Barcelona: Aedos, 1961).

7. *CDACA*, 4: 93–99, no. 43 (27 November 1143); Alan Forey, *The Military Orders from the Twelfth to the Early Fourteenth Centuries* (Toronto: University of Toronto Press, 1992), 23–25, and *The Templars in the Corona de Aragón* (Oxford: Oxford University Press, 1973), 15–24, 27, and "The Military Orders and the Spanish Reconquest in the Twelfth and Thirteenth Centuries," *Traditio* 40 (1984): 197–234; María Luisa Ledesma Rubio, *Templarios y Hospitalarios en el Reino de Aragón (Siglos XII–XIV)* (Zaragoza: Fernández-Gatell, 1984), and *Las Ordenes militares en Aragón* (Zaragoza: Caja de Ahorros de la Inmaculada, 1994).

8. Jean Delaville Le Roulx, *Cartulaire général de l'Ordre des Hospitaliers de Saint-Jean de Jérusalem*, 4 vols. (Paris: E.L. Roulx, 1894–1906), 1: 141, no. 181 (8 January 1149); María Bonet Donato, *La Orden del Hospital en la Corona de Aragón: Poder y gobierno en la Castellanía de Amposta (S. XII–XV)* (Madrid: CSIC, 1994).

9. Carlos de Ayala Martínez, ed., *Libro de privilegios de la Orden de San Juan de Jerusalén en Castilla y León (Siglos XII–XV)* (Madrid: Editorial Complutense, 1995), 322–24, no. 144 (6 August 1183); *DMP DR*, 1: 321–23, no. 2560 (April 1157); Kehr, *Papsturkunden*, 2: 554–55, no. 200 (4 November 1193); Santos García Larragueta, "La Orden de San Juan en la crísis del imperio hispánico en el siglo XII," *Hispania* 12 (1952): 483–524, and *El Gran Priorado de Navarra de la Orden de San Juan de Jerusalén* (Pamplona: CSIC, 1957); Carlos Barquero Goñi, "La Orden Militar del Hospital en La Mancha durante los siglos XII y XIII," in *Alarcos 1195: Actas del Congreso internacional conmemorativo del VIII Centenario de la Batalla de Alarcos*, ed. Ricardo Izquierdo Benito and Francisco Ruiz Gómez (Cuenca: Universidad de Castilla-La Mancha, 1996), 289–314; Jesús Manuel Molero García, "Participación de la Orden del Hospital en el avance de la frontera castellana," ibid., 331–52.

10. *DMP DR*, 1: 384–85, no. 295 (September 1169); also ibid., 1: 99–103, 120, 261, 272, 325, 344–45, 370, 388–89, nos. 77, 79, 80, 96, 212, 221, 262, 271, 288, 297.

11. Eloy Benito Ruano, "Las Ordenes militares españolas y la idea de Cruzada," *Hispania* 16 (1956): 3–15; Maur Cocheril, "Essai sur l'origine des Ordres militaires dans la peninsule ibérique," *Collectanea Ordinis Cisterciensis Reformati* 20 (1958): 346–61; 21 (1959): 228–50, 302–29; Elena Lourie, "The Confraternity of Belchite, the Ribāṭ, and the Temple," *Crusade and Colonisation*, No. II.

12. *Bullarium Ordinis Militiae de Calatrava*, ed. I. J. Ortega y Cotes, J. F. Alvarez

de Baquedano, and P. de Ortega Zúñiga y Aranda (Madrid: Antonio Marín, 1761), 2–6, 21–25; Rodrigo, *Historia*, 235, Bk. 7, ch. 14; Joseph F. O'Callaghan, "The Affiliation of the Order of Calatrava with the Order of Cîteaux," in *The Spanish Military Order of Calatrava and Its Affiliates* (London: Variorum 1975), No. I, 176–92, and "La vida de las Ordenes Militares de España según sus estatutos primitivos," in Izquierdo Benito and Ruiz Gómez, *Alarcos*, 7–30.

13. Sánchez Casabón, *Alfonso II*, 375–76, no. 279 (March 1179); Jaime Caruana Gómez de Barreda, "La Orden de Calatrava en Alcañiz," *Teruel* 8 (1952): 1–176.

14. *Bullarium Ordinis Militiae de Alcantara*, ed. Ignacio José Ortega y Cotes (Madrid: Antonio Marín, 1759), 3, 6–9, 20–21; *BC*, 22–25; Joseph F. O'Callaghan, "The Foundation of the Order of Alcántara, 1176–1218," in *Calatrava*, No. IV; Rui de Azevedo, "A Ordem militar de S. Julião do Pereiro, depois chamada de Alcântara," *AEM* 11 (1981): 713–29.

15. *DMP DR*, 1: 427–28, 460–61, nos. 327 (April 1176), 345 (April 1181); *BC*, 22–25, 36–37, 450–51; Rui de Azevedo, "As Origens da Ordem de Évora ou de Avis," *Revista de Historia* 1 (1932): 233–41; Carlos da Silva Tarouca, "As origens da Ordem dos cavaleiros de Évora e Avis, segundo as cartas do Arquivo do Cabildo da Se de Évora," *Boletin da Cidade de Évora* 5 (1947): 25–39; Miguel de Oliveira, "A Milicia de Évora e a Ordem de Calatrava," *Lusitania Sacra* 1 (1956): 51–67; Maur Cocheril, "Origine cistercienne des Ordres militaires portugais d'Avis et du Christ," in his *Études sur le monachisme en Espagne et au Portugal* (Lisbon: Bertrand, 1966), 423–32; Aurea Javierre Mur, *La Orden de Calatrava en Portugal* (Madrid: Editorial Maestre, 1952).

16. *Bullarium Equestris Ordinis Militiae Sancti Iacobi de Spatha*, ed. José López Agurleta (Madrid: Juan de Ariztia, 1719), 3–4, 5–6, 13–17; Derek W. Lomax, *La Orden de Santiago (1170–1275)* (Madrid: CSIC, 1965), 5–8, and "The Order of Santiago and the Kings of León," *Hispania* 18 (1958): 3–37; José Luis Martín, *Los orígenes de la Orden Militar de Santiago (1170–1195)* (Barcelona: CSIC, 1974), 11–19, 212–16, 240–41, 255–56, nos. 42, 50–51, 53, 65, 75, and "Orígenes de las Ordenes Militares Hispánicas: La Orden de Santiago," in Izquierdo Benito and Ruiz Gómez, *Alarcos*, 31–46; Enrique Gallego Blanco, *The Rule of the Spanish Military Order of St. James 1170–1493: Latin and Spanish Texts* (Leiden: E.J. Brill, 1971).

17. *DMP DR*, 1: 417, no. 317 (September 1173), and ibid., 1: 409–10, 415, 421, nos. 311, 315, 321; Milagros Rivera Garretas "La Orden de Santiago en Castilla la Nueva en los sighlos XII y XIII," *Las Ordenes Militares en el Mediterráneo occidental: Siglos XIII–XVIII* (Madrid: Casa de Velázquez/Instituto de Estudios Manchegos, 1989), 23–40.

18. O'Callaghan, "The Foundation of the Order of Alcántara," 481–84; Alan J. Forey, "The Order of Mountjoy" *Speculum* 46 (1971): 250–66, Ángel Blázquez y Jiménez, "Bosquejo histórico de la Orden de Monte Gaudio," *BRAH* 71 (1917): 138–72; Laurent Dailliez, *Les chevaliers de Montjoie* (Nice: Impresses Sud, 1978); Jean Delaville Le Roulx, "L'Ordre de Montjoye," *Revue de l'Orient latin* 1 (1893): 42–57; G. Velo y Nieto, *La Orden de caballeros de Monfrag* (Madrid: Otice, 1950); Miguel Muñoz de San Pedro, "La desaparecida Orden de caballeros de Monfragüe," *Hidalguía* 1 (1953): 68–76; Regina Sáinz de la Maza Lasoli, *La Orden de San Jorge de Alfama: Aproximación a su historia* (Barcelona: CSIC, 1990).

19. *Anales Toledanos I, ES* 23: 392–93; Ibn Ṣāḥīb al-Salā, *Al-Mann*, 205–33; Ibn ʿIdhārī, *Nuevos fragmentos*, 427–48, and *Al-Bayān*, 1: 3–6, 13–15; Roger de Hoveden, *Chronica*, 2: 33; *Chronica latina*, 42–43, ch. 10; Lévi-Provençal, "Recueil," 52.

20. Ramón Riu, *Sermón de la Bula de la Santa Cruzada* (Madrid, 1887), appendix; Fidel Fita, "Tres bulas inéditas de Alejandro III," *BRAH* 12 (1888): 164–68; Rivera Recio, *Toledo*, 218–19; Goñi Gaztambide, *Historia*, 94; Riley-Smith, *Crusades*, 106–7.

21. Sánchez Casabón, *Alfonso II*, 324–26, 330–31, nos. 236 (June 1177), 239 (August 1177); Antonio López Ferreiro, *Historia de la santa a.m. iglesia de Santiago de Compostela*, 11 vols. (Santiago: Imprenta del Seminario conciliar y central, 1898–1909), 4: 332, no. 49 (23, 30 October 1176); González, *Fernando II*, 453 (22 September 1177), and *Alfonso VIII*, 2: 472–74, no. 288 (August 1177).

22. Ibn ʿIdhārī, *Al-Bayān*, 1: 28–30; *Annales Compostellani, ES* 23: 323; *Chronica latina*, 42–43, ch. 10; Rodrigo, *Historia*, 248–49, Bk. 7, ch. 26; Fidel Fita, "El Concilio de Lérida en 1193 y Santa María la Real de Nájera: Bulas inéditas de Celestino III, Inocencio III y Honorio III," *BRAH* 26 (1895): 348, without citing any source, stated that Cardinal Hyacinth proclaimed a crusade. The cardinal was not in Spain at that time.

23. Marqués de Mondéjar, *Memorias históricas de la vida y acciones del Rey D. Alonso el Noble* (Madrid: Antonio de Sancha, 1783), lxx, no. 5. See James F. Powers, "The Early Reconquest Episcopate of Cuenca, 1177–1284," *CHR* 87 (2001): 1–15.

24. González, *Alfonso VIII*, 2: 528–32, nos. 319–20 (20 March 1179); Sánchez Casabón, *Alfonso II*, 376–80, nos. 280–81.

25. Ibn ʿIdhārī, *Al-Bayān*, 2: 21, 32, 39–51, 65, 69–79; Ibn Abī Zarʿ, *Rawd al-Qirtas*, 2: 578; Ibn Khaldūn, *Histoire*, 2: 203–6; al-Maqqarī, *History*, 2: 318–19, Bk. 8, ch. 3; *Annales D. Alfonsi*, 159–61; *Chronica Gothorum, PMH SS* 1: 16–17; *Anales Toledanos I, ES* 23: 393; *Chronicon Conimbricense, ES* 23: 333 and *PMH SS* 1: 3; Lucas, *Chronicon*, 4: 106–7, and *Crónica*, 405, ch. 83; González, *Fernando II*, 315–21, no. 46 (1 June 1183), and *Alfonso VIII*, 2: 701–8, no. 407.

26. *Epistolae Alexandri III, PL* 200: 1237–38, no. 1424 (23 May 1179); *MH*, 1: 18–21, no. 9. Julio González, *Alfonso IX*, 2 vols. (Madrid: CSIC, 1945) is the principal study of this reign.

27. *Epistolae Gregorii VIII, PL* 202: 1539–42 (29 October 1187); Rivera Recio, *Toledo*, 221–23, n.14 (8 May 1188); *Anales Compostellani* and *Anales Toledanos I, ES* 23: 323, 393–94; Brundage, *Canon Law and the Crusader*, 147, 154, 165–69, 179–80, 184–87.

28. AC Toledo, E.7.C (XII).15.1, published in part by Rivera Recio, *Toledo*, 225–27, n. 75 (8 June 1188, including the papal letter of 8 May).

29. Ibn ʿIdhārī, *Al-Bayān*, 1: 153; *Anales Toledanos I, ES* 23: 393.

30. Ibn ʿIdhārī, *Al-Bayān*, 1: 150–151; *Chronica regia Coloniensis, MGH SS in Usum Scholarum*, 18: 84–86; *Annales Lamberti Parvi, MGH SS* 16: 649; Bruno Meyer, "El papel de los cruzados alemanes en la reconquista de la Península Ibérica en los siglos XII y XIII," *En la España Medieval* 23 (2000): 48–56.

31. Ralph of Diceto, *Ymagines historiarum*, in *Opera historica*, 2 vols., ed. William Stubbs, Rolls Series 68 (London: Longman, 1876), 2: 65–66; Ibn ʿIdhārī, *Al-Bayān*, 1: 150–53; *Chronicon Conimbricense, ES* 23: 331 and *PMH SS* 1: 3; *Narratio de itinere navali peregrinorum Hierosolymam tendentium et Silvam capientium, A.D. 1189*, ed. C. W. David, *Proceedings of the American Philosophical Society* 81 (1939):

591–678; Gonzaga de Azevedo, *História*, 5: 10–11; Mattoso and de Sousa, *A Monarquia feudal*, 84–87.

32. Ibn 'Idhārī, *Al-Bayān*, 1: 155, 168–72; Ibn Khaldūn, *Histoire*, 2: 212; Ibn Abī Zar', *Rawd al-Qirtas*, 1: 429, 519–20; Al-Ḥimyarī, *Kitāb*, 218–23; *Al-Ḥulal*, 189; al-Maqqarī, *History*, 2: 320, Bk. 8, ch. 3; *Gesta Regis Ricardi*, 117–22; Roger de Hoveden, *Chronica*, 3: 175.

33. Ibn 'Idhāri, *Al-Bayān*, 1: 159, 174–76; Levi-Provençal, "Recueil," 64–65 (31 July 1190); al-Maqqarī, *History*, 2: 320, Bk. 8, ch. 3; *Chronica latina*, 43–44, ch. 11; Rodrigo, *Historia*, 246–47, Bk. 7, ch. 24; Lucas, *Chronicon*, 4: 106–7, and *Crónica*, 406, ch. 83; *Chrónicon de Cardeña*, ES 23: 379; Roger de Hoveden, *Chronica*, 3: 90; *CSJP*, 130–31; *CGPIII*, 107–8, ch. 33; *CSJP*, 55, ch. 33; *Gesta comitum*, 14, ch. 9 (rp), 47, ch. 24.3 (rd); Sánchez Casabón, *Alfonso II*, 684–87, 701–2, nos. 520 (7 September 1190), 533 (May 1191); González, *Alfonso IX*, 2: 66–67, 70–71, nos. 40 (15 February 1191), 43 (May).

34. Rivera Recio, *Toledo*, 228, n. 79 (25 April 1191); Kehr, *Papsturkunden*, 2: 542, no. 190 (16 April 1192).

35. AC Toledo, E.7.C (XII).16.4, partial transcription by Rivera Recio, *Toledo*, 229, n. 80 (29 October 1192); Goñi Gaztambide, *Historia*, 95–96.

36. Kehr, *Papsturkunden*, 2: 554–55, no. 200 (4 November 1193).

37. Kehr, *Papsturkunden*, 2: 555–57, 567, nos. 201 (5 November 1193), 211 (undated).

38. González, *Alfonso VIII*, 3: 105–8, no. 622 (20 April 1194), and *Alfonso IX*, 2: 116–19, no. 79; *MH*, 1: 29, no. 13 (27 May 1194); *CSJP*, 131–32; *CGPIII*, 107–8, ch. 33; *CSJP (tr)*, 55, ch. 33; *Gesta comitum*, 15–16, ch. 9 (rp), 48, ch. 24.4 (rd).

39. Rodrigo, *Historia*, 251, Bk. 7, ch. 28; *Chronica latina*, 44–45, ch. 12; Ibn 'Idhārī, *Al-Bayān*, 1: 180; Sharīf al-Gharnāṭī, *Comentario a la Qasīda maqṣūra de Ḥāzim al-Qarṭājanī*, in Huici, *Batallas*, 202.

40. Paolo Zerbi, *Papato, Impero e Respublica Christiana dal 1187 al 1198* (Milan: Università Cattolica del Sacro Cuore, 1955), 179, no. 1 (10 July 1195); AC Toledo E.7.C(XII).16.6, published in part by Rivera Recio, *Toledo*, 232, n. 84.

41. *Chronica latina*, 44–47, ch. 12–13; Rodrigo, *Historia*, 251, Bk. 7, ch. 28; *Chronicon Conimbricense*, ES 23: 333 and *PMH SS* 1: 3; *Anales Toledanos I*, ES 23: 393; Lucas, *Chronicon*, 4: 106–7, and *Crónica*, 406–8, ch. 83; Ibn 'Idhārī, *Al-Bayān*, 1: 183–90; Sharif al-Gharnāṭī, *Comentario*, in Huici, *Batallas*, 197–201 (Arabic text), 202–6 (Spanish translation); al-Marrākushī, *Kitāb*, 235–36; Ibn Abī Zar', *Rawd al-Qirtas*, 2: 440–46; al-Maqqarī, *History*, 2: 321–22, Bk. 8, ch. 3; Ibn Khaldūn, *Histoire*, 2: 212–14; Roger de Hoveden, *Chronica*, 3: 302.

42. Francisco Ruiz Gómez, "La guerra y los pactos: A propósito de la batalla de Alarcos," in Izquierdo Benito and Ruiz Gómez, *Alarcos*, 145–68; Francisco García Fitz, "La batalla en su contexto estratégico. A propósito de Alarcos," ibid., 265–82, and Jaafar Benelhaj Soulami, "La batalla de Alarcos en la mitología árabe," ibid., 283–88; Huici, *Batallas*, 137–218.

43. Rodrigo, *Historia*, 252–53, Bk. 7, ch. 30; *Chronica latina*, 47–48, ch. 14; *Gesta comitum*, 14, ch. 9 (rp), and 48, ch. 24.4; *CSJP*, 131; *CGPIII*, 108, ch. 33; *CSJP (tr)*, 55–56, ch. 33; *Chronicon Conimbricense*, ES 23: 334 and *PMH SS* 1: 3; Antonio Ubieto Arteta, "La peregrinación de Alfonso II de Aragón a Santiago de Compostela," *EEMCA* 5 (1953): 438–52.

44. Kehr, *Papsturkunden,* 2: 574, 576–78, 588, nos. 220, 221–22 (29 March 1196), 228 (28 May 1196); Fidel Fita, "Bulas históricas del reino de Navarra en los postreros años del siglo XII," *BRAH* 26 (1895): 418–22; Goñi Gaztambide, *Historia,* 100–101.

45. Lévi-Provençal, "Recueil," 66–67, no. 35 (6 August 1196); Rodrigo, *Historia,* 252–53, Bk. 7, ch. 30; *Chronica latina,* 47–50, ch. 14–15; *Anales Toledanos I, ES* 23: 394; Ibn ʿIdhārī, *Al-Bayān,* 1: 193–95; Ibn Khaldūn, *Histoire,* 2: 213–14; Lucas, *Chronicon,* 4: 108, and *Crónica,* 407–8, ch. 83, and *Vita Sancti Martini Legionensis, PL* 208: 20, 22, ch. 20, 23; Roger de Hoveden, *Chronica,* 3: 303.

46. Francisco Martinez Marina, *Teoria de las Cortes, BAE* 220: 85, no. 3 (31 October 1196); Ramón Riu, "Dos bulas inéditas de Celestino III," *BRAH* 11 (1887): 455–58; Fidel Fita, "Bulas históricas, 423–24; *DP,* 170, no. 138 (16 April 1198).

47. Rodrigo, *Historia,* 253–54, Bk. 7, ch. 32; *Chronica latina,* 50–52, ch. 16; Lucas, *Chronicon,* 4: 108, and *Crónica,* 409, ch. 83; Kehr, *Papsturkunden,* 2: 591–93, no. 230 (20 February 1197); Carl Erdmann, *Papsturkunden in Portugal* (Berlin: Weidmannsche Buchhandlung, 1927), 2: 376, no. 154 (10 April 1197); *MH,* 1: 32–34, no. 16; Zerbi, *Papato,* 180–81, nos. 2–3 (13–14 May 1197).

48 Ibn ʿIdhārī, *Al-Bayān,* 1: 199–202; *Anales Toledanos I, ES* 23: 394; Rodrigo, *Historia,* 246–47, 252–53, Bk. 7, ch. 24, 30–31; *Chronica latina,* 48–50, ch. 15; Lucas, *Chronicon,* 4: 109, and *Crónica,* 409–10, ch. 83; Roger de Hoveden, *Chronica,* 3: 90.

49. Alvar, *Textos,* 235–36, 241–42, 248.

50. *Chronica latina,* 50–52, ch. 16-18; Rodrigo, *Historia,* 253–54, 256, Bk. 7, ch. 32, 34; Lucas, *Chronicon,* 4: 110, and *Crónica,* 406, ch. 83; Roger de Hoveden, *Chronica,* 3: 91–92, and 4: 78–79; *Chrónicon Burgenese, ES* 23: 310; *CSJP,* 137–38; González, *Alfonso VIII,* 3: 365–74, 424–29, 479–84, nos. 782 (26 March 1206), 813 (29 October 1207), 845 (27 June 1209), and *Alfonso IX,* 2: 284–91, 341–45, nos. 205, 251.

51. *DP,* 168–72, 175–76, 181–82, 185, 193, 197–98, 209–15, 305–6, 332, 335–39, 347, 358, nos. 138 (16 April 1198), 140 (21 April), 144 (2 May), 152 (28 May), 157 (6 June), 170 (9 December), 181 (11 February 1199), 196 (25 May), 276 (5 June 1203), 299 (22 May 1204), 304–5 (19–20 June), 315 (16 June 1205, reg.), 331 (2 March 1206); Joseph F. O'Callaghan,"Innocent III and the Kingdoms of Castile and Leon," in *Pope Innocent III and His World,* ed. John C. Moore (Aldershot: Ashgate, 1999), 317–35; Antonio García y García, "Innocent III," ibid., 337–50.

52. *DP,* 329–30, no. 295 (14 February 1204); Ibn ʿIdhārī, *Al-Bayān,* 1: 223–26.

53. Francisco J. Miquel Rosell, *Regesta de letras pontificias del Archivo de la Corona de Aragón, sección cancillería real (pergaminos)* (Madrid: CSIC, 1945–47), 41, no. 51 (8 August 1204, reg.); *DP,* 339–41, 346–47, nos. 306 (reg.), 307 (10 November 1204), 314 (16 June 1205). *CSJP,* 135; *CGPIII,* 111–13, ch. 34; *CSJP (tr),* 56–58, ch. 34; *Gesta comitum,* 26, 51–52, ch. 10 (rp), 25.2 (rd); Zurita, *Anales,* 1: 308–12.

54. *DP,* 349–51, 367–69, nos. 318–21 (16 June 1205), 343–44 (9 June 1206).

55. *DP,* 366–67, no. 342 (26 May 1206).

56. Zurita, *Anales,* 1: 313–14; Soldevila, *Història,* 1: 226–28.

57. *DP,* 436, no. 416 (26 February 1210); Javier Gorosterratzu, *Don Rodrigo Jiménez de Rada, Gran Estadista, Escritor y Prelado* (Pamplona: Viuda de T. Bescansa, 1925), 411, no. 1; *Gesta comitum,* 17, 52, ch. 10 (rp), 25.4 (rd); Ibn Idhārī, *Al-Bayān,* 1: 258; Zurita, *Anales,* 1: 331–32.

58. *DP*, 472–76, nos. 442 (10 December 1210), 446–48 (22 February 1211); Gorosterratzu, *Rodrigo*, 414–16, nos. 8–10.

59. Matthew Paris, *Chronica Majora*, ed. H. R. Luard, 7 vols., Rolls Series 57 (London: Longman, 1872–83), 2: 559–66; Nevill Barbour, "The Embassy Sent by King John of England to Miramamolín, King of Morocco," *Al-Andalus* 25 (1960): 373–81, and "Two Christian Embassies to the Almohad Sultan Muḥammad al-Naṣir at Seville in 1211," *Actas del Primer Congreso de Estudios árabes e islámicos (Córdoba 1962)* (Madrid: Comité permanente del Congreso de Estudios árabes e islámicos, 1964), 189–213; Ibn Abī Zarʿ, *Rawd al-Qirtas*, 2: 457–60.

60. *Annales Compostellani*, and *Anales Toledanos I*, *ES* 23: 324, 394–95; Rodrigo, *Historia*, 256–57, Bk. 7, ch. 34–35; *Chronica latina*, 52–55, ch. 18–19; Lucas, *Chronicon*, 4: 111, and *Crónica*, 412–13, ch. 83; Al-Ḥimyarī, *Kitāb*, 223–28; Ibn ʿIdhārī, *Al-Bayān*, 1: 261–70; al-Marrākushī, *Kitāb*, 265; Ibn Khaldūn, *Histoire*, 2: 224; Ibn Abī Zarʿ, *Rawd al-Qirtas*, 2: 455–64; Joseph F. O'Callaghan, "The Order of Calatrava: Years of Crisis and Survival, 1158–1212," in *The Meeting of Two Worlds: Cultural Exchange Between East and West During the Period of the Crusades*, ed. Vladimir P. Goss and Christine Verzár Bornstein (Kalamazoo: Western Michigan University, 1986), 427–28.

61. Rodrigo, *Historia*, 257–58, Bk. 7, ch. 35–36; *Chronica latina*, 54–56, ch. 19–20; *Annales Compostellani* and *Anales Toledanos I*, *ES* 23: 324, 395–96; Alvar, *Textos*, 118–21; González, *Alfonso VIII*, 3: 557–58, no. 890 (1212); Goñi Gaztambide, *Historia*, 114, n. 13.

62. *DP*, 497–98, 500–501, nos. 468 (31 January 1212), 470 (4 February); Gorosterratzu, *Rodrigo*, 417, nos. 14–15; *Anales Toledanos I*, *ES* 23: 396; *Chronica latina*, 61, ch. 23; Arnald Amaury in Mondéjar, *Alonso el Noble*, Appendix, ciii–cvii.

63. For the text see *Continuatio Lambacensis*, *MGH SS* 9: 557–58.

64. Alvar, *Textos*, 91–94; Milá y Fontanals, *Trovadores*, 126–30.

65. Alvar, *Textos*, 95–96; Caesarius of Heisterbach, *Dialogus miraculorum*, ed. Joseph Strange, 2 vols. (Cologne: J.M. Heberle, 1851), 1: 303, Bk. 5, ch. 21.

66. Lucas *Chronicon*, 4: 110, and *Crónica*, 413, ch. 83; Rodrigo, *Historia*, 259–60, Bk. 8, ch. 1; *Chronica latina*, 57, ch. 21.

67. *DP*, 501–2, no. 471 (5 April 1212), and 480–81, no. 452 (fragment misdated 5 April 1211); Gorosterratzu, *Rodrigo*, 416, nos. 11, 13; Hernández, *Cartularios*, 329, 651, nos. 328 (n.d.), 649 (5 April 1212); Lucas, *Chronicon*, 4: 110, and *Crónica*, 412–13, ch.83.

68. *DP*, 503–4, no. 473; Christoph T. Maier, "Mass, the Eucharist and the Cross: Innocent III and the Relocation of the Crusade," in Moore, *Pope Innocent III*, 352–54; García y García, "Innocent III," ibid., 339–40; Alberic of Trois Fontaines, *Chronica*, *MGH SS* 23: 894–95.

69. Huici, *Batallas*, 219–327; Martín Alvira Cabrer, "De Alarcos a las Navas de Tolosa: Idea y realidad de los orígenes de la batalla de 1212," in Izquierdo Benito and Ruiz Gómez, *Alarcos*, 249–64.

70. Arnald Amaury in Mondéjar, *Alonso el Noble*, Appendix, civ, cvi; *Chronica latina*, 56–58, ch. 21; Rodrigo, *Historia*, 259–65, 273, Bk. 8, ch. 1–4, 6, 10; *Anales Toledanos I*, *ES* 23: 396–97; González, *Alfonso VIII*, 3: 568, 570, 573, nos. 897–98 (1212); Alberic of Trois Fontaines, *Chronica*, *MGH SS* 23: 894.

71. González, *Alfonso VIII*, 3: 567–68, no. 897 (1212); *Chronica latina*, 57, ch. 21.

72. González, *Alfonso VIII*, 3: 569, no. 897 (1212); Rodrigo, *Historia*, 264–68, Bk. 8, ch. 5–7; *Chronica latina*, 58–59, ch. 22; *Anales Toledanos I, ES* 23: 397; Damian Smith, "¿*Soli Hispani?* Innocent III and Las Navas de Tolosa," *Hispania Sacra* 51 (1999): 489–512.

73. Rodrigo, *Historia*, 269–72, Bk. 8, ch. 8–9; Juan Eslava Galán, "Tácticas en la Batalla de Las Navas de Tolosa," *CEM* 6–7 (1978–79): 39–53.

74. Rodrigo, *Historia*, 272–75, Bk. 8, ch. 10–11; *Chronica latina*, 61–62, ch. 24; Lucas, *Chronicon*, 4: 110, and *Crónica*, 414–15, ch. 83; *Anales Toledanos I, ES* 23: 397; Ibn ʿIdhārī, *Al-Bayān*, 1: 269–73; Al-Ḥimyarī, *Kitāb*, 276–78; Ibn Abī Zarʿ *Rawd al-Qirtas*, 2: 464–68; Ibn Khaldūn, *Histoire*, 2: 224; Alberic of Troisfontaines, *Chronica, MGH SS* 23: 894; González, *Alfonso VIII*, 3: 566–72, no. 897 (1212); *DP*, 511–15, no. 483; Ricardo of San Germano, *Chronicon, MGH SS*, 19: 335.

75. *DP*, 519–21, no. 488 (26 October 1212); González, *Alfonso VIII*, 3: 572–74, no. 898 (1212, Berenguela to Blanca); Arnald Amaury in Mondéjar, *Alonso el Noble*, Appendix, cvi; Diego García de Campos, *Planeta*, ed. Manuel Alonso (Madrid: CSIC, 1943), 181, prologue.

76. *Chronicon Conimbricense, ES* 23: 334 and *PMH SS* 1: 3; Rodrigo, *Historia*, 275–76, Bk. 8, ch. 12; *Chronica latina*, 62–64, ch. 25; Lucas, *Chronicon*, 4: 111, and *Crónica*, 414–15, ch. 83.

77. Ibn ʿIdhārī, *Al-Bayān*, 1: 271–73.

78. Rodrigo, *Historia*, 277–80, Bk. 8, ch. 13–15; *Chronica latina*, 64–69, ch. 26, 28; Lucas, *Chronicon*, 4: 111, and *Crónica*, 415–16, ch. 83; *Anales Toledanos I, ES* 23: 398–400; Ibn ʿIdhārī, *Al-Bayān*, 1: 276–77; González, *Alfonso VIII*, 3: 576, no. 900 (11 November 1212), and *Alfonso IX*, 2: 383–84, no. 284.

79. *DP*, 522–25, nos. 491 (15 January 1213), 493 (17 January); Soldevila, *Història*, 1: 233–42; Jordi Ventura, *Pere el Catòlic I Simó de Montfort* (Barcelona: Aedos, 1960).

80. *DP*, 523–34, 546–50, 553–55, nos. 492 (16 January 1213), 493–96 (17–18 January), 505 (1 June), 513–14 (1213), 515 (15 January 1214).

81. *Crònica de Jaume I*, 9 vols. ed. Joseph M. de Cascuberta and Enric Bagüe (Barcelona: Editorial Barcino, 1926–62), 1: 24–28, ch. 8; *Gesta comitum*, 17–18, ch. 10 (rp), and 52–54, Bk. 25, ch. 4 (rd); *CSJP*, 138–42; *CGPIII*, 113–15, ch. 34; *CSJP (tr)*, 59–61, ch. 34; *Chronica latina*, 66–67, ch. 27; Rodrigo, *Historia*, 181–82, Bk. 6, ch. 4; Matthew Paris, *Chronica Majora*, 2: 566–68; Zurita, *Anales*, 1: 342–49.

82. Ibn ʿIdhārī, *Al-Bayān*, 1: 273–74, 276; Ibn Abī Zarʿ, *Rawd al-Qirtas*, 2: 468–69; Rodrigo, *Historia*, 279–80, Bk. 8, ch. 15; *Chronica latina*, 67–69, ch. 28.

Chapter 4

1. *DP*, 543–45, no. 503 (19 April 1213); Demetrio Mansilla, *La documentación pontificia de Honorio III (1216–1227)* (Rome: Instituto Español de Historia eclesiástica, 1965), 76, no. 95 (September–October 1217), and *Iglesia castellano-leonesa y curia romana en los tiempos del rey San Fernando* (Madrid: CSIC, 1945), 50–53; *MH*, 1: 46, no. 25; Lucas, *Chronicon*, 4: 113 and *Crónica*, 421, ch. 88; *Chronica latina*, 72, ch. 30; García y García, "Innocent III," 343–47; Goñi Gaztambide, *Historia*, 132, 135; Peter

Linehan, *The Spanish Church and the Papacy in the Thirteenth Century* (Cambridge: Cambridge University Press, 1971), 5–6.

2. *DP*, 556, 566–68, nos. 516 (23 January 1214), 537 (23 January 1216); Mansilla, *Honorio III*, 6–8, 10, nos. 9 (10 November 1216), 11 (12 November); Gorosterratzu, *Rodrigo*, 420–21, nos. 30–32; González, *Alfonso IX*, 2: 442–44, nos. 337–38 (12 August 1216); Rodrigo, *Historia*, 281–85, Bk. 9, ch. 1–4; *Chronica latina*, 73–76, ch. 31–32; Lucas, *Chronicon*, 4: 113, and *Crónica*, 417, ch. 84; *Anales Toledanos I*, *ES* 23: 400; Ibn ʿIdhārī, *Al-Bayān*, 1: 275–80.

3. *DP*, 566–68, no. 537 (23 January 1216); Mansilla, *Honorio III*, 1–2, no. 1 (25 July 1216). See Chapter 7.

4. Lucas, *Chronicon*, 4: 113, and *Crónica*, 421–22, ch. 88; Joseph P. Donovan, *Pelagius and the Fifth Crusade* (Philadelphia: University of Pennsylvania Press, 1950); James M. Powell, *The Anatomy of a Crusade, 1213–1221* (Philadelphia: University of Pennsylvania Press, 1986); Thomas C. Van Cleve, "The Fifth Crusade," in Setton, *Crusades*, 2: 377–428.

5. Emo, *Chronicon*, *MGH SS* 23: 478–80; *Chronica regia Coloniensis (Anales Colonienses maximi)*, *Scriptores rerum Germanicarum in usum scholarum* (Hannover 1880), 239–40, and *MGH SS* 17: 829–30, and *Chronica regia Coloniensis continuatio tertia* in *Quinti Belli Sacri Scriptores minores*, ed. Reinhold Röhricht (Geneva: J. Fick, 1879), 147–52; Oliver of Paderborn, *The Capture of Damietta*, tr. John J. Gavigan (Philadelphia: University of Pennsylvania Press, 1948), 20–21; Al-Ḥimyarī, *Kitāb*, 324–26; Gonzaga de Azevedo, *História*, 5: 86, 192–93, no. 4 (13 June 1219); Letter of the Portuguese bishops, Mansilla, *Honorio III*, 76–78, no. 95 (September–October 1217); *MH*, 1: 45–47, no. 25; Goñi Gaztambide, *Historia*, 139–41; Herculano, *História*, 4: 76–95.

6. *Chronica regia Coloniensis*, *QBS*, 149–51; Letter of the Portuguese bishops, Mansilla, *Honorio III*, 76–78, no. 95; *MH*, 1: 45–47, no. 25; Reinerus Leodensis, *Chronica*, *QBS*, 329–30; Caesarius of Heisterbach, *Dialogus*, 2: 137, Bk. 8, ch. 66; Ibn Abī Zarʿ, *Rawd al-Qirtas*, 2: 523; Gosuinus, *Quomodo fuit capta Alcaser a Francis*, *PMH SS* 1: 101–4; see the same text in Antonio Brandão, *Crónicas de D. Sancho I e D. Afonso II*, ed. A. de Magalhães Basto (Lisbon: Livraria Civilização, 1945), 273–77, no. 11; Gonzaga de Azevedo, *História*, 5: 84–97.

7. Mansilla, *Honorio III*, 76–78, 106–8, 116, nos. 95 (September–October 1217)–96 (after 21 October 1217), 134 (12 January 1218), 143 (26 January); *MH*, 1: 45–49, nos. 25–26; Clemens Rodenberg, *Epistolae Saeculi XIII e Regestis Pontificum Romanorum selectae*, *MGH Epistolae Saeculi XIII*, 3 vols. (Berlin: Monumenta Germaniae Historica, 1883–94), 1: 29, 34, nos. 36, 44; *Chronica regia Coloniensis*, *QBS*, 151.

8. Mansilla, *Honorio III*, 115–16, 119–21, 123, nos. 142 (26 January 1218), 148 (30 January), 153 (31 January), and *Iglesia*, 276, no. 5; Gorosterratzu, *Rodrigo*, 429, nos. 51, 54; Goñi Gaztambide, *Historia*, 142–43.

9. Mansilla, *Honorio III*, 121, 124, 141–42, 146–47, nos. 149 (30 January 1218), 155 (31 January), 179 (10 July), 185–86 (19 August), and *Iglesia*, 275, 277–78, nos. 3, 6–7; also *Honorio III*, 6–8, 10, nos. 9 (10 November 1216), 11 (12 November); Gorosterratzu, *Rodrigo*, 185–89, 420–21, nos. 30–32; González, *Alfonso IX*, 2: 458–59, 460–61, 479, nos. 350 (26 November 1217), 352 (n.d.), 366 (26 August 1218).

246 Notes to Pages 81–85

10. Mansilla, *Honorio III*, 160–63, nos. 207 (9 February 1219), 208–9 (15 March), 210 (16 March); Gorosterratzu, *Rodrigo*, 431–32, nos. 65, 67–68; Fidel Fita, "Bernardo de Perigord, arcediano de Toledo y obispo de Zamora: Bulas inéditas de Honorio III (15 de marzo de 1219) y Nicolas IV (18 de agosto de 1291)," *BRAH* 14 (1889): 456–66.

11. Mansilla, *Honorio III*, 170, 171, 173, 177–78, nos. 223 (29 April 1219), 224 (8 May), 227 (18 May), 234–35 (26 July); Gorosterratzu, *Rodrigo*, 433, no. 71; *Anales Toledanos I, ES* 23: 401.

12. Mansilla, *Honorio III*, 207–8, 226–27, 273–74, nos. 269 (5 February 1220), 301 (4 July), 368 (13 February 1221); see other bulls relating to the twentieth, ibid., 207, 214, 217–18, 221, nos. 268, 278, 285, 291; Gorosterratzu, *Rodrigo*, 435–36, nos. 74–75; Hernández, *Cartularios*, 399–400, no. 398 (30 November 1221); Linehan, *Spanish Church*, 8–9, n. 1; *Anales Toledanos III, ES* 23: 413.

13. *BC*, 683–86 (August 1221); Joseph F. O'Callaghan, "*Hermandades* Between the Military Orders of Calatrava and Santiago During the Castilian Reconquest, 1158–1252," in *Calatrava*, No. V; Letter of the Almohad vizier to Queen Berenguela, 24 October 1221, in Ibn 'Idhārī, *Al-Bayān*, 1: 282–83.

14. Mansilla, *Honorio III*, 78, no. 96 (1217); González, *Alfonso IX*, 2: 455–56, 478, nos. 347 (28 May 1217), 365 (16 July 1218); *Anales Toledanos I, ES* 23: 401; Lucas, *Chronicon*, 4: 113–14, and *Crónica*, 419, 422, ch. 86, 89.

15. Mansilla, *Honorio III*, 251–52, 274, nos. 339–40, 369 (18 December 1220); *BC*, 55, 57, nos. 11, 13–14. See Honorius III's letter of 13 March 1221 to the archbishop of Tarragona in Peter Linehan, "Documento español sobre la Quinta Cruzada," *Hispania Sacra* 20 (1967): 177–82.

16. Ana María Barrero Garciá, "Un formulario de cancillería episcopal castellano-leonés del siglo XIII," *AHDE* 46 (1976): 703, 707–8, nos. 18–19, 29–31. Barrero believes that most of the documents in this collection can be dated between 1220 and 1226. Martín Rodríguez was bishop of Zamora from 1219 to 1230. In a formulaic reply an abbot stated that he could only pay 200 *aurei*. Honorius III ordered the master of the Temple in Jerusalem to pardon Pedro Alvítiz for debts incurred over the last seven years in the war against the Saracens; Mansilla, *Honorio III*, 324–25, no. 447 (22 June 1223). González, *Alfonso IX*, 2: 530–31, no. 415 (14 November 1221).

17. *Anales Toledanos II, ES* 23: 407; Ayala Martínez, *San Juan*, 426–27, no. 238 (8 August 1222); González, *Alfonso IX*, 1: 196–98.

18. Julio González, *Reinado y diplomas de Fernando III*, 3 vols. (Córdoba: Monte de Piedad y Caja de Ahorros de Córdoba, 1980–86), is the principal study of the reign.

19. Ibn 'Idhārī, *Al-Bayān*, 1: 287–92; al-Maqqarī, *History*, 2: 324–25, Bk. 8, ch. 3; Rachel Arié, *L'Espagne musulmane au temps des nasrides (1232–1492)* (Paris: E. de Boccard, 1973), 49–50; Cristóbal Torres Delgado, *El antiguo reino nazarí de Granada (1232–1340)* (Granada: Anel, 1974), 64–65.

20. *Chronica latina*, 84–88, 109–10, ch. 42–45, 68; .Rodrigo, *Historia*, 292, Bk. 9, ch.12; *Anales Toledanos II, ES* 23: 408; O'Callaghan, "*Hermandades*," 617–18.

21. *Chronicon de Cardeña, Anales Toledanos II*, and *Anales Toledanos III, ES* 23: 373, 408, 413; *Chronica latina*, 86–92, ch. 44–48; Rodrigo, *Historia*, 292–93, Bk. 9, ch. 12; Ibn 'Idhārī, *Al-Bayān*, 1: 287–95; Ibn Abī Zar', *Rawd al-Qirtas*, 2: 524; Juan Eslava Galán, "La campaña de Quesada (1224)," *CEM* 12–13 (1984): 5–23. On Abū Zayd see

Robert I. Burns, S.J., *Islam Under the Crusaders: Colonial Survival in the Thirteenth-Century Kingdom of Valencia* (Princeton, N.J.: Princeton University Press, 1973), 32–37, and "Almohad Prince and Mudejar Convert: New Documentation on Abū Zayd," in *Medieval Iberia: Essays on the History and Literature of Medieval Spain,* ed. Donald J. Kagay and Joseph T. Snow (New York: Peter Lang, 1997), 171–88.

22. Mansilla, *Honorio III,* 414–16, 421–22, 440–41, nos. 559–61 (3 June 1225), 569 (15 July), 585–86 (20 October); *Chronica latina,* 91–92, ch. 48; *BS,* 85–86; *MFIII,* 352 (7 September 1225); *Cantigas de Santa Maria,* ed. Walter Mettmann, 4 vols. (Coimbra: Universidade de Coimbra, 1959–72; reprint, 2 vols. Vigo: Edicions Xerais de Galicia, 1981), 1: 651–53; also see Hernández, *Cartularios,* 361–62, nos. 401–2 (20 January 1220); González, *Fernando III,* 2: 185–86, no. 153 (23 January 1222); Hilda Grassotti, "Don Rodrigo Jiménez de Rada, gran señor y hombre de negocios en la Castilla del siglo XIII," *CHE* 55–56 (1972): 281–84.

23. Mansilla, *Honorio III,* 429–32, nos. 574–76 (25–26 September 1225), and *Iglesia,* 289–91, nos. 20–22; Goñi Gaztambide, *Historia,* 150, dated this letter incorrectly in 1226; Robert I. Burns, S.J., "The Many Crusades of Valencia's Conquest (1225–1280): An Historiographical Labyrinth," in Kagay and Vann, *Social Origins,* 169.

24. *Chronica latina,* 91–95, ch. 48–50; Rodrigo, *Historia,* 294, Bk. 9, ch. 13; Ibn Abī Zarʿ, *Rawd al-Qirtas,* 2: 525; Ibn ʿIdhārī, *Al-Bayān,* 1: 295–96; Al-Ḥimyarī, *Kitāb,* 121–26; González, *Fernando III,* 3: 93–96, no. 575 (9 September 1236).

25. AHN Tumbo de Tojos Outos, fol. 52 v, cited by González, *Alfonso IX,* 1: 200. The bishop of Astorga, also preparing for the campaign, made his will at that time; *ES* 16: 229. Lucas, *Chronicon,* 4: 114, and *Crónica,* 422, ch. 89; *Chronica latina,* 94–95, ch. 50; Herculano, *História,* 4: 187–89, 328–29, 343–44; Gonzaga de Azevedo, *História,* 6: 14–19, 138–41.

26. Ibn ʿIdhārī, *Al-Bayān,* 12: 296–310; al-Maqqarī, *History,* 2: 326–28, Bk. 8, ch. 4; *Chronica latina,* 97–98, ch. 53; Arié, *L'Espagne musulmane,* 52–53; Torres Delgado, *El antiguo reino,* 75–87.

27. Gorosterratzu, *Rodrigo,* 257–59, 439, no. 90 (14 February 1228); *MFIII,* 358–59; Lucien Auvray, *Les registres de Grégoire IX,* 2 vols. (Paris: Bibliothèque des Ecoles Françaises d'Athènes et de Rome, 1896–1955), 1: 155–56, nos. 255 (8 December 1228), 329 (reg., 7 August 1229); Goñi Gaztambide, *Historia,* 153–54.

28. Lucas, *Chronicon,* 4: 114, and *Crónica,* 423, ch. 91; Auvray, *Grégoire IX,* 1: 160, 170–71, nos. 268 (reg., 19 February 1229), 283 (February–March); *Chronica latina,* 98–99, ch. 54; *Gesta comitum,* 19, ch. 11 (rd), and 57, ch. 27.2; Rodrigo, *Historia,* 293, Bk. 9, ch. 12; Linehan, *Spanish Church,* 20–34; Mansilla, *Iglesia,* 48–50.

29. Lucas, *Chronicon,* 4: 114, and *Crónica,* 423, ch. 91; *Chronica latina,* 98–99, ch. 54; Antonio C. Floriano, *Documentación histórica del Archivo Municipal de Cáceres (1229–1471)* (Cáceres: Diputación Provincial, 1987), 7–9, no. 1 (23 April 1229); AHN Poyo, cited by González, *Alfonso IX,* 1: 207; also ibid., 2: 616–19, nos. 516–518 (14, 26 December 1227; 8 January 1228).

30. Lucas, *Chronicon,* 4: 114, and *Crónica,* 423–27, ch. 91–92; *Chronicon de Cardeña,* and *Anales Toledanos II, ES* 23: 379, 409; *Chronica latina,* 100, 103–4, ch. 56, 60; Rodrigo, *Historia,* 247–48, Bk. 7, ch. 25; Ibn Abī Zarʿ, *Rawd al-Qirtas,* 2: 526; Ibn ʿIdhārī, *Al-Bayān,* 1: 320–22; al-Maqqarī, *History,* 2: 328–29, Bk. 8, ch. 4.

31. Auvray, *Grégoire IX*, 1: 339, nos. 516–17 (29 October 1230); Odoricus Raynaldus, *Annales ecclesiastici ab anno MCXCVIII ubi desinit Cardinalis Baronius*, ed. J. D. Mansi, 15 vols. (Lucca: Leonardo Venturini, 1738–47) 2: 34, anno 1230, no. 35.

32. *Chronica latina*, 101, 103, ch. 57, 60; *Annales Compostellani*, and *Chronicon Conimbricense*, *ES* 23: 324–25, 335; Lucas, *Chronicon*, 4: 114 and *Crónica*, 424, ch. 91; Rodrigo, *Historia*, 295–96, Bk. 9, ch. 14; *PMH Leges* 1.3: 619–20 (May 1229); Herculano, *História*, 4: 188–89, 331, 343–44.

33. Auvray, *Grégoire IX*, 1: 338–40, nos. 515 (31 October 1230), 518 (reg.); Goñi Gaztambide, *Historia*, 152, nn. 65–66 (29 October 1230).

34. *DP*, 567–68, no. 537 (23 January 1216). See the royal autobiography, *Crònica de Jaume I*, ed. Josep Maria Casacuberta, tr. Enric Bagüe, 9 vols. (Barcelona: Editorial Barcino, 1926–62). There is an English translation by John Forster, *The Chronicle of James I, King of Aragon, Surnamed the Conqueror*, 2 vols. (London: Chapman and Hall, 1883); Robert I. Burns, S.J., "The Spiritual Life of James the Conqueror," in his *Moors and Crusaders in Mediterranean Spain* (London: Variorum, 1978), No. I; Ferran Soldevila, *Vida de Jaume I el conqueridor* (Barcelona: Editorial Aedos, 1958), 1–87, and *Jaume I. Pere el Gran* (Barcelona: Editorial Teide, 1955), 11–17.

35. Mansilla, *Honorio III*, 298–99, 309, nos. 404 (15 June 1222), 419 (22 November); *CJI*, 1: 30–43, ch, 1–16.

36. *CAVC*, 1: 102–3, no. 16 (29 April 1225); Ambrosio Huici Miranda and María Desamparados Cabanes Pecourt, *Documentos de Jaime I de Aragón*, 5 vols. thus far (Valencia: Anubar, 1976–88), 1: 139–44, no. 67 (28 April 1225); Villanueva, *Viage*, 13: 307–13.

37. *DJI*, 1: 147–53, nos. 70 (13 August 1225), 71 (3 September), 72 (5 September), 73 (10 September); Gual Camarena, "Precedentes," 241–43, nos. 58–66 (reg.); *CJI*, 1: 62–66, ch. 25; Bernat Desclot, *Crònica*, ed. Miguel Coll i Alentorn, 5 vols. (Barcelona: Editorial Barcino, 1949–51), 2: 65–66, ch. 13; Antonio Ubieto Arteta, *Origenes del Reino de Valencia: Cuestiones cronológicos sobre su reconquista*, 2 vols. (Valencia: Anubar, 1975), 1: 32–39; Pedro López Elum, *La conquista y repoblación valenciana durante el reinado de Jaime I* (Valencia: Pedro López Elum, 1995), 27–33; Ramón Ferrer Navarro, *Conquista y repoblación del reino de Valencia* (Valencia: Del Senia al Segura, 1999), 25–28.

38. *Chronica latina*, 98–99, ch. 54; Ibn ʿIdhārī, *Al-Bayān*, 1: 321; al-Maqqarī, *History*, 2: 334, Bk. 8, ch. 4; *DJI*, 223–26, no. 119 (20 April 1229).

39. Sánchez Casabón, *Alfonso II*, 345–46, no. 255 (June 1178); *CAVC*, 1: 112–20, no. 17 (21 December 1228); Desclot, *Crònica*, 2: 66–67, ch. 14; *CJI*, 1: 118–27, ch. 47–49; al-Maqqarī, *History*, 2: 329–30, Bk. 8, ch. 4; Álvaro Santamaría, "La expansión político-militar de la Corona de Aragón bajo la dirección de Jaime I: Baleares," in *Jaime I y su época: X Congreso de Historia de la Corona de Aragón* (Zaragoza: CSIC, 1979), 91–146.

40. *CJI*, 2: 6–14, ch. 50–53; Desclot, *Crònica*, 2: 70–81, 88, ch. 15–28, 30; *CDACA*, 6: 97–101, nos. 16 (23 December 1228), 17 (28 August 1229), and 11: 3–6 (18 October 1229); John Shideler, *A Medieval Catalan Noble Family: The Montcadas, 1000–1230* (Berkeley: University of California Press, 1984).

41. *CAVC*, 1: 112–20, no, 17; *DJI*, 1: 205–11, nos. 110–11 (21 December 1228), 114 (27 December), 115 (30 December), *CDACA*, 6: 95–98, 104–11, nos. 16 (23 December 1228),

19 (17 May 1234); *CJI*, 2: 6, 8, 16, ch. 50, 55; Desclot, *Crònica*, ch. 14; Zurita, *Anales*, 1: 427–30.

42. Auvray, *Grégoire IX*, 1: 160, no. 268 (12 February 1229, reg.); Goñi Gaztambide, *Historia*, 157–58; *ES* 48: 324; Juan Tejada y Romero, *Colección de Canones y de todos los Concilios de la Iglesia de España y de América*, 7 vols. (Madrid: P. Montero, 1859–63), 3: 329–30 (canons 25–26); Mansilla, *Iglesia*, 49. Gregory IX, in an undated bull, condemned anyone fomenting conflict among the Christians; Rodenberg, *MGH Epistolae Selectae Saeculi XIII*, 1: 296, no. 379.

43. *DJI*, 1: 230–32, no. 124 (28 August 1229); *CDACA*, 6: 98–101, no. 17. Gregory IX indicated that Jaime I received the cross from the legate; Villanueva, *Viaje*, 21: 252 (28 November 1229), and 13: 313–16 (28 August); Desclot, *Crònica*, 2: 88–91, ch. 30–31; Zurita, *Anales*, 1: 436.

44. *CJI*, 2: 16–20, 24, ch. 55–57; Desclot, *Crònica*, 2: 93–95, ch. 34; *Chronica latina*, 99–100, ch. 55.

45. *CJI*, 2: 36–48, 52, ch. 58, 63–67, 69; Desclot, *Crònica*, 2: 95–109, ch. 35–37; Villanueva, *Viaje*, 21: 252 (28 November 1229); Goñi Gaztambide, *Historia*, 160–61.

46. *CJI*, 2: 56–90, ch. 71–88; Desclot, *Crònica*, 2: 109–37, ch. 38–47; *Gesta comitum*, 19, ch. 11 (rp) and 58, ch. 27.5 (rd); *Chronica latina*, 99–100, ch. 55; *CSJP*, 149; *CSJP (tr)*, 64, ch. 35; *CGPIII*, 121, ch. 35; Ramon Muntaner, *Crònica*, 9 vols., 2d ed. Enric Bagüe (Barcelona: Editorial Barcino, 1927–52), 1: 27–29, ch. 7–8; Ibn Abī Zarʿ, *Rawd al-Qirtas*, 2: 525–26; Ibn al-Abbār, quoted by al-Maqqarī, *History*, 2: 330–32, Bk. 8, ch. 4; Al-Ḥimyarī, *Kitāb*, 382–83.

47. *CJI*, 2: 122–27, ch. 108–9, and 3: 7–13, ch. 110–14; *DJI*, 1: 233–36, 247–54, 263–64, 269–72, 277–82, 286–88, 293–94, 300, 303, 318–21, 371, 379–80, 384–85, nos. 126 (12 January 1230), 127–28 (1 April), 134–39 (11 July–23 October), 146 (10 January 1231), 150 (1 March), 154–155 (8–11 July), 159 (29 September), 165 (5 April 1232), 169 (7 July), 172 (13 September), 178 (22 March 1233), 186 (8 August), 225 (13 December 1235), 235 (20 May 1236), 237 (13 October), and 2: 49, no. 284 (27 November 1238); *Liber partitionis regni Maiorice* in *CDACA*, 11: 7–141 (1 July 1232); *CJI*, 3: 7–8, ch. 110–12; Soldevila, *Vida de Jaume I*, 117–70, and *Jaume I. Pere el Gran*, 24–25; Zurita, *Anales*, 1: 470–72.

48 *CJI*, 3: 14–28, ch. 115–26; Ibn Abī Zarʿ, *Rawd al-Qirtas*, 2: 527; Al-Ḥimyarī, *Kitāb*, 371; al-Maqqarī, *History*, 2: 332, Bk. 8, ch. 4; *DJI*, 1: 274–77, 288–89, nos. 153 (17 July 1231), 160 (29 September); Louis Mas Latrie, *Traités de paix et de commerce et documents divers concernant les relations des chrétiens avec les arabes de l'Afrique septentrionale au moyen âge*, 2 vols. (Paris, 1866; reprint Philadelphia: Burt Franklin, 1963), 2: 182–85; Raynaldus, *Annales*, 2: 34, no. 34 (24 April 1235); Goñi Gaztambide, *Historia*, 162–63, n. 111; David Abulafia, *A Mediterranean Emporium: The Catalan Kingdom of Majorca* (Cambridge: Cambridge University Press, 1994).

49. Ibn Abī Zarʿ, *Rawd al-Qirtas*, 2: 525–27; al-Maqqarī, *History*, 2: 328, 339–40, Bk. 8, ch. 4–5; Rodrigo, *Historia*, 294, Bk. 9, ch. 13; Arié, *L'Espagne musulmane*, 49–58; Torres Delgado, *El antiguo reino*, 62–92.

50. Rodrigo, *Historia*, 293, 295–97, Bk. 9, ch. 12, 14–15; *Chronica latina*, 103–4, ch. 60.

51. Gorosterratzu, *Rodrigo*, 441–42, 444–45, nos. 98 (incorrectly dated 4 April 1230), 100 (7, 30 April 1231), 109 (26 June 1234), 114 (24 July); Mansilla, *Iglesia*, 299, 302–3, nos. 33 (12 June 1231), 36 (26 June 1234); Auvray, *Grégoire IX*, 1: 385, 428, 1079,

1116–17, 1215–16, nos. 606 (reg., 7 April 1231), 671 (reg., 12 June), 1987–88 (26 June 1234), 2063 (reg., 24 July), 2195 (reg., 23 October), 2300 (reg., 4 December); *BC*, 63; Juan Francisco Rivera, *El adelantamiento de Cazorla* (Toledo: Editorial Católica Toledana, 1948), 8–9 (5 June 1232, facsimile), 10–11 (24 July 1234), facsimile); Rodrigo, *Historia*, 297, Bk. 9, ch. 15; Goñi Gaztambide, *Historia*, 154–57.

52. *Chronica latina*, 103–6, 108–9, ch. 60–64, 67; Rodrigo, *Historia*, 293, 295–96, Bk. 9, ch. 12, 14–15; *Annales Compostellani, Anales Toledanos II, Anales Toledanos III, ES* 23: 325, 409, 413; Lucas, *Chronicon*, 4: 114, and *Crónica*, 427, ch 93; Ibn ʿIdhārī, *Al-Bayān*, 1: 335–36, and 2: 17, 85; Al-Ḥimyarī, *Kitāb*, 133–34; González, *Fernando III*, 3: 32–33, 43–44, 65–67, nos. 521 (24 April 1234), 531 (10 August), 550 (26 March 1235).

53. *Annales Compostellani, Anales Toledanos II*, and *Anales Toledanos III, ES* 23: 325, 409, 413; Rodrigo, *Historia*, 297–99, Bk. 9, ch. 16; Lucas, *Chronicon*, 4: 115–16, and *Crónica*, 428–31, ch. 94; *Chronica latina*, 108–17, ch. 67–73; Ibn Abī Zarʿ, *Rawd al-Qirtas*, 2: 528; Ibn ʿIdhārī, *Al-Bayān*, 2: 17, 85–86; Ayala Martínez, *San Juan*, 465, no. 266 (March 1235).

54. *Chronica latina*, 115–18, ch. 73–74; Rodrigo, *Historia*, 299, Bk. 9, ch. 17; Lucas, *Chronicon*, 4: 114, and *Crónica*, 430–31, ch. 94; al-Maqqarī, *History*, 2: 335, Bk. 8, ch. 4; Ayala Martínez, *San Juan*, 470–72, no. 268 (5 August 1237).

55. *Chronica latina*, 117–18, ch. 74, concludes at this point; Rodrigo, *Historia*, 299–301, Bk. 9, ch. 17–18, closed his history in 1237.

56. Ibn ʿIdhārī, *Al-Bayān*, 2: 106–13; Rodrigo, *Historia*, 301, Bk. 9, ch. 18; *PCG*, 2: 737, 739–41, ch. 1052–53. 1055, 1057, 1060; González, *Fernando III*, 3: 207–9, no. 666 (17 September 1240); *BC*, 73–74.

57. González, *Fernando III*, 3: 134–35, 146–48, 157–59, 173–74, 178–79, 210–15, 217, 219–26, 232–36, 281–85, nos. 607 (8 July 1237), 615 (29 January 1238), 625 (7 July), 640 (12 November), 645 (4 February 1239), 668–69 (20 February 1241), 670 (3 March), 671 (5 March), 673 (10 March), 677 (8 April), 679 (20 April), 684–85 (12 July), 686 (21 July), 723 (18 November 1244), 724 (15 February 1245), 725 (20 Febuary). The king granted the *fuero* of Córdoba to Andújar; ibid., 3: 217–18, nos. 674–75 (10, 12 March 1241). See *Fuero Juzgo en latín y castellano*, ed. Real Academia de la Historia (Madrid: Joaquín Ibarra, 1815).

58. Gorosterratzu, *Rodrigo*, 449, nos. 128–29 (3 September 1236); Raynaldus, *Annales*, 2: 154, anno 1236, no. 58 (4 September); Mansilla, *Iglesia*, 306–7, nos. 40–41 (10 October).

59. *BA*, 49 (12 April 1238); *MH*, 1: 75–76, no. 49 (29 May); Auvray, *Grégoire IX*, 3: nos. 5210 (reg.), 5132 (5 April 1240, reg.); *BC*, 73 (2 June 1240), and 685–86 (1 August 1243); O'Callaghan, "*Hermandades*," 614–16; Goñi Gaztambide, *Historia*, 155–57.

60. Al-Maqqarī, *History*, 2: 336–37, 340–44, Bk. 8, ch. 4–5, quoting the fourteenth-century historians Ibn al-Khaṭīb and Ibn Khaldūn; Arié, *L'Espagne musulmane*, 55–58; Torres Delgado, *El antiguo reino*, 95–99; L. P. Harvey, *Islamic Spain, 1250 to 1500* (Chicago: University of Chicago Press, 1990), 20–26.

Chapter 5

1. Robert I Burns, S.J., "The Many Crusades of Valencia's Conquest (1225–1280): An Historiographical Labyrinth," in Kagay and Vann, *Social Origins*, 167–77.

2. *DJI*, 1: 173, 223–26, nos. 85 (14 July 1226), 119 (20 April 1229); Gual Camarena, "Precedentes," 245, no. 71 (15 June 1231, reg.); Zurita, *Anales*, 1: 431–32.

3. *CJI*, 3: 29–44, ch. 127–37; Ibn Abī Zarʿ, *Rawd al-Qirtas*, 2: 527; Emilio Sáez, Rafael Gibert, Manuel Alvar, and Atilano G. Ruiz-Zorrilla, *Los Fueros de Sepúlveda* (Segovia: Diputación Provincial, 1953), 190–93, no. 11 (17 April 1233); *DJI*, 1: 363–65, nos. 162 (2 January 1232), 163 (March), 219–220 (11 May 1235); Gual Camarena, "Precedentes," 245, no. 72 (30 January 1232, reg.)

4. ACA Bulas pontificias, legajo 5, no. 10 (10 March 1232) published by Robert I. Burns, S.J. in his dissertation, *The Crusader Kingdom of Valencia (1238–1276): A Study in the Organization of the Mediaeval Frontier*, 3 vols. (Ph.D. dissertation, Johns Hopkins University, 1958), 3: 1032, no. 1; Francisco J. Miquel Rosell, *Regesta de letras pontificias del Archivo de la Corona de Aragón* (Madrid: Cuerpo de Archiveros, Bibliotecarios, y Arqueólogos, 1945), 62, no. 92 (10 March 1232, reg.); Zurita, *Anales*, 1: 478–79; Goñi Gaztambide, *Historia*, 163. Father Burns kindly provided me with a transcript of Gregory IX's bull.

5. *CJI*, 3: 66–111, 153–84, and 4: 7–8, 12–16, ch. 185–86, 189–91; *Chronica latina*, 105–6, ch. 64; *DJI*, 1: 312–18, 322–24, 342–45, 352–53, 366, 372, nos. 181 (5 June 1233), 182 (15 July), 183 (22 July), 184–85 (24–25 July), 189 (17 August 1233), 190 (10 November), 205 (29 December 1234), 206–8 (1–2 January 1235), 213 (8 February), 220 (11 May), 226 (23 December); Ramón de María, *El "Repartiment" de Burriana y Villarreal* (Valencia: J. Nacher, 1935); Ubieto Arteta, *Orígenes*, 1: 48, 50, 61–69; Ferrer Navarro, *Conquista*, 31–41; López Elum, *La conquista*, 33–47, 50–52; Soldevila, *Vida de Jaume I*, 171–86; Zurita, *Anales*, 1: 481–83.

6. Auvray, *Grégoire IX*, 1: 824, nos. 1490–91 (9 August 1233); Goñi Gaztambide, *Historia*, 163; Burns, "The Many Crusades," 173–74.

7. Rodenberg, *MGH Epistolae Saeculi XIII*, 1: 315–17, no. 397 (18 July 1229); Gorosterratzu, *Rodrigo*, 440–41, no. 96; *BC*, 67 (21 March 1234); Auvray, *Grégoire IX*, 1: 199, 1210, 1237–39, nos. 324 (reg., 18 July 1229), 2290 (reg., 7 November 1234), 2360–73 (27 November); Goñi Gaztambide, *Historia*, 170; Eloy Benito Ruano, "Santiago, Calatrava y Antioquía," *AEM* 1 (1964): 549–60.

8. Alvar, *Textos*, 201; Milá Fontanals, *Trovadores*, 154–55.

9. *DJI*, 1: 264–66, 268, 272–73, 339, nos. 147 (2 February 1231), 149 (26 February), 151 (4 April), 202 (13 October 1234); *CDACA*, 6: 102–4, no. 18; Raynaldus, *Annales*, 2: 114, anno 1234, no. 52 (fragment); Auvray, *Grégoire IX*, 1: 1120–22 and 2: 547–48, nos. 2072 (reg.), 2078 (reg., 1 September 1234), 3475–78 (30 January 1237); Mansilla, *Iglesia*, 307–8, no. 42 (30 January 1237); Gorosterratzu, *Rodrigo*, 454–55, no. 138; Archivo General de Navarra, cajón 2, nos. 40–42 (28 March, 1 April 1238), cited by Goni Gaztambide, *Historia*, 165, 171–74, 644, n. 2 (24 September).

10. *Annales Compostellani*, *ES* 23: 325; Sidney Painter, "The Crusade of Theobald of Champagne and Richard of Cornwall, 1239–1241," in Setton, *Crusades*, 2: 463–86.

11. *CAVC*, 1: 123–25, nos. 18 (7 February 1235), 19 (17 March); *CDACA*, 6: 104–11,

no. 19 (17 May 1234); *DJI*, 1: 357–61, no. 217 (17 March 1235); Gunnar Tilander, *Los Fueros de Aragón según el Manuscrito 458 de la Biblioteca Nacional de Madrid* (Lund: C.W.K. Gleerup, 1937), 149, Bk. 7, no. 262; Gunnar Tilander, *Vidal Mayor: Traducción aragonesa de la obra "In excelsis Dei Thesauris" de Vidal de Canellas*, 3 vols. (Lund: H. Ohlsson, 1956), 2: 467–69, Bk. 8, ley 5; Donald J. Kagay, "Structures of Baronial Dissent and Revolt Under James I (1213–1276)," *Mediaevistik* 1 (1988): 61–85; Burns, "The Many Crusades," 174.

12. Auvray, *Grégoire IX*, 2: 38–39, nos. 2527–28 (24–25 April 1235); Goñi Gaztambide, *Historia*, 164; Burns, "The Many Crusades," 174.

13. *DJI*, 1: 370–71, 373, 379–83, 385–89, nos. 224 (11 December 1235), 227 (23 December), 235 (20 May 1236), 236 (28 May), 238 (15 October), 239 (28 October); Villanueva, *Viage*, 3: 228–30 (22 April 1236), 232–33 (19 April 1238); Tilander, *Fueros*, 149, 154, Bk.7, nos. 262, 266; *CJI*, 5: 26, ch. 241; Zurita, *Anales*, 1: 508–9.

14. Auvray, *Grégoire IX*, 2: 548–54, nos. 3480 (11 February 1237), 3483 (5 February), 3484–88, 3493 (reg.); ACA Bulas pontificias, legajo 6, no. 17, published by Burns, *The Crusader Kingdom of Valencia (1238–1276)*, 3: 1093, no. 12 (9 February 1237). Father Burns kindly provided me with a transcript of this bull. Goñi Gaztambide, *Historia*, 166–67.

15. *CJI*, 4: 40–64, 85, and 5: 6–24, ch. 206–39; Desclot, *Crònica*, 2: 139–45, ch. 49; *DJI*, 2: 13–14, 19–20, nos. 243 (1 July 1237), 244 (1 August), 250 (24 January 1238).

16. Auvray, *Grégoire IX*, 2: 880–81, 905, nos. 4070 (9 February 1238), 4116 (reg., 5 March); Goñi Gaztambide, *Historia*, 167–68.

17. *CJI*, 4: 62–84, and 5: 28–88, ch. 219–30, 242–84; Desclot, *Crònica*, 2: 145–48, ch. 49; Ramon Muntaner, *Crònica*, 1: 29, ch. 9; *DJI*, 2: 21–39, nos. 252–72 (26 April to 27 September 1238).

18. A. R. Nykl, *Hispano-Arabic Poetry and Its Relations with the Old Provençal Troubadours* (Baltimore, 1946; reprint, New York: Hispanic Society, 1970), 332; Ibn Khaldūn, *Histoire*, 2: 307–11; al-Maqqarī, *History*, Appendix D, 2: lxxvi–lxxviii, and 2: 334–35, Bk. 8, ch. 4.

19. *Annales Compostellani* and *Anales Toledanos II*, ES 23: 325, 409; *Gesta comitum*, 19, ch. 11 (rp) and 58, ch. 27.5 (rd); *CSJP*, 150; *CGPIII*, 121, ch. 35; *CSJP (tr)*, 64, ch. 35; Ibn Abī Zarʿ, *Rawd al-Qirtas*, 2: 529; Ubieto Arteta, *Orígenes*, 1: 87–116; Soldevila, *Vida de Jaume I*, 187–91, 196–215; Ferrer Navarro, *Conquista*, 44–55, 85–305; Zurita, *Anales*, 1: 528–32; López Elum, *La conquista*, 57–61, 125–226.

20. *DJI*, 2: 39–40, no. 273 (28 September 1238), and 1: 388–91, nos. 239 (28 October 1236), 240 (13 November), and 2: 42, 44–45, nos. 276, 278 (18, 22 October 1238); *CDACA*, 11: 221–22; Villanueva, *Viage*, 17: 331; *CJI*, 5: 88–97, ch. 284–89; Gorosterratzu, *Rodrigo*, 458, 464–66, nos. 145 (29 April 1239), 162 (14 March 1240), 163 (16 April 1241), 164–65 (14 July); Auvray, *Grégoire IX*, 3: 18–19, 471, 615, nos. 4815, 5978, 6086.

21. *Regestum donationum regni Valentie*, in *CDACA*, 11: 151–656; María Desamparados Cabanes Pecourt and Ramón Ferrer Navarro, *Llibre del repartiment del reyne de Valencia*, 3 vols. (Zaragoza: Anubar, 1979–80); see donations of 1238–40 in *DJI*, 2: 41, 43–58, 60–75, nos. 275–81, 283, 285–91, 293–94, 296–98, 300–306, 308, 310; also from 1238 to 1252 in *CDACA* 11: 159–60, 226, 281–83, 287, 309–12, 314, 316, 318, 321, 324–25, 335,

353, 355, 357, 360, 362, 364, 366–70, 372, 376–77, 379, 382–83, 386–88, 394, 404, 407, 409–10, 412, 415, 421, 462, 483, 485, 487, 495, 499, 505, 515.

22. Manuel Dualde Serrano, ed., *Fori antiqui Valentiae* (Madrid, Valencia: Escuela de Estudios Medievales, 1967); Germà Colón and Arcadí García, eds., *Furs de Valencia*, 4 vols. to date (Barcelona: Barcino, 1970–). See these works by Robert I. Burns, S.J.: *The Crusader Kingdom of Valencia: Reconstruction on a Thirteenth-Century Frontier*, 2 vols. (Cambridge, Mass.: Harvard University Press, 1967); *Islam Under the Crusaders: Colonial Survival in the Thirteenth-Century Kingdom of Valencia* (Princeton, N.J.: Princeton University Press, 1973); *Medieval Colonialism: Postcrusade Exploitation of Islamic Valencia* (Princeton, N.J.: Princeton University Press, 1975); *Muslims, Christians and Jews in the Crusader Kingdom of Valencia: Societies in Symbiosis* (Cambridge: Cambridge University Press, 1984); *Diplomatarium of the Crusader Kingdom of Valencia: The Registered Charters of Its Conqueror, Jaume I, 1257–1276*, 2 vols. thus far (Princeton, N.J.: Princeton University Press, 1985–91).

23. Al-Ḥimyarī, *Kitāb*, 102–18.

24. *Cancioneiro da Ajuda*, ed. Carolina Michaëlis, 2 vols. (Hildesheim/New York: G. Olms, 1980) 1: 905–6, no. 466; Burns, *Diplomatarium*, vol. 2, frontispiece, translated the poem in part.

25. Burns, *Crusader Kingdom*, 1: 1–2, citing Matthew Paris, *Chronica maiora*, 3: 517, and a document in the cathedral of Valencia, dated March 1256.

26. ACA, leg. 6, Bulas pontificias, no. 19 (8 January 1239); Raynaldus, *Annales*, 2: 199, anno 1238, nos. 46–47; Auvray, *Grégoire IX*, 2: 1205, no. 4703 (reg.); Goñi Gaztambide, *Historia*, 169–70; Burns, "The Many Crusades," 175.

27. *CJI*, 6: 28–32, ch. 307; Juan Manuel Del Estal, "Alicante en la política territorial del los dos Jaimes de Aragón," *Jaime I y su época*, 1: 67; Burns, "Surrender Constitutions: The Islamic Communities of Eslida and Alfandech," in *Muslims, Christians and Jews*, 52–79.

28. González, *Fernando III*, 3: 71–73, 197–98, 248–80, nos. 554 (1 May 1235) 657 (25 November 1239), 700 (21 August 1242); Consuelo Gutiérrez del Arroyo de Vázquez de Parga, *Privilegios reales de la Orden de Santiago en la edad media* (Madrid: Junta técnica de Archivos, Bibliotecas, y Museos, n.d.), 158, 160, nos. 321 (3 February 1243), 325 (15 February); *Anales Toledanos II* and *Anales Toledanos III*, ES 23: 409, 413; PCG, 2: 741–42, 744, ch. 1060–62, 1065; Antonio Ballesteros Beretta, *La Reconquista de Murcia por el Infante D. Alfonso de Castilla* (Murcia: Academia Alfonso X el Sabio, 1959); Juan Torres Fontes, "Incorporación del reino de Murcia a la Corona de Castilla," *Fueros y Privilegios de Alfonso X el Sabio al Reino de Murcia* (Murcia: Academia Alfonso X el Sabio, 1973), xxi–xxxiii.

29. *DJI*, 2: 176–77, no. 388 (26 March 1244); Juan Torres Fontes, *Documentos del Siglo XIII* (Murcia: Academia Alfonso X el Sabio, 1969), 3–4, no. 3; *CJI*, 6: 78–87, ch, 345–49; Zurita, *Anales*, 1: 533–59, 566–67; Soldevila, *Vida de Jaume I*, 216–26; Ubieto Arteta, *Origenes*, 1: 161–66; Ferrer Navarro, *Conquista*, 57–66; López Elum, *La conquista*, 63–88.

30. *CJI*, 6: 58–101, ch. 328–60; Bernat Desclot, *Crònica*, 2: 148–53, ch. 49. See charters dated during the siege of Játiva in *DJI*, 2: 173–74, nos. 385–86, 389–92; Robert I.

Burns, S.J., and Paul Chevedden, "'The Finest Castle in the World,' " *History Today* 49 (1999): 10–17. See their book *Negotiating Cultures: Bilingual Surrender Treaties in Muslim-Crusader Spain Under James the Conqueror* (Leiden: E.J. Brill, 1999).

31. *Anales Toledanos II, ES* 23: 409; *PCG,* 2: 744, ch. 1065–66; González, *Fernando III,* 3: 287–89, 297–300, nos. 728 (8 August 1245), 733 (16 January 1246); Ayala Martínez, *San Juan,* 500–501, no. 294 (15 June 1244); Torres Fontes, *Fueros,* 11–13, 69–71, nos. 9 (16 January 1246), 52 (25 January 1260), and *Documentos,* 7–12, nos. 7 (1247), 8 (31 July 1250), 9–11 (1250), 12 (5 July), 14 (6 July).

32. Pascual Savall y Dronda and Santiago Penén y Dehesa, ed., *Fueros, observancias, y actos de corte del reino de Aragón,* 2 vols. (Zaragoza: F. Castro y Bosque, 1866), 1: 7, prologue; Augusto Quintana Prieto, *La documentación pontificia de Inocencio IV (1243–1254),* 2 vols. (Rome: Instituto Español de Historia Eclesiástica, 1987), 1: 99–100, 104–6, 120, nos. 88 (9 January 1245), 94 (25 January), 104 (15 February); Burns, "The Many Crusades," 175.

33. ACA Bulas pontificias, legajo 8, no. 20 (18 March 1246), published by Robert I. Burns, S.J., "The Loss of Provence: King James's Raid to Kidnap its Heiress (1245): Documenting a Legend," *XII Congrès d'histoire de la Couronne d'Aragon,* 3 vols. (Montpellier: Société archéologique de Montpellier, 1987–88), 3: 195–231, no. 18.

34. Bernat Desclot, *Crònica,* 2: 151–53, ch. 49; *CJI,* 7: 7–33, ch. 361–77.

35. Quintana Prieto, *Inocencio IV,* 2: 518–20, 527–28, 562–63, nos. 557–59 (12–13 November 1248), 571 (25 January 1249), 619–20 (22, 28 March 1250); Robert I. Burns, S.J., "A Lost Crusade: Unpublished Bulls of Innocent IV on al-Azraq's Revolt in Thirteenth-Century Spain," *CHR* 74 (1988): 440–49.

36. See Robert I. Burns, S.J., "The Crusade Against al-Azraq: A Thirteenth-Century Mudejar Revolt in International Perspective," *American Historical Review* 93 (1988): 80–106, and *Islam,* 323–32, 336–37; Ferrer Navarro, *Conquista,* 67–70.

37. Auvray, *Grégoire IX,* 1: 554, 778, 1151, nos. 926 (reg., 18 October 1232), 1385 (reg., June 1233), 2145 (21 October 1234); *MH,* 1: 60–61, no. 35; Antonio Brandão, *Crónicas de Sancho II e Afonso III,* ed. A. de Magalhães Basto (Porto: Livraria Civilização, 1945), 54–55, 351, no. 3.

38. *BS,* 144, 153–55, nos. 8 (31 March 1235), 19 (19 January 1236), 20 (3 November 1237), 21 (16 January 1239); Brandão, *CSII-AIII,* 352, 355–57, nos. 4, 6–7, 9; Quintana Prieto, *Inocencio IV,* 1: 203–4, 221–22, nos. 179 (5 September 1245), 193 (11 September); Gutiérrez del Arroyo, *Privilegios,* 151, 153–54, 156–57, nos. 300, 305, 309, 313–14, 317.

39. González, *Fernando III,* 1: 93–95, identified Infante Alfonso as the son of Fernando III, but the pope, on 25 November 1239, referred to "*A[lfonso], consanguineo tuo, nato clare memorie A[lfonso] regis Legionensis,*" that is, Alfonso de Molina.

40. *MH,* 1: 66–75, nos. 39–40 (25 November 1239), 41–43 (28 November), 44–47 (11 December), 48 (13 December); Auvray, *Grégoire IX,* 3: 135–37, 144–45, nos. 4969–74 (reg.), (reg.), 4994–97 (reg.), 5002 (20 December 1239); Gorosterratzu, *Rodrigo,* 318–321, 455, 461, nos. 139 (29 April 1238), 140 (6 May), 154 (3 December 1239).

41. *MH,* 1: 77–78, no. 50 (18 February 1241); Quintana Prieto, *Inocencio IV,* 1: 230–31, no. 199 (13 September 1245); González, *Fernando III,* 3: 323–25, no. 756 (27 January 1248).

42. *MH,* 1: 78–79, no. 51 (8 April 1245); Quintana Prieto, *Inocencio IV,* 1: 106–8,

112–13, 126–28, 133–34, 173–76, nos. 96 (30 January 1245), 100 (4 February), 114 (20 March), 120 (8 April), 144 (24 July); Emile Berger, *Les registres d'Innocent IV (1243–1254)*, 4 vols. (Paris: Bibliothèque des Écoles Françaises d'Athènes et de Rome, 1881–1921), 1: 182, 212, nos. 1176 (reg.), 1389.

43. Lomax, *The Reconquest*, 144, questioned the authenticity of the *Chrónica da conquista do Algarve*, *PMH SS* 1: 415–20; *Crónica de cinco reis*, ed. A. Magalhães Basto (Porto: Livraria Civilização, 1945), 202–13, ch. 4; Brandão, *CSII-AIII*, 65–144, 153, 366, no. 14 (10 March 1250); Herculano, *História*, 4: 245, 253, 255–56, 283–93, and 5: 25–26; Gonzaga de Azevedo, *História*, 6: 54–60, 81–99.

44. *Anales Toledanos II*, *Anales Toledanos III*, and *Chronicon de Cardeña*, *ES* 23: 374, 410, 413; *PCG*, 2: 742–46, ch. 1062–64, 1068–70; Al-Ḥimyarī, *Kitāb*, 147–52; al-Maqqarī, *History*, 2: 340–41, Bk. 8, ch. 5; Ibn Abī Zarʿ, *Rawd al-Qirtas*, 2: 529; Ibn ʿIdhārī, *Al-Bayān*, 3: 162–63; Ibn Khaldūn, *Histoire*, 4: 74–75; Ayala Martínez, *San Juan*, 503–4, no. 297 (10 May 1246); González, *Fernando III*, 3: 290–93, no. 730 (31 December 1245).

45. Berger, *Innocent IV*, 1: 346–48, nos. 1758, 1759 (18 March 1246), 1760 (22 March 1246); Toribio Mingüella, *Historia de la diócesis de Sigüenza y de sus obispos*, 3 vols. (Madrid: Revista de Archivos, Bibliotecas y Museos, 1900–13), 1: 600–601 (24 April); Raynaldus, *Annales*, 2: 361–62, anno 1246, no. 40 (fragment).

46. Quintana Prieto, *Inocencio IV*, 1: 195, 197, nos. 172 (1 September 1245), 174 (2 September), 181–82 (7 September), 186 (18 March 1246); *BS*, 140; Goni Gaztambide, *Historia*, 180–83, 186; María del Carmen Pescado del Hoyo, "Tres nuevos poemas medievales," *Nueva Revista de Filología Hispánica* 14 (1960): 242–50.

47. Eloy Benito Ruano, "La Orden de Santiago y el Imperio latino de Constantinopla," *Estudios Santiaguistas* (León: Colegio universitario de León, 1978), 29–60. esp. 53–60, nos. 1 (20 February 1246), 2 (11 May), 3–4 (August), 5 (11 February 1247).

48 Ibn ʿIdhārī, *Al-Bayān*, 2: 162–63, 182–87; Ibn Khaldūn, *Histoire*, 2: 242, 244, 319–22; al-Maqqarī, *History*, Appendix D, 2: lxxviii–lxxx; González, *Fernando III*, 3: 305–6, no. 739 (13 April 1246); Francisco García Fitz, "El cerco de Sevilla: Reflexiones sobre la guerra de asedio en la edad media," in *Sevilla 1248: Congreso internacional conmemorativo del 750 Aniversario de la Conquista de la Ciudad de Sevilla por Fernando III, rey de Castilla y León*, ed. Manuel González Jiménez (Madrid: Fundación Ramón Areces, 2000), 115–54.

49. *PCG*, 2: 747–48, ch. 1073. González, *Fernando III*, 1: 365–69.

50. Gorosterratzu, *Rodrigo*, 386–87, 468–69, no. 177 (15 April 1247); Berger, *Innocent IV*, no. 2538; Mansilla, *Iglesia*, 338–39, no. 68 (11 June 1247); Goñi Gaztambide, *Historia*, 184.

51. *PCG*, 2: 748–70, ch. 1075–1129; *Annales Compostellani* and *Anales Toledanos II*, *ES* 23: 325, 410; *Chronicon Conimbricense*, *ES* 23: 335 and *PMH SS* 1: 3; Ibn ʿIdhārī, *Al-Bayān*, 2: 186–89, 197; Ibn Khaldūn, *Histoire*, 2: 246, 321–22, 381–82, 384, 405, 411; Ibn ʿAbī Zarʿ, *Rawd al-Qirtas*, 2: 496–503, 529; al-Ḥimyārī, *Kitāb*, 48–54; al-Maqqarī, *History*, 2: 335, Bk. 8, ch. 4.

52. Diego Catalán and Juan Gil, eds., "Rithmi de Iulia Romula seu ispalensi urbe," *AEM* 5 (1968): 549–58; González, *Fernando III*, 1: 370–91; Lomax, *The Reconquest*, 150–54.

53. *Cancioneiro da Biblioteca antiga Colucci-Brancuti*, ed. Elza Paxeco Machado and José Pedro Machado, 8 vols. (Lisbon: Revista de Portugal, 1949–64), 5: 366–68, no. 928.

54. *PCG*, 2: 770; ch. 1130; Ibn ʿIdhārī, *Al-Bayān*, 3: 188–89; González, *Fernando III*, 1: 391–94 and 3: 408–12, no. 825 (15 June 1251) and *Repartimiento de Sevilla*, 2 vols. (Madrid: CSIC, 1951); Continuator of Lucas of Tuy, *Crónica*, 433–47, ch. 97–101; Manuel González Jiménez, *En torno a los orígenes de Andalucía: La repoblación del siglo XIII*, 2nd ed. (Seville: Universidad de Sevilla, 1988); Antonio Ballesteros, *Sevilla en el siglo XIII* (Seville: Juan Pérez Torres, 1913).

55. Gaines Post, *Studies in Medieval Legal Thought: Public Law and the State, 1100–1322* (Princeton, N.J.: Princeton University Press, 1964), 490, n. 190.

56. Nykl, *Hispano-Arabic Poetry*, 338–39.

57. Mas Latrie, *Traités*, 1: 8–9, no. 8 (9 March 1198); *DP*, 261, no. 232 (reg., April–May 1200); James W. Brodman, *Ransoming Captives in Crusader Spain: The Order of Merced on the Christian-Islamic Frontier* (Philadelphia: University of Pennsylvania Press, 1986).

58. Mansilla, *Honorio III*, 184–85, 318–19, nos. 243 (5 September 1219), 439 (13 May 1223); Andrés Giménez Soler, "Caballeros españoles en Africa y Africanos en España," *Revue hispanique* 12 (1905): 299–372.

59. Fidel Fita, "Noticias," *BRAH* 11 (1887): 456 (2 June 1192); Marie Thérèse d'Alverny, "Deux traductions latines du Coran au Moyen Age," *Archives d'histoire doctrinale et litteraire du Moyen Age* 16 (1948): 69–131; Joseph F. O'Callaghan, "The Mudejars of Castile and Portugal in the Twelfth and Thirteenth Centuries," in *Muslims Under Latin Rule, 1100–1300*, ed. James M. Powell (Princeton, N.J.: Princeton University Press, 1990), 46–50.

60. Mansilla, *Honorio III*, 435, 442, 450–52, nos. 579 (7 October 1225), 588 (27 October), 595 (20 February 1226); Gorosterratzu, *Rodrigo*, 438, no. 84; Mas Latrie, *Traités*, 1: 9–12, nos. 9 (17 May 1226), 10 (27 May 1233), 12 (12 June 1237); Raynaldus, *Annales*, 2: 129, 1235, no. 36 (15 May 1235); Ibn Abī Zarʿ, *Rawd al-Qirtas*, 2: 485–86; Benjamin Z. Kedar, *Crusade and Mission: European Approaches Toward the Muslims* (Princeton, N.J.: Princeton University Press, 1984), 124–26.

61. Quintana Prieto, *Inocencio IV*, 1: 251–52, no., 216 (24 September 1245); *BS*, 166; Mas Latrie, *Traités*, 1: 12–13, no. 13; Ibn ʿIdhārī, *Al-Bayān*, 2: 153; Burns, *Muslims, Christians and Jews*, 86.

62. Quintana Prieto, *Inocencio IV*, 1: 339–40, 344–47, 351–52, 354, nos. 325 (25 October 1246), 332–33 (31 October), 340 (11 December), 344 (19 December); *MH*, 1: 79–81, no. 52; Mas Latrie, *Traités*, 1: 13–16, nos. 14–16.

63. Quintana Prieto, *Inocencio IV*, 1: 335–36, 338–42, nos. 318 (18 October 1246), 322–23 (23 October), 326 (26 October). 328 (30 October).

64. Quintana Prieto, *Inocencio IV*, 1: 372, no. 372 (11 April 1247); Goñi Gaztambide, *Historia*, 184, n. 210.

65. Quintana Prieto, *Inocencio IV*, 2: 636–40, 642–43, nos. 710, 712, 714 (17 March 1251), 718–19 (17 April); Mas Latrie, *Traités*, 1: 16–17, no. 17; Mansilla, *Iglesia*, 59–64.

66. Quintana Prieto, *Inocencio IV*, 2: 709, no. 803 (4 October 1252); al-Ḥimyārī,

Kitāb, 54; *PCG*, 2: 747, 770–74, ch. 1072, 1131–34; *Chronicon de Cardeña*, *ES* 23: 380; González, *Fernando III*, 1: 364; Lomax, *The Reconquest*, 156.

67. Joseph F. O'Callaghan, *The Learned King: The Reign of Alfonso X of Castile* (Philadelphia: University of Pennsylvania Press, 1993), 181–97.

Chapter 6

1. González, *Alfonso IX*, 2: 23–26, no. 11 (1188); *CAI*, 184, Bk. 1, ch. 72; *Historia Roderici*, 53, ch. 14; *Chronica latina*, 52–58, 85–87, ch. 18–21, 43–44; Rodrigo, *Historia*, 256–64, Bk. 7, ch. 34–36, Bk. 8, ch. 1–14; *CJI*, 1: 112, 120–27, ch. 43, 47–49; 3: 29–34, ch. 127–31; Donald J. Kagay, *The Usatges of Barcelona: The Fundamental Law of Catalonia* (Philadelphia: University of Pennsylvania Press, 1994), 90, art. 102.

2. *LFM*, 69–70, no. 65 (28 April 1061); Kagay, *Usatges*, 117, app. 3, no. 1; Simon Barton, *The Aristocracy in Twelfth-Century León and Castile* (Cambridge: Cambridge University Press, 1997), 168–72.

3. *PCG*, 2: 736–38, 754, ch. 1054, 1090; Kagay, *Usatges*, 71, art. 26, 28; *Espéculo: Texto jurídico atribuído al Rey de Castilla Don Alfonso el Sabio*, ed. Robert A. MacDonald (Madison, Wis.: Hispanic Seminary, 1990), 2, 7, and 3, 7, 10; *Las Siete Partidas del Rey Don Alfonso el Sabio*, ed. Real Academia de la Historia, 3 vols. (Madrid: Imprenta Real, 1801), 2, 18, 22–24, 27, 29; *CAI*, 190, 202–3, Bk. 1, ch. 87, and Bk. 2, ch. 15, 17–18; Rodrigo, *Historia*, 257, Bk. 7, ch. 35; *Crónica de la población de Ávila*, ed. Ámparo Hernández Segura (Valencia: Anubar, 1965), 23–24, 39; González, *Alfonso IX*, 2: 285, 304, 341, nos 205 (26 March 1206), 219 (7 September 1207), 251 (27 June 1209); Hilda Grassotti, "El deber y el derecho de hacer guerra y paz en León y Castilla" and "Sobre la retenencia de los castillos en la Castilla medieval," in her *Estudios medievales españolas* (Madrid: Fundación Universitaria Española, 1981), 43–132, 261–81.

4. Kagay, *Usatges*, 80, art. 64, and 98, app. 1, A 2; *Historia Roderici*, 61, ch. 32; *HC*, 116–17, 133–34, Bk. 1, ch. 75, 83; Donald J. Kagay, "Army Mobilization, Royal Administration, and the Realm in the Thirteenth-Century Crown of Aragon," in *Iberia and the Mediterranean World of the Middle Ages: Essays in Honor of Robert I. Burns, S.J.*, ed. P. E. Chevedden, D. J. Kagay, and P. G. Padilla (Leiden: E.J. Brill, 1996), 95–115.

5. *CAI*, 214, Bk. 2, ch. 40–41; *PFG*, 21, v. 75, and 60–61, 116, 150, 224, vv. 194, 198, 382, 509, 749; Linehan, "The Synod of Segovia," 42–43, canon 2; *Chronica latina*, 87–88, 110–12, ch. 44, 69–70; *Espéculo*, 3,1,2; Hilda Grassotti, "La ira regia en León y Castilla," in her *Miscelánea de estudios sobre instituciones castellano-leonesas* (Bilbao: Editorial Nájera, 1978), 1–132.

6. Alfonso García Gallo, *Manual de Historia del Derecho español*, 2 vols. (Madrid: AGESA, 1967), 2: 469–71, nos. 732 (Aragonese *Fueros*, 1134), 733 (*Vidal Mayor*); *Espéculo*, 3, 5, 6, 11; *CPA*, 33, 44; *Chronica latina*, 105, 114–15, ch. 62, 72.

7. *CPA*, 19; *PFG*, 3, 13, 40, 67, 108, 116, 201, 266, vv. 10, 46, 130, 224, 356, 381, 671, 685; *CAI*, 171, 214, 238, Bk. 1, ch. 46, and Bk. 2, ch. 40, 92; González, *Repartimiento*, 2: 234–35; *CJI*, 5: 12, ch. 235; *Espéculo*, 3, 5; *Partidas* 2, 9, 3, 9–10, 12–15, 21; Reilly, *Alfonso VII*, 153.

8. *Poem of the Cid*, Spanish Text by Ramón Menéndez Pidal; English Verse

Translation by W. S. Merwin (New York: Meridian, 1975), 208–10, vv. 116–17; Rodrigo, *Historia*, 251, Bk. 7, ch. 28; Rivera, *Cazorla*, 8–9 (5 June 1232, facsimile); Auvray, *Grégoire IX*, 1: 1116–17, no. 2063 (reg., 24 July 1234); *PCG*, 2: 758, 763, ch. 1099, 1113.

9. *CJI*, 2: 10–14, ch. 52–53; Bernat Desclot, *Crònica*, 2: 70–75, ch. 15–22; *DJI*, 1: 215, no. 113 (23 December 1228); *CDACA*, 6: 97–101, nos. 16–17 (28 August 1228), and 11: 3–6 (October 1229).

10. *De Expugnatione Lyxbonensi*, 70–85, 114–16; *PMH Leges*, 1.2: 162 (28 December 1210); Mansilla, *Honorio III*, 76–78, no. 95 (October 1217); Auvray, *Grégoire IX*, 1: 36–38, 742–45, nos. 70 (5 May 1227), 1327 (26 May 1233).

11. García Gallo, *Manual*, 2: 469–70, no. 732, art. 8 (Aragonese *Fueros*, 1134); *Fuero real*, ed. Gonzalo Martínez Díez, José Manuel Asencio, and C. Hernández Alonso (Ávila: Fundación Claudio Sánchez Albornoz, 1988), 4, 19, 1; *Historia Roderici*, 60, 78, ch. 28, 43; *PFG*, 14, v. 54; Barton, *Aristocracy*, 83, app. 3, no. 13 (30 October 1165); *Chronica latina*, 112, ch. 70; Kagay, *Usatges*, 69, 90, arts. 20, 103; Reilly, *Alfonso VII*, 165–69, 235–39.

12. *Historia Roderici*, 48, ch. 4; *Chronica Gothorum*, *PMH SS* 1: 11; Hilda Grassotti, *Las instituciones feudo-vasalláticas en León y Castilla*, 2 vols. (Spoleto: Centro Italiano di Studi sull'alto Medioevo, 1969), 2: 723–893.

13. *PFG*, 3, 51, 59, 67, 108, 173, 198, 201, 206, vv. 10, 66, 192, 224, 356, 583, 661, 671, 685; *Partidas*, 2, 21, 1–24, and 2, 23, 13; Reilly, *Alfonso VII*, 214, 216; González, *Fernando III*, 1: 129–73, and *Repartimiento*, 2: 191, 226–28; Inés Carrasco, *Los cargos de la hueste real en tiempos de Alfonso X: Estudio onomasiológico* (Granada: Universidad de Granada, 1992), 89–98.

14. *DJI*, 1: 215, no. 113 (23 December 1228); *CJI*, 2: 6–8, 10, ch. 50; Bernat Desclot, *Crònica*, 2: 76–80, ch. 23–27.

15. Bernat Desclot, *Crònica*, 2: 75, ch. 22; Eloy Benito Ruano, "La Orden de Santiago y el imperio latino de Constantinopla," *Estudios santiaguistas* (León: Colegio Universitario de León, 1978), 29–60.

16. *BC*, 683–86 (1 August 1221), 686–87 (4 September 1239), 685–86 (1 August 1243); Joseph F. O'Callaghan, "*Hermandades* Between the Military Oders of Calatrava and Santiago During the Castilian Reconquest, 1158–1252," in *Calatrava*, no. V.

17. James F. Powers, *A Society Organized for War: The Iberian Municipal Militias in the Central Middle Ages, 1000–1284* (Berkeley: University of California Press, 1988); "The Creative Interaction Between Portuguese and Leonese Municipal Military Law, 1055 to 1279," *Speculum* 62 (1987): 53–80; "Two Warrior Kings and Their Municipal Militias: The Townsman-Soldier in Law and Life," in *The Worlds of Alfonso the Learned and James the Conqueror: Intellect and Force in the Middle Ages*, ed. Robert I. Burns, S.J. (Princeton, N.J.: Princeton University Press, 1985), 95–129; "Frontier Military Service and Exemption in the Municipalities of Aragon and Castile," *Military Affairs* 45 (1981): 75–78; "Frontier Competition and Legal Creativity: A Castilian-Aragonese Case Study Based on Twelfth-Century Municipal Military Law," *Speculum* 52 (1977): 465–87; "Townsmen and Soldiers: The Interaction of Urban and Military Organization in the Militias of Mediaeval Castile," *Speculum* 46 (1971): 641–55; "The Origins and Development of Municipal Military Service in the Leonese and Castilian

Reconquest, 800–1250," *Traditio* 26 (1970): 91–111; "The Municipal Militias in the Reconquest of Seville," in González Jiménez, *Sevilla*, 155–66.

18. *CPA*, 36; *PC*, 84, v. 33; *PFG*, 60–61, 116, vv. 194, 198, 382; Charles Emmanuel Dufourcq and Jean Gautier-Dalché, *Historica económica y social de la España cristiana en la edad media* (Barcelona: Ediciones Albir, 1983), 97.

19. *El Fuero de Jaca*, ed. Mauricio Molho (Zaragoza: CSIC, 1964); *El Fuero latino de Teruel*, ed. Jaime Caruana Gómez de Barreda (Teruel: Instituto de Estudios Turolenses, 1974); *Fuero de Cuenca*, ed. Rafael de Ureña y Smenjaud (Madrid: Tipografía de Archivos, 1935); James F. Powers, tr., *The Code of Cuenca: Municipal Law on the Twelfth-Century Castilian Frontier* (Philadelphia: University of Pennsylvania Press, 2000); *El Fuero de Coria*, ed. José Maldonado y Fernández del Torco (Madrid: Institución de Estudios de Administración local, 1949).

20. Powers, "Origins," 97–111, and *Society*, 16–18, 27, 31–33, 83, 97, 112–26, 147–52; 190–93, 215–30; Carrasco, *Cargos*, 89–99; O'Callaghan, *The Learned King*, 92–94, 107–9.

21. Bernat Desclot, *Crònica*, 3: 62–63, ch. 79; *De Expugnatione Lyxbonensi*, 128; *PCG*, 2: 729, ch. 1054; *Espéculo*, 3, 8, 2; *Partidas*, 2, 22, 6–7, and 2, 23, 3, and 2, 24, 4, and 2, 26, 30; Carrasco, *Cargos*, 79–83, 101–4; González, *Repartimiento*, 2: 250–51, 271–74, 277–79, 285–87.

22. Powers, *Society*, 188–205, and Table 3; *Fuero real*, 4, 19, 5; *Espéculo*, 3, 5, 1–18, and 3, 6, 1–5, and 3, 8, 1–9; *Partidas*, 2, 28, 1–11.

23. Kagay, *Usatges*, 90, art. 100–101, and "Army Mobilization," 104; Mansilla, *Honorio III*, 388–89, no. 524 (31 October 1224); Gorosterratzu, *Rodrigo*, 445, no. 114 (24 July 1234); Auvray, *Grégoire IX*, 1: 1116–17, 1210, 1215–16, nos. 2063 (reg.), 2290 (7 November 1234, reg.), 2300 (4 December); *BS*, 111–12 (29 January and 17 February 1239); Quintana Prieto, *Inocencio IV*, 1: 71–72, no. 51 (23 April 1244); Berger, *Innocent IV*, 1: 565, no. 3731 (21 March 1248); Villanueva, *Viage*, 17: 248 (6 November 1244).

24. *PFG*, 16–18, 36, 59, 90, 117, 154–55, vv. 63, 119, 192, 304, 383, 485, 524, 527; *PC*, 110, 212–14, vv. 58, 118; *CAI*, 206, Bk. 2, ch. 24; *CPA*, 46; *CJI*, 2: 86, ch. 85, and 3: 96, ch. 174, and 4: 16, ch. 191; *Alfonso X. Toledo 1984* (Toledo: Museo de Santa Cruz, 1984), figs. 1, 2, 3, 29, 30, 61, 64; Powers, *Society*, 128–32, plates 18–21, 23–25; Amparo García Cuadrado, *Las Cantigas: El Códice de Florencia* (Murcia: Universidad de Murcia, 1993), 291–308, 314–19; Sánchez Albornoz, *España*, fig. 31; John Williams, *Early Spanish Manuscript Illumination* (New York: George Braziller, 1971), plates 9a, 30, 32; Huici, *Batallas*, 285 opposite; Carrasco, *Cargos*, 120–23.

25. *CSJP*, 59; *CSJP (tr)*, 20–21, ch. 17; *CJI*, 3: 78, 94, ch. 161, 172, and 4: 6, ch. 184; García Cuadrado, *Cantigas*, 264–91; Sanchez Albornoz, *España*, figs. 31, 55–56; al-Maqqarī, *History*, 2: 287; *Alfonso X. Toledo 1984*, fig. 28.

26. Powers, *Society*, plates 9–10, 14–17; *PC*, 214, v. 118; *PFG*, 154–55, vv. 526–27; *Carmen Campidoctoris*, ed. J. Gil, in *Chronica Hispana*, 2: 105–8, lines 100–125; *CPA*, 35; *Chronica Gothorum, PMH SS* 1: 15; González, *Alfonso VIII*, 3: 484–85, no. 846 (15 July 1209); Carrasco, *Cargos*, 120–23.

27. Sánchez Albornoz, *España*, fig. 64; Powers, *Society*, plates 1–4, 7–8; John E. Keller and Richard P. Kinkade, *Iconography in Medieval Spanish Literature* (Lexington:

University of Kentucky Press, 1984), plates 15, 22; John E. Keller and Annette G. Cash, *Daily Life Depicted in the Cantigas de Santa Maria* (Lexington: University of Kentucky Press, 1998), plate 60; Anna Maria Blasco i Bardas, *Les pintures murals del Palau Reial Major de Barcelona* (Barcelona: Ajuntament de Barcelona, 1993), 11–13, 36, 39, 51, 53, 56, 61.

28. *CPA*, 44; *Carmen Campidoctoris*, lines 105–28; *CJI*, 2: 86, ch. 85, and 4: 64–66, ch. 219–20; al-Maqqarī, *History*, 2: 279; *Chronique de Saint-Maixent*, 190; *CSM* 165; Blasco i Bardas, *Pintures*, 51; Powers, *Society*, 132–33, 159–61, and plates 11, 14–15; García Cuadrado, *Cantigas*, 320–39; Joseph F. O'Callaghan, *The Cortes of Castile-León, 1188–1350* (Philadelphia: University of Pennsylvania Press, 1989), 189–90.

29. *Partidas*, 2, 23, 27; *CJI*, 3: 14, ch. 117; al-Maqqarī, *History*, 2: 286; *PC*, 207, v. 115; *CSM* 165; Huici, *Batallas*, 72.

30. *CJI*, 4: 62–64, ch. 219; *PCG*, 2: 744, ch. 1066; *CPA*, 37–38; *Espéculo*, 3, 6, 8; Reilly, *Alfonso VI*, 188, and *Alfonso VII*, 218–19; Kagay, "Army Mobilization," 106–11; Eslava Galán, "Quesada," 10–11.

31. Bernat Desclot, *Crónica*, 2: 102, ch. 36; *Chronica latina*, 62, ch. 24; *PC*, 38, 84–86, vv. 3, 34; *PFG*, 150, 197, 201, vv. 512, 657, 671; Rodrigo, *Historia*, 222, Bk. 7, ch. 2.

32. *Espéculo* 3, 5, 13; *Partidas*, 2, 23, 12–15; *Gesta comitum*, 26, 51–52, ch. 10 (rp), 25.2 (rd); *CSJP*, 135; *CSJP (tr)*, 56–58, ch. 34; *CJI*, 2: 44, ch. 65, and 4: 66–67, ch. 221; *PCG*, 2: 762, ch. 1112; Zurita, *Anales*, 1: 104–5; Blasco i Bardas, *Pintures*, 56, 72–75; García Cuadrado, *Cantigas*, 308–14.

33. *CPA*, 31, 33, 37; González, *Fernando III*, 3: 388, no. 809 (18 November 1250); *Espéculo*, 3, 5, 13–15, 18–19.

34. *Espéculo*, 2, 13, 1; *Partidas*, 2, 9, 16; *Historia Roderici*, 48, ch,. 5; Reilly, *Alfonso VI*, 137–38, and *Alfonso VII*, 163–64; Carrasco, *Cargos*, 59–70.

35. *Partidas*, 2, 22, 1–6, and 2, 23, 4–11, 16–21, *Espéculo*, 3, 6, 10; Carrasco, *Cargos*, 71–78; *CPA*, 23–26, 32–33, 37; *CAI*, 201, 207–8, 210–11, Bk. 2, ch. 14, 25, 26, 28, 33–54; *CJI*, 2: 106, ch. 98; *PCG*, 2: 764, ch. 1113; González, *Repartimiento*, 2: 249, 271, 274–79, 282–87.

36. *CAI*, 204, Bk. 2, ch. 20; *CJI*, 4: 10, ch. 187, and 2: 98, 114, ch. 93, 103; *CPA*, 41, 42, 44; *Partidas*, 2, 23, 27–29; Ibn Ṣāḥib al-Salā, *Al-Mann*, 227–32; Ibn ʿIdhārī, *Al-Bayān*, 2: 4–6, 29–30, 32; García Fitz, *Castilla y León*, 59–171, 453–55, and fig. 1.

37. *CJI*, 2: 20, 38. ch. 63, 120, and 3: 8–10, ch. 112; *CAI*, 167, 206–7, Bk. 1, ch. 36, Bk. 2, ch. 25–26; *CPA*, 18, 24–29, 35, 45–46; *PC*, 76, 80, vv. 27, 30; *CSJP*, 79–80; *CSJP (tr)*, 30–31, ch. 19; Ibn ʿIdhārī, *Nuevos fragmentos*, 160–68; *Al-Ḥulal*, 108–15; al-Maqqarī, *History*, 2: 304–7, Bk. 8, ch. 1; Ordericus, *Historia*, 405–7, Bk. 13, ch. 6; *PCG*, 2: 743, 759, 763–64, ch. 1063, 1105, 1112–13; *Partidas*, 2, 23, 16, 19–20, 30; García Fitz, *Castilla y León*, 157–60; Powers, *Society*, 151–59, plate 26; Keller and Kinkade, *Iconography*, plate 24, *CSM* 181, panel 1; García Cuadrado, *Cantigas*, 259–64.

38. Ibn Ṣāḥib al-Salā, *Al-Mann*, 137–39, 149–50, 155–56; Ibn ʿIdhārī, *Nuevos fragmentos*, 403–4, 406; Rodrigo, *Historia*, 264–68, Bk. 8, ch. 5–7; *Chronica latina*, 58–59, 110–12, ch. 22, 69–70; Lucas, *Chronicon*, 4: 116, and *Crónica*, 428–30, ch. 94. *Partidas*, 2, 27, 8; García Fitz, *Castilla y León*, 171–278, 455–57.

39. Caffaro, *De captione*, 33; *Gesta triumphalia*, 91–92; Huici, *Batallas*, 244; *PCG*, 2: 748–61, ch. 1075–1108; Rodrigo, *Historia*, 278–79, Bk. 8, ch. 14.

40. al-Maqqarī, *History*, 2: 263–70; Letters of Arnulf, *RHGF* 14: 326, and Duodechin, *MGH SS* 17: 27–28; *De Expugnatione Lyxbonensi*, 142–44, 179; Ibn ʿIdhārī, *Al-Bayān*, 1: 69–79; Caffaro, *De captione*, 34; García Fitz, *Castilla y León*, 243–44. A seam (*summa*) was about six to eight bushels, and a *sextarius* perhaps a pint or a quart.

41. *CJI*, 2: 50, ch. 69, and 3: 80, 98–100, ch. 163, 175–76; *De Expugnatione Lyxbonensi*, 142, 145; Letters of Arnulf, *RHGF* 14: 325–27, and Duodechin, *MGH SS* 17: 27–28; *Chronica Gothorum*, *PMH SS* 1: 17; *Chronica regia Coloniensis*, *QBS*, 149–50; *PCG*, 2: 762, ch. 1110; *Espéculo*, 3, 6, 9; Randall Rogers, *Latin Siege Warfare in the Twelfth Century* (Oxford: Oxford University Press, 1997), 166–69, 252–53.

42. *Gesta triumphalia*, 92; Bernardo Maragone, *Annales*, 7–8; al-Maqqarī, *History*, 2: 303; Caffaro, *De captione*, 26–27, 32–33; *CAI*, 159, 206, 214, 219, 224, Bk. 1, ch. 19, Bk. 2, ch. 24, 41, 51, 64; *De Expugnatione Lyxbonensi*, 134, 142, 147–60; Letters of Arnulf, *RHGF* 14: 325–27 and Duodechin, *MGH SS* 17: 27–28; *CJI*, 3: 72–80, ch. 157–63.

43. Caffaro, *De captione*, 26–27. Kagay, *Usatges*, 83, art. 73; *CAVC*, 1: 106, art. 19; *PCG*, 2: 761–62, ch. 1108, 1111; Paul E. Chevedden, "The Hybrid Trebuchet: The Halfway Step to the Counterweight Trebuchet," in Kagay and Vann, *Social Origins*, 179–222, and "The Artillery of King James I the Conqueror," in Chevedden, Kagay, and Padilla, *Iberia*, 47–94; also Paul E. Chevedden, Zvi Shiller, Samuel R. Gilbert, and Donald J. Kagay, "The Traction Trebuchet: A Triumph of Four Civilizations," *Viator* 31 (2000): 433–86; Rogers *Siege Warfare*, 251–73.

44. *De Expugnatione Lyxbonensis*, 134, 142, 162; *CAI*, 197, 206, Bk. 2, ch. 4–5, 25; *CPA*, 41, 44; *PCG*, 2: 761–62, ch. 1108, 1110; al-Maqqarī, *History*, 2: 303; *CJI*, 2: 50, ch. 69. and 4: 12–16, 18–24, 34–37, ch. 189, 192–95, 201–2, and 5: 56, ch. 262; *CSM*, 28; Keller and Cash, *Daily Life*, plate 20; *Espéculo*, 3, 6–9; *Partidas*, 2, 23, 23–25.

45. *CJI*, 2: 54, ch. 70; *De Expugnatione Lyxbonensi*, 130–33; *CAI*, 220, Bk. 2, ch. 55.

46. *CSJP*, 62–63, 70–72; *CSJP* (*tr*), 22–23, 26–27, ch. 18, 19; *De Expugnatione Lyxbonensi*, 136–38; *CAI*, 224, Bk. 2, ch,. 64; Rodrigo, *Historia*, 248–49, Bk. 7, ch. 26; *PCG*, 2: 749, ch. 1075.

47. *Historia Silense*, 189–94, ch. 87–90; *Chronica latina*, 36, ch. 2; Rodrigo, *Historia*, 203–5, Bk. 6, ch. 22; *CSJP*, 71–73; *CSJP* (*tr*), 25–26, ch. 19; *CAI*, 218–25, Bk. 2, ch. 50–66; *De Expugnatione Lyxbonensis*, 173–81; Robert I. Burns, S.J., and Paul E. Chevedden, *Negotiating Cultures: Bilingual Surrender Treaties in Muslim-Christian Spain Under James the Conqueror* (Leiden: E.J. Brill, 1999); Robert I. Burns, S.J., "How to End a Crusade: Techniques for Making Peace in Thirteenth-Century Valencia," in his *Moors and Crusaders*, No. IV, and "Surrender Constitutions: The Islamic Communities of Eslida and Alfandech," in his *Muslims, Christians, and Jews*, 52–79, and 288–92, nos. 1–5.

48 *Chronica latina*, 105–6, 114–17, ch. 64, 72–73; Rodrigo, *Historia*, 297–300, Bk. 9, ch. 15–17; *CJI*, 4: 6, 14, 38, 40, ch. 184–85, 189, 203, 249, and 5: 66–88, ch. 269–84; *PCG*, 2: 725, 746–47, 766–67, 770, ch. 1040, 1069–71, 1123–24, 1130.

49. *Historia Silense*, 189–90, ch. 86–87; *Chronica Gothorum*, *PMH SS* 1: 15; Caffaro, *De captione*, 28–29; *Chronica latina*, 62–64, ch. 25; Rodrigo, *Historia*, 275–76, Bk. 8, ch.12; *CJI*, 4: 40, ch. 205; *PCG*, 2: 749, ch. 1076; *Partidas*, 2, 23, 26–29.

50. *Historia Roderici*, 88–89, ch. 62; *PC*, 156–68, vv. 90–96; *CSJP*, 61–64, 70–72,

80–81; *CSJP (tr)*, 22, 26–27, 30–31, ch. 18–19; *Chronica Gothorum*, 12–13; *Chronicon de Cardeña*, *ES* 23: 379; *Chronica latina*, 100–101, ch. 56; Rodrigo, *Historia*, 247–48, Bk. 7, ch. 25; Ibn Abī Zarʿ, *Rawd al-Qirtas*, 2: 526; Huici, *Batallas*, 104–34 and appendices 1–2; *CJI*, 2: 36–44, ch. 63–65, and 4: 58–61, ch. 217–18; Reilly, *Alfonso VI*, 243–44, 348–50, and *Contest*, 112–15, 160–67, 203; Soldevila, *Jaume I*, 125–29, 196–200; García Fitz, *Castilla y León*, 288–89, 457–58.

51. Lévi-Provençal, *Histoire*, 3: 100; Elena Lourie, "A Society Organized for War: Medieval Spain," *Past and Present* 35 (1966): 69–70.

52. ʿAbd Allāh, *The Tibyān*, 114–17, ch. 7; *Chronicon Lusitanum*, *ES* 14: 416–18; Huici, *Batallas*, 19–84, especially 68 (battlefield map) and 72 (aerial photographs); Menéndez Pidal, *España*, 1: 331–41; Reilly, *Alfonso VI*, 187–90.

53. Huici, *Batallas*, 137–218, and opposite 166 (map) and opposite 168 (aerial photograph); González, *Alfonso VIII*, 1: 952–70.

54. Huici, *Batallas*, 219–330, and opposite 256, 280 (maps), and between 284–85 (photographs); González, *Alfonso VIII*, 1: 1024–47; Juan Eslava Galán, "Tácticas en la Batalla de Las Navas de Tolosa," *CEM* 6–7 (1978–79): 39–53.

55. García Fitz, *Castilla y León*, 348–405.

56. *CAI*, 205, 226, Bk. 2, ch. 22, 67; *CPA*, 35; *CSJP*, 72, 79–80, 119; Caffaro, *De captione*, 21–24, 27; Rodrigo, *Historia*, 298, Bk. 9, ch. 16; *Chronica latina*, 118, ch. 74; *CJI*, 5: 53, ch. 260; *PCG*, 2: 747–49, 751, 753, 758, ch. 1072, 1075, 1082, 1085, 1099.

57. Huici, *Batallas*, 74–75, 109–11, 142–45, 157, 163, 265–66; Reilly, *Alfonso VI*, 187–88; al-Maqqarī, *History*, 2: 313, 321–24, Bk. 8, ch. 2–4; González, *Alfonso VIII*, 3: 566–72, no. 897 (1212); García Fitz, *Castilla y León*, 353–66.

58. *DJI*, 1: 215, no. 113 (23 December 1228); *CJI*, 2: 18, 36–44, ch. 56, 63–65, and 4: 58–61, ch. 217–18; *Chronica latina*, 99–100, ch. 55.

59. *CAI*, 229, Bk. 2, ch. 73; *Historia Roderici*, 87–89, ch. 61–62; *PC*, 70–71, 81, 92, 96, 128, 136, 167, 218, vv. 23–25, 31, 40, 44–45, 74, 82, 95, 121; Powers, *Society*, ch. 7.

60. *CAI*, 167, 205–10, 212, Bk. 1, ch. 36, and Bk. 2, ch. 23–24, 27, 31, 33, 36; Caffaro, *De captione*, 28–29; Rodrigo, *Historia*, 275–75, Bk. 8, ch. 11; *CJI*, 4: 36, ch. 202.

61. *CPA*, 19; *CAI*, 167–68, 205–7, 209–10, 212, 229–31, Bk. 1, ch. 36, 39, and Bk. 2, ch. 23–24, 27, 31, 33, 36, 73–74, 78; *PC*, 72, v. 25; *PFG*, 74, v. 246; *HC*, 175, 264, Bk. 1, ch. 103, and Bk. 2, ch. 21; González, *Alfonso VIII*, 2: 931–32, no. 543 (10 March 1190); *CJI*, 4: 40, 64, ch. 205, 220; *Espéculo*, 3, 5, 7–17; *Partidas*, 2, 25,1–5, and 2, 26, 1–8, 32–34, and 2, 27, 1–10; Powers, *Society*, 165–67 (tables 1 and 2), 172–73, 249–50, n. 36, and plates 5–6.

62. Powers, *Society*, 93–111; *Liber partitionis regni Maiorice* in *CDACA*, 11: 151–656; *Regestum donationum regni Valentie* in *CDACA*, 11: 7–141 (1 July 1232); Ramón de María, *El "Repartiment" de Burriana y Villarreal* (Valencia: J. Nacher, 1935); Julio González, *Repartimiento de Sevilla*, 2 vols. (Madrid: CSIC, 1951).

63. González, *Alfonso VIII*, 3: 571, no. 897 (1212); Caesarius, *Dialogus*, 1: 303; *CAI*, 187, 202, Bk. 2, ch. 8, 14–15; *CPA*, 32, 33; *PCG*, 2: 755, 759–60, 764–65, ch. 1092, 1105–7, 1114–15.

64. *Fuero real*, 4, 16, 1–2; *CAVC*, 1: 103; *BC*, 22–25 (4 November 1187), 31–35 (16 January 1199), 38–39 (May 1205), 42–46 (20 May 1214); González, *Alfonso VIII*, 1: 602–26, and 2: 266–68, 514–15, 568–70, nos. 156 (1 February 1171), 313 (17 January 1179), 338 (2 April 1180), and 3: 306–7, 695–97, nos. 745 (10 June 1203), 982 (28 April 1215), and

Alfonso IX, 2: 548, no. 434 (22 July 1223); and *Fernando III,* 2: 60, 96–97, 178–79, 346–47, 389–90, nos. 48 (27 November 1218), 78 (16 June 1219), 147 (7 December 1221), 301 (31 January 1231), 810 (20 November 1250).

65. González, *Alfonso VIII,* 1: 625, and 3: 271–72, no. (25 July 1202), and *Fernando III,* 2: 21–22, no. 14 (9 January 1218); *Partidas,* 2, 9, 10; *CAI,* 215, Bk. 2, ch. 43; *Chronica Gothorum, PMH SS* 1: 16; Roger de Hoveden, *Chronica,* 2: 334; *CJI,* 2: 40–42, ch. 64, and 5: 62, ch. 266; Robert I. Burns, S.J., "The Medieval Crossbow as Surgical Instrument: An Illustrated Case History," in his *Moors and Crusaders,* No. VII.

66. *Partidas,* 2, 29, prologue; *CAI,* 176–77, 202–3, Bk. 1, ch. 56, 59, and Bk. 2, ch. 14, 17; *Historia Roderici,* 76, ch. 41; Fidel Fita, "Noticias," *BRAH* 11 (1887): 456 (2 June 1192); Mansilla, *Honorio III,* 450–52, no. 595 (20 February 1226); *Gesta triumphalia,* 93; González, *Alfonso VIII,* 1: 619.

67. James Brodman, "Military Redemptionism and the Castilian Reconquest, 1180–1250," *Military Affairs* 44 (1980): 24–27; "Municipal Ransoming Law on the Medieval Spanish Frontier," *Speculum* 60 (1985): 318–30; "The Origins of Hospitallerism in Medieval Catalonia," in Simon, *Iberia,* 1: 290–302; *Charity and Welfare: Hospitals and the Poor in Medieval Catalonia* (Philadelphia: University of Pennsylvania Press, 1998), 40; Charles Emmanuel Dufourcq, *L'Espagne catalane et le Maghrib aux XIIIe et XIVe siècles* (Paris: Presses Universitaires de France, 1966), 76–82; *Partidas,* 2, 29, 1–12, and 2, 30, 1–3.

68. Faustino Gazulla, "La Orden del Santo Redentor," *Boletín de la Sociedad castellonense de Cultura* 9 (1928): 90–107, 157–60, 204, 212, 370–75; 10 (1929): 38–412, 98–101, 124–26; Forey, "Mountjoy," 250–66, and *Military Orders,* 27–28; Brandão, *CSII-AII,* 261–63, no. 4 (October 1189); Hernández, *Cartularios,* 406, no. 452 (5 July 1239).

69. *DP,* 198, 281, 321, 418–19, nos. 182 (8 March 1199), 232 (reg., April–May 1200), 283 (10 July 1203), 403 (18 June 1209); Gonzalez, *Alfonso VIII,* 1: 552–54, and *Repartimiento,* 2: 42, 242, 299, 305; Robert I. Burns, "Los hospitales del reino de Valencia en el siglo XIII," *AEM* 2 (1965): 135–54.

70. James Brodman, *Ransoming Captives in Crusader Spain: The Order of Merced on the Christian-Islamic Frontier* (Philadelphia: University of Pennsylvania Press, 1986), 11–19, 128–40; *DJI,* 3: 30–31, no. 569 (1251).

71. *Partidas,* 2, 24, 7; Richard W. Unger, *The Ship in the Medieval Economy, 600–1600* (London: Croom Helm, 1980), ch. 3; Rogers, *Siege Warfare,* 201–7; *CSM* 9 (panel 5); *CSM* 15 (panels 7–8); *CSM* 25 (panel 9); *CSM* 33; *CSM* 35 (panels 4–11); *CSM* 36; *CSM* 65 (panel 4); *CSM* 95 (panels 4–10); *CSM* 112; *CSM* 115 (panel 6); *CSM* 172; *CSM* 183 (panels 3, 5–6); *CSM* 193; Keller and Kinkade, *Iconography,* plate 4 (*CSM* 33, panel 2); Keller and Cash, *Daily Life,* plates 62 (*CSM* 95B, panel 1), 63 (*CSM* 36, panel 1); Dufourcq, *L'Espagne catalane,* 36–37.

72. *HC,* 174–75, 262–64, Bk. 1, ch. 103, and Bk. 2, ch. 21; Bernardo Maragone, *Annales,* 8; *Gesta triumphalia,* 90; Caffaro, *De captione,* 22, 3; *De Expugnatione Lyxbonensi,* 53; Letters of Arnulf *RHGF* 14: 325 and Duodechin, *MGH SS* 17: 27; *Chronicon Gothorum, PMH SS* 1: 13, 15; Ralph of Diceto, *Chronica,* 2: 65–66; Gosuinus, *Quomodo fuit capta Alcaser a Francis, PMH SS* 1: 103; *Chronicon Regia Coloniensis, QBS,* 148.

73. *DJI,* 1: 187, 235–36, nos. 96 (12 October 1227), 128 (1 April 1230); Mas Latrie,

Traités, 2: 279–80; *CJI*, 2: 14, 16, 18, ch. 54–56, and 3: 14, 18, ch. 116, 118–19, and 5: 56–60, ch. 264–65. The *nau* and *taride* were sailing ships.

74. *PCG*, 2: 756, ch. 1096; González, *Repartimiento*, 1: 293–98, 516–20; *Chronica da conquista do Algarve*, *PMH SS* 1: 419; *Partidas*, 2, 24, 1–10; Florentino Pérez Embid, "La marina real castellana en el siglo XIII," *AEM* 6 (1969): 158–65; O'Callaghan, *The Learned King*, 167–68.

Chapter 7

1. Thomas Bisson, *Fiscal Accounts of Catalonia Under the Early Count-Kings (1151–1213)*, 2 vols. (Berkeley: University of California Press, 1984); Joseph F. O'Callaghan, "La financiación de la Conquista de Sevilla," in González Jiménez, *Sevilla*, 191–206.

2. James J. Todesca, "The Monetary History of Castile-León (ca. 1100–1300) in Light of the Bourgey Hoard," *American Numismatic Society Museum Notes* 33 (1988): 129–203, and "Means of Exchange: Islamic Coinage in Christian Spain, 1000–1200," in Simon, *Iberia*, 1: 232–58, and *What Touches All: Coinage and Monetary Policy in León-Castile to 1230* (Ph.D. dissertation, Fordham University, 1996); Bisson, *Accounts*, 1: 304, and *Conservation of Coinage: Monetary Exploitation and Its Restraint in France, Catalonia and Aragon (A.D. 1000–c. 1225)* (New York: Oxford University Pres, 1979), 74–81.

3. *Chronica Naierensis*, 156, Bk. 3, ch. 21; *Historia Roderici*, 78, ch. 43; *Chronica latina*, 81, 89, 112, ch. 38, 46, 70; *Al-Ḥulal*, 95; González, *Fernando II*, 390, and *Fernando III*, 1: 125–27, 177, 479; Grassotti, *Instituciones*, 2: 755–56, 763–66.

4. Imperiale di Sant'Angelo, *Genova*, 1: 206–9, no. 167 (September 1146); Rodrigo, *Historia*, 263, Bk. 8, ch. 3; González, *Alfonso VIII*, 1: 1011–14.

5. Eloy Benito Ruano, "La Orden de Santiago y el imperio latino de Constantinopla," *Estudios santiaguistas* (León: Colegio Universitario de León, 1978), 29–60, esp. 53–60, nos. 1–5; Todesca, "Monetary History," 163.

6. Reilly, *Alfonso VII*, 226–27; González, *Fernando III*, 1: 490–92.

7. Loewenfeld, *Epistolae*, 63, no. 130 (1 July 1089); *DP*, 53–54, 58–59, 69–70, 339–41, nos. 34 (16 March 1095), 39 (May–December 1098), 50 (23 May 1116), 307 (10 November 1204); and *Honorio III*, 148–49, no. 188 (5 October 1218); Ubieto Arteta, *Pedro I*, 235–36, 292, nos. 21 [1095], 58 [1098]; Paul F. Kehr, *Das Papsttum und die Königreiche Navarra und Aragon bis zur Mitte des XII. Jahrhunderts* (Berlin: Akademie der Wissenschaften, 1928), 55–58, nos. 1 (1095), 2 (1099).

8. *DMP DR*, 1: 250, no. 202 (13 December 1143); Lucius II, *Epistolae*, *PL* 179: 860–61, no. 26 (1 May 1144); Alexander III, *Epistolae*, *PL* 200: 1237–38, no. 1424 (23 May 1179); *DP*, 193, no. 170 (9 December 1198); *MH*, 1: 50–51, no. 27 (11 January 1218); Herculano, *Historia*, 3: 109–11, 318–20, and 4: 57–58, 307–8.

9. Rivera Recio, *Toledo*, 222–24, n. 74 (8 May 1188); Lucas, *Chronicon*, 4: 113, and *Crónica*, 421, ch. 88; Goñi Gaztambide, *Historia*, 134–35; Linehan, *Spanish Church*, 5–8; Brundage, *Canon Law and the Crusader*, 147, 185–87.

10. *Chronica latina*, 57, ch. 21; Mansilla, *Honorio III*, 13–14, 29–31, 103–4, 122–23, 127–28, 144, 147–48, 155, 159–60, 174–75, nos. 16 (1 December 1216), 35 (13 February

1217), 131 (12 January 1218), 152 (31 January), 162 (24 February), 182 (before 24 July), 187 (5 October), 197 (29 November), 205 (19 January 1219), 230 (28 May 1219).

11. Mansilla, *Honorio III*, 76–78, 106–8, 160–61, 207–8, 214, 217–18, 221, nos. 95–96 (1217), 134, 207 (9 February 1219), 268–69 (4–5 February 1220), 278 (29 April), 285 (21 May), 291 (17 June); Gorosterratzu, *Rodrigo*, 431, 435–36, nos. 65 (28 January 1219), 74–75; González, *Fernando III*, 1: 279–80, 461; Linehan, *Spanish Church*, 9, n. 1, citing AC Toledo, A6.H.1.8d (4 February 1220); *BS*, 70, 616, nos. 3, 12.

12. Mansilla, *Honorio III*, 225–27, 237–38, 242–43, 290, 396, 438–39, 454, nos. 299–300 (1 July 1220), 301 (4 July), 319 (4 September), 326 (22 September), 390 (15 January 1222), 535 (30 January 1225), 584 (19 October), 598 (7 April 1226); Paul Freedman, "Two Letters of Pope Honorius III on the Collection of Ecclesiastical Revenues in Spain," *Church, Law and Society in Catalonia, 900–1500* (Aldershot: Ashgate/Variorum, 1994), No. VI: 37–40, nos. 1 (23 August 1222), 2 (1 September); González, *Fernando III*, 1: 461; Linehan, *Spanish Church*, 19.

13. Goni Gaztambide, *Historia*, 171–78, 644, no. 2 (24 September 1238); Quintana Prieto, *Inocencio IV*, 2: 519–20, no. 559 (13 November 1248); José Font Rius, *Rationes Decimarum Hispaniae (1279–1280)*, 2 vols. (Barcelona: CSIC, 1946–47). 1: viii.

14. González, *Alfonso VIII*, 2: 522–24, no. 344 (18 June 1180), and *Alfonso IX*, 2: 125–29, 306–9, nos. 84 (1194), 221 (1208). For a comparison with France see Giles Constable, "The Financing of the Crusades in the Twelfth Century," in *Outremer: Studies in the History of the Crusading Kingdom of Jerusalem Presented to Joshua Prawer*, ed. Benjamin Z. Kedar, Hans Eberhard Mayer, and R. C. Smail (Jerusalem: Yad Izhak ben-Zvi Institute, 1982), 64–88.

15. Gonzalo de Berceo, *Vida de Santo Domingo*, in *Obras completas de Gonzalo de Berceo* (Logroño: Instituto de Estudios riojanos, 1974), 28–32, vv. 130–58; *ES*, 16: 237; *CSJP*, 77; *CSJP (tr)*, 29, ch. 19; Lema Pueyo, *Alfonso I*, 446–48, no. 284 (4 September 1134); Zurita, *Anales*, 1: 86–87, 106–7.

16. González, *Alfonso VIII*, 2: 522–24, no. 344 (1180), and *Alfonso IX*, 2: 99–100, 264–65, nos. 65 (29 March 1193), 189 (25 September 1204); Mansilla, *Honorio III*, 316–17, no. 436 (10 April 1223); Rodrigo, *Historia*, 262–63, Bk. 8, ch. 4.

17. *CDACA*, 8: 64–67, no. 21 (December 1180); Bisson, *Accounts*, 1: 138, and *Crown of Aragon*, 54–55; Goñi Gaztambide, *Historia*, 72, n. 31; *Chronica latina*, 57, ch. 21; Mansilla, *Honorio III*, 76–78, no. 95 (1217); Bernat Desclot, *Crònica*, 2: 70, ch. 15; *DJI*, 205–6, 229–30, nos. 110 (21 December 1228), 123 (27 August 1229).

18. *Cortes de los antiguos reinos de León y Castilla*, 5 vols. (Madrid: Real Academia de la Historia, 1861–1903), 1: 38, canon 16; *HC*, 430, Bk. 3, ch. 7; Erdmann, *Papsturkunden*, 198–203, no. 40 (September 1143); *ES*, 16: 487–88, no. 29 (6 January 1154).

19. Hernández, *Cartularios*, 530, no. 644 (5 April 1208); González, *Alfonso VIII*, 2: 774–75, no. 451 (21 April 1186), and 3: 716–17, nos. 995–96 (15 February 1216); Mansilla, *Honorio III*, 67, 74, nos. 84 (25 August 1217), 93 (25 September); Linehan, *Spanish Church*, 111.

20. Mansilla, *Honorio III*, 162–63, 414–16, 440–41, nos. 210 (16 March 1219), 559–60 (3 June 1225), 585–86 (20 October).

21. Gorosterratzu, *Rodrigo*, 257–59, 439–40, nos. 90–91 (14 February 1228); Auvray, *Grégoire IX*, 1: 155–56, 202, 1116–17, nos. 255 (8 December 1228), 329 (7 August 1229), 2063 (5 June 1232), 2195 (23 October 1234); *BS*, 103–4, no. 11 (23 October 1234).

22. Gorosterratzu, *Rodrigo,* 449, no. 128 (3 September 1236); Auvray, *Grégoire IX,* 2: 473–74, nos. 3315–16 (reg.); Linehan, *Spanish Church,* 111–12, citing AC León, doc. 1564; Goñi Gaztambide, *Historia,* 153–57.

23. Gorosterratzu, *Rodrigo,* 468–69, no. 177 (15 April 1247); Berger, *Innocent IV,* 1: 377, no. 2533; Mansilla, *Iglesia,* 57; Goñi Gaztambide, *Historia,* 184; Ana Rodríguez López, "La política eclesiástica de la monarquía castellano-leonesa durante el reinado de Fernando III (1217–1252)," *Hispania* 48 (1988): 37; Clementino Sanz y Díaz, *Reseña cronológica de algunos documentos conservados en el archivo de la catedral de Cuenca* (Cuenca: Calasanz, 1965), no. 77 (30 April 1250).

24. Antonio Ballesteros, "Las Cortes de 1252," *Anales de la junta para ampliación de estudios e investigaciones científicas* 3 (1911): 114–43, art. 44; Antonio López Ferreiro, *Fueros municipales de Santiago y de su tierra* (Santiago de Compostela: Imprenta del Seminario, 1895), 386, art. 69; *Fuero real* 1, 5, 4; O'Callaghan, *Cortes,* 132–33, and *The Learned King,* 53–54.

25. Auvray, *Grégoire IX,* 1: 36–38, 742–46, nos. 70–71 (5 May 1227), 1327 (26 May 1233), 1328–29 (reg.); *MH,* 1: 60–61, no. 35 (21 October 1234); Caetano de Sousa, *Provas,* 1: 50–54, no. 22 (January 1238); Gorosterratzu, *Rodrigo,* 455, no. 140 (6 May 1238).

26. Mansilla, *Honorio III,* 127–28, 161–62, 274–75, nos. 162 (24 February 1218), 209 (15 March 1219), 369 (13 February 1221); Auvray, *Grégoire IX,* 1: 1215–16, no. 2300 (4 December 1234, reg.), and 2: 473–74, nos. 3315–16 (3 September 1236, reg.).

27. O'Callaghan, *Cortes,* 130–51; Evelyn Procter, *Curia and Cortes in León and Castille, 1072–1295* (Cambridge: Cambridge University Press, 1980), 186–203.

28. Gambra, *Alfonso VI,* 2: 273–75, 295–98, nos. 105 (7 February 1190), 114 (31 March 1091); González, *Alfonso IX,* 2: 306–8, 547–48, 571–72, nos. 221 (February 1208), 433 (4 July 1223), 459 (28 July 1225); Claudio Sánchez Albornoz, "Notas para el estudio del *Petitum,*" *Estudios sobre las instituciones medievales españolas* (México: Universidad Autónoma de México, 1965), 483–614; Procter, *Curia,* 25–29, 53–54.

29. Bisson, *Conservation,* 199–200, no. 1 (4 April 1118), and *Accounts,* 1: 134–36, 140–43, and 2: 86, 198–99, 213, 240–42, nos. 27 (March c. 1174–75); 105 (11–12 August 1200), 115 (19 November 1205), 130 (30 December 1210); Kagay, *Usatges,* 107, app. 1, no. 4 (1118); *CAVC,* 1: 67, art. 18 (1188); *CJI,* 2: 6–8, ch. 50; Ferran Soldevila, "A propòsit del servei del bovatge," *AEM* 1 (1964): 573–88; Zurita, *Anales,* 1: 367, 478–79 (17 December 1232).

30. Bisson, *Conservation,* 199–200, no. 1 (4 April 1118); Kagay, *Usatges,* 107, app. 1, no. 4, and 79, art. 62; Kehr, *Papsturkunden,* 2: 389–90, no. 76 (1155); Villanueva, *Viage,* 6: 241 (1174); Freedman, *Vic,* 77–78; Todesca, "What Touches All," ch. 7 and ch. 9.

31. Bisson, *Conservation,* 81–85, 201, no. 3 (c. 1174); Sánchez Casabón, *Alfonso II,* 264–65, no. 184; Kehr, *Papsturkunden,* 1: 559, no. 238 (4 September 1191); Todesca, "What Touches All," 341.

32. *DP,* 199–200, nos. 183–84 (5 April 1199); Thomas N. Bisson, "Sur les origines du *monedatge: Quelques textes inédits,*" *Annales du Midi* 85 (1973): 99–100, no. 1 (1197), and *Conservation,* 86–86, 90, 203–4 no. 6 (5 April 1199).

33. González, *Alfonso IX,* 2: 236–37, no. 167 (March 1202), and *Alfonso VIII,* 3: 702–4, no. 986 (4 September 1215); Procter, *Curia,* 54–57, 82–85; O'Callaghan, *Cortes,* 133–35.

34. Thomas N. Bisson, "An 'Unknown Charter' for Catalonia (d. 1205)," in *Album Elemér Mályusz* (Brussels: Librairie Encyclopedique, 1976), 61–76, and *Conservation*, 88–96; *CDACA*, 8: 106, no. 39 (1 March 1209); Zurita, *Anales*, 1: 313–14.

35. *DJI*, 1: 44–46, 96–101, and 2: 385–88, nos. 13 (5 September 1218), 41 (18 March 1223), 42 (19 April), 238 (15 October 1236); Ángel Canellas López, *Colección diplomática del Concejo de Zaragoza, 1119–1276*, 2 vols. (Zaragoza: Catedra Zaragoza de la Universidad, 1972), 1: 140–42, no. 49 (1221); *CJI*, 4: 82–83, ch. 230; Zurita, *Anales*, 1: 509, 545, 560.

36. *PMH Leges* 1.2: 183 (1254), 188 (1250), 192 (1253), 196–97 (18 March 1255), and (16 March), 202–10 (1261); Herculano, *Hiistória*, 5: 133–35, 149–52, 167–73; Claudio Sánchez Albornoz, *La curia regia portuguesa: Siglos XII y XIII* (Madrid: Junta para Ampliación de Estudios e Investigaciones científicas, 1920), 156–58.

37. Olivia Remie Constable, *Trade and Traders in Muslim Spain: The Commerical Realignment of the Iberian Peninsula, 900–1500* (Cambridge: Cambridge University Press, 1994), 9, n. 14: "The term *paria* derives from either the Arabic *bara'* (to be free, acquitted, cleared [of debt] or *bara'* (which in some forms means to donate, give or concede)."

38. José María Lacarra, "Aspectos económicos de la sumisión de los reinos de taifas (1010–1102)," *Homenaje a Jaime Vicens Vives*, 1: 254–77, reprinted in his *Colonización, parias, repoblación y otros estudios* (Zaragoza: Anubar 1981); MacKay, *Spain*, ch. 1; Kennedy, *Muslim Spain*, 124–29.

39. Villanueva, *Viage*, 6: 326 (1090), and 10: 184 (1048); Prosper Bofarull y Moscaró, *Los Condes de Barcelona vindicados y cronología y genealogía de los reyes de España*, 2 vols. (Barcelona: J. Oliveres y Montmany, 1836), 2: 14 (1048), 17 (1056), 27 (1050); *LFM*, 1: 144–50, 518–20, 524–27, nos. 148 (1058), 149 (1063), 489 (1056), 492 (1076); *Historia Roderici*, 52–54, 69, 94–95, ch. 14–15, 37–42, 70.

40. José María Lacarra, "Dos tratados de paz y alianza entre Sancho el de Peñalén y Moctadir de Zaragoza (1069 y 1073)," *Homenaje a Johannes Vincke*, 2 vols. (Madrid: CSIC, 1962–1963), 1: 122–34, and *Documentos*, 1: 472, nos. 2 (1091), 3, 94 (1086–1094); Menéndez Pidal, *España*, 1: 206, 356, 376–88, 941–44, and 2: 712–13; Kehr, "Cuándo y cómo," 304, 319–20; Ibn al-Kardabūs, *Kitábu-l-iktifá*, in al-Maqqarī, *History*, 2: xxix.

41. *Crónica del Obispo Don Pelayo*, 73, 80; *Historia Silense*, 197–98, 202, 206–7, ch. 93, 95, 99–100, 104–5; Al-Ḥimyarī, *Kitāb*, 324; Alexandre Bruel, *Recueil des chartes de l'Abbaye de Cluny*, 6 vols. (Paris: Imprimerie Nationale, 1876–1903), 4: 809; *Chronicon Compostellanum*, *ES* 23: 327; Lucas, *Chronicon*, 4: 96; Dozy, *Recherches*, 161–62, 223, 225–26; Menéndez Pidal, *España*, 1: 135–45, 151–53, 166; Hilda Grassotti, "Para la historia," in her *Miscelánea*, 135–225, and *Instituciones*, 2: 739–42; Charles Julian Bishko, "Fernando I and the Origins of the Leonese Castilian Alliance with Cluny," in his *Studies in Medieval Spanish Frontier History* (London: Variorum, 1980), No. II, and "Liturgical Intercession at Cluny for the King-Emperors of León," *Studia Monastica* 3 (1961): 53–76.

42. Ibn al-Kardabūs, *Kitábu-l-iktifá*, in al-Maqqarī, *History*, 2: xxvii–xxviii.

43. Bruel, *Cluny*, 4: 627–29, 697–98, 809–10, nos. 3509 (10 July 1077), 3562 (c. 1080), 3638 (Easter 1090).

44. *The Tibyān*, 104, 130–33, ch. 6, 8; *Historia Roderici*, 49–51, ch. 7–9; *Al-Ḥulal*, 55; al-Maqqarī, *History*, 2: 270–73; Menéndez Pidal, *España*, 1: 257–58, 299–300; Kennedy, *Muslim Spain*, 146–49; Reilly, *Alfonso VI*, 83–84.

45. Rodrigo, *Historia*, 204–5, Bk. 6, ch. 22; al-Maqqarī, *History*, 2: 262–64; Ibn al-Kardabūs, *Kitábu-l-iktifá*, ibid., 2: xxix–xxxi.

46. *The Tibyān*, 130–31, ch. 8; Ibn Khaldūn, *Histoire*, 2: 81; al-Maqqarī, *History*, 2: 270, Ibn al-Kardabūs, *Kitábu-l-iktifá*, ibid., 2: xxxiv, xl; *Historia Roderici*, 60, ch. 29; *PCG*, 2: 559, 565, ch. 890, 896; Menéndez Pidal, *España*, 1: 393, 395–96, 406; Grassotti, *Instituciones*, 2: 742–50.

47. *Historia Roderici*, 51, 68–69, 86, ch. 31, 36, 58; Ibn ʿIdhārī, *Nuevos Fragmentos*, 65–67, and *Al-Bayān*, in Reinhardt Dozy, *Histoire des musulmanes d'Espagne*, new ed. Evariste Lévi-Provençal, 3 vols. (Leiden: E.J. Brill, 1932), 3: 231, Appendix II; Ibn al-Kardabūs, *Katábu-l-iktifá*, in al-Maqqarī, *History*, 2: xxxii, xxxix; Ibn Alcama, in *PCG*, 2: 565, ch. 896; *Carmen Campidoctoris*, 107, v. 85; Menéndez Pidal, *España*, 1: 360, 390.

48 *CAI*, 162–64, 169, 239–40, 242, Bk. 1, ch. 27–29, 41, and Bk. 2, ch. 93, 96; Ibn Khaldūn, *Histoire*, 2: 187; Rodrigo, *Historia*, 232, Bk. 7. ch. 11.

49. *CDACA*, 4: 47–48, 174–75, 315–16, nos. 20 (24 July 1136), 63 (September 1150), 129 (23 June 1158); Imperiale di Sant'Angelo, *Genova*, 1: 247–49, no. 196 (June 1149); Sánchez Casabón, *Alfonso II*, 94–96, 116–17, 147–50, 168–69, nos. 56 (5 November 1168), 72 (11 November 1169), 90 (4 June 1170), 106 (April 1171); Ibn Ṣāḥib al-Salā, *Al-Mann*, 146–51, 154–62, 193–95; Ibn ʿIdhārī, *Nuevos fragmentos*, 411–12, 418–19, 421–26, 439–42; al-Marrākushī, *Kitāb*, 170–71; al-Maqqarī, *History*, 2: 318–19, Bk.8, ch. 3; Ibn Khaldūn, *Histoire*, 2: 200–2; *Anales Toledanos I, ES* 23: 392; Zurita, *Anales*, 1: 259, 267–68.

50. *Chronica latina*, 89, ch. 46; *CJI*, 1: 64, ch. 25, and 3: 25, ch. 123; *DJI*, 1: 274–277, no. 153 (17 June 1231).

51. *Chronica latina*, 97, ch. 53; Gonzalez, *Fernando III*, 1: 308, 311, 499, citing the *Crónica de Castilla*, fol. 177r.

52. Ibn ʿIdhārī, *Al-Bayān*, 2: 17, 83, 85; Ibn Khaldūn, *Histoire*, 4: 173, set the annual tribute at 400,000 gold pieces, a sum approximating the 365,000 dinars cited by Ibn ʿIdhārī. *Chronica latina*, 108–9, ch. 67; Gonzalez, *Fernando III*, 1: 319–22, 391, 499–500; O'Callaghan, *The Learned King*, 174–77.

53. *Chronica latina*, 108–9, 148, ch. 67, 73; Rodrigo, *Historia*, 301, Bk. 9, ch. 18; *PCG*, 2: 736, ch. 1048; Ibn Abī Zarʿ, *Rawd al-Qirtas*, 2: 528.

54. *PCG*, 2: 741–42, ch. 1060–62; *Anales Toledanos II* and *Anales Toledanos III, ES* 23: 409, 413; González, *Fernando III*, 1: 343–45.

55. *PCG*, 2: 745, ch. 1069; *Crónica de Alfonso X*, ed. Manuel González Jiménez (Murcia: Real Academia Alfonso X el Sabio, 1998), 5–6, ch. 1; Gonzalez, *Fernando III*, 1: 361–63, 500.

56. *Chronica latina*, 109, ch. 67; González, *Fernando III*, 1: 299, 499, citing the *Crónica de Castilla*, fol. 73; Ibn ʿIdhārī, *Al-Bayān*, 2: 162–63; *PCG*, 2: 749, ch. 1076.

57. Bisson, *Accounts*, 2: 259–61, nos. 142 (15 October 1148), 143 (3 December); Huici, *Batallas*, 219.

58. González, *Alfonso VIII*, 1: 249–50, and 3: 344, 710–11, nos. 769 (8 December 1204), 991 (20 December 1215); Brandão, *CSI-AII*, 283–85, no. 15 (November 1208), and *CSII-AIII*, 364–65 (n.d.).

59. Sánchez Casabón, *Alfonso II*, 814, no. 628 (December 1194); Bisson, *Accounts*, 1: 129–42, and "Las finanzas del joven Jaime I (1213–1228)," *Jaime I y su época*, 192, no. 1 (23 January 1216); *DP*, 568, no. 538 (reg., 1216); *CJI*, 1: 22, 30, ch. 6, 11; *DJI*, 1: 39–40, 126–27, 222–23, 289–90, nos. 10 (1 January 1218), 57 (16 June 1224), 118 (3 April 1229), 161 (9 October 1231); Forey, *The Templars*, 29–30; Huici, *Batallas*, 227; Carlos Marichalar, *Colección diplomática de Don Sancho el Fuerte* (Pamplona: Editorial Arambarú, 1934), 102, no. 56 (12 May 1212).

60. *DJI*, 1: 189–90, 299, nos. 98 (14 February 1228), 168 (6 May 1232); Marichalar, *Sancho VII*, no. 176 (February 1231); *CJI*, 2: 80, ch. 82, and 3: 80–84, ch. 164, and 4: 56, ch. 216, and 6: 12–14, ch. 295.

61. Mansilla, *Honorio III*, 324–25, no. 447 (22 June 1223); Forey, *Templars*, 388–90, no. 20 (21 May 1253); Eloy Benito Ruano, "La Banca Toscana y la Orden de Santiago," in his *Estudios*, 61–153, nos. 1 (9 September 1238), 2 (24 September 1245), 3 (3 February 1248), 4 (4 February), 5 (5 June), 6 (17 July 1249), 7–8 (30 August 1250), 9 (17 May 1253), 10 (18 March 1258), 11 (17 September), 12 (4 December 1274), 13 (5 March 1291).

62. *PCG*, 2: 737, 739, 742, 744, ch. 1052–53, 1055, 1060–62, 1065. Jaime I used the word *manlevar* to describe his loans; *CJI*, 2: 80, ch. 82, and 4: 56, ch. 216.

63. Luciano Serrano, "El canciller de Fernando III de Castilla," *Hispania* 1 (1941): 37–40; González, *Fernando III*, 3: 429, no. 842 (22 April 1252), and *Repartimiento*, 1: 279–80, 311–12, 361–63, and 2: 65–66, 113–14, 118, 176–77, 233, 247, 263; Nina Melechen, *The Jews of Medieval Toledo: Their Economic and Social Contacts with Christians from 1150 to 1391* (Ph.D. dissertation, Fordham University, 1999), ch. 6. The Jewish names are given as they appear in the documents.

64. González, *Fernando III*, 1: 502, and 3: 336, no. 765 (21 June 1248), and *Repartimiento*, 1: 184, n. 140.

65. Hilda Grassotti, "Un empréstito para la conquista de Sevilla. Problemas históricos que suscita," *Miscelánea*, 225–73; Procter, *Curia*, 201.

66. Mansilla, *Iglesia*, 210, 213–14; Vicente Beltrán de Heredia, *Cartulario de la Universidad de Salamanca*, 4 vols. (Salamanca: Universidad de Salamanca, 1970–1973), 1: 606–7, no. 23 (1254); López Ferreiro, *Fueros*, 363–88 (15 February 1253), *leyes* 25–27, 31, 33–34, 42.

67. González, *Alfonso IX*, 2: 264, no. 189 (1204); Ciriaco Miguel Vigil, *Colección histórico-diplomática del ayuntamiento de* Oviedo (Oviedo: Pardo-Gusano, 1889), 46, no. 22 (1 February 1258); Hilda Grassotti, "Alfonso IX y el origen de los empréstitos," *CHE* 69 (1987): 218–20; O'Callaghan, *The Learned King*, 170.

68. *Memorial Histórico Español*, 50 vols. (Madrid: Real Academia de la Historia, 1851–1963), 1: 69, no. 33 (18 June 1255); Alberto Martín Expósito and José María Monsalvo, *Documentación medieval del Archivo municipal de Ledesma* (Salamanca: Universidad de Salamanca, 1986), 36–40, no. 3 (6 October 1255); Juan Agapíto y Revilla, *Los privilegios de Valladolid* (Valladolid: Sociedad Castellana de Excursiones, 1906), 48–49, no. 29–XI. (6 November 1255); Julián Sánchez Ruano, *El Fuero de Salamanca* (Salamanca: S. Cerezo, 1870), 166 (7 April 1256); Antonio Ballesteros Beretta, *Alfonso X el Sabio* (Barcelona: El Albir, 1984), 1074, no. 315 (to Ribadavia, 30 June 1256). O'Callaghan, *Cortes*, 133.

69. González, *Fernando III*, 1: 502–3, and 3: 415–16, no. 829 (20 August 1251); Grassotti, "Un empréstito," 261–65.

Chapter 8

1. Mansilla, *Honorio III*, 430–32, nos. 575–76 (26 September 1225), and *Iglesia*, 289–91, nos. 21–22.

2. Rodrigo, *Historia*, 235, Bk. 7, ch. 14; *Poema de Almería*, in *CAI*, 256, lines 38–48; Christoph Maier, *Crusade Propaganda and Ideology: Model Sermons for the Preaching of the Cross* (Cambridge: Cambridge University Press, 2000), and *Preaching the Crusades: The Mendicant Friars and the Cross in the Thirteenth Century* (Cambridge: Cambridge University Press, 1994).

3. See the text in *De Expugnatione Lyxbonensi*, 70–85. Isidore of Seville, *Etymologiarum sive Originum Libri* XX, ed. W. M. Lindsay, 2 vols. (Oxford: Clarendon Press, 1911), Bk. 18, ch. 1–2.

4. *De Expugnatione Lyxbonensi*, 130–33, 147–59; Jonathan Phillips, "Ideas of Crusade and Holy War in *De Expugnatione Lyxbonensi*," in *Holy Land, Holy Lands, and Christian History*, ed. Robert Swanson, *Studies in Church History* 36 (2000): 123–141.

5. Alvar, *Textos trovadorescos*, 84–88.

6. *Chronica latina*, 60, ch. 23; Lucas, *Chronicon*, 4: 110, and *Crónica*, 414, ch. 83.

7. *CJI*, 2: 36, 52, ch. 61–62, 69; Bernat Desclot, *Crònica*, 2: 131–32, ch. 40.

8. Brundage, *Canon Law and the Crusader*, 17–18, and chs. 2–3, and "The Votive Obligations of Crusaders: The Development of a Canonistic Doctrine," *Traditio* 24 (1968): 77–118, and "A Note on the Attestation of Crusaders' Vows," *CHR* 52 (1966): 234–39, and "*Cruce signari*: The Rite for Taking the Cross in England," *Traditio* 22 (1966): 289–310; Kenneth Pennington, "The Rite for Taking the Cross in the Twelfth Century," *Traditio* 30 (1974): 429–35; Michael Markowski, "*Crucesignatus*: Its Origins and Early Usage," *Journal of Medieval History* 10 (1984): 157–65.

9. Alejandro Olivar, *El Sacramentario de Vich* (Barcelona: CSIC, 1953), 173–76, 215–17, nos. 258–59, 297, and cviii–cix (Bibliothèque de Avignon, MS 178, fol. 155), and *Sacramentarium Rivipullense* (Madrid: CSIC, 1964), 216, no. 377.

10. *Gesta comitum*, 7, 11, 13, 33, 37, 48, ch. 4 (rd), 8–9, 11–12 (rp), 16 (rd); Lucas of Túy, *Vita Sancti Martini*, PL 208: 13–14, ch. 5–6; *CAI*, 191, ch. 90; *The Pilgrim's Guide to Santiago de Compostela*, tr. William Melczer (New York: Italica, 1993), 56–60; *Partidas*, 1, 8–9. Luis Vázquez de Parga, José María Lacarra, and Juan Uría Riu, *Las peregrinaciones a Santiago de Compostela*, 3 vols. (Madrid: CSIC, 1948), 1: 136–38, cite pilgrimage vows from the eleventh-century Ceremonial of Roda and Lleida.

11. Rodrigo, *Historia*, 139, Bk. 6, ch. 26; Ubieto Arteta, *Pedro I*, 113, n. 6 and 115, n. 9, and "La participación navarro-aragonesa en la primera cruzada," *Príncipe de Viana* 8 (1947): 370, nn. 8, 30.

12. *Liber Maiolichinus*, 137–40, no. 1 (September 1113); *DP*, 79–80, no. 62 (2 April [1121–24]); *HC*, 379, Bk. 2, ch. 78; Ordericus, *History*, 410, Bk. 13, ch. 8; *CSJP*, 80–81; *CGPIII*, 67, ch. 19; *CSJP (tr)*, 30–31, ch. 19; *CAI*, 237, Bk. 2, ch. 90; Erdmann, *Papsturkunden*, 202–3, no. 40 (1143), canon 21; Goñi Gaztambide, *Historia*, 67, 76–78.

13. *Annales D. Alfonsi*, 155; *Chronica Gothorum*, 13–14; Eugenius III, *Epistolae, PL* 180: 1203 (13 April 1147); *DP*, 94–96, 116–17, nos. 78 (27 April 1148), 98 (1155); *CDACA*, 4: 314–15, 320–21, nos. 128 (22 June 1148), 133 (24 September 1153); Kehr, *Papsturkunden*, 1: 373–77, no. 70 (24 September 1153); Goñi Gaztambide, *Historia*, 67, 76–78, 86, 93–94, 643, appendix 1.

14. *BS*, 17–18; Martín, *Santiago*, 255–56, no 75 (3 August 1175); *Materials for the History of Thomas Becket, Archbishop of Canterbury*, ed. J. C. Robertson, 7 vols., Rolls Series (London: Longman, 1875–1885), 7: 517–18; *Gesta Regis Henrici Secundi*, ed. William Stubbs, 2 vols., Rolls Series (London: Longman, 1867), 1: 30; Fidel Fita, "Tres bulas inéditas de Alejandro III," *BRAH* 12 (1888): 167–68 (23 March 1175); Rivera Recio, *Toledo*, 222–23, n. 14 (8 May 1188).

15. Ralph of Diceto, *Ymagines historiarum*, 2: 65–66; Kehr, *Papsturkunden*, 2: 554–55, 572–73, nos. 200 (4 November 1193), 217 (19 March 1196); Zerbi, *Papato*, 179–81, nos. 1 (10 July 1195), 2 (13 May 1197), 3 (14 May); Rivera Recio, *Toledo*, 232, n. 84; Erdmann, *Papsturkunden*, 368–69, 376, nos. 148 (22 July 1195), 154 (10 April 1197); Martinez Marina, *Teoria, BAE* 220: 85, no. 3 (31 October 1196).

16. *DP*, 329–30, 472–73, 497–98, 500–501, nos. 295 (14 February 1204), 442 (10 December 1210), 468 (31 January 1212), 470 (4 February 1212); González, *Alfonso VIII*, 3: 568, 573, nos. 897–98 (1212); Lucas, *Chronicon*, 4: 110, and *Crónica*, 413, ch. 83; Rodrigo, *Historia*, 259, 261–62, 265, Bk. 8, ch. 1, 3, 6; Arnald Amaury, in Mondéjar, *Alonso el Noble*, Appendix, cvi.

17. Mansilla, *Honorio III*, 76–78, 170, 251, 273–74, nos. 95–96 (1217), 223 (29 April 1219), 339 (18 December 1220), 368 (13 February 1221); *MH*, 1: 45–49, no. 25; Gosuinus, "Quomodo fuit capta Alcaser a Francis," *PMH SS* 1: 102; *Chronica regia Coloniensis*, QBS, 148; Barrero Garciá, "Un formulario," 703, no. 18; *Anales Toledanos II, ES* 23: 407.

18. Mansilla, *Honorio III*, 119–21, 161–63, nos. 148 (30 January 1218), 208–9 (15 March 1219), 210 (16 March). Rodrigo Díaz de los Cameros took the cross, "*licet esset cruce signatus in subsidium Terre Sancte*"; Rodrigo, *Historia*, 291, Bk. 9, ch. 11; González, *Alfonso IX*, 1: 200; Hernández, *Cartularios*, 399–400, no. 398 (30 November 1221); *PFG*, 77. 84, 132, vv. 253, 279, 445; Gonzalo de Berceo, "El Duelo que fizo la Virgen María el día de la Pasión de su fijo Jesu Cristo," in *Obras*, 429, 441, vv. 16, 105. Alfonso X, *Setenario*, ed. Kenneth H. Vanderford (Madrid, 1945; reprint Barcelona: Editorial Crítica, 1984), 220–21, ley 102; José María Garate Córdoba, *Espiritu y Milicia en la España medieval* (Madrid: Publicaciones Españolas, 1967).

19. Rodrigo, *Historia*, 292, Bk. 9, ch.12; *Chronica latina*, 87, ch. 44; Mansilla, *Honorio III*, 429–32, 440–41, nos. 574–76 (26 September 1225), 585–86 (20 October); Auvray, *Grégoire IX*, 2: 38–39, 880–81, nos. 2527–28 (24–25 April 1235), 4070 (9 February 1238); *MFIII*, 352 (7 September 1225); Gorosterratzu, *Rodrigo*, 386–87, 441, 468–69, nos. 98 (7 April 1230), 177 (15 April 1247); Mansilla, *Iglesia*, 299, no. 33 (12 June 1230); Berger, *Innocent IV*, 1: 346, 377, nos. 1758 (22 March 1246), 2533 (15 April 1247); Minguella, *Sigüenza*, 1: 600–601 (24 April 1246).

20. *CAVC*, 1: 102–3, no. 16 (29 April 1225); Bernat Desclot, *Crònica*, 2: 88–91, ch. 30–31; Villanueva, *Viaje*, 21: 252 (28 November 1229); Zurita, *Anales*, 1: 478–79; Auvray, *Grégoire IX*, 1: 824, nos. 1490–91 (9 August 1233); *DJI*, 1: 388–89, no. 239 (28 October 1236); *CJI*, 5: 26, ch.241; Quintana Prieto, *Inocencio IV*, 2: 518–20, 527–28, 562–63, nos.

557 (12 November 1248), 558–59 (13 November), 571 (25 January 1249), 619–20 (22, 28 March 1250); Burns, "A Lost Crusade," 440–49.

21. Lucas, *Chronicon*, 4: 114, and *Crónica*, 422, ch. 89; *MH*, 1: 60–61, 66–75, 77–79, nos. 35 (21 October 1234), 39 (25 November 1239), 40–48, 50 (18 February 1241), 51 (8 April 1245); Quintana Prieto, *Inocencio IV*, 1: 106–8, 133–34, nos. 96 (30 January 1245), 120 (8 April).

22. Marius Ferotin, *Le Liber ordinum en usage dans l'église wisigothiue et mozarabe d'Espagne du Ve au Xie siècle* (Paris, 1904; reprint Rome: Edizione Liturgiche, 1996), 150.4–8, 152.7–22, 153.21–23, 28–40, and 444.14–21; Clemens Blume, "Hymnodica Gothica," *Analecta Hymnica Medii Aevi* 27 (1897): 269; Francisco de Berganza, *Antigüedades de España*, 2 vols. (Madrid: Francisco del Hierro, 1772), 2: 684–86, Apendice, ch. 18; Sánchez Albornoz, *España*, 1: 240–41, fig. 32; Michael McCormick, *Eternal Victory: Triumphal Rulership in Late Antiquity: Byzantium and the Early Medieval West* (Cambridge: Cambridge University Press, 1986), 308–14.

23. Olivar, *El Sacramentario de Vich*, 180–81, no. 267, and *Sacramentarium Rivipullense*, 224–25, nos. 393–94.

24. Berganza, *Antigüedades*, 2: 685, Apendice, ch. 18; McCormick, *Eternal Victory*, 57–58, 313. See the votive masses of the cross in Olivar, *El Sacramentario de Vich*, 122, no. 186, and *Sacramentarium Rivipullense*, 173–74, 202, nos. 260, 340, and the masses of the Holy Cross and of the feast of the Exaltation of the Holy Cross (14 September) in the *Missale Romanum*.

25. Ubieto Arteta, *Pedro I*, 115, n. 9; González, *Alfonso VIII*, 3: 570, no. 897 (1212); *Poema de Alfonso XI*, 515, v. 1269.

26. *CAI*, 197–98, Bk. 2, ch. 6.

27. Rodrigo, *Historia*, 260, Bk,. 8, ch. 1; *DP*, 503–4, no. 473 (1212); Christoph T. Maier, "Mass, the Eucharist and the Cross: Innocent III and the Relocation of the Crusade," in Moore, *Pope Innocent III*, 352–54, and García y García, "Innocent III and the Kingdom of Castile," ibid., 339–40; Alberic of Troisfontaines, *Chronicon, MGH SS* 23: 894–95.

28. Sharīf al-Gharnāṭī, in Huici, *Batallas*, 203; *HC*, 379, Bk. 2, ch. 78; *CAI*, 213, 227–28, Bk. 2, ch. 38, 69–70; *De Expugnatione Lyxbonensi*, 56–57, 68–69, 84, 126.

29. Rodrigo, *Historia*, 269–71, Bk. 8, ch. 8–9; *Chronica latina*, 61, ch. 24; Bernard of Clairvaux, *De laude novae militiae, PL* 182: 922, ch. 1.

30. Bernat Desclot, *Crònica*, 2: 86–87, 102, 132, 134, ch. 30, 36, 46–47; *CJI*, 3: 70, 108, ch. 156, 183, and 4: 20, 58, ch. 194, 217, and 5: 8, 14, ch. 232, 236; Burns, "The Spiritual Life," 10–14.

31. *PC*, 160, 162, 166, 210, vv. 93–95, 116; *PFG*, 142, vv. 481–82.

32. *CAI*, 213, Bk. 2, ch. 38; *De Expugnatione Lyxbonensi*, 134–35; *Indiculum fundationis monasterii beati Vincentii, PMH SS* 1: 92; Theodor Klauser, *A Short History of the Western Liturgy: An Account and Some Reflections*, 2nd ed. (Oxford: Oxford University Press, 1979), 135.

33. *Historia Roderici*, 88, 91, 93, ch. 62, 66, 68; *CAI*, 227, Bk. 2, ch. 69.

34. Rodrigo, *Historia*, 272–73, Bk. 8, ch. 10.

35. *CJI*, 2: 18, 24, ch. 56–57; Bernat Desclot, *Crònica*, 2: 98, 102, ch. 35–36.

36. *CPA*, 24, and 17, 19, 27; *PC*, 98, v. 46.

37. Erdmann, *Origin*, 35–56; Ferotin, *Liber ordinum*, 152, Berganza, *Antigüedades*, 2: 684–85.

38. Ibn Ḥayyān, in al-Maqqarī, *History*, 2: 265–270, Bk. 7, ch. 5; Erdmann, *Origin*, 139; Ferreiro, "Barbastro," 133–35; Fita, "Concilio nacional de Palencia," 231; *Alfonso X. Toledo 1984*, fig. 24; Etelvina Fernández González, "Iconografía y leyenda del Pendón de Baeza," *Medievo Hispano: Estudios in Memoriam del Profesor Derek W. Lomax* (Madrid: Sociedad Española de Estudios medievales, 1995), 141–58; González, *Fernando II*, 350.

39. Rodrigo, *Historia*, 261–62, 265, 273, Bk. 8, ch. 3, 6, 10; González, *Alfonso VIII*, 3: 568, 570, 573, nos. 897–98 (1212); Alberic of Trois Fontaines, *Chronicon*, MGH SS 23: 894–95; Arnald Amaury, in Mondéjar, *Alonso el Noble*, Appendix, cvi, cxxiii.

40. José Gómez Pérez, "La más antigua traducción de las Crónicas del Toledano," *Hispania* 22 (1962): 361–62; Diego Ortiz de Zúñiga, *Anales eclesiásticos y seculares de la muy noble y muy leal ciudad de Sevilla, metropolí de Andalucía*, ed. Antonio María Espinosa y Carzel, 2 vols. (Madrid: Imprenta Real, 1795; reprint Sevilla: Guadalquivir, 1988), 1: 146; *CSM* 181.

41. *CAI*, 174, 176, Bk. 1, ch. 52, 56; Ordericus, *History*, 410–11, Bk. 13, ch. 8.

42. *CAI*, 176, 205, 207, 210, 227, Bk. 1, ch. 55, and Bk. 2, ch. 22, 26, 33, 69.

43. Caesarius, *Dialogus*, 2: 137, Bk. 8, ch. 66; *CJI*, 2: 40, 84, 86, ch. 63, 84–85; Continuator of Lucas, *Crónica*, 438, ch. 98; *PC*, 88, 122, vv. 36, 68; *PFG*, 150, v. 511; *CPA*, 25; *PCG*, 2: 726–27, ch, 1044.

44. *CAI*, 176, Bk. 1, ch. 55; Erdmann, *Origin*, 6, 14, 20–21; Castro, *Realidad*, 336.

45. *Historia Silense*, 190–92, ch. 87–89; *Chronica Naierensis*, 158–59, Bk. 3, ch. 7; Rodrigo, *Historia*, 189–91, Bk. 6, ch. 11; *PCG*, 2: 486–87, ch. 807; Fletcher, *Saint James's Catapult*, 296–97; Castro, *Realidad*, 331–32, 353–54; Sánchez Albornoz, *España*, 1: 268.

46. See the privilege of 844 in López Ferreiro, *Historia*, 2: 132–37.

47. López Ferreiro, *Historia*, 2:75–76, 83, 130–46 accepted the privilege as authentic; but Sanchez Albornoz, *Espana*, 1: 268, and José Barreiro Somoza, *El señorío de la iglesia de Santiago de Compostela (Siglos IX–XIII)* (La Coruña: Editorial Diputación Provincial, 1987), 324–26, did not. Rodrigo, *Historia*, 133, Bk. 4, ch. 13; *PCG*, 2: 360–61, ch. 629.

48 See the illustrations in Castro, *Realidad*, 349–50.

49. See illustrations in Castro, *Realidad*, 331–32, 359, n. 25, and facing page 332; Sánchez Albornoz, *España*, 1: 273–75.

50. Gonzalo de Berceo, "La Estoria de Sennor Sant Millán, tornada de Latín en Romançe," in *Obras*, 174–75, vv. 362–64, and *Vida de San Millán*, vv. 362–64, 420–32, 437–39, 446, 459–79; Dutton, *La Vida de San Millán*, 2–21. According to Pelayo of Oviedo, before the battle of Simancas God plunged the whole world into darkness for an hour as a sign of a future Christian victory. Pérez de Urbel, *Sampiro*, 325, 343, ch. 22, 29; *Chronica Naierensis*, 131, Bk. 2, ch. 29.

51. Lucas, *Chronicon*, 4: 114–15, and *Crónica*, 423–25, ch. 91; *PCG*, 2: 726–27, ch, 1044; Diego Catalán, *La Estoria de Espanna de Alfonso X: Creación y Evolución* (Madrid: Universidad Autónoma de Madrid, 1992), 97, n. 27.

52. Lucas, *Chronicon*, 4: 105, and *Crónica*, 393–97, ch. 69. Lucas's *Vita Sancti Isidori* in *Acta Sanctorum*, April, vol. 1, is not reliable. Rodrigo, *Historia*, 232, Bk. 7, ch. 11; *PCG*, 2: 660, ch. 981; Sánchez Albornoz, *España*, 1: 277. See n. 38 above.

53. Rodrigo, *Historia*, 243, Bk. 7, ch. 21; Lucas, *Chronicon*, 4: 114, and *Crónica*, 425, ch. 91; Continuator of Lucas, *Crónica*, 442, 444, ch. 100–101.

54. *CJI*, 1: 20, ch. 5; *Crónica de los Estados peninsulares (Texto del Siglo XIV)*, ed. Antonio Ubieto Arteta (Granada: Universidad de Granada, 1955), 122; *CSJP*, 63–64 ch. 18; *CSJP (tr)*, 23, ch. 18; Riley-Smith, *The First Crusade*, 6, 85–86, 91, 94, 103, 105, 123, 193–194; Erdmann, *Origin*, 134–35, 273–80; Samantha Riches, *St. George, Hero, Martyr, and Myth* (Stroud: Sutton, 2000). The mounted figure of St. George appears in the north arch in the royal pantheon in San Isidro of León, a work completed between 1160 and 1170.

55. Rodrigo, *Historia*, 178, Bk. 6, ch. 1; *PCG*, 2: 476, ch. 794; Zurita, *Anales*, 1: 104–5; Regina Sainz de la Maza Lasoli, *La Orden de San Jorge de Alfama. Aproximación a su historia* (Barcelona: CSIC, 1990); Burns, *Crusader Kingdom*, 1: 182–83, 457–58.

56. *CJI*, 2: 84, ch. 84, and 7: 52–55, ch. 389–90; *CSJP*, 154; *CSJP (tr)*, 66, ch. 35; Zurita, *Anales*, 1: 454; Burns, "The Spiritual Life," 12, and *Crusader Kingdom*, 1: 12, 249.

57. *Chronica latina*, 59–60, ch. 22–23; Lucas, *Chronicon*, 4: 110, and *Crónica*, 415; Rodrigo, *Historia*, 268–69, ch. 7–8; Alberic of Trois Fontaines, *Chronicon*, MGH SS 23: 894–95.

58. Mansilla, *Honorio III*, 76–77, no. 95 (1217); *PFG*, 123, v. 408.

59. Etienne Delaruelle, "Essai sur la formation de l'idée de la croisade," *Bulletin de la litterature ecclésiastique* 42 (1941): 103; Bernard of Clairvaux, *Epistolae*, nos. 363, 458, and *Liber de Laude Novae Militiae*, ch. 1, PL 182: 566, 672, 922; H. E. J. Cowdrey, "Martyrdom and the First Crusade," in *Crusade and Settlement*, ed. Peter W. Edbury (Cardiff: University College, 1985), 46–56.

60. *Prefatio de Almería*, 267, lines. 381–82; Letters of Duodechin, MGH SS 17: 28, and Arnulf, *RGHF* 14: 327; *Chronica latina*, 46, ch. 13; Francisco Rades y Andrada, *Chronica de las tres Ordenes y Cavallerías de Sanctiago, Calatrava y Alcántara* (Toledo: Juan de Ayala, 1572), *Chronica de la Orden de Calatrava*, fol. 20v.

61. *DP*, 500–1, no. 470 (4 February 1212); Rodrigo, *Historia*, 271, 275, Bk. 8, ch. 9, 11; González, *Alfonso VIII*, 3: 571, no. 897 (1212); *CJI*, 4: 44, ch. 207; *PCG*, 2: 738, ch. 1054; *Chronica da conquista do Algarve*, PMH SS 1: 418, 420.

62. *PFG*, 161, v. 549; *Espéculo* 3, 7, 11; *Partidas*, 2, 25, 3; Juan Manuel, *Libro de los estados*, BAE 51: 294, 324–25, Bk. 1, ch. 30, 76.

63. *CAI*, 178, Bk. 1, ch. 60–61; *CJI*, 2: 48, ch. 68; *Chronica da conquista do Algarve*, PMH SS 1: 418; Bernat Desclot, *Crònica*, 2: 136, ch. 47.

66.4 *Chronique d'Albelda*, 23, ch. 35; MS A of *Chronique prophétique*, 4, ch. 3; Pérez de Urbel, *Sampiro*, 309–10, 323, 325, ch. 16–17, 22; *Historia Roderici*, 56, 88–89, 91–92, ch. 20, 62, 66; *Chronica latina* 36, ch. 2.

65. *CAI*, 209, Bk. 2, ch. 29; *Chronica latina*, 46, 55, 100, ch. 13, 19, 56; Rodrigo, *Historia*, 251, ch. 29; Lucas, *Chronicon*, 4: 108, and *Crónica*, 407, ch. 83; *CJI*, 2: 118, ch. 105.

66. *PC*, 92, 96, 122, 158, 218, vv. 40, 43, 69, 90, 120, 122; *PFG*, 23, 29, 80, 148, vv. 80, 98–100, 267, 503.

67. *Annales D. Alfonsi*, 155–56.

68. *CAI*, 206, 209–11, 222, Bk. 2, ch. 23, 30, 33–34, 59; Caffaro, *De captione*, 26.

69. Rodrigo, *Historia*, 273, Bk. 8, ch. 10; *Chronica latina*, 62, 116, ch. 25, 73; *CJI*, 4: 62, ch. 219.

70. *PC*, 164, v. 95; *PFG*, 82, v. 271.

71. *CAI*, 222, Bk. 2, ch. 59; *De Expugnatione Lyxbonensi*, 174–75; *CJI*, 5: 86–88, ch. 282; Bernat Desclot, *Crònica*, 2: 136, ch. 47; *PC*, 80, vv. 30, 128.

72. *Chronica latina*, 116, ch. 73; Rodrigo, *Historia*, 298, Bk. 9, ch. 16; *PCG*, 2: 767, ch. 1123.

73. Ibn Ḥayyān, in al-Maqqarī, *History*, 2: 270; Ibn ʿIdhārī, *Nuevos fragmentos*, 123; *PFG*, 16, Bk. 3, vv. 89–90; *CAI*, 212, Bk. 2, ch. 36; Lema Pueyo, *Alfonso I*, 135, 184–86, nos. 88, 122; Lacarra, *Documentos*, 1: 70–71, no. 56 (1118).

74. Rodrigo, *Historia*, 205–7, Bk. 6, ch. 24; *Chronique de Saint-Maixent*, 156; Ubieto Arteta, *Pedro I*, 251–52, no. 30 (5 April 1097); José María Lacarra, "La Iglesia de Tudela entre Tarazona y Pamplona (1119–1143)," *EEMCA* 5 (1952): 420, 427–34; Olivar, *El Sacramentario de Vich*, 192–93, 273–74, nos. 285, 342, and *Sacramentarium Rivipullense*, 127–28, no. 143.

75. *Historia Roderici*, 92–93, 96–97, ch. 67–68, 72–73; *CAI*, 225, Bk. 2, ch. 66; *De Expugnatione Lyxbonensi*, 180–81; Ralph of Diceto, *Ymagines Historiarum*, 2: 66; *Chronica latina*, 64–65, 94, ch. 26, 50; *CJI*, 2: 118, ch. 105; *Chronica da conquista do Algarve*, *PMH SS* 1: 418.

76. *Chronica latina*, 117, ch. 73–74; Rodrigo, *Historia*, 299, Bk. 9, ch. 17; *PCG*, 2: 746–47, 767, ch. 1071, 1125.

77. Ferotin, *Liber ordinum*, 154.12–13, 155.7–11, 20–24; Berganza, *Antigüedades*, 2: 685–86, Apendice, ch. 18; McCormick, *Eternal Victory*, 311–12.

78. *CAI*, 180, Bk. 1, ch. 66, and 223–25, Bk. 2, ch. 61–63, 66.

79. *CAI*, 230, Bk. 2, ch. 73–79; *Chronica latina*, 47, 64, 94, 118, ch. 13, 25, 50, 74; al-Maqqarī, *History*, 322, Bk. 8, ch. 3.

80. *CAI*, 231, Bk. 2, ch. 78; Villanueva, *Viage*, 5: 250–251; Rodrigo, *Historia*, 299–300, Bk. 9, ch. 17.

81. *PC*, 158, v. 91, and 94, v. 41; *PFG*, 84, v. 277.

82. González, *Alfonso VIII*, 1: 1003–4, and *Alfonso IX*, 1: 207.

83. Ibn Ḥayyān, in al-Maqqarī, *History*, 2: 270; Sharīf al-Gharnāṭī, in Huici, *Batallas*, 203; Castro, *Realidad*, 419–29; Sánchez Albornoz, *España*, 1: 303–4.

Chapter 9

1. Vincentius Hispanus, cited by Post, *Studies*, 490, n. 190; Álvaro Pelayo, *Espelho*, 258; Alfonso de Cartagena, *Discurso sobre la precedencia del Rey católico sobre el de Inglaterra en el Concilio de Basilea*, BAE 116: 210.

2. O'Callaghan, *The Learned King*, 163–97, 234–51; Miguel Ángel Manzano Rodríguez, *La intervención de los benimerines en la peninsula ibérica* (Madrid: CSIC, 1992), 1–80; Goñi Gaztambide, *Historia*, 187–204.

3. Mercedes Gaibrois de Ballesteros, *Historia del Reinado de Sancho IV de Castilla*, 3 vols. (Madrid: Revista de Archivos, Bibliotecas, y Museos, 1922), 2: 167–97,

294–97, and 3: ccl–cclvii, nos. 384–86; José Manuel: Nieto Soria, *Sancho IV, 1284–1295* (Palencia: La Olmeda, 1994), 112–13, 117–30; Manzano Rodríguez, *Intervención*, 81–157; Goñi Gaztambide, *Historia*, 204–5.

4. Antonio de Benavides, *Memorias de Fernando IV*, 2 vols. (Madrid: José Rodríguez, 1860), 2: 621–26, nos. 416–19; César González Mínguez, *Fernando IV de Castilla (1295–1312): La Guerra civil y el Predominio de la Nobleza* (Valladolid: Universidad de Valladolid, 1974), 273–300, 322–26; Dufourcq, *L'Espagne catalane*, 387–404; Manzano Rodríguez, *Intervención*, 158–88; Goñi Gaztambide, *Historia*, 208–5, 221–31, 263–81.

5. *Crónica de Fernando IV*, ch. 17, *BAE* 66: 163.

6. Juan Manuel, *Libro de los estados*, *BAE* 51: 294, Bk. 1, ch. 30.

7. Álvaro Pelayo, *Espelho*, 12; Huici, *Batallas*, 331–87; Manzano Rodríguez, *Intervención*, 215–64; Goñi Gaztambide, *Historia*, 316–31.

8. Joseph F. O'Callaghan, "Castile, Portugal, and the Canary Islands: Claims and Counterclaims, 1344–1479," *Viator* 24 (1993): 289–91; Antonio Rumeu de Armas, *España en el África atlántica*, 2 vols. (Madrid: CSIC, 1956–57), 2: 1–2, no. 1.

9. Juan Gil de Zamora, *Liber de preconiis Hispaniae*, 21–23, 75, 235; Manzano Rodríguez, *Intervención*, 266–308; Goñi Gaztambide, *Historia*, 331–35.

10. Pedro López de Ayala, *Rimado de Palacio*, ed. Germán Orduña (Madrid: Castalia, 1987), 187–88, vv. 339–40; Goñi Gaztambide, *Historia*, 336–70.

11. Juan Rodríguez Puértolas, "El Libro de la Consolación de España: Una meditación sobre la Castilla del Siglo XV," *Miscelánea de Estudios medievales* 1 (1972): 205.

12. Fernán Pérez de Guzmán, *Generaciones y Semblanzas*, ed. J. Domínguez Bordona (Madrid: Espasa-Calpe, 1965), 27–28, 118; I. I. Macdonald, *Don Fernando de Antequera* (Oxford: Dolphin, 1948).

13. *Cancionero castellano del Siglo XV*, ed. R. Foulché-Delbosc, 2 vols. (Madrid: Bailly-Bailliére, 1912–15), 2: 314, 332, 367, 425, nos. 602, 686; 770; Alfonso de Cartagena, *Discurso sobre la precedencia del Rey católico sobre el de Inglaterra en el Concilio de Basilea*, *BAE* 116: 221–222.

14. Diego de Valera, *Epistola 21*, *BAE* 116: 27; Goñi Gaztambide, *Historia*, 380–94, 671–76, no. 15.

15. Goñi Gaztambide, *Historia*, 392–93 (2 January 1492); Tarsicio de Azcona, *Isabel la Católica* (Madrid: BAC, 1964), 499–556; Miguel Ángel Ladero Quesada, *Castilla y la conquista del Reino de Granada* (Granada: Diputación Provincial de Granada, 1987), and *La España de los Reyes Católicos* (Madrid: Alianza, 1999), 379–400.

16. Alfonso de Cartagena, *Alegaciones formuladas para defender ante el Papa en Basilea el derecho de los reyes de Castilla sobre las Canarias*, in García Gallo, *Manual*, 2: 628, no. 848; O'Callaghan, "Castile, Portugal, and the Canary Islands," 300–303.

17. Rodrigo Sánchez de Arévalo, *Vergel de los Principes*, *BAE* 116: 312; Diego de Valera, *Epistola 24*, *BAE* 116: 31.

18. Bailey W. Diffie and George D. Winius, *Foundations of the Portuguese Empire, 1415–1580* (Minneapolis: University of Minnesota Press, 1977), 44–73; Goñi Gaztambide, *Historia*, 465–76.

19. Goñi Gaztambide, *Historia*, 629, 639–40.

Bibliography

Narrative Sources: Christian

Alberic of Trois Fontaines. *Chronicon. MGH SS* 23: 631–950.

Amato of Montecassino. *Storia de' Normanni*. Ed. Vincenzo de Bartholomaeis. *Fonti per la Storia d'Italia* 76. Rome: Tipografia del Senato, 1935.

Anales Toledanos I. ES 23: 382–401.

Anales Toledanos II. ES 23: 402–10.

Anales Toledanos III. ES 23: 411–24.

Annales Complutenses. ES 23: 311–15.

Annales Compostellani. ES 23: 318–25.

Annales D. Alfonsi Portugallensium regis. Ed. Monica Blöcker-Walter. *Alfons I. von Portugal. Studien zu Geschichte und Sage des Begründers der Portugiesischen Unabhängigkeit*. Zurich: Fretz und Wasmuth, 1966. 155–56.

Annales Lamberti Parvi. MGH SS 16: 645–50.

Arnulf. *Epistola Arnulfi ad Milonem Episcopum Morinensem. PMH SS* 1: 406–7. *De Ulixbona Saracensis erepta. RHGF* 14: 325–27.

Bernardo Maragone. *Gli Annales Pisani*. Ed. Michele Lupo Gentile. *Raccolta degli Storici Italiani* 6. Parts 2–3. Bologna: N. Zanichelli, 1936.

Bernat Desclot. *Crònica*. 5 vols. Ed. Miguel Coll i Alentorn. Barcelona: Editorial Barcino, 1949–51.

Caffaro. *De captione Almarie et Tortuose*. Ed. Antonio Ubieto Arteta. Valencia: Anubar, 1973.

Caffaro di Caschifellone. *Ystoria de captione Almarie et Tortose*. In *Annali genovesi*. Ed. Luigi T. Belgrano and Cesare Imperiale. *Fonti per la storia d'Italia* 11. Genoa: Istituto Storico Italiano, 1890. 79–89.

Carmen Campidoctoris. Ed. Juan Gil. In *Chronica Hispana Saeculi XIII*. Pars I. 105–8.

Chronica Adefonsi Imperatoris. Ed. Antonio Maya Sánchez. In *Chronica Hispana Saeculi XII*. Pars I. 109–248.

Chronica Adefonsi Imperatoris. Ed. Luis Sánchez Belda. Madrid: CSIC, 1950.

Chronica Breve. PMH SS 1: 22–23.

Chrónica da conquista do Algarve. PMH SS 1: 415–420.

Chronica Gothorum. PMH SS 1:8–17.

Chronica Hispana Saeculi XII. Pars I. Ed. Emma Falque, Juan Gil and Antonio Maya. *Corpus Christianorum. Continuatio Mediaevalis* 71. Turnhout: Brepols, 1990.

Chronica Hispana Saeculi XIII. Ed. Luis Charlo Brea, Juan A. Estévez Sola, and Rocío Carande Herrero. *Corpus Christianorum. Continuatio Mediaevalis* 73. Turnhout: Brepols, 1997.

Chronica latina regum Castellae. Ed. Luis Charlo Brea. *Chronica Hispana Saeculi XIII.* 7–118.

Chronica regia Coloniensis (Anales Colonienses maximi). MGH SS 17: 723–847.

Chronica regia Coloniensis (Anales Colonienses maximi). Scriptores rerum Germanicarum in usum scholarum. Hannover, 1880.

Chronica regia Coloniensis continuatio tertia. In Röhricht. *QBS.* 147–52.

Chronica Naierensis. Ed. Juan A. Estévez Sola. *Chronica Hispana Saeculi XII. Pars II. Corpus Christianorum. Continuatio Mediaevalis* 71A. Turnhout: Brepols, 1995.

Chronicon Alcobacense. PMH SS 1: 20–22.

The Chronicle of James I, King of Aragon, surnamed the Conqueror. Tr. John Forster. 2 vols. London: Chapman and Hall, 1883.

The Chronicle of San Juan de la Peña: A Fourteenth-Century Official History of the Crown of Aragón. Tr. Lynn H. Nelson. Philadelphia: University of Pennsylvania Press, 1991.

Chronicon Barcinonense I. ES 28: 323–27.

Chronicon Barcinonense II. ES 28: 328–33.

Chronicon Burgense. ES 23: 306–11.

Chronicon de Cardeña. ES 23: 371–81.

Chronicon Complutense sive Alcobacense. PMH SS 1: 17–19. *ES* 23: 316–18.

Chronicon Conimbricense. PMH SS 1: 2–7. *ES* 23: 330–56.

Chronicon Durtusense I. In Villanueva, *Viage.* 5: 233–36.

Chronicon Durtusense II. In Villanueva, *Viage.* 5: 236–40.

Chronicon Lamecense. PMH SS 1: 19–20.

Chronicon Laurbanense. PMH SS 1: 20.

Chronicon Lusitanum. ES 14: 402–19.

Chronicon Massiliense. ES 28: 338.

Chronicon Rivipullense. In Villanueva, *Viage.* 5: 241–49.

Chronicon Rotense. In Villanueva, *Viage.* 15: 332–35.

Chronicon Turonensis. RHGF 12: 461–78.

Chronicon Ulianense. ES 28: 334–37.

Chronique d'Alphonse III. In *Chroniques asturiennes.* 31–59.

La Chronique de Saint-Maixent, 751–1140. Ed. Jean Verdon. Paris: Société de l'Édition Les Belles Lettres, 1979.

La Chronique de Saint-Pierre-le-Vif de Sens dite de Clarius. Chronicon Sancti Petri Vivi Senonensis. Ed. Robert Henri Bautier and Monique Gilles. Paris: CNRS, 1979.

Chronique d'Albelda. In *Chroniques asturiennes.* 10–30.

Chronique latine des rois de Castille jusqu'en 1236. Ed. Georges Cirot. Bordeaux: Feret et Fils, 1913.

Chronique prophétique. In *Chroniques asturiennes.* 1–9.

Chroniques asturiennes (fin IXe siècle). Ed. Yves Bonnaz. Paris: CNRS, 1987.

Continuatio Hispana. MGH Auctores Antiquissimi XI. *Chronica Minora* 2: 323–68.

Continuatio Lambacensis. MGH SS 9: 556–61.

Crónica de Alfonso III. Ed. Zacarias García Villada. Madrid: Sucesores de Rivadeneyra, 1918.

Crónica de Alfonso X. Ed. Manuel González Jiménez. Murcia: Real Academia Alfonso X el Sabio, 1998.

Crónica de cinco reis. Ed. A. Magalhães Basto. Porto: Livraria Civilização, 1945.

Crónica de Fernando IV. BAE 66: 91–172.

Crònica de Jaume I. Ed. Joseph M. de Cascuberta and Enric Bagüe. 9 vols. Barcelona: Editorial Barcino, 1926–62.

Crónica de Juan II. BAE 68: 277–695.

Crónica de la población de Ávila. Ed. Ámparo Hernández Segura. Valencia: Anubar, 1965.

Crónica de 1344 que ordenó el Conde de Barcelos don Pedro Afonso. Ed. Diego Catalán and María Soledad. Madrid: Gredos, 1977.

Crónica de los Estados peninsulares (Texto del Siglo XIV). Ed. Antonio Ubieto Arteta. Granada: Universidad de Granada, 1955.

Crónica de San Juan de la Peña. Ed. Antonio Ubieto Arteta. Valencia: Anubar, 1961.

Crónica del Obispo Don Pelayo. Ed. Benito Sánchez Alonso. Madrid: Sucesores de Hernando, 1924.

Crònica general de Pere III el Cerimoniós dita comunament Crònica de San Joan de la Penya. Ed. Amadeu-J. Soberanas Lleó. Barcelona: Alpha, 1961.

Crónica latina de los reyes de Castilla. Ed. María Desamparados Cabanes Pecourt. Valencia: Anubar, 1964.

Crónica latina de los reyes de Castilla. Ed. Luis Charlo Brea. Cádiz: Universidad de Cádiz, 1984.

Crónica Najerense. Ed. Antonio Ubieto Arteta. Valencia: Anubar, 1966.

De expugnatione Lyxbonensi. The Conquest of Lisbon. Ed. and tr. Charles W. David. New York: Columbia University Press, 1936; reprint 2001.

De expugnatione Scalabis. PMH SS 1: 93–95.

Diego Enríquez del Castillo. *Crónica de Enrique IV. BAE* 70: 99–222.

Diego de Valera. *Doctrinal de los Principes.* In Penna. *Prosistas. BAE* 116: 173–204.

———. *Memorial de diversas hazañas. BAE* 70: 1–98.

Duodechin. In *Annales Sancti Disibodi, MGH SS* 17: 27–28.

Emo. *Chronicon. MGH SS* 23: 465–523.

Estoria de Espanna. See *Primera Crónica General.*

Gesta comitum Barchinonensium. Ed. L. Barrau Dihigo and J. Massó Torrents. Barcelona: Fundació Concepció Rabell i Cibils and Institut d'Estudis Catalans, 1924.

Gesta regis Henrici II. Ed. William Stubbs. 2 vols. Rolls Series 49. London: Longman, 1867.

Gesta triumphalia per Pisanos facta de captione Hierusalem et civitatis Maioricarum et aliarum civitatum et de triumpho habito contra Ianuenses. Ed. Michele Lupo Gentile. Raccolta degli Storici Italiani 6, Part 2. Bologna: N. Zanichelli, 1936.

Gosuinus. *Quomodo fuit capta Alcaser a Francis. PMH SS* 1: 101–4.

Guibert de Nogent. *Dei gesta per Francos et cinq autres textes.* Ed. R. B. C. Huygens. Turnhout: Brepols, 1996.

Helmold. *Chronica Slavorum. MGH SS* 21: 1–99.

Hernando del Pulgar. *Crónica de los señores reyes católicos Don Fernando y Doña Isabel de Castilla y Aragón. BAE* 70: 225–563.

Historia Compostellana. Ed. Emma Falque. *Corpus Christianorum. Continuatio Mediaevalis* 70. Turnhout: Brepols, 1988.

Historiae Francicae fragmentum. RHGF 11: 160–62; 12: 1–8.

Historia Roderici. In *Chronica Hispana Saeculi XII.* Pars I: 3–98.

Historia Silense. Ed. Justo Pérez de Urbel and Atilano González Ruiz-Zorrilla. Madrid: CSIC, 1959.

Historia translationis Sancti Isidori. Ed. J. A. Estévez Sola. *Chronica Hispana Saeculi XIII.* 119–79.

Hugh of Fleury. *Historia. RHGF* 12: 792–99.

Indiculum fundationis monasterii beati Vincentii. PMH SS 1: 90–93.

Isidore of Seville. *Historia de regibus Gotorum, Wandalorum et Suevorum. MGH Auctores Antiquissimi* XI. *Chronica Minora.* 2: 267–303.

John of Hexham. *Historia.* In Simeon of Durham. *Opera Omnia.* Ed. Thomas Arnold. 2 vols. London: Longmans, Green, 1882–85.

The Latin Chronicle of the Kings of Castile. Tr. Joseph F. O'Callaghan. Tempe, Ariz.: ACMRS, 2002.

Liber Maiolichinus de gestis Pisanorum illustribus. Ed. Carlo Calisse. *Fonti per la storia d'Italia* 29. Rome: Istituto Storico Italiano, 1904.

Lucas of Túy. *Chronicon Mundi.* In *Hispania Illustrata.* Ed. Andreas Schott. 4 vols. Frankfort: Claudius Marnius et Heredes Joannis Aubrii, 1603–08. 4: 1–116.

———. *Crónica de España.* Ed. Julio Puyol. Madrid: Revista de Archivos, Bibliotecas y Museos, 1926.

———. *Vita Sancti Isidori. Acta Sanctorum,* April. 1.

———. *Vita Sancti Martini Legionensis. PL* 208: 9–21.

Matthew Paris. *Chronica Majora.* Ed. H. R. Luard. 7 vols. Rolls Series. London: Longman, 1872–83.

Narratio de itinere navali peregrinorum Hierosolymam tendentium et Silvam capientium, A.D. 1189. Ed. C. W. David. *Proceedings of the American Philosophical Society* 81 (1939): 591–678.

Oliver of Paderborn. *The Capture of Damietta.* Tr. John J. Gavigan. Philadelphia: University of Pennsylvania Press, 1948.

Ordericus Vitalis. *The Ecclesiastical History of Ordericus Vitalis.* Ed. and tr. Marjorie Chibnall. Oxford: Clarendon Press, 1978.

Pedro López de Ayala. *Crónica del rey don Pedro. BAE* 66: 393–614.

Pelayo of Oviedo. *Crónica del Obispo Don Pelayo.* Ed. Benito Sánchez Alonso. Madrid: Sucesores de Hernando, 1924.

Poema de Almería. Prefatio de Almaria. In *Chronica Hispoana Saeculi XII.* Pars I: 255–67.

Prelog, Jan. *Die Chronik Alfons' III. Untersuchung und kritische Edition der vier Redaktionen.* Frankfurt-am-Main: Peter D. Lang, 1980.

Primera Crónica General. Ed. Ramón Menéndez Pidal. 2 vols. Madrid: Editorial Gredos, 1955.

Ralph of Diceto. *Ymagines historiarum.* In *Opera historica.* 2 vols. Ed. William Stubbs. Rolls Series 68. London: Longman, 1876.

Ramon Muntaner. *Crònica*. 9 vols. 2nd ed. Enric Bagüe. Barcelona: Editorial Barcino, 1927–52.

Reinerus Leodensis. *Chronica*. In Röhricht, *QBS*: 329–30.

Ricardo of San Germano. *Chronicon. Chronicon, MGH SS* 19: 335. Raccolta degli Storici italiani 7.2: 34–46.

Robert of Torigny. *Chronica. MGH SS* 6: 475–535.

Rodrigo Jiménez de Rada. *Historia de rebus Hispanie sive Historia Gothica*. Ed. Juan Fernández Valverde. *Corpus Christianorum. Continuatio Mediaevalis* 72. Turnhout: Brepols, 1987.

———. *De rebus Hispaniae*. In *Opera*. 1–208.

———. *Historia arabum*. In *Opera*. 242–83.

———. *Opera*. Ed. Francisco de Lorenzana. Madrid: 1793; reprint Valencia: Anubar, 1968.

Roger de Hoveden. *Chronica*. Ed. William Stubbs. 4 vols. Rolls Series 51. London: Longman, Green, 1868–71.

Röhricht, Reinhold. *Quinti Belli Sacri Scriptores minores*. Geneva: Fick, 1879.

Sampiro, su crónica y la monarquía leonesa en el siglo X. Ed. Justo Pérez de Urbel, Madrid: CSIC, 1952.

Snorre Sturlason. *Heimskringla*. Tr. Erling Monsen and A. H. Smith. Cambridge: W. Heffer, 1932.

Suger. *Vita Ludovici Grossi. PL* 186: 1253–1340.

Vita Paschali II. In *Liber Pontificalis*. 2nd ed. Louis Duchesne. 3 vols. Paris: E. de Boccard, 1955–57. 2: 296–310.

Vita S. Anastasii, PL 149: 423–34.

Vita Sancti Olegarii, ES 29: 472–99.

Vita S. Theotonii. PMH SS 1: 79–88.

William of Malmesbury. *Historia novella*. Ed. William Stubbs. 2 vols. London: Longman, 1887–89.

Wolf, Kenneth Baxter. *Conquerors and Chroniclers of Early Medieval Spain*. Liverpool: Liverpool University Press, 1990.

Narrative Sources: Muslim

ʿAbd Allāh. *The Tibyan: Memoirs of ʿAbd Allāh b. Buluggin, last Zirid Emir of Granada*. Tr. Amin T. Tibi. Leiden: E.J. Brill, 1986.

———. *El Siglo XI en 1ª Persona: Las "Memorias" de ʿAbd Allah, último rey Zirí de Granada destronado por los Almorávides (1090)*. Tr. Évariste Lévi-Provençal and Emilio García Gómez. Madrid: Alianza, 1980.

———. "Les Mémoires de ʿAbd Allāh, dernier roi Ziride de Grenade." Tr. Évariste Lévi-Provençal. *Al Andalus* 3 (1935): 233–344; 4 (1936–39): 29–143; 6 (1941):1–63.

Al-Ḥimyari. *Kitāb ar-Rawd al-Miʿṭar*. Tr. María del Pilar Maestro González. Valencia: Anubar, 1963.

Al-Ḥulal al-Mawshiyya: Crónica árabe de las dinastías almorávide, almohade, y ben-imerín. Tr. Ambrosio Huici Miranda. Tetuán: Editora Marroquí, 1951.

Al-Maqqarī. *The History of the Mohammedan Dynasties in Spain.* Tr. Pascual de Gayangos. 2 vols. London: W.H. Allen, 1840–43.

Al-Marrākūshī. *Kitāb al-Mu'jib fi Taljis Ajbar al-Magrib: Lo Admirable en el Resumen de las Noticias del Magrib.* Tr. Ambrosio Huici Miranda. Tetuán: Editoria Marroquí, 1955.

Bosch Vila, Jacinto. "Al-Bakri: Dos fragmentos sobre Barbastro." *EEMCA* 3 (1947–48): 242–61.

Crónica anónima de ʿAbd al-Rahman III al-Naṣir. Ed. Évariste Lévi-Provençal and Emilio García Gómez. Madrid-Granada: CSIC, 1950.

Huici, Ambrosio. *Colección de crónicas árabes de la reconquista.* 3 vols. Tetuán: Editora Marroquí, 1954.

Ibn ʿAbd al-Ḥakam. *Conquista de Africa del Norte y de España.* Tr. Eliseo Vidal Beltrán. Valencia: Anubar, 1966.

Ibn Abī Zarʿ. *Rawd al-Qirtas.* Tr. Ambrosio Huici Miranda. 2 vols. Valencia: Anubar, 1964.

Ibn al-Kardabūs, *Kitábu-l-iktifá.* In al-Maqqari, *History.* 2: xxii–xlviii.

Ibn ʿIdhārī. *Al-Bayān al-Mugrib.* Ed. Évariste Lévi-Provençal, Georges Colin, and I. ʿAbbas. 4 vols. Paris: P. Geuthner, 1930; Leiden: E.J. Brill 1948; Beirut: Dar al-Thaqafair, 1967.

———. *Al-Bayān al-Mugrib fi Ijtiṣār ajbar Muluk al-Andalus wa al-Magrib.* Tr. Ambrosio Huici. 2 vols. Tetuán: Editora Marroquí, 1954.

———. *Al-Bayan al-Mugrib: Nuevos fragmentos almorávides y almohades.* Tr. Ambrosio Huici Miranda. Valencia: Anubar, 1963.

Ibn Khaldūn. *Histoire des Berbères et des dynasties musulmanes de l'Afrique septentrionale.* Tr. Baron de Slane. 4 vols. Paris: P. Geuthner, 1852–56.

Ibn Ṣaḥib al-Sala. *Al-Mann bil-Imama.* Tr. Ambrosio Huici Miranda. Valencia: Anubar, 1969.

ʿIsa ibn Ahmad al-Razi. *Anales palatinos del Califa de Córdoba Al-Ḥakam II.* Tr. Emilio García Gómez. Madrid: Sociedad de Estudios y Publicaciones, 1967.

Documentary Sources

Agapíto y Revilla, Juan. *Los privilegios de Valladolid.* Valladolid: Sociedad Castellana de Excursiones, 1906.

Alberigo, Giuseppe, et al. *Conciliorum oecumenicorum decreta.* 2nd ed. Freiburg-im-Breisgau: Herder 1962.

Alexander II. *Epistolae. PL* 146: 1279–1436.

Alexander III. *Epistolae. PL* 200.

Alfonso X. *Espéculo: Texto jurídico atribuído al Rey de Castilla Don Alfonso el Sabio.* Ed. Robert A. MacDonald. Madison, Wis.: Hispanic Seminary, 1990.

———. *Fuero real.* Ed. Gonzalo Martínez Díez, José Manuel Asencio, and C. Hernández Alonso. Ávila: Fundación Claudio Sánchez Albornoz, 1988.

————. *Las Siete Partidas del Rey Don Alfonso el Sabio.* Ed. Real Academia de la Historia. 3 vols. Madrid: Imprenta Real, 1801.

————. *Setenario.* Ed. Kenneth H. Vanderford. Madrid, 1945. Reprint Barcelona: Editorial Crítica, 1984.

Amari, Michele. *I diplomi arabi del Real Archivio fiorentino.* 2 vols. Florence: Felice LeMonnier, 1863.

Auvray, Lucien. *Les registres de Grégoire IX.* 2 vols. Paris: Bibliothèque des Écoles Françaises d'Athènes et de Rome, 1896–1955.

Baer, Fritz. *Die Juden im christlichen Spanien.* Berlin: Schocken, 1936.

Ballesteros, Antonio. "Las Cortes de 1252." *Anales de la junta para ampliación de estudios e investigaciones científicas.* 3 (1911): 114–43.

Barrero Garciá, Ana María. "Un formulario de cancillería episcopal castellano-leonés del siglo XIII." *AHDE* 46 (1976): 671–712.

Beltrán de Heredia, Vicente. *Cartulario de la Universidad de Salamanca.* 4 vols. Salamanca: Universidad de Salamanca, 1970–73.

Benavides, Antonio de. *Memorias de Fernando IV.* 2 vols. Madrid: José Rodríguez, 1860.

Berger, Émile. *Les registres d'Innocent IV (1243–1254).* 4 vols. Paris: Bibliothèque des Écoles Françaises d'Athènes et de Rome, 1881–1921.

Blanco Lozano, Pilar. *Colección diplomática de Fernando I (1037–1065).* Leon: CSIC, 1987.

Bofarull, Próspero de, et al., eds. *Colección de documentos inéditos del Archivo General de la Corona de Aragón.* 41 vols. Barcelona: Imprenta del Archivo, 1847–1910.

Bruel, Alexandre. *Recueil des chartes de l'Abbaye de Cluny.* 6 vols. Paris: Imprimrie Nationale, 1876–1903.

Bullarium equestris Ordinis Militiae Sancti Iacobi de Spatha. Ed. José López Agurleta. Madrid: Juan de Ariztia, 1719.

Bullarium Ordinis Militiae de Alcantara. Ed. Ignacio José Ortega y Cotes. Madrid: Antonio Marín, 1759.

Bullarium Ordinis Militiae de Calatrava. Ed. Ignacio José Ortega y Cotes, J. F. Alvarez de Baquedano, and P. de Ortega Zúñiga y Aranda. Madrid: Antonio Marín, 1761.

Burns, Robert I., S.J. *Diplomatarium of the Crusader Kingdom of Valencia: The Registered Charters of Its Conqueror, Jaume I, 1257–1276.* 2 vols. thus far. Princeton, N.J.: Princeton University Press, 1985–91.

————. "A Lost Crusade: Unpublished Bulls of Innocent IV on al-Azraq's Revolt in Thirteenth-Century Spain." *CHR* 74 (1988): 440–49.

Cabanes Pecourt, María Desamparados, and Ramón Ferrer Navarro. *Llibre del repartiment del reyne de Valencia.* 3 vols. Zaragoza: Anubar, 1979–80.

Caetano de Sousa, Antonio. *Provas da História genealogica da Casa Real Portugueza.* 4 vols. Ed. Manuel Lopes de Almeida and Cesar Pegado. Coimbra: Atlantida, 1946–52.

Calixtus II. *Epistolae. PL* 163: 1073–1414.

Canellas López, Angel. *Colección diplomática del Concejo de Zaragoza, 1119–1276.* 2 vols. Zaragoza: Catedra Zaragoza de la Universidad, 1972.

Canivez, Joseph M. *Statuta capitulorum generalium Ordinis Cisterciensis.* 8 vols. Louvain: Revue d'Histoire Ecclésiastique, 1933–41.

Caruana Gómez de Barreda, Jaime. *El Fuero latino de Teruel.* Teruel: Instituto de Estudios Turolenses, 1974.

Colón, Germà, and Arcadí García, eds. *Furs de Valencia.* 4 vols. thus far. Barcelona: Barcino, 1970–.

Cortes de los antiguos reinos de Aragón y Valencia y principado de Cataluña. 26 vols. Madrid: Real Academia de la Historia, 1896–1922.

Cortes de los antiguos reinos de León y Castilla. 5 vols. Madrid: Real Academia de la Historia, 1861–1903.

D'Albon, Marquis. *Cartulaire du Temple.* Paris: H. Champion, 1913.

De Ayala Martínez, Carlos, ed. *Libro de privilegios de la Orden de San Juan de Jerusalén en Castilla y León (Siglos XII–XV).* Madrid: Editorial Complutense, 1995.

Delaville Le Roulx, Jean. *Cartulaire général de l'Ordre des Hospitaliers de Saint-Jean de Jérusalem.* 4 vols. Paris: E.L. Roulx, 1894–1906.

Documentos Medievais Portugueses. Documentos régios. I. Ed. Rui Pinto de Azevedo. Lisbon: Academia Portuguesa da Historia, 1958.

Dualde Serrano, Manuel. *Fori antiqui Valentiae.* Madrid, Valencia: Escuela de Estudios Medievales, 1967.

Edgington, Susan. "The Lisbon Letter of the Second Crusade." *Historical Research* 69 (1996): 328–39.

Erdmann, Carl. *Papsturkunden in Portugal.* Berlin: Akademie der Wissenschaften in Gottingen, 1970.

Eugenius III. *Epistolae. PL* 180: 1003–1612.

Ferotin, Marius. *Le Liber ordinum en usage dans l'église wisigothique et mozarabe d'Espagne du Ve au Xie siècle.* Paris, 1904. Reprint Rome: Edizione Liturgiche, 1996.

Fita, Fidel. "Bulas históricas del reino de Navarra en los postreros años del siglo XII." *BRAH* 26 (1895): 417–59.

———. "Tres bulas inéditas de Alejandro III." *BRAH* 12 (1888): 164–68.

Floriano, Antonio C. *Documentación histórica del Archivo Municipal de Cáceres (1229–1471).* Cáceres: Diputación Provincial, 1987.

Font Rius, José. *Rationes Decimarum Hispaniae (1279–1280).* 2 vols. Barcelona: CSIC, 1946–47.

Fuero Juzgo en latín y castellano. Ed. Real Academia de la Historia. Madrid: Joaquín Ibarra, 1815.

Gallego Blanco, Enrique. *The Rule of the Spanish Military Order of St. James 1170–1493. Latin and Spanish Texts.* Leiden: E.J. Brill, 1971.

Gelasius II, *Epistolae. PL* 163: 473–512.

González, Julio. *Repartimiento de Sevilla.* 2 vols. Madrid: CSIC, 1951.

Gutiérrez del Arroyo de Vázquez de Parga, Consuelo. *Privilegios reales de la Orden de Santiago en la edad media.* Madrid: Junta técnica de Archivos, Bibliotecas, y Museos, n.d.

Hernández, Francisco J. *Los cartularios de Toledo. Catálogo documental.* Madrid: Fundación Ramón Areces, 1985.

———. "Las Cortes de Toledo de 1207." In *Las Cortes de Castilla y León en la Edad Media. Actas de la Primera Etapa del Congreso Científico sobre la Historia de las Cortes de Castilla y León, Burgos, 30 de Septiembre a 3 de Octubre de 1986.* 2 vols. Valladolid: Cortes de Castilla y León, 1988–89. 1: 219–63.

Huici Miranda, Ambrosio, and María Desamparados Cabanes Pecourt. *Documentos de Jaime I de Aragón.* 5 vols. thus far. Valencia: Anubar, 1976–88.

Imperiale di Sant'Angelo, Cesare, ed. *Codice diplomatico della Repubblica di Genova.* 2 vols. Rome: Tipografia del Senato, 1936–42.

Innocent III. *Epistolae. PL* 214–16.

Kagay, Donald J. *The Usatges of Barcelona: The Fundamental Law of Catalonia.* Philadelphia: University of Pennsylvania Press, 1994.

Kehr, Paul. *Papsturkunden in Spanien: Vorarbeiten zur Hispania Pontificia.* 2 vols. Berlin: Weidmannsche Buchhandlung, 1926.

Lacarra, José María. *Documentos para el estudio de la reconquista y repoblación del valle del Ebro.* 2 vols. Valencia: Anubar, 1982.

Lema Pueyo, José Ángel. *Colección diplomática de Alfonso I de Aragón y Pamplona (1104–1134).* San Sebastián: Eusko-Ikaskuntza, 1990.

Lévi-Provençal, Évariste. *Documents inédits d'histoire almohade. Fragments manuscrits du legajo 1919 du fonds arabe de l'Escorial.* Paris: P. Geuthner, 1928.

———. "Un recueil des lettres officielles almohades." *Hesperis* 28 (1941): 1–80.

Liber Feudorum Maior. Cartulario real que se conserva en el Archivo de la Corona de Aragón. Ed. Francisco Miquel Rosell. 2 vols. Barcelona: CSIC, 1945–47.

Liber partitionis regni Maiorice. CDACA. 11: 7–141.

Loewenfeld, Samuel, ed. *Epistolae pontificum Romanorum ineditae.* Leipzig: Veit, 1885.

López Ferreiro, Antonio. *Fueros municipales de Santiago y de su tierra.* Santiago de Compostela: Imprenta del Seminario, 1895.

Lucius II. *Epistolae. PL* 179: 819–935.

Maldonado y Fernández del Torco, José, ed. *El Fuero de Coria.* Madrid: Institución de Estudios de Administración local, 1949.

Mansi, Joannes Dominicus. *Sacrorum Conciliorum nova et amplissima collectio.* 53 vols. in 60. Paris: H. Welter, 1901–27.

Mansilla, Demetrio. *La documentación pontificia de Honorio III (1216–1227).* Rome: Instituto Español de Historia eclesiástica, 1965.

———. *La documentación pontificia hasta Inocencio III (965–1216).* Rome: Instituto Español de Estudios eclesiásticos, 1955.

María, Ramón de. *El "Repartiment" de Burriana y Villarreal.* Valencia: J. Nacher, 1935.

Marichalar, Carlos. *Colección diplomática del rey don Sancho VII el Fuerte de Navarra.* Pamplona: Editorial Arambarú, 1934.

Martín Expósito, Alberto, and José María Monsalvo. *Documentación medieval del Archivo municipal de Ledesma.* Salamanca: Universidad de Salamanca, 1986.

Mas Latrie, Louis de. *Traités de paix et de commerce et documents divers concernant les relations des chrétiens avec les arabes de l'Afrique septentrionale au moyen âge.* 2 vols. Paris, 1866. Reprint Philadelphia: Burt Franklin, 1963.

Materials for the History of Thomas Becket, Archbishop of Canterbury. Ed. J. C. Robertson. 7 vols. Rolls Series. London: Longman, 1875–85.

Memorial Histórico Español. 50 vols. Madrid: Real Academia de la Historia, 1851–1963.

Miguel Vigil, Ciriaco. *Colección histórico-diplomática del ayuntamiento de* Oviedo. Oviedo: Pardo-Gusano, 1889.

Miquel Rosell, Francisco J. *Regesta de letras pontificias del Archivo de la Corona de Aragón. Sección cancillería real (pergaminos)*. Madrid: CSIC, 1945–47.

Molho, Mauricio, ed. *El Fuero de Jaca*. Zaragoza: CSIC, 1964.

Monumenta Henricina. 15 vols. Coimbra: Commisão executiva das Commemorações do V Centenario da Morte do Infante D. Henrique, 1960–74.

Muñoz, Tomás. *Colección de fueros municipales y cartas pueblas de los reinos de Castilla, León, Corona de Aragón y Navarra*. Madrid: José María Alonso, 1847.

Olivar, Alejandro. *El Sacramentario de Vich*. Barcelona: CSIC, 1953.

———. *Sacramentarium Rivipullense*. Madrid: CSIC, 1964.

Paschal II. *Epistolae. PL* 163: 9–469.

Portugaliae Monumenta Historica a saeculo octavo post Christum usque ad quintum decimum. Leges et Consuetudines. 1. Lisbon: Academia Real das Ciências de Lisboa, 1856.

———. *Scriptores*. 1. Lisbon: Academia Real das Ciências de Lisboa, 1856.

Powers, James F. *The Code of Cuenca: Municipal Law on the Twelfth-Century Castilian Frontier*. Philadelphia: University of Pennsylvania Press, 2000.

Quintana Prieto, Augusto. *La documentación pontificia de Inocencio IV (1243–1254)*. 2 vols. Rome: Instituto Español de Historia Eclesiástica, 1987.

Rassow, Peter. "Die Urkunden Kaiser Alfons VII von Spanien," *Archiv für Urkundenforschung* 10 (1928): 327–468; 11 (1930): 66–137.

Regestum donationum regni Valentie. CDACA 11: 151–656.

Reuter, Abiah Elisabeth. *Chancelarias Medievais Portugueses*. Coimbra: Universidad de Coimbra, 1938.

Riu, Ramón. "Dos bulas inéditas de Celestino III." *BRAH* 11 (1887): 455–458.

Rodenberg, Clemens. *Epistolae Saeculi XIII e Regestis Pontificum Romanorum selectae. MGH Epistolae Saeculi XIII*. 3 vols. Berlin: Monumenta Germaniae Historica, 1883–94.

Rymer, Thomas. *Foedera, conventiones, litterae et cuiuscunque acta publica inter reges Angliae et alios quovis imperatores, reges, pontifices, principes*. 10 vols. The Hague: Joannes Neaulme, 1739–45.

Sáez, Emilio, and Carlos Sáez, eds. *El fondo español del Archivo de la Academia de las Ciencias de San Petersburgo*. Alcalá de Henares: Universidad de Alcalá, 1993.

Sáez, Emilio, Rafael Gibert, Manuel Alvar, and Atilano G. Ruiz-Zorrilla. *Los Fueros de Sepúlveda*. Segovia: Diputación Provincial, 1953.

Salarrullana, José, and Eduardo Ibarra. *Documentos correspondientes al reinado de Sancho Ramírez*. 2 vols. Zaragoza: M. Escar, 1904–13.

Sánchez Belda, Luis. "Notas de diplomática: En torno a tres diplomas de Alfonso VII." *Hispania* 11 (1951): 58–61.

Sánchez Casabón, Ana Isabel. *Alfonso II, Rey de Aragón, Conde de Barcelona y Marqués de Provenza: Documentos (1162–1196)*. Zaragoza: CSIC, 1995.

Sánchez Ruano, Julián. *El Fuero de Salamanca*. Salamanca: S. Cerezo, 1870.

Savall y Dronda, Pascual, and Santiago Penèn y Dehesa, ed. *Fueros, observancias, y actos de corte del reino de Aragón*. 2 vols. Zaragoza: F. Castro y Bosque, 1866.

Tejada y Romero, Juan. *Colección de Canones y de todos los Concilios de la Iglesia de España y de América*, 7 vols. Madrid: P. Montero, 1859–63.

Tilander, Gunnar, ed. *Los Fueros de Aragón según el Manuscrito 458 de la Biblioteca Nacional de Madrid.* Lund: C. W. K. Gleerup, 1937.

————. *Vidal Mayor. Traducción aragonesa de la obra "In excelsis Dei Thesauris" de Vidal de Canellas.* 3 vols. Lund: H. Ohlsson, 1956.

Torres Fontes, Juan. *Documentos del Siglo XIII.* Murcia: Academia Alfonso X el Sabio, 1969.

————. *Fueros y Privilegios de Alfonso X el Sabio al Reino de Murcia.* Murcia: Academia Alfonso X el Sabio, 1973.

Ubieto Arteta, Antonio. *Colección diplomática de Pedro I de Aragón y Navarra.* Zaragoza: CSIC, 1951.

Ureña y Smenjaud, Rafael de. *Fuero de Cuenca.* Madrid: Tipografía de Archivos, 1935.

Literary Sources

Alfonso X. *Cantigas de Santa Maria.* Ed. Walter Mettmann. 4 vols. Coimbra: Universidade de Coimbra, 1959–72. Reprint, 2 vols. Vigo: Edicions Xerais de Galicia, 1981.

Alfonso de Cartagena. *Alegaciones formuladas para defender ante el Papa en Basilea el derecho de los reyes de Castilla sobre las Canarias.* In García Gallo, *Manual.* 2: 628, no. 848.

————. "Discurso sobre la precedencia del Rey católico sobre el de Inglaterra en el Concilio de Basilea." *BAE* 116: 205–34.

Alvar, Carlos. *Textos trovadorescos sobre España y Portugal.* Madrid: Cupsa, 1978.

Álvaro Pelayo. *Espelho dos reis.* Ed. Miguel Pinto de Meneses. 2 vols. Lisbon: Universidade de Lisboa, 1956.

Bernard of Clairvaux. *Epistolae.* In *Opera.* Ed. Jean Leclercq and Henri Rochais. 8 vols. Rome: Editiones Cistercienses, 1955–77.

————. *Liber de Laude Novae Militiae. PL* 182: 921–39.

Caesarius of Heisterbach. *Dialogus miraculorum.* Ed. Joseph Strange. 2 vols. Cologne: J.M. Heberle, 1851.

Cancionero castellano del siglo XV. Ed. R. Foulché-Delbosc. 2 vols. Madrid: Bailly-Bailliére, 1912–15.

Cancioneiro da Ajuda. Ed. Carolina Michaëlis. 2 vols. Hildesheim/New York: G. Olms, 1980.

Cancioneiro da Biblioteca antiga Colucci-Brancuti. Ed. Elza Paxeco Machado and José Pedro Machado. 8 vols. Lisbon: Revista de Portugal, 1949–64.

Catalán, Diego, and Juan Gil, eds. "Rithmi de Iulia Romula seu ispalensi urbe." *AEM* 5 (1968): 549–58.

Diego García de Campos. *Planeta.* Ed. Manuel Alonso. Madrid: CSIC, 1943.

Diego de Valera. *Doctrinal de Principes. BAE* 116: 173–204.

————. *Epistolas. BAE* 116: 1–54.

Fernán Pérez de Guzmán. *Generaciones y Semblanzas.* Ed. J. Domíinguez Bordona. Madrid: Espasa-Calpe, 1965.

Goldin, Frederick. *Lyrics of the Troubadours and Trouvères: Original Texts with Translations and Introductions.* Garden City, N.Y.: Doubleday Anchor, 1973.

Gonzalo de Berceo. *El Duelo que fizo la Virgen María el día de la Pasión de su fijo Jesu Cristo.*" *Obras completas.* 427–57.

———. "La Estoria de Sennor Sant Millán, tornada de Latín en Romançe." *Obras completas.* 125–92.

———. *Obras completas.* Logroño: Instituto de Estudios Riojanos, 1974.

———. *Vida de Santo Domingo de Silos. Obras completas.* 7–124.

———. *La Vida de San Millán de la Cogolla.* Ed. Brian Dutton. London: Tamesis, 1967.

Isidore of Seville. *Etymologiarum sive Originum Libri XX.* Ed. W. M. Lindsay. 2 vols. Oxford: Clarendon Press, 1911.

Juan Gil de Zamora. *Liber de preconiis Hispaniae.* Ed. Manuel de Castro. Madrid: Universidad de Madrid, 1955.

———. "Liber de preconiis numantine." Ed. Fidel Fita. "Dos libros inéditos de Gil de Zamora." *BRAH* 5 (1884): 131–200.

Juan Manuel. *Libro de los estados. BAE* 51: 278–364.

Libro de Alexandre. In *Poetas castellanos anteriores al siglo XV.* Ed. Tomás Antonio Sánchez, Pedro José Pidal, and Francisco Janer. Madrid: M. Rivadeneyra, 1864.

Lida de Malkiel, María Rosa. "La Garcineida de García de Toledo." *Nueva Revista de Filología hispánica* 7 (1953): 246–58.

Martín de Córdoba, Fray. *Jardín de las doncellas.* In Penna, *Prosistas. BAE* 117: 67–120.

Pedro López de Ayala. *Rimado de Palacio.* Ed. Germán Orduña. Madrid: Castalia, 1987.

Penna, Mario, and Fernando Rubio, eds. *Prosistas castellanos del siglo XV.* 2 vols. *BAE* 116, 2: 171. Madrid: Real Academia Española, 1959.

Pescador del Hoyo, María del Carmen. "Tres nuevos poemas medievales." *Nueva Revista de Filología Hispánica* 14 (1960): 242–50.

The Pilgrim's Guide to Santiago de Compostela. Tr. William Melczer. New York: Italica, 1993. *Poem of the Cid.* Spanish text by Ramón Menéndez Pidal. English verse translation by W. S. Merwin. New York: Meridian, 1975.

The Poem of the Cid. Tr. Rita Hamilton and Janet Perry. London: Penguin Books, 1984.

Poema de Alfonso XI. Ed. Yo Ten Cate. Madrid: CSIC, 1956.

Poema de Fernán González. Ed. A. Zamora Vicente. Madrid: Espasa-Calpe, 1946.

Rodrigo Sánchez de Arévalo. *Vergel de los Principes. BAE* 116: 311–43.

Rodríguez Puértolas, Juan. "El Libro de la Consolación de España. Una Meditación sobre la Castilla del Siglo XV." *Miscelánea de Estudios medievales* 1 (1972): 189–212.

Secondary Works

Abulafia, David. *A Mediterranean Emporium: The Catalan Kingdom of Majorca.* Cambridge: Cambridge University Press, 1994.

———. *The Western Mediterranean Kingdoms, 1200–1500: The Struggle for Dominion.* London: Longman, 1997.

Al-Azmeh, Aziz. "Mortal Enemies, Invisible Neighbors: Northerners in Andalusi Eyes." In Salma Khadra Jayyusi, ed., *The Legacy of Muslim Spain.* 2 vols. Leiden: E.J. Brill, 1994. 259–72.

Alfonso X. Toledo 1984. Toledo: Museo de Santa Cruz, 1984.

Alvira Cabrer, Martín. "De Alarcos a las Navas de Tolosa: Idea y realidad de los orígenes de la batalla de 1212." In Izquierdo Benito and Ruiz Gómez, *Alarcos*. 249–64.

Arié, Rachel. *L'Espagne musulmane au temps des nasrides (1232–1492)*. Paris: E. de Boccard, 1973.

Arrarás, Joaquín, ed. *Historia de la Cruzada Española*. 35 vols. Madrid: Ediciones españolas, 1939–43.

Arvizu, Fernando de. "Las Cortes de León de 1188 y sus Decretos." In *El Reino de León en la Alta Edad Media*, vol. 1, *Cortes, Concilios y Fueros*. 11–142.

Azcona, Tarsicio de. *Isabel la Católica*. Madrid: BAC, 1964.

Azevedo, Rui de. "A Ordem militar de S. Julião do Pereiro, depois chamada de Alcântara." *AEM* 11 (1981): 713–29.

————. "As Origens da Ordem de Evora ou de Avis." *Revista de Historia* 1 (1932): 233–41.

Baer, Yitzhak. *A History of the Jews in Christian Spain*. 2 vols. Philadelphia: Jewish Publication Society, 1961.

Balaguer, Federico. "Los límites del obispado de Aragón y el concilium de Jaca de 1063." *EEMCA* 4 (1950): 68–138.

Ballesteros Beretta, Antonio. *Alfonso X el Sabio*. Barcelona: El Albir, 1984.

————. *La marina cantabra*. Santander: Diputación Provincial, 1968.

————. *La Reconquista de Murcia por el Infante D. Alfonso de Castilla*. Murcia: Academia Alfonso X el Sabio, 1959.

————. *Sevilla en el siglo XIII*. Sevilla: Juan Pérez Torres, 1913.

Barbero, Abilio, and Marcelo Vigil. *Sobre los orígenes sociales de la Reconquista*. Barcelona: Ariel, 1974.

Barbour, Nevill. "The Embassy Sent by King John of England to Miramamolín, King of Morocco." *Al-Andalus* 25 (1960): 373–381.

————. "Two Christian Embassies to the Almohad Sultan Muḥammad al-Nāṣir at Seville in 1211." *Actas del Primer Congreso de Estudios árabes e islámicos (Córdoba 1962)*. Madrid: Comité permanente del Congreso de Estudios árabes e islámicos, 1964. 189–213.

Barkai, Ron. *Cristianos y musulmanes en la España medieval (El enemigo en el espejo)*. Madrid: Rialp, 1984.

Barquero Goñi, Carlos. "La Orden Militar del Hospital en La Mancha durante los siglos XII y XIII." In Izquierdo Benito and Ruiz Gómez, *Alarcos*. 289–314.

Barreiro Somoza, José. *El señorío de la iglesia de Santiago de Compostela (Siglos IX–XIII)*. La Coruña: Editorial Diputación Provincial, 1987.

Barton, Simon. *The Aristocracy in Twelfth-Century Leon and Castile*. Cambridge: Cambridge University Press, 1997.

————. "A Forgotten Crusade: Alfonso VII and the Campaign for Jaén (1148)." *Historical Research* 73 (2000): 312–20.

Benelhaj Soulami, Jaafar. "La batalla de Alarcos en la mitología árabe." In Izquierdo Benito and Ruiz Gómez, *Alarcos*. 283–88.

Benito Ruano, Eloy. "La Banca Toscana y la Orden de Santiago." *Estudios Santiaguistas*. 61–153.

————. *Estudios Santiaguistas*. León: Colegio Universitario de León, 1978.

————. "La Orden de Santiago y el Imperio latino de Constantinopla." *Estudios Santiaguistas*. 29–60.

————. "Las Ordenes Militares españolas y la idea de Cruzada." *Hispania* 16 (1956): 3–15.

————. "Santiago, Calatrava y Antioquía." *AEM* 1 (1964): 549–60.

Bennett, Matthew. "Military Aspects of the Conquest of Lisbon, 1147." In Phillips and Hoch, *Second Crusade*. 71–89

Berganza, Francisco de. *Antigüedades de España*. 2 vols. Madrid: Francisco del Hierro, 1772.

Berry, Virginia G. "The Second Crusade." In Setton, *Crusades*. 1: 463–512.

Bishko, Charles Julian. "Fernando I and the Origins of the Leonese-Castilian Alliance with Cluny." *Studies*. No. II.

————. "Liturgical Intercession at Cluny for the King-Emperors of León." *Studia Monastica* 3 (1961): 53–76.

————. "Peter the Venerable's Journey to Spain." In Giles Constable and James Kritzeck, eds., *Petrus Venerabilis, 1156–1956: Studies and Texts Commemorating the Eighth Centenary of His Death*. Rome: Herder, 1956. 163–76.

————. "The Spanish and Portuguese Reconquest, 1095–1492." In Setton, *Crusades*. 3: 396–456.

————. *Studies in Medieval Spanish Frontier History*. London: Variorum, 1980.

Bisson, Thomas N. *Conservation of Coinage: Monetary Exploitation and its Restraint in France, Catalonia and Aragon (A.D. 1000–c. 1225)*. New York: Oxford University Press, 1979.

————. "Las finanzas del joven Jaime I (1213–1228)." *Jaime I y su época*. 161–208.

————. *Fiscal Accounts of Catalonia Under the Early Count-Kings (1151–1213*. 2 vols. Berkeley: University of California Press, 1984.

————. *The Medieval Crown of Aragon: A Short History*. Oxford: Clarendon Press, 1986.

————. "Sur les origines du *monedatge*: Quelques textes inédits." *Annales du Midi* 85 (1973): 91–104.

————. "An 'Unknown Charter' for Catalonia (d. 1205)." *Album Elemér Mályusz: Szekesfehévár-Budapest 1972*. Brussels: Librairie Encyclopédique, 1976. 61–76.

Blasco i Bardas, Anna Maria. *Les pintures murals del Palau Reial Major de Barcelona*. Barcelona: Ajuntament de Barcelona, 1993.

Blázquez y Jiménez, Ángel. "Bosquejo histórico de la Orden de Monte Gaudio." *BRAH* 71 (1917): 138–72.

Blume, Clemens. "Hymnodica Gothica." *Analecta Hymnica Medii Aevi* 27 (1897): 1–275.

Bofarull y Moscaró, Prosper. *Los Condes de Barcelona vindicados y cronología y genealogía de los reyes de España*. 2 vols. Barcelona: J. Oliveres y Montmany, 1836.

Boissonade, Pierre. "Cluny, la Papauté et la première grande Croisade internationale contre les Sarrasins d'Espagne." *Revue des questions historiques* 60 (1932): 257–301.

————. "Les premiers croisades françaises en Espagne." *Bulletin Hispanique* 36 (1934): 5–28.

Bonet Donato, María. *La Orden del Hospital en la Corona de Aragón: Poder y gobierno en la Castellanía de Amposta (S. XII–XV)*. Madrid: CSIC, 1994.

Bonnaz, Yves. "Divers aspects de la continuité wisigothique dans la monarchie asturienne." *Mélanges de la Casa de Velázquez* 12 (1976): 81–99.

Brandão, Antonio. *Crónicas de D. Sancho I e D. Afonso II*. Ed. A. de Maglahães Basto. Lisbon: Livraria Civilização, 1945.

———. *Crónicas de D. Sancho II e D. Afonso III*. Ed. A. de Magalhães Basto Porto: Livraria Civilização, 1945.

Brodman, James W. *Charity and Welfare: Hospitals and the Poor in Medieval Catalonia*. Philadelphia: University of Pennsylvania Press, 1998.

———. "Military Redemptionism and the Castilian Reconquest, 1180–1250." *Military Affairs* 44 (1980): 24–27.

———. "Municipal Ransoming Law on the Medieval Spanish Frontier." *Speculum* 60 (1985): 318–30.

———. "The Origins of Hospitallerism in Medieval Catalonia." In Simon, *Iberia*. 1: 290–302.

———. *Ransoming Captives in Crusader Spain: The Order of Merced on the Christian-Islamic Frontier*. Philadelphia: University of Pennsylvania Press, 1986.

Brundage, James A. "*Cruce signari*: The Rite for Taking the Cross in England." *Traditio* 22 (1966): 289–310.

———. "Holy War and the Medieval Lawyers." In Murphy, *The Holy War*. 99–140.

———. *Medieval Canon Law and the Crusader*. Madison, Wis.: University of Wisconsin Press, 1969.

———. "A Note on the Attestation of Crusaders' Vows." *CHR* 52 (1966): 234–39.

———. "The Votive Obligations of Crusaders: The Development of a Canonistic Doctrine." *Traditio* 24 (1968): 77–118.

Burman, Thomas E. *Religious Polemic and the Intellectual History of the Mozarabs, c. 1050–1200*. Leiden: E.J. Brill, 1994.

Burns, Robert I., S.J. "Almohad Prince and Mudejar Convert: New Documentation on Abū Zayd." In Donald J. Kagay and Joseph T. Snow, eds. *Medieval Iberia: Essays on the History and Literature of Medieval Spain*. New York: Peter Lang, 1997. 171–88.

———. "The Crusade Against al-Azraq: A Thirteenth-Century Mudéjar Revolt in International Perspective." *American Historical Review* 93 (1988): 80–106.

———. *The Crusader Kingdom of Valencia (1238–1276): A Study in the Organization of the Mediaeval Frontier*. 3 vols. PhD dissertation. Johns Hopkins University, 1958.

———. *The Crusader Kingdom of Valencia: Reconstruction on a Thirteenth-Century Frontier*. 2 vols. Cambridge, Mass.: Harvard University Press, 1967.

———. "How to End a Crusade: Techniques for Making Peace in Thirteenth-Century Valencia." *Moors and Crusaders* No. IV.

———. *Islam Under the Crusaders: Colonial Survival in the Thirteenth-Century Kingdom of Valencia*. Princeton, N.J.: Princeton University Press, 1973.

———. "Los hospitales del reino de Valencia en el siglo XIII." *AEM* 2 (1965): 135–54.

———. "The Loss of Provence: King James's Raid to Kidnap Its Heiress (1245):

Documenting a Legend." *XII Congrès d'histoire de la Couronne d'Aragon.* 3 vols. Montpellier: Société Archéologique de Montpellier, 1987–88. 3: 195–231.

———. "A Lost Crusade: Unpublished Bulls of Innocent IV on al-Azraq's Revolt in Thirteenth-Century Spain." *CHR* 74 (1988): 440–49.

———. "The Many Crusades of Valencia's Conquest (1225–1280): An Historiographical Labyrinth." In Kagay and Vann, *Social Origins.* 167–77.

———. *Medieval Colonialism: Postcrusade Exploitation of Islamic Valencia.* Princeton, N.J.: Princeton University Press, 1975.

———. "The Medieval Crossbow as Surgical Instrument: An Illustrated Case History." *Moors and Crusaders* No. VII.

———. *Moors and Crusaders in Mediterranean Spain.* London: Variorum, 1978.

———. *Muslims, Christians and Jews in the Crusader Kingdom of Valencia: Societies in Symbiosis.* Cambridge: Cambridge University Press, 1984.

———. "Muslims in the Thirteenth-Century Realms of Aragon: Interaction and Reaction." In Powell, *Muslims Under Latin Rule.* 57–102.

———. "The Spiritual Life of James the Conqueror." *Moors and Crusaders* No. I.

———. "Surrender Constitutions: The Islamic Communities of Eslida and Alfandech." *Muslims, Christians and Jews.* 52–79.

———, ed. *The Worlds of Alfonso the Learned and James the Conqueror: Intellect and Force in the Middle Ages.* Princeton, N.J.: Princeton University Press, 1985.

Burns, Robert I., S.J., and Paul Chevedden. "The Finest Castle in the World." *History Today* 49 (1999): 10–17.

———. *Negotiating Cultures: Bilingual Surrender Treaties in Muslim-Crusader Spain Under James the Conqueror.* Leiden: E.J. Brill, 1999.

Cadoux, C. John. *The Early Christian Attitude to War.* New York: Seabury, 1982.

Cantarino, Vicente. "The Spanish Reconquest: A Cluniac Holy War Against Islam?" In *Islam and the West,* ed. Khalil I. Semaan. Albany: State University of New York Press, 1980. 82–109.

Carrasco, Inés. *Los cargos de la hueste real en tiempos de Alfonso X. Estudio onomasiológico.* Granada: Universidad de Granada, 1992.

Caruana Gómez de Barreda, Jaime. "La Orden de Calatrava en Alcañiz." *Teruel* 8 (1952): 1–176.

Castro, Américo. *La realidad histórica de España.* Ed. ren. México: Porrua, 1962.

Catalán, Diego. *La Estoria de Espanna de Alfonso X: Creación y Evolución.* Madrid: Universidad Autónoma de Madrid, 1992.

Chevedden, Paul E. "The Artillery of King James I the Conqueror." In Chevedden, Kagay, and Padilla, *Iberia.* 47–94.

———. "The Hybrid Trebuchet: The Halfway Step to the Counterweight Trebuchet." In Kagay and Vann, *Social Origins.* 179–222.

Chevedden, Paul E., Zvi Shiller, Samuel R. Gilbert, and Donald J. Kagay. "The Traction Trebuchet: A Triumph of Four Civilizations." *Viator* 31 (2000): 433–86.

Chevedden, Paul E., Donald J. Kagay, and P. G. Padilla, eds. *Iberia and the Mediterranean World of the Middle Ages: Essays in Honor of Robert I. Burns, S.J.* Leiden: E.J. Brill, 1996.

Cocheril, Maur. "Essai sur l'origine des Ordres militaires dans la peninsule ibérique."

Collectanea Ordinis Cisterciensis Reformati 20 (1958): 346–61; 21 (1959): 228–50, 302–29.

———. "Origine cistercienne des Ordres militaires portugais d'Avis et du Christ." In his *Études sur le monachisme en Espagne et au Portugal.* Lisbon: Bertrand, 1966. 423–32.

Colbert, Edward. *The Martyrs of Córdoba (850–859): A Study of the Sources.* Washington, D.C.: Catholic University of America Press, 1962.

Collins, Roger. *The Arab Conquest of Spain, 710–797.* Oxford: Blackwell, 1989.

———. *Early Medieval Spain: Unity in Diversity, 400–1000.* New York: St. Martin's Press, 1983.

Constable, Giles. "The Financing of the Crusades in the Twelfth Century." In Benjamin Z. Kedar, Hans Eberhard Mayer, and R.C. Smail, ed. *Outremer: Studies in the History of the Crusading Kingdom of Jerusalem presented to Joshua Prawer.* Jerusalem: Yad Izhak ben-Zvi Institute, 1982. 64–88.

———. "A Note on the Route of the Anglo-Flemish Crusaders of 1147." *Speculum* 28 (1953): 525–28.

———. "The Second Crusade as Seen by Contemporaries." *Traditio* 9 (1953): 213–79.

Constable, Olivia Remie. *Trade and Traders in Muslim Spain: The Commerical Realignment of the Iberian Peninsula, 900–1500.* Cambridge: Cambridge University Press, 1994.

Coope, Jessica A. *The Martyrs of Córdoba: Community and Family Conflict in an Age of Mass Conversion.* Lincoln: University of Nebraska Press, 1995.

Corral Val, Luis. *Los monjes soldados de la Orden de Alcántara en la Edad Media: Su Organización institucional y vida religiosa.* Madrid: Castellum, 1999.

Cowdrey, H. E. J. "The Genesis of the Crusades: The Springs of Western Ideas of Holy War." In Murphy. *Holy War.* 9–32.

———. "Martyrdom and the First Crusade." In Peter W. Edbury, ed., *Crusade and Settlement.* Cardiff: University College Cardiff, 1985. 46–56.

Daniel, Norman. *Islam and the West: The Making of an Image.* Edinburgh: University of Edinburgh Press, 1960.

D'Alverny, Marie Thérèse. "Deux Traductions latines du Coran au Moyen Âge." *Archives d'histoire doctrinale et litteraire du Moyen Âge* 16 (1947): 69–131.

D'Alverny, Marie Thérèse, and Georg Vajda. "Marc de Tolède, traducteur d'Ibn Tumart." *Al-Andalus* 16 (1951):99–140, 249–307; 17 (1952): 1–56.

Dailliez, Laurent. *Les chevaliers de Montjoie.* Nice: Impresses Sud, 1978.

Delaville Le Roulx, Jean. "L'Ordre de Montjoye." *Revue de l'Orient latin* 1 (1893): 42–57.

Defourneaux, Marcelin. *Les français en Espagne aux XIe et XIIe siècles.* Paris: Presses Universitaires de France, 1949.

———. "Louis VII et les souverains espagnols." *Estudios dedicados a Menéndez Pidal.* 6: 647–61

Del Estal, Juan Manuel. "Alicante en la política territorial del los dos Jaimes de Aragón." *Jaime I y su época.* 1: 65–80.

Delaruelle, Etienne. "Essai sur la formation de l'idée de croisade." *Bulletin de littérature ecclésiastique publié par l'Institut catholique de Toulouse* 42 (1941): 24–45, 86–103.

————. *L'idée de croisade au Moyen Âge*. Turin: Bottega d'Erasmo, 1980.

Diffie, Bailey W., and George D. Winius. *Foundations of the Portuguese Empire, 1415–1580*. Minneapolis: University of Minnesota Press, 1977.

Donovan, Joseph P. *Pelagius and the Fifth Crusade*. Philadelphia: University of Pennsylvania Press, 1950.

Dozy, Reinhart. *Histoire des musulmanes d'Espagne*. Ed. Evariste Lévi-Provençal. 3 vols. Leiden: E.J. Brill, 1932.

————. *Recherches sur l'histoire et la littérature de l'Espagne pendant le moyen âge*. 3d ed. 2 vols. Paris, Maisonneuve, 1881.

Durán Gudiol, Antonio. *La Iglesia de Aragón durante los reinados de Sancho Ramírez y Pedro I, 1062–1104*. Rome: Iglesia nacional española, 1962.

Dufourcq, Charles Emmanuel. *L'Espagne catalane et le Maghrib aux XIIIe et XIVe siècles*. Paris: Presses Universitaires de France, 1966.

————. *L'Ibérie chrétienne et le Maghreb XIIe-XIVe siècles*. Aldershot: Variorum, 1990.

Dufourcq, Charles Emmanuel, and Jean Gautier-Dalché. *Historica económica y social de la España cristiana en la edad media*. Barcelona: Ediciones Albir, 1983.

Dunlop, D. M. "A Christian Mission to Muslim Spain in the Eleventh Century." *Al-Andalus* 17 (1952): 263–90.

Egger, Nelly. "El paso por Galicia de un Rey de Noruega en el siglo XII." *Estudios en Homenaje a Don Claudio Sánchez Albornoz en sus 90 Años*. 3 vols. Buenos Aires: Instituto de Historia de España, 1983. 2: 267–74.

Erdmann, Carl. "Der Kreuzzugsgedanken in Portugal." *Historische Zeitschrift* 141 (1930): 23–53.

————. *The Origin of the Idea of the Crusade*. Tr. Marshall W. Baldwin and Walter Goffart. Princeton, N.J.: Princeton University Press, 1977.

————. *Das Papsttum und Portugal im ersten Jahrhundert der portugiesische Geschichte*. Berlin: Weidmannsche Buchhandlung, 1928.

Eslava Galán, Juan. "La campaña de Quesada (1224)." *CEM* 12–13 (1984): 5–23.

————. "Tácticas en la Batalla de Las Navas de Tolosa." *CEM* 6–7 (1978–79): 39–53.

Estepa Díez, Carlos. "Las Cortes del Reino de León." In *El Reino de León en la Alta Edad Media*. 181–282.

Estudios dedicados a Menéndez Pidal. 7 vols. Madrid: Patronato Marcelino Menéndez Pelayo, 1950–62.

Fernández de Navarrete, Miguel. "Disertación histórica sobre la parte que tuvieron los españoles en las guerras de ultramar o de las cruzadas." *Memorias de la Real Academia de la Historia* 5. Madrid: Real Academia de la Historia, 1817.

Fernández González, Etelvina. "Iconografía y leyenda del Pendón de Baeza." *Medievo Hispano. Estudios in Memoriam del Profesor Derek W. Lomax*. Madrid; Sociedad Española de Estudios medievales, 1995. 141–58.

Ferreiro, Alberto. "The Siege of Barbastro, 1064–65: A Reassessment." *Journal of Medieval History* 9 (1983): 129–44.

Ferreira Alemparte, Jaime. *Arribadas de Normandos y Cruzados a las Costas de la Península Ibérica*. Madrid: Sociedad Española de Estudios Medievales, 1999.

————. "Asentamiento y extinción de la Orden Teutónico en España. La En-

comienda de Santa María de Castellanos de la Mota de Toro (1222–1556)."
BRAH 168 (1971): 227–74.

———. "España y Alemania en la Edad Media." *BRAH* 170 (1973): 319–76.

Ferrer Navarro, Ramón. *Conquista y repoblación del reino de Valencia.* Valencia: Del Senia al Segura, 1999.

Fita, Fidel. "Actas del Concilio de Clermont (18 nov. 1130): Revisión crítica." *BRAH* 4 (1884): 360–66.

———. "Bernardo de Perigord, arcediano de Toledo y obispo de Zamora: Bulas inéditas de Honorio III (15 de marzo de 1219) y Nicolao IV (18 de agosto de 1291)." *BRAH* 14 (1889): 456–66.

———. "Biografía inédita de Alfonso IX, Rey de León, por Gil de Zamora." *BRAH* 13 (1888): 291–95.

———. "Biografías de San Fernando y de Alfonso el Sabio por Gil de Zamora." *BRAH* 5 (1885): 302–28.

———. "Bula inédita de Honorio II." *Estudios históricos.* 4: 19–31.

———. "El Concilio de Lérida en 1193 y Santa María la Real de Nájera: Bulas inéditas de Celestino III, Inocencio III y Honorio III." *BRAH* 26 (1895): 352–83.

———. "El Concilio nacional de Burgos en 1080: Nuevas Ilustraciones." *BRAH* 49 (1906): 339–84.

———. "El Concilio nacional de Palencia en el año 1100 y el de Gerona en 1101." *BRAH* 24 (1894): 215–35.

———. "Concilios nacionales de Salamanca en 1154 y Valladolid en 1155." *BRAH* 24 (1894): 467–75.

———. "Cortes y usages de Barcelona en 1064: Textos inéditos." *BRAH* 17 (1890): 385–428.

Estudios históricos. 8 vols. Madrid: Fortanet, 1884.

———. "Noticias." *BRAH* 11 (1887): 456.

———. "Primera legación del Cardenal Jacinto en España: Bulas inéditas de Anastasio IV. Nuevas luces sobre el Concilio nacional de Valladolid (1155) y otros datos inéditos." *BRAH* 14 (1889): 530–55.

———. "Santuario de Atocha (Madrid): Bulas inéditas del siglo XII." *Estudios históricos* 4 (1885): 1–18.

———. "La sínagoga de Córdoba." *BRAH* 5 (1884): 361–99.

———. "Tres bulas inéditas de Alejandro III." *BRAH* 12 (1888): 167–68.

Fletcher, Richard. *Moorish Spain.* Berkeley: University of California Press, 1992.

———. *The Quest for El Cid.* New York: Alfred Knopf, 1990.

———. "Reconquest and Crusade in Spain, c. 1050–1150." *Transactions of the Royal Historical Society* 5th ser. 37 (1987): 31–48.

———. *Saint James' Catapult. The Life and Times of Diego Gelmírez of Santiago de Compostela.* Oxford: Clarendon Press, 1984.

Flórez, Enrique, et al. eds. *España Sagrada.* 52 vols. Madrid: Antonio Marín et al., 1754–1918.

Flori, Jean. *La Guerre sainte: La formation de l'idée de Croisade dans l'Occident chrétien.* Paris: Presses Universitaires de France, 2001.

————. "Reforme, *reconquista,* croisade (L'idée de reconquête dans la correspondance pontificale d'Alexandre II à Urbain II). In *Croisade et Chevalerie (XIe-XIIe siécles).* Paris: De Boeck & Larcier, 1998. 51–80.

Forey, Alan J. "The Emergence of the Military Order in the Twefth Century." *Journal of Ecclesiastical History* 36 (1985): 175–95.

————. "The Military Orders and the Spanish Reconquest in the Twelfth and Thirteenth Centuries." *Traditio* 40 (1984): 197–234.

The Military Orders from the Twelfth to the Early Fourteenth Centuries. Toronto: University of Toronto Press, 1992.

————. "The Order of Mountjoy" *Speculum* 46 (1971): 250–66.

————. *The Templars in the Corona de Aragón.* London: Oxford University Press, 1973.

————. "The Will of Alfonso I of Aragón and Navarre." *Durham University Journal* 73 (1980): 59–65.

Freedman, Paul H. "Archbishop Berenguer Seniofred de Lluça and the Gregorian Reform in Catalonia." In *Church, Law and Society* No. III.

————. *Church, Law and Society in Catalonia 900–1500.* Aldershot: Ashgate/ Variorum, 1994.

————. *The Diocese of Vic: Tradition and Regeneration in Medieval Catalonia.* New Brunswick, N.J.: Rutgers University Press, 1983.

————. "Two Letters of Pope Honorius III on the Collection of Ecclesiastical Revenues in Spain." In *Church, Law and Society* No. VI.

Fuentes Ganzo, Eduardo. *Las Cortes de Benavente (El Siglo de Oro de una Ciudad leonesa). Benavente: 1164–1230.* Benavente: Fomento Esla, 1996.

Gaibrois de Ballesteros, Mercedes. *Historia del Reinado de Sancho IV de Castilla.* 3 vols. Madrid: Revista de Archivos, Bibliotecas, y Museos, 1922.

Gambra, Andrés. *Alfonso VI. Cancillería, Curia e Impero.* 2 vols. León: Centro de Estudios e Investigación "San Isidoro," 1997.

Garate Córdoba, José María. *Espiritu y Milicia en la España medieval.* Madrid: Publicaciones Españolas, 1967.

García de Cortázar, José Ángel. *El dominio del monasterio de San Millán de la Cogolla. Siglos X–XV: Introducción a la historia rural de la Castilla altomedieval.* Salamanca: Universidad de Salamanca, 1969.

————. *Organización social del espacio en la España medieval. La Corona de Castilla en los Siglos VIII a XV.* Madrid: Ariel, 1985.

García Cuadrado, Amparo. *Las Cantigas: El Códice de Florencia.* Murcia: Universidad de Murcia, 1993.

García Gallo, Alfonso. *Manual de historia del derecho español.* 2 vols. Madrid: Agesa, 1967.

García Guijarro, Luis. *Papado, cruzadas, órdenes militares, siglos XI–XIII.* Madrid: Cátedra, 1995.

García Fitz, Francisco. "La batalla en su contexto estratégico. A propósito de Alarcos." In Izquierdo Benito and Ruiz Gómez. *Alarcos.* 265–82.

————. *Castilla y León frente al Islam: Estrategías de expansión y tácticas militares (Siglos XI–XIII).* Seville: Universidad de Sevilla, 1998.

————. "El cerco de Sevilla: Reflexiones sobre la guerra de asedio en la edad media." In González Jiménez. *Sevilla.* 115–54.

García Larragueta, Santos. *El Gran priorado de Navarra de la Orden de San Juan de Jerusalén.* Pamplona: CSIC, 1957.

———. "La Orden de San Juan en la crísis del imperio hispánico en el siglo XII." *Hispania* 12 (1952): 483–524.

García y García, Antonio. "Innocent III and the Kingdom of Castile." In Moore, *Pope Innocent III.* 337–50.

Gaudefroy-Demomboynes, Maurice. *Muslim Institutions.* London: Allen and Unwin, 1950.

Gazulla, Faustino. "La Orden del Santo Redentor." *Boletín de la Sociedad castellonense de Cultura* 9 (1928): 90–107, 157–60, 204, 212, 370–75; 10 (1929): 38–41, 98–101, 124–26.

Gilchrist, John. "The Papacy and the War Against the 'Saracens,' 795–1216." *International History Review* 10 (1988): 174–97.

Giménez Soler, Andrés. "Caballeros españoles en Africa y Africanos en España." *Revue hispanique* 12 (1905): 299–372.

Gómez Pérez, José. "La más antigua traducción de las Crónicas del Toledano." *Hispania* 22 (1962): 357–71.

Goñi Gaztambide, José. *Historia de la bula de la cruzada en España.* Vitoria: Editorial del Seminario, 1958.

Gonzaga de Azevedo, Luiz. *História de Portugal.* 6 vols. Lisbon: Biblion, 1940–42.

González, Julio. *Alfonso IX.* 2 vols. Madrid: CSIC, 1944.

———. *Regesta de Fernando II.* Madrid: CSIC, 1943.

———. *Repoblación de Castilla la nueva.* 2 vols. Madrid: Universidad Complutense, 1975.

———. *Reinado y Diplomas de Fernando III.* 3 vols. Córdoba: Monte de Piedad y Caja de Ahorros, 1980–86.

———. *El reino de Castilla en la época de Alfonso VIII.* 3 vols. Madrid: CSIC, 1960.

González Jiménez, Manuel. *En torno a los orígenes de Andalucía. La repoblación del siglo XIII.* 2nd ed. Seville: Universidad de Sevilla, 1988.

———. "¿Re-conquista? Un estado de la cuestión." In Eloy Benito Ruano. *Tópicos y realidades de la Edad Media.* Madrid: Real Academia dẽ la Historia, 2000. 155–78.

———. *La Repoblación de la Zona de Sevilla durante el Siglo XIV.* 2nd ed. Seville: Universidad de Sevilla, 1993.

———, ed. *Sevilla 1248. Congreso internacional conmemorativo del 750 Aniversario de la Conquista de la Ciudad de Sevilla por Fernando III, rey de Castilla y León.* Madrid: Fundación Ramón Areces, 2000.

González Mínguez, César. *Fernando IV de Castilla (1295–1312): La Guerra civil y el Predominio de la Nobleza.* Valladolid: Universidad de Valladolid, 1974.

Gorosterratzu, Javier. *Don Rodrigo Jiménez de Rada, Gran Estadista, Escritor y Prelado.* Pamplona: Viuda de T. Bescansa, 1925.

Grandá Gallego, Cristina. "Otra imagen del guerrero cristiano (su valoración positiva en testimonios del Islam)." *En la España medieval* 5, 1 (1986): 471–80.

Grassotti, Hilda. "Alfonso IX y el origen de los empréstitos." *CHE* 69 (1987): 217–24.

———. "El deber y el derecho de hacer guerra y paz en León y Castilla." *Estudios.* 43–132.

————. "Don Rodrigo Jiménez de Rada, gran señor y hombre de negocios en la Castilla del siglo XIII." *CHE* 55–56 (1972): 90–113.

————. *Estudios medievales españolas.* Madrid: Fundación Universitaria Española, 1981.

————. *Las instituciones feudo-vasalláticas en León y Castilla.* 2 vols. Spoleto: Centro Italiano di Studi sull'alto Medioevo, 1969.

————. "La ira regia en León y Castilla." *Miscelánea.* 1–132.

————. *Miscelánea de estudios sobre instituciones castellano-leonesas.* Bilbao: Editorial Nájera, 1978.

————. "Para la historia del botín y de las parias." *Miscelánea.* 135–225.

————. "Sobre la retenencia de los castillos en la Castilla medieval." *Estudios* 261–81.

————. "Un empréstito para la conquista de Sevilla. Problemas históricos que suscita." *Miscelánea.* 225–73.

Gual Camarena, Miguel. "Precedentes de la Reconquista valenciana." *Estudios medievales* 1 (1952):167–246.

Gutton, Francis. *L'Ordre de Calatrava.* Paris: P. Lethielleux, 1955.

Handler, Andrew. *The Zirids of Granada.* Coral Gables, Fla.: University of Miami Press, 1994.

Hartigan, R. "Saint Augustine on War and Killing." *Journal of the History of Ideas* 27 (1966): 195–204.

Harvey, L. P. *Islamic Spain, 1250 to 1500.* Chicago: University of Chicago Press, 1990.

Herculano, Alexandre. *História de Portugal desde o começo da monarquia até o fim do reinado de D. Afonso III.* 9th ed. 8 vols. Lisbon: Bertrand, n.d.

Hillgarth, Jocelyn. *The Spanish Kingdoms, 1250–1516.* 2 vols. Oxford: Clarendon Press, 1976–78.

————. *The Problem of a Catalan Mediterranean Empire, 1229–1327.* English Historical Review Supplement 8. London: Longman, 1975.

Homenaje a Jaime Vicens Vives. 2 vols. Barcelona: Universidad de Barcelona, 1965–67.

Housley, Norman. *The Later Crusades: From Lyons to Alcazar 1274–1580.* Oxford: Oxford University Press, 1992.

Huici Miranda, Ambrosio. *Las grandes batallas de la reconquista durante las invasiones africanas (Almorávides, Almohades y Benimerines).* Madrid: CSIC, 1956.

————. *Historia política del imperio almohade.* 2 vols. Tetuán: Editora Marroqui, 1956.

Izquierdo Benito, Ricardo, and Francisco Ruiz Gómez, eds. *Alarcos 1195. Actas del Congreso internacional conmemorativo del VIII Centenario de la Batalla de Alarcos.* Cuenca: Universidad de Castilla-La Mancha, 1996.

Jaime I y su época: X Congreso de Historia de la Corona de Aragón. Zaragoza: CSIC, 1979–80.

Jaspert, Nikolas. "*Capta est Dertosa, clavis christianorum:* Tortosa and the Crusades." In Phillips and Hoch, *The Second Crusade.* 90–110.

Javierre Mur, Aurea. *La Orden de Calatrava en Portugal.* Madrid: Editorial Maestre, 1952.

Johnson, James Turner. *The Holy War Idea in Western and Islamic Traditions.* University Park: Pennsylvania State University Press, 1997.

Kagay, Donald J. "Army Mobilization, Royal Administration, and the Realm in the

Thirteenth-Century Crown of Aragon." In Chevedden, Kagay, and Padilla, *Iberia*. 95–115.

———. "Structures of Baronial Dissent and Revolt under James I (1213–1276)." *Mediaevistik* 1 (1988): 61–85.

Kagay, Donald J., and Theresa M. Vann, eds. *On the Social Origins of Medieval Institutions: Esssays in Honor of Joseph F. O'Callaghan*. Leiden: E.J. Brill, 1998.

Kedar, Benjamin. *Crusade and Mission: European Approaches Toward the Muslims*. Princeton, N.J.: Princeton University Press, 1984.

Kehr, Paul F. "Cómo y cuándo se hizo Aragón feudatario de la Santa Sede." *EEMCA* 1 (1945): 285–326.

———. "El Papado y los reinos de Navarra y Arag;on hasta medios del siglo XII." *EEMCA* 2 (1946): 74–186.

———. *Das Papsttum und der katalanische Prinzipat bis zur Vereinigung mit Aragon*. Berlin: Preussische Akademie der Wissenschaften, 1926.

———. *Das Papsttum und die Königreiche Navarra und Aragon bis zur Mitte des XII. Jahrhunderts*. Berlin: Akademie der Wissenschaften, 1928.

Keller, John E., and Annette Grant Cash. *Daily Life Depicted in the Cantigas de Santa Maria*. Lexington: University of Kentucky Press, 1998.

Keller, John E., and Richard P. Kinkade. *Iconography in Medieval Spanish Literature*. Lexington: University of Kentucky Press, 1984.

Kennedy, Hugh. *Muslim Spain and Portugal: A Political History of Al-Andalus*. London: Longman, 1996.

Klauser, Theodor. *A Short History of the Western Liturgy: An Account and Some Reflections*. 2nd ed. Oxford: Oxford University Press, 1979.

Kritzeck, James. *Peter the Venerable and Islam*. Princeton, N.J.: Princeton University Press, 1964.

Lacarra, José María. *Alfonso el Batallador*. Zaragoza: Guara, 1978.

———. "Aspectos económicos de la sumisión de los reinos de taifas (1010–1102)." *Homenaje a Jaime Vicens Vives*. 1: 254–77.

———. *Colonización, parias, repoblación y otros estudios*. Zaragoza: Anubar 1981.

———. "La conquista de Zaragoza por Alfonso I, 18 diciembre 1118." *Al-Andalus* 12 (1947): 65–96.

———. "Dos tratados de paz y alianza entre Sancho el de Peñalén y Moctadir de Zaragoza (1069 y 1073)." *Homenaje a Johannes Vincke*. 2 vols. Madrid: CSIC, 1962–63. 1: 122–34.

———. "La Iglesia de Tudela entre Tarazona y Pamplona (1119–1143)." *EEMCA* 5 (1952): 417–34.

———, ed. *La Reconquista española y la repoblación del país*. Zaragoza: CSIC, 1951.

Ladero Quesada, Miguel Ángel. *Castilla y la conquista del Reino de Granada*. Granada: Diputación Provincial de Granada, 1987.

———. *La España de los Reyes Católicos*. Madrid: Alianza, 1999.

Lapiedra Gutiérrez, Eva. *Cómo los musulmanes llamaban a los cristianos hispánicos*. Alicante: Instituto de Cultura Juan Gil Albert, 1997.

Le Tourneau, Roger. *The Almohad Movement in North Africa in the Twelfth and Thirteenth Centuries*. Princeton, N.J.: Princeton University Press, 1969.

Ledesma Rubio, María Luisa. *Las Ordenes militares en Aragón.* Zaragoza: Caja de Ahorros de la Inmaculada, 1994.

———. *Templarios y Hospitalarios en el Reino de Aragón (Siglos XII–XIV).* Zaragoza: Fernández-Gatell, 1984.

Lévi-Provençal, Évariste. *Histoire de l'Espagne musulmane.* 3 vols. Leiden: E.J. Brill, 1950.

Linehan, Peter. "Documento español sobre la Quinta Cruzada." *Hispania Sacra* 20 (1967): 177–82.

———. *History and the Historians of Medieval Spain.* Oxford: Clarendon Press, 1993.

———. "Religion, Nationalism and National Identity in Medieval Spain and Portugal." *Studies in Church History* 18 (1982): 161–99.

———. *The Spanish Church and the Papacy in the Thirteenth Century.* Cambridge: Cambridge University Press, 1971.

———. *Spanish Church and Society, 1150–1300.* London: Variorum, 1983.

———. "The Synod of Segovia (1166)." *Bulletin of Medieval Canon Law* 10 (1980): 31–44.

Livermore, Harold. "The 'Conquest of Lisbon' and its Author." *Portuguese Studies* 6 (1990): 1–16.

Lomax, Derek W. *La Orden de Santiago (1170–1275).* Madrid: CSIC, 1965.

———. "The Order of Santiago and the Kings of León." *Hispania* 18 (1958): 3–37.

———. *The Reconquest of Spain.* London: Longman, 1978.

Lopes, David. "O Cid Portugues: Giraldo sem pavor." *Revista de Historia portuguesa* 1 (1941): 93–110.

López Elum, Pedro. *La conquista y repoblación valenciana durante el reinado de Jaime I.* Valencia: Pedro López Elum, 1995.

López Ferreiro, Antonio. *Historia de la santa a.m. iglesia de Santiago de Compostela.* 11 vols. Santiago: Imprenta del Seminario conciliar y central, 1898–1909.

Lourie, Elena. "The Confraternity of Belchite, the Ribāṭ, and the Temple." *Crusade and Colonisation* No. II.

———. *Crusade and Colonisation: Muslims, Christians and Jews in Medieval Aragon.* London: Variorum, 1990.

———. "A Society Organized for War: Medieval Spain." *Past and Present* 35 (1966): 54–76.

———. "The Will of Alfonso I, el Batallador, King of Aragon and Navarre: A Reassessment." *Crusade and Colonisation.* No. III.

———. "The Will of Alfonso I of Aragon and Navarre: A Reply to Dr. Forey." *Crusade and Colonisation.* No. IV.

Macdonald, D. B. "Djihad." *Encyclopedia of Islam* 1 (1934): 1041–42. Reprint "Djihad." *Shorter Encyclopedia of Islam,* ed. H. A. R. Gibb and J. H. Kramers. Ithaca, N.Y.: Cornell University Press, 1974. 89.

Macdonald, I. I. *Don Fernando de Antequera.* Oxford: Dolphin, 1948.

MacKay, Angus. *Spain in the Middle Ages: From Frontier to Empire, 1000–1500.* New York: St. Martin's Press. 1977.

Madelung, W. "Jihād." *Dictionary of the Middle Ages* 7 (1986): 110–11.

Maier, Christoph T. *Crusade Propaganda and Ideology: Model Sermons for the Preaching of the Cross.* Cambridge: Cambridge University Press, 2000.

————. "Mass, the Eucharist and the Cross: Innocent III and the Relocation of the Crusade." In Moore. *Pope Innocent III.* 352–54.

————. *Preaching the Crusades: The Mendicant Friars and the Cross in the Thirteenth Century.* Cambridge: Cambridge University Press, 1994.

Mansilla Reoyo, Demetrio. *Iglesia castellano-leonesa y curia romana en los tiempos del rey San Fernando.* Madrid: CSIC, 1945.

Manzano Rodríguez, Miguel Ángel. *La intervención de los benimerines en la peninsula ibérica.* Madrid: CSIC, 1992.

Marçais, Georges. "Ribāṭ." *Encyclopedia of Islam* 3 (1936): 1150–53. Reprint "Ribāṭ." *Shorter Encyclopedia of Islam.* 473–5.

Markowski, Michael. "*Crucesignatus*: Its Origins and Early Usage." *Journal of Medieval History* 10 (1984): 157–65.

Markus, Robert A. "Saint Augustine's Views on the Just War." *Studies in Church History* 20 (1983): 1–13.

Martín, José Luis. *Los orígenes de la Orden Militar de Santiago (1170–1195).* Barcelona: CSIC, 1974.

————. "Orígenes de las Ordenes Militares Hispánicas: La Orden de Santiago." In Izquierdo Benito and Ruiz Gómez, *Alarcos.* 31–46.

Martínez Marina, Francisco. *Teoría de las Cortes. BAE* 219–20.

Mattoso, José, and Armindo de Sousa. *A Monarquia feudal (1096–1480).* In José Mattoso, ed., *História de Portugal.* 8 vols. Lisbon: Editorial Estampa, 1997–99. vol. 2.

Mayer, Hans Eberhard. *The Crusades.* Tr. John Gillingham. New York: Oxford University Press, 1972.

Maravall, José Antonio. *El concepto de España en la edad media.* 2nd ed. Madrid: Instituto de Estudios Políticos, 1964.

McCormick, Michael. *Eternal Victory: Triumphal Rulership in Late Antiquity, Byzantium and the Early Medieval West.* Cambridge: Cambridge University Press, 1986.

McCrank, Lawrence J. "The Foundation of the Confraternity of Tarragona by Archbishop Oleguer Bonestruga, 1126–1129." In *Medieval Frontier History.* No. III.

————. *Medieval Frontier History in New Catalonia.* Aldershot: Variorum, 1996.

————. "Norman Crusaders in the Catalan Reconquest: Robert Burdet and the Principality of Tarragona, 1129–55." In *Medieval Frontier History* No. IV.

————. "La restauración y la reconquista abortiva de Tarragona, 1076–1108." *CHE* 61–62 (1979): 145–245.

————. "Restoration and Reconquest in Medieval Catalonia: The Church and Principality of Tarragona, 971–1177." PhD dissertation, University of Virginia, 1974.

Melechen, Nina. *The Jews of Medieval Toledo: Their Economic and Social Contacts with Christians from 1150 to 1391.* PhD dissertation, Fordham University, 1999.

Memorias para la vida del santo Rey Don Fernando III. Ed. Miguel de Manuel Rodríguez. Madrid, 1800. Reprint Barcelona: El Albir, 1974.

Menéndez Pidal, Ramón. *La España del Cid.* 4th ed. 2 vols. Madrid: Espasa-Calpe, 1947.

————. *The Spaniards in Their History.* Tr. Walter Starkie. New York: W.W. Norton, 1950.

Meyer, Bruno. "El papel de los cruzados alemanes en la reconquista de la Península Ibérica en los siglos XII y XIII." *En la España Medieval* 23 (2000): 48–56.

Milá y Fontanals, M. *De los trovadores de España: Estudio de lengua y poesía provenzal.* Barcelona: Joaquín Verdaguer, 1861.

Mingüella, Toribio. *Historia de la diócesis de Sigüenza y de sus obispos.* 3 vols. Madrid: Revista de Archivos, Bibliotecas y Museos, 1900–13.

Molero García, Jesús Manuel. "Participación de la Orden del Hospital en el avance de la frontera castellana." In Izquierdo and Ruiz Gómez, *Alarcos.* 331–52.

Mondéjar, Marqués de. *Memorias históricas de la vida y acciones del rey D. Alonso el Noble, octavo del nombre.* Madrid: Antonio de Sancha, 1783.

Montenegro y Arcadio del Castillo, Isabel. "Don Pelayo y los orígenes de la reconquista." *Hispania* 180 (1992): 5–32.

Moore, John C., ed. *Pope Innocent III and His World.* Aldershot: Ashgate, 1999.

Muñoz de San Pedro, Miguel. "La desaparecida Orden de caballeros de Monfragüe." *Hidalguía* 1 (1953): 68–76.

Murphy, Thomas P., ed. *The Holy War.* Columbus: Ohio State University Press, 1976.

Musto, Ron. *The Catholic Peace Tradition.* Maryknoll, N.Y.: Orbis, 1986.

Nelson, Lynn. "Rotrou of Perche and the Aragonese Reconquest." *Traditio* 26 (1970): 113–33.

Nieto Soria, José. *Sancho IV, 1284–1295.* Palencia: La Olmeda, 1994.

Nykl, A. R. *Hispano-Arabic Poetrty and its Relations with the Old Provençal Troubadours.* Baltimore, 1946. Reprint. New York: The Hispanic Society, 1970.

O'Callaghan, Joseph F. "The Affiliation of the Order of Calatrava with the Order of Cîteaux." In *The Spanish Military Order of Calatrava* No. I.

———. *Alfonso X and the Cantigas de Santa Maria: A Poetic Biography.* Leiden: E. J. Brill, 1998.

———. *Alfonso X, the Cortes and Government in Medieval Spain.* Aldershot: Ashgate/Variorum, 1998.

———. "Castile, Portugal, and the Canary Islands: Claims and Counterclaims, 1344–1479." *Viator* 24 (1993): 287–309.

———. *The Cortes of Castile-León, 1188–1350.* Philadelphia: University of Pennsylvania Press, 1989.

———. "La financiación de la Conquista de Sevilla." In González Jiménez, *Sevilla.* 191–206.

———. "The Foundation of the Order of Alcántara, 1176–1218." In *The Spanish Military Order of Calatrava* No. IV.

———. "*Hermandades* Between the Military Orders of Calatrava and Santiago During the Castilian Reconquest, 1158–1252." In *The Spanish Military Order of Calatrava* No. V.

———. *A History of Medieval Spain.* Ithaca, N.Y.: Cornell University Press, 1975.

———. "Innocent III and the Kingdoms of Castile and León." In Moore. *Pope Innocent III.* 317–35.

———. "The Integration of Christian Spain into Europe: The Role of Alfonso VI of León-Castile." In Reilly, *Santiago.* 101–20.

———. *The Learned King: The Reign of Alfonso X of Castile.* Philadelphia: University of Pennsylvania Press, 1993.

———. "The Mudejars of Castile and Portugal in the Twelfth and Thirteenth Centuries." In Powell, *Muslims Under Latin Rule*. 46–53.

———. "The Order of Calatrava: Years of Crisis and Survival, 1158–1212." In Vladimir P. Goss and Christine Verzár Bornstein, eds., *The Meeting of Two Worlds: Cultural Exchange Between East and West During the Period of the Crusades*. Kalamazoo: Western Michigan University Press, 1986. 419–30.

———. "Sobre los orígenes de Calatrava la nueva." *The Spanish Military Order of Calatrava* No. III.

———. *The Spanish Military Order of Calatrava and Its Affiliates*. London: Variorum 1975.

———. "Una nota sobre las llamadas Cortes de Benavente." In *Alfonso X, the Cortes and Government*. No. X.

———. "La vida de las Ordenes Militares de España según sus estatutos primitivos." In Izquierdo Benito and Ruiz Gómez, *Alarcos*. 7–30.

Oliveira, Miguel de. "A Milicia de Évora e a Ordem de Calatrava." *Lusitania Sacra* 1 (1956): 51–67.

Oliver Asín, Jaime. "Origen árabe de 'rebato,' 'arrobda,' y sus homónimos." *Boletín de la Real Academia Española* 15 (1928): 347–95, 496–542.

Ortiz de Zúñiga, Diego. *Anales eclesiásticos y seculares la muy noble y muy leal ciudad de Sevilla, metropolí de Andalucía*. Ed. Antonio María Espinosa y Carzel. 2 vols. Madrid: Imprenta Real, 1795. Reprint Sevilla: Guadalquivir, 1988.

Painter, Sidney. "The Crusade of Theobald of Champagne and Richard of Cornwall, 1239–1241." In Setton, *Crusades*. 2: 463–86.

Partner, Peter. *God of Battles: Holy Wars of Christianity and Islam*. Princeton, N.J.: Princeton University Press, 1997.

Pennington, Kenneth. "The Rite for Taking the Cross in the Twelfth Century." *Traditio* 30 (1974): 429–35.

Pérez Embid, Florentino. "La marina real castellana en el siglo XIII." *AEM* 6 (1969): 158–65.

Phillips, Jonathan. "Ideas of Crusade and Holy War in *De Expugnatione Lyxbonensi* (*The Conquest of Lisbon*)." In Robert Swanson, ed., *Holy Land, Holy Lands, and Christian History. Studies in Church History* 36 (2000): 123–41.

———. "St. Bernard of Clairvaux, the Low Countries and the Lisbon Letter of the Second Crusade." *Journal of Ecclesiastical History* 48 (1997): 485–97.

Phillips, Jonathan, and Martin Hoch, eds. *The Second Crusade: Scope and Consequences*. Manchester: Manchester University Press, 2001.

Post, Gaines. *Studies in Medieval Legal Thought: Public Law and the State, 1100–1322*. Princeton, N.J.: Princeton University Press, 1964.

Powell, James M. *The Anatomy of a Crusade, 1213–1221*. Philadelphia: University of Pennsylvania Press, 1986.

———, ed. *Muslims Under Latin Rule, 1100–1300*. Princeton, N.J.: Princeton University Press, 1990.

Powers, James F. "The Creative Interaction Between Portuguese and Leonese Municipal Military Law, 1055 to 1279." *Speculum* 62 (1987): 53–80.

———. "The Early Reconquest Episcopate of Cuenca, 1177–1284." *CHR* 87 (2001): 1–15.

———. "Frontier Competition and Legal Creativity: A Castilian-Aragonese Case Study Based on Twelfth-Century Municipal Military Law." *Speculum* 52 (1977): 465–87.

———. "Frontier Military Service and Exemption in the Municipalities of Aragon and Castile." *Military Affairs* 45 (1981): 75–78.

———. "The Municipal Militias in the Reconquest of Seville." In González Jiménez. *Sevilla.* 155–66.

———. "The Origins and Development of Municipal Military Service in the Leonese and Castilian Reconquest, 800–1250." *Traditio* 26 (1970): 91–111.

———. *A Society Organized for War: The Iberian Municipal Militias in the Central Middle Ages, 1000–1284.* Berkeley: University of California Press, 1988.

———. "Townsmen and Soldiers: The Interaction of Urban and Military Organization in the Militias of Mediaeval Castile." *Speculum* 46 (1971): 641–55.

———. "Two Warrior Kings and Their Municipal Militias: The Townsman-Soldier in Law and Life." In Burns, *Worlds.* 95–129.

Procter, Evelyn. *Curia and Cortes in León and Castille, 1072–1295.* Cambridge: Cambridge University Press, 1980.

Rades y Andrada, Francisco. *Chronica de las tres Ordenes y Cavallerías de Sanctiago, Calatrava y Alcántara.* Toledo: Juan de Ayala, 1572.

Rassow, Peter. "La cofradía de Belchite." *AHDE* 3 (1926): 200–226.

Raynaldus, Odoricus. *Annales ecclesiastici ab anno MCXCVIII ubi desinit Cardinalis Baronius.* Ed. J. D. Mansi. 15 vols. Lucca: Leonardo Venturini, 1738–47.

Reilly, Bernard F. *The Contest of Christian and Muslim Spain, 1031–1157.* Cambridge: Blackwell, 1992.

———. *The Kingdom of León-Castilla Under King Alfonso VI, 1065–1109.* Princeton, N.J.: Princeton University Press, 1988.

———. *The Kingdom of León-Castilla Under King Alfonso VII, 1126–1157.* Philadelphia: University of Pennsylvania Press, 1998.

———. *The Kingdom of León-Castile Under Queen Urraca, 1109–1126.* Princeton, N.J.: Princeton Univesity Press, 1982.

———. *The Medieval Spains.* Cambridge: Cambridge University Press, 1993.

———, ed. *Santiago, Saint-Denis, and Saint Peter: The Reception of the Roman Liturgy in León-Castile in 1080.* New York: Fordham University Press, 1985.

El Reino de León en la Alta Edad Media. Vol. 1. *Cortes, Concilios y Fueros.* León: Centro de Estudios e Investigación "San Isidoro", 1988.

Riches, Samantha. *St. George, Hero, Martyr, and Myth.* Stroud: Sutton, 2000.

Riley-Smith. Jonathan. *The Crusades: A Short History.* New Haven, Conn: Yale University Press, 1987.

———. *The First Crusade and the Idea of Crusading.* Philadelphia: University of Pennsylvania Press, 1986.

———. *What Were the Crusades?* London: Macmillan, 1977.

Rivera Garretas, Milagros. "La Orden de Santiago en Castilla la Nueva en los siglos XII y XIII." *Las Ordenes Militares en el Mediterráneo occidental. Siglos XIII–XVIII.* Madrid: Casa de Velázquez/Instituto de Estudios Manchegos, 1989. 23–40.

Rivera Recio, Juan Francisco. *El adelantamiento de Cazorla.* Toledo: Editorial Católica Toledana, 1948.

———. *La Iglesia de Toledo en el siglo XII (1086–1208).* 2 vols. Rome: Instituto Español de Historia Ecclesiástica, 1966–76.

Robinson, I. S. "Gregory VII and the Soldiers of Christ." *History* 58 (1973): 169–92.

Rodríguez López, Ana. *La consolidación territorial de la monarquía feudal castellana. Expansión y fronteras durante el reinado de Fernando III.* Madrid: CSIC, 1995.

———. "La política eclesiástica de la monarquía castellano-leonesa durante el reinado de Fernando III (1217–1252)." *Hispania* 48 (1988): 7–48.

Rogers, Donna. "Christians and Moors in *Ay Jherusalem!*" In Barbara N. Sargent-Baur, ed., *Journeys Toward God: Pilgrimage and Crusade.* Kalamazoo: Western Michigan University Press, 1992. 127–34.

Rogers, Randall. *Latin Siege Warfare in the Twelfth Century.* Oxford: Clarendon Press, 1997.

Rousset, Paul. *Histoire des croisades.* Paris: Payot, 1957.

Ruiz Gómez, Francisco. "La guerra y los pactos. A propósito de la batalla de Alarcos." In Izquierdo Benito and Ruiz Gómez, *Alarcos.* 145–68.

Rumeu de Armas, Antonio. *España en el Africa atlántica.* 2 vols. Madrid: CSIC, 1956–57.

Runciman, Steven. *A History of the Crusades.* 3 vols. Cambridge: Cambridge University Press, 1953.

Russell, Frederick. *The Just War in the Middle Ages.* Cambridge:Cambridge University Press, 1975.

Safran, Janina M. "Identity and Differentiation in Ninth-Century al-Andalus." *Speculum* 76 (2001): 573–98.

Sáinz de la Maza Lasoli, Regina. *La Orden de San Jorge de Alfama. Aproximación a su historia.* Barcelona: CSIC, 1990.

Sánchez Albornoz, Claudio. *La curia regia portuguesa: Siglos XII y XIII.* Madrid: Junta para Ampliación de Estudios e Investigaciones científicas, 1920.

———. *España, un enigma histórico.* 2nd ed. 2 vols. Buenos Aires: Editorial Sudamericana, 1962.

———. *Estudios sobre las instituciones medievales españolas.* México City: Universidad Autónoma de México, 1965.

———. "The Frontier and Castilian Liberties" In A. R. Lewis and T. F. McGann, eds., *The New World Looks at Its History.* Austin: University of Texas Press, 1965. 26–46.

———. "Notas para el estudio del *Petitum.*" *Estudios.* 483–614.

———. "La potestad real y los señoríos en Asturias, León y Castilla." *Estudios.* 791–822.

Sánchez Candeira, Alfonso. "Las cruzadas en la historiografía española de la época." *Hispania* 20 (1960): 325–67.

Santamaría, Álvaro. "La expansión politico-militar de la Corona de Aragón bajo la dirección de Jaime I: Baleares." In *Jaime I y su época.* 91–146.

Sanz y Díaz, Clementino. *Reseña cronológica de algunos documentos conservados en el archivo de la catedral de Cuenca.* Cuenca: Calasanz, 1965.

Serrano, Luciano. "El canciller de Fernando III de Castilla." *Hispania* 1 (1941): 3–40.

———. *El obispado de Burgos y Castilla primitiva desde el Siglo V al XIII.* 3 vols. Madrid: E. Maestre, 1935.

Setton, Kenneth M., ed. *A History of the Crusades.* 5 vols. Philadelphia and Madison: University of Pennsylvania Press and University of Wisconsin Press, 1955–85.

Shideler, John. *A Medieval Catalan Noble Family: The Montcadas, 1000–1230.* Berkeley: University of California Press, 1984.

Silva Tarouca, Carlos da. "As origens da Ordem dos cavaleiros de Évora e Avis, segundo as cartas do Arquivo do Cabildo da Se de Évora." *Boletin da Cidade de Évora* 5 (1947): 25–39.

Simon, Larry, ed. *Iberia and the Mediterranean World of the Middle Ages: Studies in Honor of Robert I. Burns, S.J.* Leiden: E.J. Brill, 1995.

Smith, Damian J. "¿'Soli Hispani'? Innocent III and Las Navas de Tolosa." *Hispania Sacra* 51 (1999): 489–512.

Sobreques i Vidal, Santiago. *Els grans comtes de Barcelona.* Barcelona: Aedos, 1961.

Soldevila, Ferran. *Historia de Catalunya.* 3 vols. Barcelona: Alpha, 1962.

———. *Jaume I. Pere el Gran.* Barcelona: Editorial Teide, 1955.

———. "A propòsit del servei del bovatge." *AEM* 1 (1964): 573–87.

———. *Vida de Jaume I el Conqueridor.* Barcelona: Aedos, 1958.

Stalls, Clay. *Possessing the Land: Aragon's Expansion into Islam's Ebro Frontier under Alfonso the Battler, 1104–1134.* Leiden: E.J. Brill, 1995.

———. "The Relationship Between Conquest and Settlement on the Aragonese Frontier of Alfonso I." In Simon, *Iberia.* 1: 216–31.

Swift, Louis J. *The Early Fathers on War and Military Service.* Wilmington, Del.: Michael Glazier, 1983.

Todesca, James J. "Means of Exchange: Islamic Coinage in Christian Spain, 1000–1200." In Simon, *Iberia.* 1: 232–58.

———. "The Monetary History of Castile-León (ca. 1100–1300) in Light of the Bourgey Hoard." *American Numismatic Society Museum Notes* 33 (1988): 129–203.

———. *What Touches All: Coinage and Monetary Policy in León-Castile to 1230.* PhD dissertation, Fordham University, 1996.

Torres Delgado, Cristóbal. *El antiguo reino nazarí de Granada (1232–1340).* Granada: Anel, 1974.

Tyerman, Christopher. *The Invention of the Crusades.* Toronto: University of Toronto Press, 1998.

Ubieto Arteta, Antonio. "La creación de la cofradía militar de Belchite." *EEMCA* 5 (1952): 427–34.

———. *Orígenes del Reino de Valencia: Cuestiones cronológicos sobre su reconquista.* 2 vols. Valencia: Anubar, 1975.

———. "La participación navarro-aragonesa en la primera cruzada." *Principe de Viana* 8 (1947): 357–83.

———. "La peregrinación de Alfonso II de Aragón a Santiago de Compostela." *EEMCA* 5 (1953): 438–52.

Unger, Richard W. *The Ship in the Medieval Economy, 600–1600.* London: Croom Helm, 1980.

Van Cleve, Thomas C. "The Fifth Crusade." In Setton, *Crusades.* 2: 377–428.

Vázquez de Parga, Luis, J. M. Lacarra, and J. Uría. *Las peregrinaciones a Santiago de Compostela.* 3 vols. Madrid: CSIC, 1948–49.

Velo y Nieto, G. *La Orden de caballeros de Monfrag.* Madrid: Otice, 1950.

Ventura, Jordi. *Alfons el Cast: El primer comte rei.* Barcelona: Aedos, 1961.

———. *Pere el Catòlic I Simó de Montfort.* Barcelona: Aedos, 1960.

Verdon, Jean. "Une source de la reconquête d'Espagne: La Chronique de Saint-Maixent." *Mélanges offerts á René Crozet.* 2 vols. Poitiers: Société d'Études Medievales, 1966. 1: 273–82.

Villanueva, Jaime. *Viage literario a las iglesias de España.* 22 vols. Madrid: Imprenta Real, 1803–52.

Villey, Marcel. *La Croisade: Essai sur la formation d'une théorie juridique.* Paris: J. Vrin, 1942.

Von Grunebaum, Gustave. *Medieval Islam: A Study in Cultural Orientation.* Chicago: University of Chicago Press, 1961.

Wasserstein, David. *The Rise and Fall of the Party Kings: Politics and Society in Islamic Spain, 1003–1086.* Princeton, N.J.: Princeton University Press, 1985.

Watt, W. Montgomery. "Islamic Conceptions of Holy War." In Murphy, *The Holy War.* 141–56.

Williams, John. *Early Spanish Manuscript Illumination.* New York: George Braziller, 1977.

Williams, John Bryan. "The Making of a Crusade: The Genoese Anti-Muslim Attacks in Spain, 1146–1148." *Journal of Medieval History* 23 (1997): 30–53.

Wolf, Kenneth B. *Christian Martyrs in Muslim Spain.* Cambridge: Cambridge University Press, 1988.

———. "Christian Views of Islam in Early Medieval Spain." In John Victor Tolan, ed., *Medieval Christian Perspectives of Islam: A Book of Essays.* New York: Garland, 1995.

———. "The Earliest Latin Lives of Muḥammad." In Michael Gervers and Ramzi Jibran Bikhazi, eds., *Conversion and Community: Indigenous Christian Communities in Islamic Lands, Eighth to Eighteenth Centuries.* Toronto: Pontifical Institute of Mediaeval Studies, 1990. 89–101.

———. "The Earliest Spanish Christian Views of Islam." *Church History* 55 (1986): 281–93.

Zacour, Norman. *Jews and Saracens in the Consilia of Oldradus de Ponte.* Toronto: Pontifical Institute of Mediaeval Studies, 1990.

Zerbi, Paolo. *Papato, Impero e Respublica Christiana dal 1187 al 1198.* Milan: Università Cattolica del Sacro Cuore, 1955.

Zurita, Jerónimo. *Anales de la Corona de Aragón.* Ed. Ángel Canellas López. 9 vols. Zaragoza: CSIC, 1967–85.

Index

ʿAbd Allāh, king of Granada, xiii, 9, 30, 167–68
Abraham: prophet, 15; Jewish lender, 173
Abrantes, 54
Abū ʿAbd Allāh Muḥammad al-Nāṣir, Almohad caliph. *See* al-Nāṣir
Abū Bakr al-Turṭūshī, historian, 141
Abū Hazam, governor of Córdoba, 95
Abū Muḥammad, al-Bayāsī. *See* al-Bayāsī
Abū ʿUmar ibn Shushan, *almojarife*, 171, 173
Abū Yaʿqūb Yūsuf al-Mustanṣir, Almohad caliph. *See* al-Mustanṣir
Abū Yaʿqūb Yūsuf I, Almohad caliph, 55
Abū Yaḥyā, king of Mallorca, 90
Abū Yūsuf Yaʿqūb al-Manṣūr, Almohad caliph. *See* al-Manṣūr
Abū Zakariyāʾ, Ḥafṣid emir of Tunis, 104
Abū Zayd, king of Valencia, 84–85, 90, 93, 99–100, 102, 119, 169
Abulafia, Jewish lender, 173
Abū-l-Hasan ʿAlī al-Saʿid, Almohad caliph. *See* al-Saʿid
Abū-l-Muṭarrif ibn ʿAmira, poet, 104
Abū-l-ʿUlā Idrīs al-Maʿmūn, Almohad caliph, 85, 87, 118, 164, 169
Acre, 80
Adalid, cavalry commander, 133
Ademuz, 66
Adrian IV, pope, 50–51
Afonso, count of Boulogne, 185. *See* Afonso III
Afonso I Henriques of Portugal, 41–44, 47–49, 51–52, 54, 57, 76, 127, 133, 141, 147, 155, 182, 203

Afonso II of Portugal, 79, 156, 171
Afonso III of Portugal, 110–11, 119, 122, 150, 163, 200
Africa, 4, 7, 16, 54, 92, 120, 150, 214–15
Agarenes, 15
Ager, 26
Agnello, bishop of Fez, 118–19
Aimery, viscount of Narbonne, 36
Airald, count of Braine, 59
Aix, 103
Al-Andalus, 8, 9, 12, 30, 37, 71, 76, 81, 84
Alange, battle (1230), 88, 94, 139, 141, 196–97, 202
Alarcón, hospital, 147
Alarcos, battle (1195), 61–63, 141–44, 163, 171, 179–80, 182–83, 200, 202, 207
Alarde, muster, 129
Al-Azraq, crusade, 107–8, 157, 185
Albacor, Muslim rebel, 107
Albarracín, 168
Al-Bayāsī, 84, 87, 169
Alberic of Trois Fontaines, chronicler, 70, 191
Albigensians, 20, 65, 69, 75, 78
Albufeira, 110
Alburquerque, 85, 159
Alcácer do Sal, 35, 47, 59; crusade, 78–80, 97, 126, 135, 138–39, 149, 157, 159, 183, 193, 198
Alcaide, castellan, 125
Alcalá de Chivert, 100
Alcalá de Guadaira, 112
Alcalá de Henares, treaty (1308), 211
Alcalá de los Gazúles, 116
Alcalá del Río, 113
Alcalde, urban magistrate, 129

Alcañiz, 54–55, 100, 106
Alcántara, Order of, 52, 54–55, 75, 82, 96
Alcaraz, 106, 205
Alcira, 106–7
Alcobaça, Abbot Fernando, 79, 159
Alcolea, bridge, 94
Alcoraz, battle (1096), 31, 141, 197
Alcoy, 107
Alentejo, 51, 59, 80, 99, 108, 141
Alexander II, pope, 24–27, 29, 32, 48, 50, 190, 209
Alexander III, pope, 55–57, 76, 156, 182
Alexander IV, pope, 172
Alfajar de Pena, 109
Alfaqueque, ransomer, 148
Alférez, standardbearer, 133
Alfonso, bishop of Cuenca, 85
Alfonso, Infante. *See* Alfonso X
Alfonso I of Aragón, 36–41, 48, 52, 133–34, 140–41, 158, 181, 192, 200
Alfonso II of Aragón, 51, 56, 60–62, 90, 106, 158, 162–63, 168–69, 171
Alfonso II of Asturias, 6, 7
Alfonso III of Asturias, 6, 7, 186
Alfonso VI of León-Castile, 6–7, 23–24, 29, 34–35, 41, 139–42, 147, 152, 162, 166–67, 202, 205
Alfonso VII of León-Castile, 41–42, 44–50, 52, 124–25, 139–40, 153–54, 161, 168, 182, 191, 196, 203–4, 206
Alfonso VIII of Castile, 51, 55–57, 61–63, 66–76, 106, 124, 132, 140–44, 146–47, 152, 154, 158–59, 161, 163–64, 171, 179–80, 182–83, 187, 189, 191, 200, 202, 205, 207
Alfonso IX of León, 57, 60–64, 69, 76, 78, 80–83, 87–89, 93, 97, 109, 124, 139, 141–42, 152, 158, 162–64, 174, 183, 196–97, 202
Alfonso X of Castile-León, 8, 96, 106–7, 111, 113, 122, 126, 129, 150, 161, 169–70, 173–75, 184, 200, 210
Alfonso XI of Castile-León, 4, 7, 17, 211–12
Alfonso Álvarez de Villasandino, poet, 213
Alfonso Téllez de Meneses, 85–86, 96, 159
Alfonso de Cartagena, bishop of Burgos, 4, 210, 213, 215
Alfonso de Molina, Infante, 94, 109, 122, 185
Algarve, 58–59, 80, 93, 99, 108–10
Algeciras, 210–12
Algeria, 7
Al-Hasan, lord of Salé, 119

Al-Himyarī, geographer, xii, 12, 120
Aliaguilla, 85
Alicante, 105–7
Aljarafe of Seville, 112, 114
Aljustrel, 108
Almada, 43
Al-Manṣūr, Almohad caliph, 59, 61, 63, 141–42
Al-Manṣūr, Muslim warrior. *See* Almanzor
Almanzor, 17, 95, 202–3, 207
Al-Maqqarī, historian, xii, 88, 95, 144
Al-Marrākushī, historian, xii
Almazán, 45
Almenar, 118, 168
Almería, 42, 44–45, 48–49, 92, 97, 135, 138, 140, 149, 154, 178, 182, 199, 203, 211
Almizra, treaty (1244), 106
Almocadén, infantry commander, 133
Almogàvers, almogávares, soldiers, 94, 129, 134
Almohads, 1, 41, 47–48, 50–52, 55–57, 59, 61–68, 74, 76, 78–80, 83–87, 89–90, 97, 99, 112, 114, 118, 142–44, 146, 153, 163, 169, 212
Almojarife, tax official, 171, 173
Almoravids, 1, 9, 12, 15, 16, 30–31, 34, 36–37, 41, 130, 132, 139, 141–42, 144, 152, 162, 168, 187, 192, 200, 202–3, 207
Al-Muqtadir, king of Zaragoza, 26, 167
Al-Mustanṣir, Almohad caliph, 78, 83
Al-Mustaʿīn, king of Zaragoza, 31, 168
Al-Muʿtamid, king of Seville, 167–68
Al-Mutawwakil, king of Badajoz, 167
Al-Mutawwakil ibn Hūd, king of Murcia, 106
Al-Nāṣir, Almohad caliph, 66–72, 74–75, 142–43, 178–80
Alphonse Jourdain, count of Toulouse, 35, 41
Alpuente, 168
Al-Qādir, king of Toledo and Valencia, 31, 167–68
Al-Rashīd, Almohad caliph, 118
Al-Rundī, poet, 117
Al-Saʿīd, Almohad caliph, 119–20
Al-Shaqaf, Sevillan leader, 114
Álvar Pérez de Castro, 94, 96
Álvaro Pelayo, bishop of Silves, 4, 7, 210–11
Alvarus of Córdoba, Mozarabic author, 16
Alvor, 58, 110
Amat, archbishop of Bordeaux, 205
Amposta, 52
Anales Toledanos I, 67, 70
Anastasius, monk of Cluny, 10
Anastasius IV, pope, 47–48

Andalucía, 8, 57, 61, 74, 93, 97, 107, 122, 135, 140–42, 160, 204
Andrew of London, crusader, 43
Andújar, 48, 84, 87
Anjou, 69
Antequera, 213
Antioch, battle (1098), 197; patriarch, 101
Aquitaine, 26
Arabs, 1, 30, 72, 166, 202
Aragón, Aragonese, 1, 2, 7, 23–25, 31, 33, 35, 40–41, 50–52, 55–56, 59, 68, 81, 99, 102–3, 105–9, 113, 120, 139, 148–49, 152, 155–57, 163–64, 168–69, 171–72, 179, 187, 197, 199, 210–11, 213
Archers, 129
Arcos, 56, 116
Ares, 100
Arjona, 93–94, 97, 110
Arles, 36, 91, 103
Armies, formation, 125–29
Arms and armor, 139–32
Arnald Amaury, archbishop of Narbonne, 68, 70–72, 75, 183
Arnaldo, bishop of Astorga, 45, 199
Arnaldo, Master, physician, 69
Arnold, count of Aerschot, 43
Aspàreg, archbishop of Tarragona, 90, 157, 159, 177
Asperges me, 203–4
Astorga, 174; bishop, 4, 45, 199
Asturias, Asturias-León, 1–7, 16–17, 185, 194
Atlantic Ocean, 35, 120
Auch, 26, 63, 101, 103
Augustine of Hippo, 13–14
Aurora lucis rutilat, 179
Ávila, 125, 144, 190; friars, 54; *Chronicle*, 194
Avis, Order of, 54, 110
Ay Jherusalem!, 111
Ayamonte, 109–10
Aznalfarache, 113–14

Babylon, 15
Badajoz, 23, 30, 51, 78–79, 85, 87–89, 94, 97, 108, 139, 141, 143, 147, 166
Baeza, 71, 74–75, 84, 94–95, 140, 143, 168, 196; bishop, 206; *pendón*, 191–92, 197, 199
Baghdad, 87, 92, 122
Bairén, 106, 189
Baldwin II, Emperor of Constantinople, 111–12, 128, 154

Balearic Islands, 23, 90, 209; crusade, 35–36
Bankers, Tuscan and Lombard, 172
Banners, religious, 190–93
Barbastro, 24–27, 29, 31, 48, 190
Barbero, Abilio, historian, 17
Barcelona, 24, 31, 79, 91, 119, 148–49, 171; archdeacon, 126; assembly (1131), 38; bishop, 90–91, 180; cathedral, 188; coinage, 163–64; counts, 9, 33, 35, 50, 68, 152, 155; Curia (1064), 26; Curia (1228), 90, 102, 159, 163; murals, 130, 132; sacristan, 126
Barton, Simon, historian, 46
Basel, Council (1435), 210, 213
Basilicas, Roman, 187
Battles, 140–43; triumphal return from, 206–8
Bay of Biscay, 107, 113, 119–20, 150
Bayonne, 119
Béarn, 69. *See* Guillem de Montcada
Beatus of Liébana, 130
Beja, 108
Belchite, *Militia Christi*, 39–40
Benavente, 94; Curia (1202), 164; Curia (1228), 48
Berbers, 1, 68, 72
Berenguela, Infanta, daughter of Alfonso VIII, 63–64, 70, 72, 81, 84
Berenguela, Infanta, sister of Fernando III, 84
Berenguela, wife of Alfonso VII, 139, 207
Berenguer de Palou, bishop of Barcelona, 90–91, 180
Berenguer de Santa Eugènia, crusader, 92
Berenguer Ramon II, count of Barcelona, 166
Berenguer, bishop of Vic, 32
Bernard, abbot of Clairvaux, 42–43, 178, 188, 199
BernardAtó of Carcassonne, 37
Bernard de Sauvetot, archbishop of Toledo, 30–31, 37, 180, 187, 205
Bernat de Santa Eugènia, crusader, 128
Bernat Desclot, chronicler, xii
Bernat, count of Besalú, 33
Béziers, 36
Biar, 56, 106
Bishko, Charles Julian, historian, 18, 166
Bishops: military service, 126–27; property of deceased, 179
Bisson, Thomas, historian, 152, 163
Blanche of Castile, queen of France, 72
Blasco de Alagón, crusader, 99–100
Blessed Bread, 189

Bogarra, 106
Bonnaz, Yves. Historian, 18
Booty, 146–47
Bordeaux, archbishop of, 63, 101, 205
Borja, 37
Borriana, 100, 103, 106, 140, 172, 188
Borriol, 100
Boso, cardinal, papal legate, 35–36
Bovatge, bovaticum, 90, 100, 162–63, 175
Braga, 31, 34, 43, 126, 178
Brittany, 69
Brundage, James A., historian, 20, 25
Bugia, 119
Burgos, 85, 153, 175, 177, 207; Curia (1224), 112, 184
Burgundy, ducal house, 24, 26
Burns, Robert I., historian, 19, 102, 108, 198
Byzantine-Arabic Chronicle of 741, 16
Byzantines, 14

Cabo São Vicente, 58
Cabriel river, 106
Cacela, 109
Cáceres, 55, 75, 82–83, 88, 94; friars, 54
Cádiz, 79. 109, 116, 212
Caesarius of Heisterbach, 69
Caffaro, Genoese historian, 45
Calatayud, 37
Calatrava la vieja, 52–53, 71; Calatrava la nueva, 74, 200
Calatrava, Order of, 52–55, 59–62, 65, 67, 70–71, 74–75, 82, 84–85, 88, 94, 96, 101, 128, 147–48, 178–79, 183, 198
Calixtus II, pope, 38–39, 48–49, 181
Calpe, 56
Cambrai, 69
Cambrils, 91
Canary Islands, 4, 214
Cantabrian mountains, 1
Cantigas de Santa Maria, xii, 149; *Cantiga* 63, 130; *Cantiga* 126, 147; *Cantiga* 165, 132; *Cantiga* 181, 191; *Cantiga* 205, 85–86
Cantillana, 113
Capilla, 87, 140, 205, 207
Captives, 147–49
Cardona, viscount of, 103
Carinthia, 54
Carmona, 112–13, 139, 171
Carrión, Curia (1224), 84, 87, 184
Carroz, Catalan admiral, 150

Cartagena, 107
Castel de Dueñas (Calatrava la nueva), 179
Castel Voltorno, 24
Castelló de la Plana, 100, 106
Castielfabib, 66
Castile, Castile-León, Castilians, 1, 2, 7, 23, 33, 51, 56, 62–64, 81–82, 85, 87, 93–94, 99, 106, 110–13, 120, 122, 129, 140, 149, 152, 158, 160, 163–64, 166, 169–70, 174–75, 184, 187, 191, 194, 199, 202, 209–14
Castles, 124–25
Castro, Américo, literary historian, 11
Castrotoraf, hospital, 147
Castrourdiales, 119
Casualties, 147–48
Catalonia, Catalans, 1, 7, 23, 33, 35–36, 48, 52, 55, 90–92, 100, 102–4, 113, 122, 127, 129, 149–50, 152–53, 162–66, 172, 175, 180, 193, 197–98, 211
Cazola, treaty (1179), 56
Cazorla, 93
Celestine III, pope, 59–63, 83, 118, 163, 182–83. *See also* Hyacinth
Census, papal, 155–56
Centulle of Bigorre, 37
Ceremonial of Cardeña, 186
Cervera, 100
Ceuta, 215
Champagne, 101
Chevedden, Paul, historian, 26, 138
Christian of Gistel, crusader, 43
Chronicle of 754, 5, 16
Chronicle of 1344, 17
Chronicle of Albelda, 4–6, 16
Chronicle of Alfonso III, 4
Chronicle of Alfonso X, 170
Chronicle of Alfonso the Emperor, xii
Chronicle of Ávila, 194
Chronicle of Cardeña, 120
Chronicle of Jaime I, xii
Chronicle of Nájera, 17
Chronicle of San Juan de la Peña, xii
Chronicle of Silos, xii, 4, 6, 17, 24, 194
Churches, consecration of, 204–6
Cid, the, 17, 30–31, 133, 141, 168, 188–89, 202–5, 207
Cintius, Master, papal tax collector, 156
Cîteaux, General Chapter, 54
Ciudad Real, 61, 67, 87
Ciudad Rodrigo, 197

Clavijo, battle (834), 194
Clement III, pope, 57–58, 156, 182
Clement IV, pope, 212
Clermont: Councils (1095), 32–33, 180;
    Council (1130), 38
Cluny, monastery, 24, 166–67
Cogolludo, hospital, 147
Coimbra, 7, 23, 26, 194; Cortes (1261), 165;
    prior of Santa Cruz, 183
Coinage, 152–53
Collins, Roger, historian, 18
Cologne, crusaders, 42
Compostela. *See* Santiago de Compostela
Concordat of 1851, 215
Constantina, 113
Constantine, Roman emperor, 13, 179, 198
Constantinople, 74; Latin Empire of, 107, 112,
    128, 154
Corbins, battle (1124), 38
Córdoba, 47; 55; 78–79, 85, 87–88, 108, 113, 117,
    125, 135, 146, 160, 168, 170, 173, 184, 203–7;
    caliphate, 1, 23, 152, 166; conquest, 92–99
Coria, 129, 205
Covadonga, battle, 5
Coves de Vinromá, 100
Cowdrey, H. E. J., historian, 14, 25
Crónica de Alfonso X, 195
Crónica de Castilla, 169
Cross, wearing of the, 180–85
Crossbowmen (*ballesteros*), 129
Crusade, idea, 17–21
Crusades (Holy Land): First, 8, 31–32, 35, 48,
    181; Second, 41–50, 75, 178, 181; Third, 57,
    76, 156, 180, 182; Fourth, 72; Fifth, 78–80,
    83–84, 97, 156–57, 183
Crusades (Spain): Alarcos, 61–63, 141–44;
    Almería, 44–45, 48–49; Balearic Islands,
    35–36; Córdoba, 92–99; Jaén, 110–12; Las
    Navas, 66–76; Lisbon, 41–44; Mallorca,
    89–92; Peñíscola, 89; Portuguese, 108–9;
    Seville, 112–17; Silves, 58–59; Tortosa, 46;
    Valencia, 99–105; Zaragoza, 36–39
Cuart de Poblet, battle (1094), 31, 141, 189, 202
Cuenca, 55–56, 63, 160; bishop, 95, 206; *fuero*,
    129; hospital, 147
Cullera, 104
Cutanda, battle (1120), 37, 141

Damietta, 83
Daroca, 37; Curia (1223), 164

Dartmouth, 43
David, Don, Jewish lender, 173
De expugnatione Lyxbonensi, 178
Decima, ecclesiastical tax, 157–59, 209
Deeds of the Counts of Barcelona, xii
Delaruelle, Etienne, historian, 199
Denia, 23, 37, 47, 56, 104, 106, 168
Denmark, 58
Diego García, chancellor of Castile, 72
Diego Gelmírez, archbishop of Compostela,
    39, 48, 54, 149, 177, 181, 187
Diego López de Haro, lord of Vizcaya, 37, 182
Diego Pérez de Vargas, crusader, 200
Diego de Valera, historian, 213, 215
Domingo Pérez de Toro, royal *portero*, 174–75
Domingo, bishop of Morocco, 118
Dominicans in Morocco, 118, 148
Donation of Constantine, 29
Dueñas (Calatrava la nueva), 74
Duero (Douro) river, 1, 42, 174
Dufourcq, Charles-Emmanuel, historian, 128

Ebles de Roucy, count, 27, 29
Ebro river, 30–31, 36–38, 40, 46–47, 55
Écija, 94, 96
El Collado de Berninches, hospital, 147
El Puerto de Santa María, 116, 212
Elvas, 87–88, 139, 185
Empréstitos, 173–76
England, English crusaders, 54, 59, 68, 123, 179
Enrique I of Castile, 78, 81, 152, 159, 164
Enrique III of Castile-León, 214
Enrique IV of Castile-León, 215
Enrique of Trastámara, 7
Ermengol III, count of Urgell, 26, 32, 166
Esteban Illán, *alcalde* of Toledo, 171
Esteban, bishop of Huesca, 37, 159
Estevão, archbishop of Braga, 156
Estoria de Espanna, 114, 120, 170, 196
Eudes, duke of Burgundy, 30
Eugenius III, pope, 42, 45–48, 181
Eulogius of Córdoba, Mozarabic author, 16
Évora, 51, 59–60; bishop, 183; knights, 54, 59;
    hospital, 147
Exea, ransomer, 148
Extremadura, 85, 175
Ezekiel, prophet, 6

Fáfila, duke, 5
Falco Pererius, papal tax collector, 157

Faro, 79, 110, 150
Ferdinand and Isabella, 2, 7, 213–15
Fernán González, count of Castile, 17, 184, 195, 202–3, 207
Fernán Pérez de Guzmán, historian, 213
Fernán Rodríguez, *el Castellano*, 197
Fernando, abbot of Alcobaça, 79, 159
Fernando, Infante, 66–7, 183
Fernando I of León-Castile, 4, 7, 9, 11, 23–24, 166, 194, 196
Fernando II of León, 50–51, 56–75, 76, 152, 191, 197
Fernando III of Castile-León, 8, 12, 81–88, 93–97, 101–2, 106, 108–23, 125, 132, 139–40, 152–53, 155, 158–61, 164, 169–70, 172–75, 177, 184–85, 191, 197, 201, 203–5, 207, 211
Fernando IV of Castile-León, 211
Fernando de Antequera, Infante, 213
Fernando de Serpa, Infante, 109, 122, 185
Fernando Díaz de Asturias, count, 33
Fernando Suárez, crusader, 66
Ferran de San Martín, crusader, 127
·Fez, 118
Fiscal accounts of Catalonia, 152
Flanders, Flemings, 42–43, 189
Fletcher, Richard, historian, 18
Folquet de Marselha, troubadour, archbishop of Toulouse, 68, 179
Fondarella, Curia (1173), 162
Fonsadera, tax, 129, 154
Formentera, 35, 92
Forum regni Valentie, 104
Fraga, battle (1134), 40, 46, 141, 158, 181, 192, 194
France, French crusaders, 7, 24, 27, 31, 35–37, 48, 59, 68–69, 71, 103, 123, 152, 179–80, 183, 187
Francis of Assisi, 118
Franciscans in Morocco, 118–19, 148
Franco, Francisco, 19
Frederick II, Holy Roman Emperor, 79, 101
Frisia, Frisian crusaders, 42, 58, 79
Fuero Juzgo (*Forum Iudicum*), 96
Fueros of Jaca, Teruel, Cuenca, Coria, 129

Galicia, 35, 43, 63, 79, 94, 149, 174–75, 199
Gallia Gothica, 7
García IV Ramírez of Navarre, 40–41
Gascony, 69, 82
Gaston IV of Béarn, 34, 37

Gautier-Dalché, Jean, historian, 128
Gavaudan, troubadour, 68–69
Gelasius II, pope, 37, 40
Genesis, Book of, 15
Genoa, Genoese, 35–36, 44–46, 49, 64–65, 92, 119, 122, 140, 149, 154, 203
George, count of Wied, 79
Geraldo the Fearless, 135, 140
Gerena, 113
Germany, German crusaders, 59, 79
Gevora river, 141
Gibraltar, 79, 211–12; Strait, 1, 9, 35, 66, 210–12
Gil García de Azagra, knight of Santiago, 89
Gilabert de Croyles, crusader, 128
Gilbert of Hastings, bishop of Lisbon, 44, 47, 50
Gilchrist, John, historian, 13
Girona (Gerona), 36, 149; bishop, 90, 126; Curia (1188), 162; sacristan of, 126
Gog, 6
Gómez, Master of Calatrava, 97
Goñi Gaztambide, José, historian, xi, 19, 24–25, 37, 113, 160
González, Julio, historian, 127, 153, 155, 170
Gonzalo, archbishop of Toledo, 58
Gonzalo de Berceo, poet, 17, 184, 195–97
Gonzalo García, papal tax collector, 157
Granada, 1, 3, 9, 23, 30, 37, 51, 85, 88, 93, 97, 99, 112, 114, 117, 122, 132, 167–70, 173, 209–14
Grassotti, Hilda, historian, 153, 174
Greek fire, 113, 138, 150
Gregory VII, pope, 14, 27, 29, 50, 155, 209
Gregory VIII, pope, 57, 156
Gregory IX, pope, 87–93, 96–98, 100–103, 105, 108–9, 118, 122, 126–27, 149, 157, 159–62, 184–85
Gregory of Sant'Angelo, cardinal, 60–62
Guadalerzas, hospital, 147
Guadalete river, battle (711), 5, 74, 184, 202, 204
Guadalquivir river, 1, 51, 62, 94, 96, 110, 113–14
Guadiana river, 1, 51, 58, 87–88, 108–9, 111, 140–42
Guerau de Cervelló, crusader, 127
Guibert de Nogent, chronicler, 31
Guifré, bishop of Barbastro and Roda, 40
Guifré, bishop of Narbonne, 25
Guilhem Ademar, troubadour, 69
Guillaume, archbishop of Bordeaux, 70
Guillem, count of Cerdanya, 33

Guillem de Montcada, viscount of Béarn, 90–91, 127, 132, 190
Guillem de Montgrí, archbishop of Tarragona, 92
Guillem Jordá, count of Cerdanya, 33
Guillem Ramon, count of Cerdanya, 33
Guillena, 113
Guillermo Pérez de Calzada, abbot of Sahagún, 116
Guimaraes, Curia (1250), 165
Guislabert, count of Rousillon, 33
Gutierre, bishop-elect of Córdoba, 111, 113, 122, 126, 184, 206

Ḥafṣids of Tunis, 104, 114
Hebrew Scriptures, 12–13, 15
Henry II, king of England, 50, 182
Henry, count of Bar, 59
Henry, count of Burgundy, 34, 41
Hervey de Glanvill, crusader, 43
Hillgarth, Jocelyn, historian, 3
History of Rodrigo (*Historia Roderici*), 17, 201
Holy Land, 20, 24, 29, 32–35, 37–39, 43, 45, 47, 49, 50, 52, 56–58, 60, 63, 75, 78–80, 85, 89, 93, 97, 101–3, 108, 110–11, 120, 155, 157–58, 163, 178, 180–83, 185, 209
Holy Redeemer, Order of the, 148
Holy Roman Empire, 116
Holy Sepulchre, 39–41, 48, 179
Holy War, 7–14
Honorius III, pope, 78, 80–83, 85, 97, 118, 155–59, 161, 172, 177, 184
Hospital, Order of the, 40–41, 48, 52, 55, 59–60, 70, 76, 79, 82, 84, 91, 100, 120, 128, 156–57, 164, 172
Hospitals, 147–48
Huesca, 31, 65, 141, 159, 164, 197, 205; Cortes (1247), 107; Curia (1221), 164
Huete, 55, 147
Hug de Forcalquer, Master of the Hospital, 100
Hug, count of Empúries, 127
Huguccio, papal tax collector, 156–57
Ḥusām ibn Razīn, king of Albarracín, 168
Hyacinth, cardinal, 47–48, 55, 76, 177, 182. *See also* Celestine III

Ibiza, 35–36, 92
Ibn Abī Zarʿ, historian, xii, 92, 118, 170

Ibn al-Abbār, historian, 92, 104
Ibn al-Aḥmar, king of Granada, 93–95, 97, 106, 110, 112, 117, 122, 169–70
Ibn Ḥayyān, historian, 26–27, 190
Ibn Ḥazm of Córdoba, author, 167
Ibn Hūd, king of Murcia and Valencia, 87–88, 92, 94–95, 99, 105, 139, 141, 169–70
Ibn Idhārī, historian, xiii, 9, 169
Ibn Juib, Sevillan leader, 114
Ibn Khaldūn, historian, xii, 114
Ibn Maḥfūt, king of Niebla, 93, 114, 116, 169–70
Ibn Mardanīsh, king of Valencia, 47, 51, 152, 168–69
Ibn Ṣāḥib al-Salā, historian, xiii
Ibn Shālib, Jewish envoy, 167
Ifrīqīya, 114
Innocent II, pope, 38, 40
Innocent III, pope, 64–66, 69, 72, 78, 80, 97, 118, 132, 148, 156, 159, 163, 183, 187, 200
Innocent IV, pope, 107–8, 110–12, 119–20, 122, 149, 157, 160–61, 184–85
Isidore of Seville, 191, 194, 196–97, 199; *History of the Gothic Kings of Spain*, 4, 6
Ishmael, Ishmaelites, 6, 15, 202
Italy, 14, 26, 149

Jaca: coinage, 152, 163–64; *fuero*, 129; Council (1063), 26
Jaén, 46–47, 56, 79, 84–85, 88, 92, 94–95, 97, 99, 110–12, 117, 132, 135, 140, 170
Jaime I, king of Aragón, 78, 89–92, 97, 99–108, 117, 119, 122, 124, 126, 132–34, 139–41, 144, 147, 150, 159, 163–65, 169, 172, 184–85, 188, 190, 193, 197–98, 200–203, 205, 211
Jaime II, king of Aragón, 210–11
Játiva, 37, 56, 106, 117, 168
Jean de Mathe, founder of the Order of the Trinity, 148
Jean Halgrin d'Abbeville, cardinal bishop of Santa Sabina, 88, 90, 184
Jerez, 56, 112, 116, 140, 171, 194, 196, 211
Jérica, 168
Jerome, bishop of Valencia, 127, 188–89, 207
Jerusalem, 31–34, 38, 40, 42, 44, 47–48, 50, 52, 54, 57, 60, 102, 179–82, 187; Latin Kingdom, 65, 128, 155, 157
Jesus of Nazareth, 16, 139, 180
Jews, 12, 25, 70, 155, 171, 173, 175
Jihād, xiv, 11

Jizya, poll tax, 12

João, archbishop of Braga, 43, 126, 178, 203, 205

John, king of England, 66–67

John of Brienne, former king of Jerusalem, 84

Joshua, Book of, 12

Juan, archbishop of Toledo, 54, 177–78

Juan, bishop of Osma, chancellor of Castile, xii, 67, 71, 95, 169, 173, 205–6

Juan II of Castile-León, 213

Juan Gil de Zamora, Fray, historian, 7, 212

Juan Manuel, author, 200, 211

Júcar river, 99, 104, 106

Jucef, *alfaqui*, and son Jucef, 173

Judah Maccabee, 12

Juslibol, castle, 33, 181

Kharaj, land tax, 12

La Higueruela, battle (1431), 213

La Merced, Order of (Mercedarians), 118, 148–49

Lacarra, José María, historian, 29

Lagos, 58

Lanfranc Cigala, troubadour, 101

Laredo, 119

Las Huelgas de Burgos, Cistercian convent, 72, 146, 157, 207

Las Navas de Tolosa, battle (1212), 66–76, 78, 97, 123–24, 132, 140–44, 146, 154, 156, 159, 163, 172, 179, 183, 187, 189, 191, 198, 200, 202–3, 207

Lateran Council: First, 38, 49; Fourth, 78, 85, 88, 93, 96, 107, 109, 156

Latin Chronicle of the Kings of Castile, xii, 7, 67, 71, 84, 144, 169, 179, 184, 188, 198, 200, 203

Lavaur, Council (1211), 75

Leadership, military, 133–34

Lebrija, 116

Ledesma, 175

Leiria, Cortes (1254), 165

León, 45, 178; church of San Isidro, 191, 196; Council (1135), 124; Curia (1063), 26; Curia (1188), 124; Curia (1208), 162; kingdom, 1, 7, 23, 33, 41, 54, 59, 62–64, 81–82, 93–94, 111–12, 125, 152, 158, 160, 162–64, 174–75, 191, 197, 199, 203

León-Castile, 4, 24, 34, 39, 41

Leonor, wife of Alfonso VIII, 67

Leopold VI, duke of Austria, 74

Lérida. *See* Lleida

Lescar, bishop, 205

Lévi-Provençal, Évariste, historian, xii

Liber ordinum, 185, 206

Libro de Alexandre, 17

Libro de la consolación de España, 212

Linehan, Peter, historian, 3

Liria, 168

Lisbon, 35, 51, 54–55, 58–59; bishop, 44, 47, 50, 60, 183; crusade, 41–44, 46–47, 49, 79–80, 110, 119, 126, 135, 138–40, 149, 178, 182, 187, 189, 199, 204–5

Liturgical preparations for battle, 185–90

Livermore, Harold, historian, 42

Lleida (Lérida), 90, 166, 172; Council (1229), 184; Curia (1218); 23, 36, 46, 52, 164

Loans, 171–73

Logroño, 62

Lomax, Derek, historian, 3, 18, 120, 157

Lope, Master, 95, 205

Lope Fernández Ain, bishop of Morocco, 119–20

Lora del Río, 113

Lorca, 107

Louis VII of France, 50

Louis VIII of France, 72

Louis IX of France, 105

Louis, landgrave of Thuringia, 59

Lucas, bishop of Tuy, 12, 87–88; *Chronicle of the World*, xii; *Liber de miraculis Sancti Isidori*, 196

Lucena, battle (1126), 37, 141

Lucius II, pope, 39, 41

Lucius III, pope, 54, 56

Lugo, 173

Lyon: First Council (1245), 107, 110–12, 172; Second Council (1274), 211

Maccabees, Book of, 60

MacKay, Angus, historian, 19, 122, 166

Magacela, 94

Magnates, 127–28

Málaga, 23, 92, 97, 152

Malagón, 71, 140

Mallorca, 36, 48, 64–65, 76, 181; crusade, 89–92, 97, 100, 105, 124, 126–27, 135, 141, 144, 149–50, 159, 163, 172, 184, 188, 190, 202

Manlieva, loan, 173
Mansilla, Demetrio, historian, 160
Mantua, bishop, 119
Marcabrú, troubadour, 46
Marīnid dynasty, 114, 210–12
Mark of Toledo, 10, 118
Marrakech, 75, 118
Marseille, 92
Martín de Córdoba, Fray, 17
Martín Muñiz, crusader, 8, 184
Martín Muñiz Falcón, crusader, 87
Martín of Pisuerga, archbishop of Toledo, 62, 118, 127
Martín Rodríguez, bishop of Zamora, 83, 184
Martos, 84, 87, 200
Martyrdom, idea of, 12, 199–201
Matthew Paris, chronicler, 67, 105, 120
Maurice Bourdin, archbishop of Braga, 34
Mauricio, bishop of Burgos, 85, 177
Mauritania, 4, 7, 16
Mayer, Hans Eberhard, historian, 20
Mazalquivir, 215
McCrank, Lawrence, historian, 32
Mecca, 120
Medellín, 94
Medina Sidonia, 140
Mediterranean Sea, 14, 35
Melilla, 215
Menéndez Pidal, Ramón, historian, 9, 18, 25
Menorca, 35, 92, 169
Mequinenza, 40, 46
Mérida, 31, 75, 78, 88, 97, 139, 141
Mértola, 51, 108
Mesnada, 125–27
Miguel de Fabra, Dominican preacher, 91, 180
Military discipline, 129
Military expenses, 153–55
Military Orders, 52–55, 124, 128, 147–48, 159, 172, 182
Militias, urban, 125
Miramamolín. *See* al-Nāṣir
Miranda del Rey, 142
Missa in tempore belli, 186
Moabites. *See* Almoravids
Mondoñedo, 173
Moneda forera, 163–65, 174, 176
Monetaticum, Monedatge, Moneda forera, 163–65
Monfrag (Monfragüe), Order of, 55

Monreal, *militia Christi*, 40, 48
Monsanto, 54
Montánchez, 88
Montaticum, 66
Monte de Pantaleu, 91
Monteagudo, treaty (1291), 210
Montearagón, monastery, 197
Montemayor, 8
Montenegro, Isabel, historian, 18
Montiel, battle (1143), 189, 206–7
Montpellier, 172
Monzón, 52, 100; Curia (1232), 184; Curia (1236), 102, 163–64, 184
Moors, 7, 9, 12, 16, 84, 90, 120, 186, 196, 200–201, 205, 211–13
Morella, 100
Morocco, 1, 7, 30, 54, 56, 61, 64, 67, 71, 78, 83, 87, 92, 94, 99, 110, 114, 122, 142, 166, 168–69, 179–80, 202, 210, 212; projected crusade, 117–20
Mosques, cleansing, 204–6
Mount Joy (Monte Gaudio), Order of, 55
Moura, 108
Moya, hospital, 147
Mozarabic liturgy, 186
Mozarabs, 10, 38
Mudejars, 14, 122, 155; revolt (1264), 198, 210
Muḥammad, Muslim prophet, 11, 12, 15, 16–17, 30, 69, 84, 87, 116, 177, 193, 204–5, 212–13
Muḥammad XII (Boabdil), king of Granada, 214
Mula, 107
Muluia river, 210
Municipalities, military obligation, 128–29
Munio Alfonso, *alcaide* of Toledo, 181, 189
Murcia, 37, 47, 56, 85, 87, 97, 99, 105–7, 117, 122, 152, 166, 168–70, 173
Muret, battle (1213), 75
Murviedro, 168

Nájera, Curia of (1180), 158
Nantes, bishop, 70
Narbonne: archbishop, 68, 70–72, 75; bishop, 25; Council (1129), 39; ecclesiastical province, 25, 91, 101, 103, 119; viscount, 36
Naval forces, 149–50
Navarre, 1, 7–8, 23–24, 33, 56, 59, 61, 64, 74, 81, 101–2, 157, 171–72, 183, 187
Nicholas, bishop of Silves, 59

Niebla, 51, 93, 110, 114, 116, 169–70, 210
Nîmes, 36
Normandy, 26, 42
Numbers of soldiers, 143–45
Nunyo Sanç, count of Roselló, Cerdanya, and
    Conflent, 90, 127

Oleguer, archbishop of Tarragona, 39–40, 48,
    177, 181
Oliver Asín, Jaime, arabist, 11
Oloron, bishop, 205
Oran, 215
Ordericus Vitalis, historian, 40, 49, 181
Oreja, 203
Orense, 158, 173–74
Ourique, battle (1139), 41, 141
Oviedo, 6, 175, 186

Paderne, 110
Palencia, 45, 85, 159; Council (1129), 159
Palestine, 11, 157
Palma de Mallorca, 36, 91, 139–40, 180, 193,
    198, 205
Palmela, 43, 79
Pamplona, bishop, 171
Papal taxation for the Holy Land, 155–58
Parias, tribute, 155, 165–71, 176
Paschal II, pope, 9, 33–36, 38, 48, 177, 209
Paterna, Aldea de los Judíos del Rey, 173
Peace and Truce of God, 26, 47, 89–90, 102,
    162
Pedro, archbishop of Compostela, 54, 58, 89,
    156
Pedro, bishop of León, 178
Pedro, bishop of Zaragoza, 37
Pedro, brother of Afonso I, 42
Pedro, Infante of Portugal, 92
Pedro I of Aragón, 31, 33, 49, 155, 181, 187, 190,
    197
Pedro II of Aragón, 63–66, 70–71, 75–76, 90,
    132, 141–43, 155, 158, 162–64, 171–72, 182, 187,
    198
Pedro III of Aragón, 211
Pedro IV of Aragón, xii
Pedro Alvítiz, Master of the Temple in Spain,
    80, 83, 172
Pedro Gutiérrez, 34
Pedro López de Ayala, historian, 212
Pedro Pitões, bishop of Porto, 43, 126, 178, 187

Pedro the Cruel, king of Castile, 7
Peire d'Alvernha, troubadour, 48
Peire Vidal, troubadour, 63
Pelagius, bishop-elect of Lod, 157
Pelagius, cardinal, 79
Pelay Pérez Correa, Master of Santiago, 97,
    106, 111–13, 128, 133, 154, 193, 200
Pelayo, bishop of Oviedo, chronicler, 4
Pelayo, king of Asturias, 5, 18
Peñiscola, 89, 97, 100, 188
Pere, archbishop of Tarragona, 108
Pere Nolasc, founder of the Order of
    La Merced, 148
Pero da Ponte, poet, 104, 116
Peter the Venerable, abbot of Cluny, 10
Petitum, tax, 162
Petronila, daughter of Ramiro II of Aragón,
    41
Philip Augustus, king of France, 67, 69
Phillips, Jonathan, historian, 42
Pierre, archbishop of Narbonne, 104
Pietro, archbishop of Pisa, 35–36, 48, 181
Pillage and devastation, 134–35
Pisa, 35–36, 48–49, 64–65, 92, 122, 149, 181
Pius VI, pope, 215
Plasencia, bishop, 94
Poem of Almería, 45
Poem of Fernán González, xii, 17, 184, 188, 193,
    198, 200, 202, 204
Poem of the Cid, xii, 126, 188, 190, 193, 204
Poitou, count of, 69
Polpis, 100
Porches, 110
Portimão, 58–59
Porto, 42, 119, 126, 161, 165, 178, 187
Porto, cardinal bishop, 65
Portopí, battle, 91, 141, 144, 180, 188, 190, 193,
    201
Portugal, Portuguese, 3, 23, 33, 35, 41–44,
    50–52, 54–55, 58–59, 71, 74, 79–80, 87, 97, 99,
    108–10, 113, 120, 122, 132, 139, 150, 152, 156–57,
    161, 165, 171, 182, 187, 200, 202, 205, 211,
    214–15
Portuguese Chronicle, 41
Preaching, crusade, 177–80
Priego, 171
Privilege of the Vows: of San Millán, 196; of
    Santiago, 195
Processions in Rome, 187

Prophetic Chronicle, 4–6, 15–16
Provence, 69, 78
Puerto del Muradal (Despeñaperros), 61, 67, 71, 142
Puig de la Cebolla (Puig de Santa Maria), 102, 132, 141, 144, 172, 188, 198, 200, 203
Pyrenees mountains, 1, 35

Quadrillero, company commander, 146–47
Quantum predecessores, crusading bull, 42
Quesada, 84, 92–94, 97, 160
Qur'ān, 10, 11, 15, 118

Raimbaut de Vaqueiras, troubadour, 64
Raimundo, archbishop of Toledo, 42, 177–78, 206–7
Ralph Viel, crusader, 42
Ramiro I of Aragón, 25
Ramiro II of Aragón, 40–41
Ramiro I of Asturias, 194–95
Ramiro II of Asturias, 195
Ramón, abbot of Fitero, 52
Ramon, count of Pallars, 37
Ramon Berenguer I, count of Barcelona, 23, 25, 152, 166
Ramon Berenguer II, count of Barcelona, 32, 166
Ramon Berenguer III, count of Barcelona, 35, 155, 162, 181
Ramon Berenguer IV, count of Barcelona, 41–42, 44–49, 51–52, 168, 171, 182
Ramon Berenguer d'Ager, crusader, 128
Ramón Bonifaz of Burgos, 112–13, 150, 175
Ramon de Montcada, lord of Tortosa, 127, 190
Ramon de Penyafort, Dominican canonist, 91
Ramon Guillem, bishop of Barcelona, 36
Ransoming captives, 148–49
Raymond VI, count of Toulouse, 30, 75
Reconquest: idea of, 3; neglect of, 212–14; providential character of, 201–2; reconquest and crusade, 17–22
Reilly, Bernard F., historian, 125, 144
Reina, 113
Remondo, bishop of Segovia, first archbishop of Seville, 116
Requena, 81
Revenues, royal, 153–55

Rheims, Council (1148), 45
Rhinelanders, crusaders, 79
Ribadavia, 175
Ribāṭ, 12, 40, 52
Richard of Camwill, crusader, 59
Riding styles, 130
Riley-Smith, Jonathan, historian, 20
Rivera Recio, Juan Francisco, historian, 58
Robert Burdet, Norman knight, 39, 192
Robert Crispin, 26
Robert de Sabloil, crusader, 59
Robert of Ketton, translator, 10
Rocamadour, French Marian shrine, 191
Rodrigo, archdeacon of León, 160
Rodrigo, Visigothic king, 5, 8, 72, 95, 184, 202, 213
Rodrigo Díaz de Vivar, see Cid, the
Rodrigo González de Lara, count, 34
Rodrigo Jiménez de Rada, archbishop of Toledo, 33, 69, 72, 87, 93, 97, 104, 112, 118, 127, 144, 146, 154, 156–57, 159–62, 177, 180, 183–84, 189, 198, 200, 203–5; crusades, 80–84; *History of the Affairs of Spain*, xii; *History of the Arabs*, 16
Rodrigo Sánchez de Arévalo, 215
Rodríguez López, Ana, historian, 160
Roman liturgy, missal, 186
Rome, Romans, 14, 16, 64, 68, 70, 109, 157, 172
Rota, 79
Rotrou of Perche, crusader, 35
Rousset, Paul, historian, 20
Runciman, Sir Steven, historian, 20

Sacramentary: Gelasian, 186; Gregorian, 186, 205; Ripoll, 180, 186, 205; Vich, 180, 186, 205
Sado river, 79
Sahagún, treaty (1158), 50–51
Saher of Archelle, crusader, 43
Saindo of Sandwich, crusader, 59
Sainte Chapelle, 105
Saints, appearance in battle and invocation, 193–99
Salado, battle (1340), 187, 211–12
Salamanca, 202; hospital, 147; University, 174–75
Salé, 119, 212
Salou, 91
Salvatierra, 61, 67, 71, 74, 159, 179

Sampiro, bishop of Astorga, chronicler, 4, 11, 16
San Esteban, 171
San Feliu de Guixols, abbot, 90, 126, 150
San Isidoro de León, 191
San Jorge de Alfama, Order of, 55, 198
San Jorge de Borqueras, 197
San Juan de la Peña, monastery, 197
San Julián del Pereiro, Order of, 54–55, 75, 82
San Miguel de Cuxá, monastery, 181
San Millán de la Cogolla, 194–97, 199
San Pedro de Arlanza, monastery, 207
San Sebastián, 119
Sánchez Albornoz, Claudio, historian, 9, 19
Sancho, Infante, son of Alfonso VI, 34
Sancho II of Castile, 4, 133
Sancho III of Castile, 50–52
Sancho IV of Castile-León, 210–11
Sancho IV of Navarre, 166
Sancho VI of Navarre, 81
Sancho VII of Navarre, 51, 62–64, 70–71, 80–82, 97, 102, 142, 171–72, 183
Sancho I of Portugal, 57–59, 63, 76, 133, 140, 152, 156, 182–83
Sancho II of Portugal, 87, 89, 108–10, 122, 127, 161, 171, 185
Sancho I Ramírez of Aragón and Navarre, 8, 26–27, 152, 155, 166, 197
Sanlúcar, 114
Santa Cruz, 94
Santa Elena, 142, 191
Santa Eulalia of Barcelona, hospital, 149
Santa María de Faro, 79, 110, 150
Santa María de los Martyres, 200
Santa María del Puerto. *See* El Puerto de Santa María
Santa Olalla, hospital, 147
Santa Ponça, 91
Santander, 119
Santarém, 42, 59
Santiago. *See* St. James
Santiago, Order of, 52, 54–55, 62, 65, 70, 82, 84–85, 93–94, 106, 108–13, 119, 128, 147–48, 160, 172, 182, 200
Santiago de Compostela, 79, 84, 88–89, 95, 97, 173, 194–95, 199, 207; archbishops, 62, 182; Council (1125), 39; pilgrimage, 24–25, 43, 50, 70, 180

Santo Domingo de la Calzada, 148
Santo Domingo de Silos, 148
Saracens, 15, 25, 31, 36, 39, 45, 51–52, 60, 64, 68, 72, 75, 85, 87, 103, 109–10, 124, 149, 183, 185, 192, 198, 200, 205
Savaric de Mauleón, crusader, 82
Sax, 106
Sayf al-Dawla (Zafadola), king of Córdoba, 168
Segorbe, 99, 168
Segovia, 81, 95, 157–58; Council (1166), 51
Serpa, 108–9
Sertella, 66
Setton, Kenneth, historian, 20
Seville, 23, 31; 47, 51, 63, 66, 74, 79, 85, 88–89, 97, 99, 110, 118, 120, 126, 129, 135, 138, 140, 142, 148, 150, 154, 160, 166–68, 173, 175, 184, 191, 193, 196–97, 204, 206, 210–11; archbishop, 116; conquest, 112–17; Cortes (1250), 133; Cortes (1252), 161, 174; repopulation, 126–27, 129, 133, 146–47
Sheepwalks (*cañadas*), 8
Sicily, 211
Siege warfare, 135–40
Siena, bankers, 172
Sigurd, king of Norway, 35
Silves, crusade (1189), 58–59, 76, 109–10, 135, 140, 149, 182
Simancas, battle of (939), 195
Simon de Montfort, 75
Simon of Dover, crusader, 43
Sintra, 35
Sisnando, count, 30
Slavs, 20
Smith, Damian, historian, 9
Spain: loss and recovery, 4–7; Roman diocese, 4
Spanish Civil War, 19
St. Emilian. *See* San Millán de la Cogolla
St. George, 92, 194, 197–99
St. James, 54, 88, 189, 191, 193–97, 199
St. John Lateran, 70
St. Michael the Archangel, 187, 194
St. Victorian, martyr, 197
Standards, military, 132–33
Stipends, *soldadas, stipendia*, 127, 153–54
Sueiro, bishop of Évora, 79, 126, 183
Sueiro, bishop of Lisbon, 79, 126, 183
Suger, abbot of St. Denis, 29

Supply, military, 132
Syria, Calatrava in, 101

Tablada, 113
Tagus river, 1, 44, 51, 54–55, 62, 75, 140, 142, 187
Taifas, 23, 26, 29–30, 41, 168, 176
Talavera, hospital, 147
Tangier, 117, 215
Tarazona, 37, 56
Tarifa, 210–11
Tarragona, 9, 31–32, 39–40, 48, 90–91, 101–3,
    119, 166, 192; archbishops, 104, 126, 150, 177;
    Curia (1235), 102
Tavira, 200–201, 205
Taxation, extraordinary, 162–65
Te Deum laudamus, 72, 203–4, 207
Tello, bishop of Palencia, 85, 87, 159, 205
Tello Alfonso, frontiersman, 96
Temple, Order of, 34, 40–41, 48, 52, 55, 59–60,
    70, 76, 79–80, 82–84, 91, 120, 128, 156,
    163–64, 171–72, 188
Tercias, 87, 112–13, 155, 158–62, 209
Teresa, daughter of Alfonso VI, 34, 41
Teruel, 51, 66, 100, 103; *fuero*, 129; hospital, 148
Thibault I, king of Navarre, 101–2, 119, 157
Thomas à Becket, 182
Tingitana, province, 7, 215
Todesca, James, historian, 154, 163
Toledo, 1, 4, 6, 9, 23, 30, 47, 52, 54, 56, 61–62,
    67, 70–71, 74, 81–82, 84, 96, 106, 135, 139– 40,
    142–44, 146, 148, 157, 159, 166–67, 171, 173,
    183, 189, 193, 202–7; archbishops, 42, 45, 62,
    118, 127, 161, 177–78, 180, 182, 187; *fuero*, 116;
    hospital, 147
Tomar, 59
Torres Novas, 59
Tortosa, 36, 52, 79, 90, 100, 135, 149–50, 166,
    168, 171; crusade, 42, 44, 46, 49, 182; Curia
    (1225), 89, 184
Toulouse, Council (1118), 37
Tours, Council (1163), 50
Trebuchet, 138–39
Trebujena, 116
Triana, suburb of Seville, 114, 138, 150
Trinity, Order of, 118, 148–49
Triumphal return from battle, 206–8
Trujillo, 94; Order of, 55
Tudela, 30, 37, 205
Tudellén, treaty (1151), 47, 56

Tunis, 7, 104, 106–7, 110, 112, 114, 119, 150, 210
Túy, 173
Twentieth of ecclesiastical revenue, 156–58
Tyerman, Christopher, historian, 20

Úbeda, 71, 74, 84, 93–94, 140, 143, 168
Uclés, battle (1108), 34, 141; encomienda of
    Santiago, 54; hospital, 147
Urban II, pope, 9, 30–35, 38, 46, 48, 177–78,
    180–81, 209
Urraca, queen of León-Castile, 39
Usatges of Barcelona, 92, 125
'Uthmān, king of Valencia, 167

Valencia, 23, 30–31, 35–36, 47, 51, 56, 66, 81–82,
    84, 89–91, 106–8, 117, 119, 122–24, 127,
    134–35, 140–41, 147–48, 150, 166–67, 198,
    202, 205, 207; crusade, 19, 99–100, 102–5,
    163–64, 172, 184, 201, 203–5, 207;
    repartiment, 147
Valladolid, 112, 175; Council (1143), 159, 181;
    Council (1155), 47, 182
Vasconia, 7
Vatican Council, Second, 215
Vejer, 116
Vic, 163
Victory, celebration of, 203–4
Vigil, Marcelo, historian, 17
Vilches, 191
Villafamés, 100
Villena, 106
Vincentius Hispanus, canonist, 116, 210
Visigothic Code, 96
Visigoths, 1, 3–8, 16, 17, 68, 117, 185–86, 190,
    202, 204, 212
Vow, crusading, 180–85

Wends, 45
William, count of Holland, crusader, 79–80
William VIII, duke of Aquitaine, 26
William VI, lord of Montpellier, 35–36, 41,
    44, 46
William Viel, crusader, 42

Yucef, Don, Jewish lender, 173
Yūsuf ibn Tāshufīn, Almoravid emir, 141–43

Zag de la Maleha, tax farmer, 173
Zag, *almojarife*, and sons, 173

Zallāqa (Sagrajas), battle (1086), 30, 62,
141–44, 147, 168
Zamora: bishop, 83, 183; cantor and
archdeacon, 156; Curia (1221), 83
Zaragoza, 9, 23, 26, 30–31, 39–40, 51, 54,
56, 56, 100, 134–35, 140–41, 158–59,
166, 168, 187, 190, 197, 200, 206;
crusade, 36–39, 48, 181; Curia (1235),
102

Zayyān ibn Saʿd ibn Mardanīsh, king of
Valencia, 90, 93, 99, 103–5, 107, 141
Zeid Aazon, king of Salé (al-Hasan, son of
Abū Zayd), 119
Ziza, *alfaqui*, 173
Zorita, 171
Zulema, royal envoy to Granada, 173
Zurita, Jerónimo, historian, 100, 122, 162, 184,
197